THE MOSES COMPLEX

UTE HOLL

THE MOSES COMPLEX

FREUD, SCHOENBERG, STRAUB/HUILLET

TRANSLATED FROM THE GERMAN
BY MICHAEL TURNBULL

DIAPHANES

CONTENTS

1. INTRODUCTION

I have been a stranger in a strange land
Exodus 2:22.

"We are strangers," is a worn-out Christian sentence.
But consider for a moment the potential that lies within it.
In it lies the potential for reversion [Umkehrung].
Jacob Taubes[1]

1.1. BEFORE THE LAW

The Moses complex, so the premise of the following deliberations, raises the question of the transformation of the political under media conditions, under new and unknown media conditions. Exile, desert, and camp are the constellations from which the emergence of a coming society is perceived. In speaking of a politics of sounds and images, I don't mean emotions or effects but the construction of effective spaces and people's distribution and connection within them. The Moses complex is about the difficulty of realizing this emerging politics without imagining it. It marks the problem of not simply being able to fall back on memory but having to continually rewrite and reconstruct it. Its temporality isn't linear or simple but recursive and complex. Writing will have been there, inscribed, when Moses is called before the law through smoke, fire, and mountain thunder. Numbers will have been there, but only when Moses counts his people, in order to make tribes, armies, gangs, families from them, does counting become the organization of people in space. Cultural techniques

1 Jacob Taubes, *The Political Theology of Paul*, Stanford 2004, p. 60.

bring symbolic systems retrospectively into the arena, but they also distort them. Because recursions are constitutive, things don't remain with a politics of identities. People can always be counted or added up anew or differently if you want. Identity and knowledge are generated from gaps, and can only be gained recursively. Moses admittedly has to make his first distinction out of nothing: burning bush—voice; thing—God; noise—message. Not imagination but attention, recursion, decision. If he hears nothing, he can move on with his sheep. If he hears a call, he has to answer it. An imposition provokes responsibility. The Moses complex is about recognition from decisions, relationships, rifts, from the blind typographic blank, the fraudulent vanishing point of painting, the logic of signification, and the constitutive relationships in sound and cinema.

In the following a Moses complex will be discussed in relation to musical composition, cinema, and psychoanalysis as cultural theory. Schoenberg.[2] Straub/Huillet. Freud. It isn't shown in images, meanings, or in a logic of representations, but in constellations and relations that bring about image and sound spaces. Forces and power relationships, which as politics underlie new perceptual spaces, the behavior and action they initiate, and their results, can be located in connections and transmissions, rifts and caesuras, but also in latencies, temporal shifts, and stratifications.

The Moses complex deals with monotheism as a problem of conceiving the unconceivable under respective historical conditions. It isn't about the "terrible abstraction" that George Steiner saw as provocation and "Jewish extortion,"[3] but rather a caesura and a resulting "now of discernability."[4]

For this reason I don't examine the meanings of sounds or images but the texture and connectivity of tones and shots. Here lies the media aspect of the Moses complex: to bring out the underlying and imperceptible structure or order of

2 In the following, except in quotations and citations by others, Schoenberg will be spelled with "oe," the way he wanted after 1933. See a letter from June 25, 1947: "My name should be written with oe. I changed it after coming to America because so few printers had the letter ö, and I wanted to avoid the spelling 'Schonberg'." Arnold Schoenberg *Letters*, ed. Erwin Stein, trans. Eithne Wilkins and Ernst Kaiser, London/Boston 1964, p. 9. This spelling will also be used retrospectively here for the Arnold Schoenberg before 1933, who he will have become from the perspective of later exile.

3 Most recently in an interview to mark his 85th birthday: George Steiner, "Pessimisten sind lächerlich," in *Die Zeit*, no. 17, April 16, 2014, p. 45.

4 Translated from Anselm Haverkamp, "Kritik der Gewalt und die Möglichkeit von Gerechtigkeit: Benjamin in Deconstruction," in Anselm Haverkamp (ed.), *Gewalt und Gerechtigkeit. Derrida – Benjamin*, Frankfurt/Main 1994, pp. 7–50: 34ff.

possible relationships within artworks and practices. This order is prematurely, and under changing media conditions, attributed to the divine, especially when its orders seem to come from nowhere. The appearance of gods is supposed in lights, sounds, and symbols, from electromagnetic fields and electronic circuitry. But gods should conversely be understood as the ideas implicit to media setups, which, beyond short-term individual interests, maintain wider collective processes and procedures in the long term. Gregory Bateson described this in 1967: "I suggest that one of the things that man has done through the ages to correct for his short-sighted purposiveness is to imagine personified entities with various sorts of supernatural power, i.e., *gods*. These entities, being fictitious persons, are more or less endowed with cybernetic and circuit characteristics."[5] Bateson's ecological, feedback media gods are too kindly conceived for the twentieth century, in which the circuits overheated and anyone issuing an order was greeted as God or Führer. Violence rules before the law, "the force that comes from within to remind us that law is always an authorized force."[6]

The unkind and inhuman God of Moses in Exodus reveals himself as a terrifying media agent. This is why the Moses figure insistently returns in the arts and sciences of the twentieth century. It corresponds to the fact that the media initially remain concealed when new laws come in with them. When Moses climbs the mountain, the tablets on which the caesuras of writing will turn out to be there already, while the people are still camping in the desert, playing, getting up to mischief, becoming violent, looking for the "liberator and lawgiver."[7] But some kind of perhaps conceivable legalism [for want of a more exact English term, the word is used throughout this book to translate *Gesetzlichkeit*, in the sense of a system that operates according to a law, as distinct from, although overlapping with, "legality" and "legal system," *trans.*] must also have already been there for the lawless in the camp, otherwise the absence of a leader wouldn't have been noticed. The connections only become apparent with the interruption of the cycles: when tablets are broken, rocks blasted, waters parted, worldly goods and evil distributed. This always comes with unconceivable violence. New

5 Gregory Bateson, "Letter to Warren McCulloch," December 20, 1967, in Gregory Bateson, "*'They threw God out of the garden': letters from Gregory Bateson to Philip Wylie and Warren McCulloch*," ed. Rodney E. Donaldson, *CoEvolution Quarterly*, 32 (winter), 1982, pp. 62–67: 65.

6 Jacques Derrida, "Force of Law: the 'Mystical Foundation of Authority'," in Jacques Derrida, *Acts of Religion*, ed. Gil Anidjar, New York 2002, p. 233.

7 Sigmund Freud, *Moses and Monotheism*, ed. Katherine Jones, London 1939, p. 29.

media, according to a distinction made by Walter Benjamin, generally appear to preserve the law, or more simply to serve the preservation of law as data processors, but nonetheless violently assert new law in their transparency.[8] The violence can be felt, while the media aspect can only be recognized in the rift and break. When Walter Benjamin compares sovereign justice, as an inherent principle of divine purpose, and the obvious manifestation of power in mythical law as forms of violence in his text "Critique of Violence," from 1920, he marks the exact poles that Moses and Aaron occupy in dealing with the question of images as one of violence in the twentieth century: unconceivable against conceivable violence. Against the advent of a law-destroying, bloodless yet lethal, suddenly striking force whose form evades knowledge, Benjamin sets a law-giving, boundary-drawing, threatening, fault-finding, and bloody—in that it applies to "bare life"[9]—mythical power. Both belong together, as Samuel Weber makes clear in his commentaries on the text.[10]

The Moses complex and its various reprises in the twentieth century provoke media-theoretical questions, while calling media theory into question at the same time. Proceeding from an obvious void, a radical not knowing, emergence from the unknown, the Moses complex examines the context of a history that is held together by an enormous, latent, non-specific violence. It explores oppression, persecution, and liberation, the question of what a people should be at all according to the law and the forms and possibilities of historiography. It deals with the inhumanity of perception and decision in pure form, whether media, musical, mathematical, machinical. In this respect the Moses complex is terrifying. It's complex, because its topological space is differentiated as a relationship of ratios, resonances, and interferences. Its place is exile.

The following study takes its starting point from the film MOSES UND ARON, realized in 1974 by Jean-Marie Straub and Danièle Huillet after much preparation and research. The filmmakers had been involved with the work since 1959, through many stations of a European exile, in search of a place where, safe from

8 See Walter Benjamin, "Critique of Violence", in Walter Benjamin, *Reflections. Essays. Aphorisms. Autobiographical Writings*, ed. and intro. Peter Demetz, New York 1986, pp. 277–300: 284.

9 Ibid., p. 184.

10 See Samuel Weber, "In the Name of the Law," in *Deconstruction and the Possibility of Justice*, ed. Drucilla Cornell, Michel Rosenfeld and David Gray Carlson, New York 1992, pp. 232–258; and Samuel Weber, "Deconstruction before the Name: Some Preliminary Remarks on Deconstruction and Violence," in *Cardozo Law Review*, vol. 13 / 1991–1992, pp. 1188–1191.

Straub being called up to the ongoing war in Algeria, they could make their films in peace—politically, economically, aesthetically. Straub and Huillet set new technical-acoustic parameters in their filming of Arnold Schoenberg's opera *Moses und Aron*, but above all they raised basic questions about political thought, action, and behavior proceeding from operations in the acoustic and the optic. When Straub and Huillet cause rifts to appear between structure and things, between the linguistic and the physical, they are working with the potential of resistance in seeing and hearing, demanding attention, distinction, decision, answer. The film MOSES UND ARON deals with a politics derived from calculated aesthetic operations, in order to make precepts, commands, and laws palpable in bodies. The experiment puts seeing and hearing to the test in relation to law and obedience. This politics of tones and images examines, with Schoenberg, the state of the political before the law. Like Schoenberg, Straub and Huillet turn their attention to a historical moment in which the law is suspended. Aesthetic politics before the law doesn't happen outside of concepts but in view of the constitutive lack of appropriate ones.

The film by Straub and Huillet is a transfer of Schoenberg's musical principles into cinematic form. Aspects of Schoenberg's musical procedure are only described in the following in so far as they are important for Straub/Huillet's film project. Yet within this framework it's clear that Schoenberg also conceived his operas in the light of media aesthetics. This applies both to his interest in the implementation of media techniques and to his principle of thinking in relationships and differences. The long composition time of the opera *Moses und Aron*, which Schoenberg began in Europe during the 1920s, resumed in 1933 in American exile, interrupted, and finally abandoned, covers his struggle against anti-Semitism and fascism, and his involvement with the Jewish project of Zionism.[11] Media-theoretical correspondences can be found between Schoenberg's aesthetic procedures and his political strategies.

Aside from the opera by Arnold Schoenberg and the film by Jean-Marie Straub and Danièle Huillet, the Moses complex includes a third work, which examines the violence of the twentieth century as a history of the suspended law and thus of perception and its interruption: the text *Moses and Monotheism*, on which Sigmund Freud worked from 1913 onward, regularly abandoned and

11 See Alexander Ringer, "Schoenberg and the Politics of Jewish Survival," in *Journal of the Arnold Schoenberg Institute*, vol. III, no. 1, March 1979, pp. 11–48.

took up again, and finally completed in a third version in London exile in 1938.[12] In this book Freud attempted to "[reduce] religion to the status of a neurosis of mankind," that is to infer the "grandiose powers"[13] of the collective from individual psychology. He, too, was now interested in what drives the many, what the collective historically shifts and postpones, in layers and dynamics beyond the logic of Oedipus, beyond any kind of Hellenism. Before being compelled to leave Austria by the National Socialists in 1938, Freud was sure that his project would provoke "the greatest resentment of the powers that be."[14] In this book he calls for an observation of the symptomatic, that is, to look in between forms for cracks and scars in order to diagnose the latently potent historical power of suppressed emotions waiting to break out again under pressure. Jacob Taubes, asking about "the political potentials in theological metaphors," thus reversing Carl Schmitt's project of inquiry into the "theological potential of legal concepts,"[15] sees a further stratification of procedures and texts, and another rift: "I believe that Freud, so to speak, enters into the role of Paul, of the Paul who supposedly brings redemption only phantasmatically, while Freud realizes it through this new method of healing, which is not only an individual method, but also a theory of culture."[16] In the symptoms he discerns, Freud sees a fundamental social injury, the moment in which something was decided fundamentally wrongly and thus can fundamentally be reversed. Freud too deals with the relationship between legalism and violence in the context of Jewish exile and genocide, which he, like Schoenberg—and presumably also Benjamin—anticipated with shocking precision. But he doesn't imagine it. Rather he suggests a procedure for recognizing and then preventing it, for discontinuing it. Freud's text can be understood as the draft of a media historiography that teaches us to recognize historicity in the symptoms of its circularly causal logics, in repetitions and distortions.

The project of bringing together the written, acoustic, and visual textures relating to "Moses" into a single context is called a *complex* in as much as they all have to do power relations that, subsequent to the Books of Exodus and

12 For a philologically exact reconstruction along the manuscripts see Ilse Grubrich-Simitis, *Freuds Moses-Studie als Tagtraum. Ein biographischer Essay*, revised edition, Frankfurt/Main 1994.

13 Freud, *Moses and Monotheism*, p. 91.

14 Ibid.

15 Jacob Taubes, *The Political Theology of Paul*, Stanford 2004, p. 69.

16 Ibid., p. 95.

Numbers, are put to work through numbers and counting, numbering off, enumeration, and scanning. Cultural techniques are understood as negotiation and intervention, not as an anthropological unconscious. If, as Mary Douglas writes in an ethnographical decoding of the book of Numbers, culture should be described as a differentiated pattern of claims, and community as a field of relationships,[17] in the Moses complex these relationships are constituted structurally, non-mimetically, as relationships without an image. The critique of depiction and representative forms was crucial to new music and the new cinema of the 1960s and 70s.[18] No one then assumed a hard and fast reality before the cinema projected it into the world. However, Straub and Huillet's techniques differ fundamentally from the cinematic forms that were being discussed in France and Italy under the impact of semiotic theories. Straub/Huillet don't refer to semiotic procedures of subjectivization, but rather to the necessary materialization and embodiment of all signs and rules. Their method corresponds closest to the thought of Roman Jakobson, who semiotically derives the inseparability of materiality and meaning.[19] For Straub/Huillet the problem of legalism is also the remanence of signs in the physical, and their insistence on the behavior of bodies. Here they meet Sigmund Freud.

When Straub and Huillet plan and edit shots in relation to one another, they follow Schoenberg in implementing relationships of numbers and frequencies in the varied materialities of a real world, so that unimaginable spaces and directions emerge. They sink texts and verses into bodies as language, into actor's bodies, singers' bodies, farmers' bodies, and into landscapes, so as to visualize an aesthetic of resistance.

The fact that the perception of rhythmic, mathematical, and frequency ratios by the senses, through hearing and seeing, can never be "pure" is the central subject matter of the Moses opera. Where mathematically pure ratios are realized through instruments, technical setups, and materials, new effects and

17 See Mary Douglas, *In the Wilderness. The Doctrine of Defilement in the Book of Numbers* (Sheffield 1993), paperback reprint 2004, p. 43.

18 In 1974, when Straub and Huillet were editing their film, a ten-year-long debate within semiotic film theory on cinematic structural relationships was reaching its height. See Umberto Eco, "Articulations of the Cinematic Code," in Bill Nichols (ed.), *Movies and Methods*, Berkeley 1976, pp. 590–607; and Pier Paolo Pasolini, *Empirismo eretico*, Milan 1972.

19 In a series of lectures in winter 1942/43 in New York, Roman Jakobson also in exile, developed the idea that sound and meaning can never be separated from one another. See Roman Jakobson, *Six leçons sur le son et le sens* (1942/43), Paris 1976, p. 22.

affects are produced for new and real relationships, human, non-human, and inhuman. In Schoenberg's opera, in resonance with the acoustics of the surroundings, unconceivably beautiful sound unfurls, and this is what is perceived, not the mathematics of the tonal relationships. The operations of strict relationships, when they encounter matter, make their effects visible in the protagonists, in Moses and Aron, [20] the People of Israel, the people in the opera, and equally its audience, a heterogeneous people of the world. With Straub and Huillet the *dispositif* of the cinema emerges as a space in which these relationships can both be experienced and observed. Arnold Schoenberg's music of twelve sequentially related tones and its transfer into film thus raises the question of the poetology of media-technical setups in regard to possible coming communities, societies, legalisms. In this complex Hölderlin notes that poetology sounds fine but realizes violence.[21] Finally, Freud's Moses text opens up a perception of the historical and historiographical dimensions of this media politics.

The Moses complex derives its actuality from recalling the emergence of cultures as fields of mutually engendering relationships. From the perspective of media studies, which is a science of differential relationships between materialities and immaterialities, noises and messages, channels and signals, apparatuses and perceptions, the relationship to God or gods turns out to be one between people and their systems of thought. So media studies argues against fundamentalism, whether ontological, anthropological, or technicistic.

The figure of Moses is a decisive node in the network of a discourse that is now being invoked and loudly proclaimed as the Jewish-Christian tradition. This discourse has the tendency to deny that violence was and is constitutive to it foundation and covenant, as sacrifice, command, regime. It equally tends to deny that there are three great monotheistic religions that have to deal with

20 Translator's note: In order to underline the book's specific reference to Arnold Schoenberg's opera, this figure is generally referred to in Schoenberg's deviant spelling. Exceptions are made, however, when the figure is mentioned in wider cultural contexts, in quotations from the Bible, or from the English translation of Schoenberg's libretto by Allen Forte, which appears in parallel with the German text in the vocal score by Winfried Zillig (Mainz 1957) and uses the conventional spelling "Aaron." The pronunciation of Aron, "Ah-ron," differs from the English "Air-ren" and the Hebrew "Ah-ha-ron." Interestingly, Schoenberg names Moses in the English spelling, not the usual German "Mose" (pron. "Moz-zuh"), both of which differ from the Hebrew "Mo-sheh."

21 See Friedrich Hölderlin, "'The declining fatherland ...'" in Friedrich Hölderlin, *Essays and Letters*, ed. and trans. Jeremy Adler and Charlie Louth, London, 2009, pp. 271–276.

violence at the foundation of their covenant. Currently, arguably not by chance at the end of the culture of printing, this tradition is again being invoked in a Moses-complex boom as the question of what a people is and who belongs to it—in Germany once again as the question of exclusion, once again as the demonization of a cultural minority.[22] But what is the question to which the answer is the people? One about Rousseau's sovereignty, the *volonté générale*, about Marx's proletariat? About the exclusive organization of counting votes after the German, Anglo-Saxon, or Swiss model? The structural question of what or who is to be counted, symbolized, represented or not? The aesthetic question of visibility, of the place where the people appears and thus calls for politics? What, in this field, do conflict, controversy, or resistance mean? What kind of politics can sounds and images, tones and takes offer in this context? For Straub and Huillet the people is present when it appears in a place where it isn't expected, isn't envisaged, isn't conceived. Or where it resists. Showing this is not only cinematically complex but also requires the making of images outside of figurations, conventions, and laws.

Four constellations manifest the Moses complex as one that has at its core to do with media and collectives: first, the relationship between migration, medium, and law; second, the relationship between counting and ratios; third the relationship between the law and the people; and fourth, the relationship, which represents the actual urgency of the subject, between exile and space.

1.2. MEDIUM, MIGRATION

The Moses complex is about the simultaneous emergence or birth of a law, a nation, and a historical media culture. This constellation is admittedly the more complex historically, both in regard to the systems of writing in the transmission of the Bible and to the inscription of the law.[23] It has hence been

22 See the essay by Alfred Bodenheimer, *Haut Ab!*, Göttingen 2012.

23 For the basis of writing and the materiality of writing in the context of the Hebrew Bible see Alexander Achilles Fischer, *Der Text des Alten Testaments. Neubearbeitung der Einführung in die Biblia Hebraica von Ernst Würthwein*, Stuttgart 2009. The fact that the Decalogue is an asynchronous compilation of historically heterogeneous ethical and cultural precepts was already supposed by Martin Buber, *Moses*, Zurich 1948, p. 176.

summarized as the "agonizing research history of the Sinai pericope."[24] Media theories have repeatedly constructed their own Sinai situations. Despite the differences between the historical-materialist media theories of Walter Benjamin or Bertolt Brecht, the models of the Canadian school, or Gilbert Simondon's differentiation of mechanical, industrial, and postindustrial technical objects as evolutionary forms, correspondences appear between radical media changes and juridical constitutions. Gregory Bateson's ecological-cybernetic thought, together with systems-theoretical media theory, discourse-analytical, and media-archaeological studies or research into cultural techniques, reminds us that the transcendent is better initially understood as a material and operational relay on which social processes are regulated through recursion. The technical, aesthetic, and political spheres are made dependent on one another in this monitoring circuit. Only in this sense can the Old Testament be understood as the implementation of a universal order: "One law shall be to him that is homeborn, and unto the stranger that sojourneth among you."[25] The law always needs to be reconceived on the arrival of new strangers, if you decide not to combat unfamiliarity but to optimize communication.

The "Sinai pericope" was already governed by the dazzlement and latency that would characterize the Moses complex in the twentieth century. Indistinguishable, awe-inspiring fire, smoke, and thunder compel necessary distinctions: call, dictation, and inscription, which are then understood as law. The imposition of a distinction, of having to decide without knowledge, is the constitutive void, the constitutive *off* at the center of media science. The difficulty of differentiation is the cause of the latency, and hesitation, faltering that interrupt events and writing about them. Even Moses has no interest at first in becoming the speaker of a downtrodden class. Twice he must climb Mount Sinai to fetch the laws that God has inscribed on the stone tablets.[26] God provides the tablets the first time, but the second time Moses has to hack them out himself, so that only the writing, and no longer its medium, is of divine origin. Law and cultural

24 Translated from Matthias Köckert, "Wie kam das Gesetz an den Sinai?," in *Vergegenwärtigung des Alten Testaments. Beiträge zur biblischen Hermeneutik. Festschrift für Rudolf Smend zum 70. Geburtstag*, ed. Christoph Bultmann and others, Göttingen 2002, pp. 13–27: 15. Translation from p. 27: "Once the Decalogue was inscribed on the tablets in Deuteronomy, it could no longer be missing as such on Mount Sinai."

25 Exodus 12:49, *The Bible. Authorized King James Version*, ed. intro. and notes by Robert Carroll and Stephen Prickett, Oxford, New York 1997.

26 Exodus 32:16.

techniques superimpose. But only when both noise and signal come into view and a decision is necessary and taken does it become clear which law has been in effect all the while. The Moses complex is recursive; there will never be a definitive work on Moses.

Once the emergence of a new medium releases an excess of possibilities, decisions, practices, relationships, and meaning, corresponding cultural techniques, regulations, and precepts organize this surplus and assert differences from which new and unknown social forms develop. The dynamic of migration, medium, and legalism also determined the transmission, transcription, and editing of the Moses story. For the exiled People of Israel it was the introduction of writing that tied the complex of freedom, autonomy, fear, and law into a bundle and a covenant. Media thinking unties it again. It understands *dispositifs*—that is, power relationships that proceed from forms of data processing and circulation, and establish new spaces and correspondingly new controls—as the relay of a legalism that can come into conflict with juridical systems.[27]

Contemporary experience includes the networking and restructuring of knowledge and relationships by media setups at a speed that disallows their accompanying observation by an individual political consciousness. The statistically regulated dynamic logic of big data renders both the psycho-logic of individual subjects and the "grandiose powers" of religion as mass psychology inoperative. This is where questions about coming societies begin: the link between connectivity and collectivity in electronics points beyond simple mass psychology. Straub and Huillet's version of the Moses opera also marks a turning point in this political respect: in 1974, parallel with the individualized search engines of Horst Herold, president of the BKA, the Federal Criminal Police Office of Germany, they made clear that the people must be spoken about differently from masses, and also differently from statistics. Their approach to cinema, which was uniquely able to connect the particular and the mass from the very beginning, is correspondingly resistive. With their cinema Straub and Huillet anticipate the question of the political aspect of new media.

In both Schoenberg's opera and the film Moses und Aron conflict and action, which primarily means acts of speech, take place before the law. The lawless camp as socially, politically, and aesthetically unorganized space and time determines the artistic constellations and solutions of the libretto and *mise en*

27 See Cornelia Vismann, *Medien der Rechtsprechung*, Frankfurt/Main 2011.

scène. This was quickly identified by critics of the opera: "Pure art, subject to no law except its own, is equivalent to the omnipotent deity Moses encounters on Sinai."[28] This will by examined more closely in the following for the cinema: what laws of the medium and what media laws intervene in art and its forms? What forms and operations remain before the law? What does media art mean and what does it accomplish? Whom does it bear upon, and how? The matter in question is the coming of the media.

Arnold Schoenberg's opera and Straub/Huillet's film show that long times in the wilderness and desert are the precondition for reaching the place before the law and so, as the Moses of the opera dictatorially demands, to "purify your thinking." The aesthetic and political aspects of this wilderness of perception can be reconstructed historically, but require times of blank hearing and seeing, of hesitation and decision. The growing of the desert is suddenly a question of time. How must we listen, and in what direction, to hear the grind of stone on stone? What is at stake is the paradoxical mission of liberating a people, of forming a free people, and thus Moses' claim in the opera: " [...] der Mensch ist unabhängig und tut, was ihm beliebt aus freiem Willen [(...) man is independent and does what pleases him, according to free will]."[29] The advice Moses gives the people, now only represented by a couple of warriors, at the end of the opera, to go into the wasteland, there to remain forever before the law, can be seen as totalitarian or anarchic: "Aber in der Wüste seid ihr unüberwindlich [But even in the wasteland you shall be victorious]."[30] This argumentation is continued in the strategies of nomadism.[31] Chantal Akerman described this superhuman effort as a necessary part of the liberation of all oppressed people: "The 40 years the Jews spent in the desert to lose all trace of slavery: something the blacks and the concentration camp victims didn't have."[32] Today the Mediterranean is the

28 Daniel Albright, "Series Editor's Foreword," in Charlotte M. Cross, Russell A. Berman, *Political and Religious Ideas in the Works of Arnold Schoenberg*, New York 2000, pp. xvi/xvii.

29 Arnold Schönberg, *Sämtliche Werke*, section III, stage works, series A, vol. 8, parts 1 and 2, *Moses und Aron. Oper in drei Akten*, ed. Christian Martin Schmidt, Mainz 1977, act III, p. 503 (quoted as Schönberg, *Moses und Aron*, score). The English translation, by Allen Forte, appears in parallel with the German text in Arnold Schoenberg, *Moses und Aron. Oper in drei Akten, vocal score, prep. Winfried Zillig, Mainz 1957, act III,* unpaginated.

30 Ibid.

31 Gilles Deleuze and Félix Guattari, "1227: Treatise on Nomadology: The War Machine," in *A Thousand Plateaus. Capitalism and Schizophrenia*, ed. Brian Massumi, Minneapolis 1987, pp. 351–424.

32 Chantal Akerman quoted from Nicole Brenez, *Chantal Akerman, The Pajama Interviews*, Vienna 2011, p. 61f.

wasteland of the migrants: monstrous blue-eyed death stares back; European voraciousness is a sailing casino called Costa Concordia, giving Africa the slip again.[33]

1.3. THE PEOPLE

In talking about people, the people, the multiple people, does it make a difference whether they are refugees, strangers, travelers, migrants, exiles? How does the emergence of masses, multitudes, mobs, movements, communities, collectives, bands, or swarms relate to the law? When does flight turn into colonization? What is the situation before the law? What is the camp? How does the people relate to the camp? Why do the tent cities that have sprung up in the early twenty-first century in cities, not in the desert of the refugees, call themselves camps, protest camps? In parks and squares, Tahrir, Zuccotti, Gezi, or Nahda, forms of power and the political before the law are being staged and improvised. The concept of the camp is no longer the same as in the twentieth century. But it is always linked with violence. The people camp in the desert, the mountain swathed in smoke; God, who has borne the people on the wings of an eagle into liberation, announces himself in a trumpet call, presses and urges, signals commands. The genealogy of the people is linked to the history of violent transmission. How can we think of a collective of hearing and seeing, of the visual and audible? A collective that has always been constitutively linked, below the threshold of perception, by the cultural and media organization of the senses? A collective whose visibility, speaking, hearing, and acting is apportioned to media faculties that relate to one another through administrative, scientific, and cultural channels? Jacques Rancière sees the principle identity of politics and "aestheticization" in modernity as arising from these constellations. Hence "the autonomization of aesthetics as a new nexus between the order of the logos and the partition of the perceptible [as] part of the modern configuration of politics."[34] While the organization of a Greek people in a

33 See FILM SOCIALISME, F/CH 2010, dir. Jean-Luc Godard, various formats, HDTV, 102 min.

34 Jacques Rancière, *Dis-agreement. Politics and Philosophy*, trans. Julie Rose, Minneapolis 1999, p. 58.

city state, requires "the lack of any vacuum, [and a] saturation of the space and time of the community,"[35] at least in his theory, the modern sovereign people demonstrates its political concentration in the setting of breaks, absences, and gaps. It "reveal[s] the noncount" to those it excludes, and distances itself from the "toiling, suffering population, the ignorant masses, the rabble bound or unbound."[36] Anyone who gives voice to this radical gap "between real justice, resembling divine proportion, and democratic stagings of wrong, assimilated to the reign of injustice,"[37] who argues and acts in the sense of a communal archi-politics, is called a terrorist. The film by Straub and Huillet opens and frames its discussion of the people with exactly these two poles of fundamental political opposition: with the Luther Bible and the dedication to Holger Meins; between the account of divinely legitimized terror and the remembrance of a filmmaker and colleague who, as Rancière put it, "adopted as [his] political task the requirement of achieving community *arkhe*, its internalization and promotion of total awareness of it."[38] However, all "promotion of total awareness" in Holger Meins' film OSKAR LANGENFELD. 12 MAL [Oskar Langenfeld. 12 Times] (FRG 1967) is achieved through precise shots and sharply analytical montage that don't allow a nostalgic proximity to ordinary people. The film shows the abandonment of figures such as Langenfeld, a homeless man with tuberculosis in Berlin, Kreuzberg. Twelve months in the life of this ragman are put together like a Way of the Cross or as a reminiscence of Godard's VIVRE SA VIE [My Life to Live] (F 1962).[39] So Holger Meins' work is both a reference to cultural and cinema history and a rehabilitation of ordinary people in film.

The people is the real subject of cinema, which not only convened its folk in the collective of an auditorium and the shared experience of a public screening[40] but also, and from the very beginning, formed national and international presentation networks, a virtual cinema people between Los Angeles and New York, Moscow and Vladivostok, Bombay and Jakarta that was able to have the same film experiences from the 1920s onward. This relationship between

35 Ibid., p. 67.
36 Ibid., p. 80.
37 Ibid., p. 81.
38 Ibid., p. 80.
39 See Harun Farocki, "Das Vorbild jeder stilisierten Jugendunsicherheit muss James Dean sein," in Gerd Conradt (ed.), *Starbuck Holger Meins. Ein Porträt als Zeitbild*, Berlin 2001, pp. 178–182: 181.
40 See Heide Schlüpmann, "Das Aufklärungsversprechen des Kinos oder: die Ablösung der Metaphysik durch die Medien," in *montage AV "Erfahrung,"* 19/1 2010, pp. 161–174.

cinema as the first mass medium and a virtual people of viewers is also a part of the Moses complex in the twentieth century. While no constitution has ever made room for the people as "rabble," that opposite of the sovereign people, the "uncounted"[41] and non-registered could appear for the first time on the cinema screen without being theatrically staged. Dziga Vertov gives prominent place to an infamous bunch of ne'er-do-wells and alcoholics, to the mad and the indigent, thus allowing them to become and participate in the coming people. The problem and the challenge of cinema as a cultural technique will remain that of developing a sense of where expulsion from the official people takes place, where one of us, on the street, is uncounted, *sans papiers*, or suddenly no longer counts.

"[...] when I walk along the street and each person looks at me to see if I'm a Jew or a Christian"[42]—so Arnold Schoenberg begins his comments, in a letter to Wassily Kandinsky dated May 4, 1923, on an incident in 1921 in Mattsee near Salzburg, when he was forbidden by municipal resolution to vacation there with his family.[43] Schoenberg contrasts points of view as behavior: "You will call it a regrettable individual case if I too am affected by the results of the anti-Semitic movement. But why do people not see the bad Jew as a regrettable individual case, instead as what's typical? [...] But it isn't an individual case, that is, it isn't merely accidental. On the contrary, it is all part of a plan."[44] Action grows out the way in which people look at you, diagnoses or prophesies Schoenberg in 1923: "But what is anti-Semitism to lead to if not to acts of violence?"[45]

In order to begin to perceive those who find themselves looked at as other, spaces of hearing and seeing have to be understood and exploded and a space opened up that causes people to appear, to become visible, where there was otherwise nothing to be heard or seen, or nothing was supposed to be heard or seen. The creation of spaces of ideas is the problem of the works associated with the Moses complex. To do this they invent new aesthetic procedures of narrating history, arranging tones, differentiating languages and images in opera,

41 Rancière, *Dis-agreement*, p. 80.

42 Arnold Schoenberg to Wassily Kandinsky, Mödling, Austria, May 4, 1923, in Schoenberg, *Letters*, p. 89.

43 See Hans Heinz Stuckenschmidt, *Schoenberg – His Life, World and Works*, Richmond 1977 p. 274.

44 Arnold Schoenberg to Wassily Kandinsky, May 4, 1923, in Schoenberg, *Letters*, p. 90.

45 Ibid., p. 92.

cinema, or dream bodies. Schoenberg, Straub/Huillet, Freud. It has to do with art as a space for people.

When describing art as resistance in his commentary on the films of Danièle Huillet and Jean-Marie Straub, Gilles Deleuze speaks of the lack of the people. Proceeding from a remark by Paul Klee, "The people are missing," he explains to the students at the IDHEC, the French state film school in Paris: "The people are missing and at the same time, they are not missing. The people are missing means that the fundamental affinity between a work of art and a people that does not yet exist is not, will never be clear. There is no work of art that does not call on a people who does not yet exist."[46] Art is supposed to bring forth the people it is about. Recursively. Proleptically. The people is an act of creation. The people marks the awareness gap from which it can be experienced as strange. This is a constitutive void that draws attention to the circularly causal production of cultural perception.

From the structural perspective, and likewise as an effect of a void, Ernesto Laclau has described a constitution of the people in the *futurum exactum* of possible appellation. From the "pure" structure of difference and ratio, and in the linguistic practice of combination and substitution, fully in the spirit of Saussure, he outlines the process of designation that causes a people or the people or simply people to appear as the result of a subsequent signification. He rehabilitates the term "populist" through showing that it is itself the strategic exclusion of an unpredictable plurality or mass from political thought. In a "populist reason," the logic or reason of the popular—which is distinguished in its own freedom not only from the sociologically described *Volk* and the ideologically invoked *völkisch* [literaly "ethinic," "of the people," but we should not forget the National Socialist overtones of the word, *trans.*] in German, from the Hispanic/Latin American *pueblo* and *popular*, and altogether from the *demos*—the people for Laclau appears as a complex of discursive differentiations and relationships that is realized among folks themselves. This, however, is precisely what makes the people real and effective, and brings real action or behavior into the arena: "'The people' is not something of the nature of an ideological expression, but a real relation between social agents. It is, in other terms, one

46 Gilles Deleuze, "What is the Creative Act?" in Gilles Deleuze, *Two Regimes of Madness. Texts and Interviews 1975–1995. Semiotext(e)*, New York 2007, pp. 317–329: 329.

way of constituting the unity of the group."[47] It is the aim of all the Moses works by Freud, Schoenberg, Straub and Huillet, by Deleuze, Douglas, Assmann, Laclau, and Taubes, to awaken an awareness of unheard and unseen but operative relationships in noises and sounds, in landscapes and historical constellations, between and among different people. Yet they all point out the terrible violence that ensues when strangers remain strange in a strange land.

The people arises as a difference phenomenon. In the network of difference relationships there is principally no center, only a "differential ensemble,"[48] which is brought into play by the discourse as "any complex of elements in which *relations* play the constitutive role,"[49] be it linguistic, acoustic, or optical. The political comes into view in the collapse or destruction of signification as a system, because only then can new combinations of elements be produced. An empty signifier, writes Laclau, would only be "a sequence of sounds." [50] The politics of the desert, as Schoenberg's precondition of liberation, could hardly be described more precisely: a new space can only unfurl from the leveling and equal distribution of the twelve tones related only to one another. Laclau even brings in the difficult concept of purification at this point: an empty signifier must be "deprived of any signifying function"[51] in order to reveal the system of signification and make it operative. Thus political activity always means keeping open the irreducible gap between words and things, so that criticism can be deployed as a question of the power of appellation and the foundation of a discourse with its rhetorical differentiations. Laclau encounters the Moses complex in the constitutive failure of every appellation and designation. In Schoenberg's opera Moses realizes, in his dramatic collapse at the end of act II, that he can't lead the people, can't be a leader, but can only keep open the gaps and caesuras in the linguistic system, and thus has to become the people he liberates. With Schoenberg it's a despairing Moses who calls "O Wort, du Wort, das mir fehlt! [O word, thou word, that I lack!]."[52] Laclau points out that the lacking word, which both breaks off and renews Moses' mission, is the beginning of every

47 Ernesto Laclau, *On Populist Reason*, London 2005, p. 73.
48 Ibid., p. 69.
49 Ibid., p. 68.
50 Ernesto Laclau, "Why do Empty Signifiers Matter to Politics?" in Ernesto Laclau, *Emancipation(s)*, London, New York 1996, pp. 36–45: 36.
51 Ibid., p. 65.
52 Schönberg, *Moses und Aron*, score II, act II, bars 1133–1136.

resistant rhetorical strategy to turn the foreign into the people. The popular limps in on semantic crutches, in torn garb: "The political construction of the people is, for that reason, essentially catachrestial."[53] Jackals, Arabs, Niggaz. A residue of strangeness must remain, to avoid pure order. For Laclau a people is characterized by its resistance to integration into symbolic systems: "The 'people' will always be something more than the pure opposite of power. There is a Real of the 'people' which resists symbolic integration."[54] The people means dealing with strangers. But there are historical differences within the network of signifiers and representation in Latin American, German, French, or Jewish contexts under Peronism, fascism, Zionism, or present-day globalized capitalism. Continuous renegotiation is necessary. The people doesn't insist as a sovereign but as a difference phenomenon, as the effect of a difference that it must simultaneously keep open in speech, music, movement, and montage.

With this strategy a different kind of counting comes into play from the one Jacques Rancière criticizes as a police method, as upholding the state, repressive, and exclusive.[55] It's a counting of the uncounted, and can admittedly only appear as conflict and claim, as an interruption of the course of events, an upsetting of the balance. This new counting, which is likewise used in the non-linear aesthetic of Schoenberg and Straub/Huillet, also involves subjectivization processes that, at the end of the age of printing and in the era of big data, are no longer covered by Rancière's logic of the "literary animal."[56] Different people show up in singular and unforeseeable forms. These new forms of the multiple and varied people were already being sought in the twentieth century and its projects of the disorganization and equalization of signs and tones, its projects of nomadism. The beginning of an unknown constellation isn't heralded by a number or the difference between 0 and 1, but by emptiness, noise, and awe, the perception of which initially requires a decision. The film MOSES UND ARON opens with this. There's something stirring in the bush; a noise is about to evolve into sound.

53 Laclau, *On Populist Reason*, p. 72.

54 Ibid., p. 152.

55 Rancière, *Dis-agreement*, p. 36: "Political subjectivation produces a multiple that was not given in the police constitution of the community, a multiple whose count poses itself as contradictory in terms of police logic. The commons, the people, are the first of these multiples that split up the community."

56 Ibid., p. 37.

In this book the evocation of a people is considered in the light of media-theoretical studies that depart, at the end of the Gutenberg era, from the idea of nations, masses, and the collective, and examined as a question of the texture of affiliations, connections, bodies, and controls. Works of art don't only address a not yet existing people; they also construct it in their execution. Commenting on Straub and Huillet's take on the people, Jacques Rancière argues in the sense of the distribution and organization of sensualism, and therefore media-theoretically: "The people are missing. You don't need Klee and Deleuze to know."[57] And he adds that with Straub and Huillet the people "is what is spoken by bodies taking its part. And, of course, everything plays out in the specificity of this embodiment."[58] But it's also crucial that this decision remains recursive: only the decision, and not without violence, shows the nature of the captivity, of the camp that provoked it and what can come of it. The decision evokes a memory and a future.

1.4. NUMBERS

The film Moses und Aron opens with two numerical reminders: a page from the Luther Bible of 1523, Exodus 32:25–28, which tells of the murder of three thousand men ordered by Moses when he returned from the mountain and finds the people worshipping other gods. After the production titles there is the briefest of dedications to Holger Meins recalling his cinematic method of mercilessly throwing the life of the infamous (un-famous) Oskar Langenfeld into relief in twelve murderous strategies in order to ask what the life actually is for which all battles are fought. For Straub and Huillet there's obviously a correspondence in Meins' undramatic uniformity to Schoenberg's compositional technique, but this could equally be interpreted as the reckoning and vengeful Old Testament power. The number twelve is compelling. Holger Meins' shots strive against this power twelve times. Schoenberg forcefully dissolves its hierarchy into twelve

57 Jacques Rancière, "Arithmetics of the People," http://www.diagonalthoughts.com/?p=1605 (accessed June 8, 2015). Originally published as "Arithmétiques du peuple (Rohmer, Godard, Straub)," *Trafic*, no. 42, summer 2002.

58 Ibid., p. 185.

equal relationships between the semitones. first counting, then distinction, then a new beginning.[59] Straub and Huillet transfer this to the cinema.

While the film was being made the German police was beginning to count differently. “The police have become aware,” wrote the inventor of the INPOL system, Horst Herold, “that in as much as they fight crime they actually represent a gigantic enterprise of data processing.”[60] The gathering, storage, combination, and processing of thousands of data led to an overwhelming quantity of crime statistics. During the system’s first year it netted around 52,000 people. Its first international success came in 1975, when at the push of a button its database of the numbers of stolen vehicles was delivered to Stockholm, where a group calling itself the Kommando Holger Meins had stormed the German Embassy. Herold, the bringer of new media, and thus of a legalism that could correct “the enormous superstructure of laws and decrees from which the actual conditions have long since moved away,” called on the basis of these new media techniques for the police to take on the “state’s task of shaping the future.”[61] Very soon the rank and file old lawyers were murmuring against him on the basis of the old data system.

In the Old Testament the relationship between space, community, law, and history is recurrently taken up as a relationship between counting and numbers. In her astonishing reading of the book of Numbers, Mary Douglas has shown that this book, thought to have been put together from heterogeneous sources and edited late, actually follows an exact logic of non-linear construction. Its structure is not only determined by doubling and repetition but also by a circular logic that connects laws and legends in mutual commentaries like *ritornelli*. “We are so used to linear writing that it is a shock at first to imagine a whole law book or epic constructed as if it were a sonnet with a very definite rhyming system.”[62] She also compares its combinatory construction, in reference to an early text by Miriam Hansen, with the principle of montage in film.[63] As in all the books of the

59 See Thomas Macho, “Zeit und Zahl. Kalender und Zeitrechnung als Kulturtechnik,” in Sybille Krämer, Horst Bredekamp (eds.), *Bild – Schrift – Zahl*, Munich 2003, pp. 179–192: 180. “Counting is older than numbers” (translated from ibid.).

60 Translated from Horst Herold, *Kriminalität und Gesellschaft. Rationalisierung und Automation in der Verbrechensbekämpfung*, RIAS Funkuniversität 1975 (79th lecture series, broadcast Monday July 7, 1975), typescript copy of the RIAS manuscript, Berlin 1975, p. 2.

61 Ibid., p. 61.

62 Douglas, *In the Wilderness*, p. xxiii.

63 Ibid., p. xxviii.

Pentateuch the description of cultural techniques is also their incorporation, transmission, and reflection. This particularly applies to their linguistic collocation, in whose strict structure practical knowledge is conveyed.

The book of Numbers is about counting people, the people, about census, which Jacques Rancière called the most important apparatus of contemporary law enforcement.[64] Douglas in no way describes this counting as a precise classification system. For Deleuze and Guattari enumeration marks the transition from the machinery of state to the war machine. The numerical principle of organization belongs to the state's deployment of armies, but on the other hand the state takes on the martial form of traversing the country through its enumeration of the people: "Its numerical organization into tens, fifties, hundreds, thousands, etc., and the associated spatial organization were obviously adopted by State armies, but basically bear witness to a military system specific to the great nomads of the steppes [...] Moses got the idea from his father-in-law, Jethro the Kenite: he used it as an organizational principle for the march and migration, and applied it himself to the military domain."[65] During an exodus, on the run, in exile, the distinction between the self and the other is renegotiated. Douglas also subscribes to this theory in reconstructing the situation of an army of refugees numbering several thousand claiming previously settled land in the Near East.

According to Mary Douglas the editors of the book of Numbers were priests who were not in the least interested in the establishment of rules of inclusion and exclusion, but were concerned, on the contrary, with the avoidance or at least moderation of "populist xenophobia."[66] The book was written in order to discover ways of integrating strangers. Correspondingly different from the book of Exodus, the figure of Moses in Numbers is the gentle head of a mixed enclave community and, just like the one in the opera libretto, a typical representative of an egalitarian society. "The Moses described in the book of Numbers is the only kind of leader that a sectarian enclave can tolerate: a charismatic leader who never speaks in his own name, who is always the servant of God."[67] Douglas also develops this egalitarian culture as an aesthetic model, as a "surprisingly

64 See Rancière, *Dis-agreement*, p. 21–43.
65 Deleuze/Guattari, *A Thousand Plateaus*, p. 118.
66 Douglas, *In the Wilderness*, p. 39.
67 Ibid., p. 58.

open political vision [...] supported by the cosmopolitan literary style," as the model of a non-hierarchical, complementary institutional organization of contrapuntal thought. The relationship structures of these cultures were ensured through common rules about impurity, not as laws but as an agreement to prevent disease and contamination under the conditions of migration and the camp. In such a "benign doctrine of defilement" it is not the stranger who is excluded: "Contact with a foreigner is not defiling, only idolatry." Douglas sees the aniconic aspect of this society as a "cohesion of dissent"[68] in the common rejection of idols. She suggests a reading of Korah's revolt and destruction as a governmental attack on the priestly caste, reported by the priests from their perspective as historical losers. The King James Bible correspondingly tells of "two hundred and fifty princes of the assembly, famous in the congregation, men of renown," who "rose up before Moses"[69] for the community of refugees against the claim of Moses and Aaron to speak in the name of God. Moses as a sectarian leader doesn't see the rebels as operating against him personally but as "gathered together against the LORD" and murmuring against Aaron.[70] The earth devours two hundred and fifty ritually distinguished men and all their households. Walter Benjamin uses this episode of enumerated violence to exemplify the sudden striking of divine power to secure its rights over the living and "for the sake of the living,"[71] and differentiates it from the bloodletting of bare life as practiced by the Greek deities. Jacques Derrida further differentiates this as a distinction between Greek and Jewish law-making. The primitive Greek blood sacrifice is contrasted with the "absolute imperative"[72] of the sixth commandment, "Thou shalt not kill." For Benjamin the destruction of Korah's people is an annihilation of the "privileged Levites,"[73] and in this respect his argumentation doesn't differ from Mary Douglas's later anthropological interpretation.[74] Samuel Weber, drawing on a Zwingli Bible, conversely objects that "the violence, as Benjamin suggests, is not simply retaliation on a privileged priestly class, but rather on the representatives of the community, who rose

68 Ibid., p. 41.
69 Numbers 16:2.
70 Numbers 16:11.
71 Benjamin, "Critique of Violence," p. 297.
72 Derrida, "Force of Law," p. 288.
73 Benjamin, "Critique of Violence," p. 297.
74 See Samuel Weber, "In the Name of the Law" and "Deconstruction before the Name."

up against Moses and Aaron in the name of the people whom they represent: 'Now we've had enough. For the entire community is sacred'."[75] The problem of advocacy disturbs the Exodus and makes people resistive. Everyone counts, but no one speaks for himself. After the company of Korah has been swallowed up, the people murmur all the more.[76] So the Bible text to which Benjamin refers doesn't tell "a completely different story,"[77] as Weber protests; it is more that all translations and interpretations take sides, for which they have to decide. What is the problem represented by the mass migration of foreigners? How should it be approached? What legal forms are useful in this circumstance? How forward-looking is it to portray truth and legalism as exclusive? Mary Douglas's philological-anthropological reconstruction of a society of different strangers who have to come to a recursive understanding and should never be counted down to two poles is just as unequivocal.

Even cursory readings of Moses' strategies in regard to the people, foreignness, and violence according to the logic of numbers and payback show how precisely the Moses figure in Arnold Schoenberg's libretto and opera is put together from various Old Testament layers but is still contemporarily biographical. Schoenberg's Moses is a protean figure that adopts heterogeneous positions and carries on a kind of soliloquy along the texts and stages of exile. So with Schoenberg the "Now we've had enough!" with which Korah rises up against Moses and his claim "to speak [...] in the name of the entire community he is held to represent"[78] comes at the beginning of the third, discontinued act of the opera, which Moses, speaking as always, opens with "Aron, nun ist es genug! [Aaron, now this must cease!]," to which Aron, who has hitherto sung and is suddenly disturbingly human in his speaking voice, answers: "Willst du mich morden? [Will you then kill me?]"[79] In the context of the biblical quotation Moses would be speaking as the rebel Korah against himself. The answer that Schoenberg's Moses then gives to Schoenberg's Aron explicitly corresponds to Benjamin's assertion that divine power must be exerted "over all life for the

75 Samuel Weber, "Deconstruction before the Name." The King James version of Numbers 16:3 says "*Ye take* too much upon you."

76 Numbers 16: 41.

77 Weber, "Deconstruction before the Name," p. 1188.

78 Ibid.

79 Schoenberg, *Moses und Aron*, vocal score, act III, unpaginated.

sake of the living,"[80] so it seems likely that Schoenberg was thinking about Benjamin's "Critique of Violence" while he was writing the libretto: "Es geht nicht um *dein* Leben ... [It is not a matter of *your* life ...]";[81] it's for the sake of the living. Samuel Weber's reading, drawing on a radically reformed Bible translation, shows that the German text can be read as nothing less than "demonically equivocal":[82] "The destruction of Korah can be read [...] as the eruption of violence interrupting the claim to speak lawfully in the name of the other," but also "in [...] the opposite sense, as the reinstatement of this very claim."[83] The binary opposites of Greek and Jewish tradition, democracy and permanent revolution, tallying votes and advocacy, sedentary and nomadic, which echo in the discourse of the Moses figure, and not only in Schoenberg's opera, also need to be deconstructed and increased to triple and multiple models. Then it can certainly be shown that "deconstruction is justice."[84] Moses doesn't represent a distinct historical figure but a complex of negotiations that Sigmund Freud will ascribe to various historical layers of traumatic events and their working through. Schoenberg's Moses is at most characterized by repeatedly wanting to withdraw from his pre-eminent mission, by his procrastination. Only if observed as a texture of relationships, rhythms, numbers, and paybacks, as undertaken by Mary Douglas, can the Moses texts, operas, and films be understood as dealing with "populist xenophobia."[85]

It will be seen that the radically egalitarian Moses in the book of Numbers corresponds both to the radically relational procedures of Schoenberg's composition in twelve equally related tones and to the practice of the segmented distribution of bodies and spaces in Straub and Huillet's film. What can be experienced in cinema doesn't result from the depiction of a previously existing reality but from the constellation of shots and spatial division. The strictly egalitarian formalism and constructivism of twelve-tone composition comes from a radical unwillingness to compromise in Schoenberg's work. While Theodor W. Adorno criticizes twelve-tone composition as a lugubrious Enlightenment dialectic, Schoenberg's attitude is neither dialectic nor eschatological but

80 Benjamin, "Critique of Violence," p. 297.
81 Schoenberg, *Moses und Aron*, vocal score, act III, unpaginated (emphasis added).
82 Weber, quoting Benjamin, "Deconstruction before the Name," p. 1188.
83 Ibid.
84 Derrida, "*Force of Law*," p. 243.
85 Douglas, *In the Wilderness*, p. 39.

committed to philosophical and historical irreconcilability from the point of view of exile. The new sound spaces he opens up don't provide a home; they are expansive, unpredictable, awe-inspiring, recursive spaces for strangers in strange lands.

Arnold Schoenberg, who, as letters to students and friends document, decidedly and energetically returned to Judaism after the so-called Mattsee episode and reports of anti-Semitic activities at the Bauhaus, had been committed to the Zionist movement since 1924.[86] After Max von Schilling, president of the Prussian Academy of Sciences, announced his intention to purge the institution of Jewish elements and influences in 1933, Schoenberg resigned from his professorship of composition in Berlin and went via Paris and Arcachon into exile in New York. There, in October and in English, he wrote the first version of his famous "Four-Point Program for Jewry." After working on it for five years he deposited the typescript at the Writer's Registration Bureau of the Authors' Club Inc., in Hollywood, the heart of California's film and dream industry. "Registered 11/29, 1938 at 3:45 PM,"[87] the text begins with a list of numbers; in retrospect one could say an enumeration of lists:

> 500,000 Jews from Germany, 300,000 from Austria, 400,000 from Czechoslovakia, 500,000 from Hungary, 60,000 from Italy—more than one million and eight hundred thousand Jews will have to migrate in how short a time, one does not know. May God provide there will not be an additional 3,500,000 from Poland, 900,000 from Rumania, 240,000 from Lithuania and 160,000 from Latvia—almost 5,000,000; and Yugoslavia with 64,000, Bulgaria with 40,000 and Greece with 80,000 might follow at once, not to speak of other countries, which are at present less active. Is there room in the world for almost 7,000,000 people?[88]

86 For the reports and rumors of the anti-Semitic attitudes of Bauhaus associates, which were the reason why Schoenberg turned down Kandinsky's suggestion of applying for the directorship of the Weimar Academy of Music, explaining himself in letters on April 20 and May 5, 1923, see Stuckenschmidt *Schoenberg – His Life, World and Work.*

87 Arnold Schoenberg, "A Four-Point Program for Jewry," in *Journal of the Arnold Schoenberg Institute*, vol. III, no. 1, March 1979, pp. 48–67.

88 Ibid., p. 49.

This enumeration is disturbing in how precisely it prophesies, despite its numerical approximations, what will happen and how people will be counted off. In 1938 at the latest the coming catastrophe had become calculable for Schoenberg, not in the singularity of biographies but counted in numbers. "In retrospect," writes Alexander L. Ringer, "the sheer numerical weight of the article and speeches, calculations, aphorisms and miscellaneous notes from those hectic initial months in exile appears staggering."[89] The numbers initially produce an equality that permits no difference between the assimilated and the non-assimilated, between rich and poor, East and West. Schoenberg, who leaves no doubt in his text that he himself would lead a Jewish society in an authoritarian manner and as a sovereignty beyond democratic law,[90] also makes clear that the simple rescue of a community could lie in equal distribution, the rescue of a people that in 1938 was only equal before death, not before the law. Here Schoenberg also considers every individual and the possibility of a very large number, which he calculates down to the last penny: "The immediate goal of my efforts is the commitment of all Jews in all countries to a monthly contribution of two *Marks* per head for several months,"[91] he wrote while still in Arcachon, before departing by ship to exile in New York. In 1938 he thus drafted the plan to realize the Promised Land himself without further ado, to push through the project of self-created spaces, in Africa if need be, as had been discussed in 1905. He was thinking of a potential space, preferably able to defend itself:

"How different would be today's Jewish situation were there now an independent state in Uganda, founded in about 1905, counting perhaps a population of five to ten million, able to provide homes for ten to twenty millions in addition, independent economically, perhaps also provided with a modern armament

89 Alexander L. Ringer, "Arnold Schoenberg and the Politics of Jewish Survival," p. 33.

90 See Schoenberg, who gives an example of necessarily authoritarian leadership of a society in "A Four-Point Program for Jewry": "I was a kind of dictator in 1920, in a musical society, erected by myself in my ideas and on the whole successful," p. 55. See also Bluma Goldstein, "Schoenberg's *Moses und Aron*. A Vanishing Biblical Nation," in Charlotte M. Cross, Russell A. Berman (eds.), *Political and Religious Ideas in the Works of Arnold Schoenberg*, New York 2000, pp. 159–192: "Among Schoenberg's most troubling characteristics, especially given what he suffered as a result of fascist rule, were his antidemocratic and authoritarian predilections and solutions, blatantly apparent in Moses's autocratic rule over the Israelites at the conclusion of *Moses und Aron*, in the authoritarian organizational structure planned for the Jewish Unity Party and elsewhere as well," ibid., p. 187.

91 Note by Arnold Schoenberg, *quoted from* Ringer, "Arnold Schoenberg and the Politics of Jewish Survival," p. 33.

and even perhaps not without political and diplomatic influence."[92] In exile an idea becomes concrete. Space emerges through violence. Like Moses, Schoenberg will never enter a promised land as a territory. He maps the road to it in the opera *Moses und Aron.*

1.5. EXILE

Complementary to circularly causal argumentation, the Moses complex evidently includes the retrospect in which camp, desert, and exile are recognized as such. Bluma Goldstein, who as a literary scholar applied herself early on to the Moses complex,[93] tells of only understanding in a later rereading of the opera libretto how prominent are the changes to the biblical text that Arnold Schoenberg made from the early 1920s onward in the awareness of his own danger from the "swastika-wearers."[94] Goldstein, having studied the opera for many years, discerns a "systematic editing, restructuring, and rewriting the record of Moses's divine commission as liberator and architect of the nation Israel."[95] The opera, she says, doesn't describe a historical, physical land grab but the spiritual state of people in exile. The liberation it deals with is from mental not physical shackles.[96] The historicity and physicality of colonization in the biblical narrative are systematically replaced by exercises in spiritual liberation, and the God who announces himself in the book of Exodus as historical, namely as the God of Abraham, Isaac, and Jacob, becomes an abstract and ahistorical

92 Ibid., p. 56.

93 Bluma Goldstein, *Reinscribing Moses: Heine, Kafka, Freud, and Schoenberg in a European Wilderness*, Cambridge 1992.

94 See Schoenberg's letter to Albert Einstein on January 1, 1924: "While abroad I am considered one of the leading musicians, for some inexplicable reason people in Germany are quite happy to ignore the ascendancy of my music in order to prevent it being linked with my name. In this, in the hatred against me, Jews and the relevant swastika-wearers are in one mind." Translated from *Journal of the Arnold Schoenberg Institute*, vol. X, no. 2, November 1987, p. 153.

95 Goldstein, "Schoenberg's *Moses und Aron*," p. 159.

96 "Moses's concern, in *Moses und Aron*, is not with the actuality of Egyptian oppression and enslavement, but rather with the spiritual impoverishment of a people too preoccupied with the transitory and the quotidian; and the promised land – here associated not with a place or territory for settlement but with a spiritual state of absolute devotion to an abstract deity – is divested of its reality as a discursive site of national identity in the biblical text." Goldstein, "Schoenberg's *Moses und Aron*," p. 161.

principle in the opera. Its film version by Jean-Marie Straub and Danièle Huillet, however, draws attention to the fact that its musical realization represents a "specificity of this embodiment,"[97] a re-materialization and decisive historicization of the Exodus and of exile. Through the film's precise deployment of aesthetic and media procedures it reveals Schoenberg's own method and his interventions into the biblical sources.[98]

The opera and therefore the film begin with the calling of Moses and his reluctance to understand what he has heard and to accept what is being imposed on him. This moment, which in both opera and film sets the radically existential tone, is still the topos for every blockbuster: the call-up to a mission of liberation. Here Goldstein points out the first departure of the libretto from the Bible: in the book of Exodus God has seen and heard the suffering of his people—"I have surely seen the affliction of my people which *are* in Egypt, and have heard their cry by reason of their taskmasters: for I know their sorrows" (Exodus 3:7)—but in Schoenberg's libretto it is Moses himself who must have seen and heard what is going on:

> Du hast die Greuel gesehen,
> die Wahrheit erkannt:
> so kannst du nicht anders mehr:
> du musst dein Volk daraus befrein!

> You've seen your kindred enslaved,
> the truth you've known;
> so you can do nothing else.
> Therefore you must set you folk free![99]

97 Rancière, "Arithmetics of the People."

98 George Steiner, who apparently didn't know the film, also accentuates the opera's intended materialization: "What Schoenberg had in mind is something very different from an ordinary operatic ballet. It is a total dramatic integration of voice, bodily motion and orchestral development." George Steiner, "Schoenberg's *Moses und Aron*," in George Steiner, *A Reader*, London 1984, pp. 234–245: 243.

99 Schönberg, *Moses und Aron*, score I, act I, bars 23–27.

The first liberation would be from self-induced anesthesia, from the blindness and deafness with which we keep the responsibility for violence and horror at arm's length. Schoenberg, in his music, and Straub/Huillet, more radically in their images, systematically deprive the Moses story of any transcendence: in the opera God no longer speaks after his first call, and, as Goldstein puts it, becomes the *deus absconditus* who characterized the cinema history of the twentieth century.[100] Moses defends this spiritual abandonment, or, as Siegfried Kracauer also put it from the experience of exile, the "ideological vacuum" in which no one can live and breathe,[101] almost beyond endurance against his brother Aron, who wishes to have the divine manifest and the new land as a proper new home, who wants to be sure of the guidance and protection of God in pillars of cloud and fire, in wonders, in images, and things. The figure of Aron is thus conceived closer to the text and probably also closer to the spirit of the book of Exodus. The figure of Moses demands the experience of radical insecurity as the precondition for social communication and commitment. The unconceivability and ineffability of a god and the ambiguity of the idea, not the safe realm of a present god, are the political preconditions of the twentieth century. This is where modernist aniconism begins.[102]

The opera therefore doesn't begin in a concrete situation, as told in the Bible and as described by Martin Buber in his Moses book, which he published in 1944 in Jerusalem, in his eyes only conditionally in exile. Buber takes an anthropological slant, observing the Palestinian Bedouins: "Moses, grazing his father-in-law's sheep, drives them across the familiar steppe, as we hear from the Bedouins of this region that they take to the mountain in the early summer, where their herds can find food that is still fresh."[103] In contrast to Buber's location of the foreign in a particular landscape, the opera and film situate the burning bush in an undefined wilderness, a non-place, an acoustically amor-

100 Goldstein, "Schoenberg's *Moses und Aron*," p. 166. For the *deus absconditus*, particularly in the works of Robert Bresson and his successors, see Ute Holl, "Vom Teuflischen, der Kybernetik und der Ethik des Kinos in Robert Bressons Le diable probablement (1977)" in *RISS, Zeitschrift für Psychoanalyse*, special edition on cinema, ed. Andreas Cremonini, Zurich 2009, pp. 53–76.

101 Siegfried Kracauer, *Theory of Film. The Redemption of Physical Reality*, Princeton 1997, p. 295 f.

102 Gertrud Koch has devoted an outstanding critique of mimesis to the figure of an "image of the imageless": Gertrud Koch, "In Sachen Moses gegen Aron. Die Kritische Theorie und das Kino," in Koch, *Die Einstellung ist die Einstellung. Visuelle Konstruktionen des Judentums*, Frankfurt/Main 1992, pp. 12–114.

103 Translated from Buber, *Moses*, p. 51.

phous, sandy space to which Moses, old and already disillusioned, has dragged himself. “Bist weit genug gegangen [You have gone far enough now],”[104] says the voice that differentiates itself in Schoenberg’s first few bars from a humming of soloists into individual singers and a four-part chorus, which is then designated the “Voice from the Burning Bush.” In Straub and Huillet’s film this sequence, like all others, is set in an entirely concrete yet historically stratified environment, in a historical interstice. This book’s examination of the opera and film will show how Straub and Huillet’s palimpsest-like historicization of Schoenberg’s work reconstructs a specific historical power relationship. Where Schoenberg causes the space of the biblical narrative to emerge in a confrontation of counting and singing, mathematics and music, purity and spatiality, Straub and Huillet return the conflict to a historicity of the physical, which must of course always resonate in Schoenberg’s music to be audible at all.

In the media setups, voices, movements, and sounds of the opera and film, reality is created from differentiations that undermine the homogeneity and hierarchy of an imagined pure space. The ambivalence, or as Adorno thought, the dialectic of monotheism becomes a political issue. If it is denied, the Promised Land doesn’t become a new experience but a nostalgic demand for a home.[105] A politics of tones and images, however, as found in these works on Moses, remains dependent on and oriented to the experience of becoming alien. Its exploration here may remain an awkward attempt to approach a world in which 65 million[106] migrants are currently en route, having left or been driven out of countries that were once theirs for an uncertain, desolate outland where in most cases they are again threatened, expelled, or killed. Today, as in Schoenberg’s time, migrants retort with counter-stories, counter-memories, counter-identities, counter-religions.[107] Under what conditions are these visible and audible? At what point do they turn into a violence of enumeration?

104 Schönberg, *Moses und Aron*, score I, act I, bars 12–13.

105 Sidra De Koven Ezrahi has written from the perspective of Jewish experience and in regard to an omnipresent exile: “One could even go so far as to argue that monotheism evolved into a strategy for making the world into one’s home, preparing the way for eliminating exile altogether as a category of experience.” Sidra De Koven Ezrahi, “Our Homeland, The Text … Our Text, The Homeland … Exile and Homecoming in the Modern Jewish Imagination,” in *Michigan Quarterly Review* 31, no. 4, 1992, pp. 463–497: 471.

106 *Global Trends 2015*, UNHCR, June 20, 2016.

107 See Jan Assmann, *Moses the Egyptian. The Memory of Egypt in Western Monotheism*, Cambridge 1997, p. 3

When does exile become occupation or colonization? Or a war machine? This is the final layer of the questions raised in this book.

This attempt to reconstruct a Moses complex remains incomplete and goes round in circles. Sigmund Freud, in his foreword to the third supplement to his Moses book, wrote wittily and elegantly in 1938: "To my critical faculties this treatise, proceeding from a study of the man Moses, seems like a dancer balancing on one toe."[108] Jan Assmann, who in his extensive contribution to the Moses complex from the perspective of a history of memory also sees it as a negotiation of the confrontation with the alien, observes that the desert diverts all Moses researches from their intended path: "All those who turned the kaleidoscope and contributed a new variation on the story of Moses wrote a different text than what they intended to write. [...] It is as if the story of Moses the Egyptian had a life of its own, incorporating itself in different versions: passing through the media and the conceptual frameworks of theology, Freemasonry, philosophy, history, literature and psychoanalysis."[109] Let's give the kaleidoscope another turn, adding a media-theoretical question: what does it mean to give people a text to read?

108 Freud, *Moses and Monotheism*, p. 95.
109 Assmann, *Moses the Egyptian*, pp. 165–166.

2. SOUND, SPACE, POLITICS

> Schoenberg's method is analogous to a society
> in which the emphasis is on the group
> and the integration of the individual in the group.
> *John Cage*[1]

2.1. FORMED SPACES: OPERA HOUSE, MOVIE THEATER

In the beginning a sound fills the theater, no more than a breath, which slowly, a little tinny at first, captures the ear and connects it to a wider space: "O ______ O ______ O______O."[2] It causes the space to vibrate with mutually modulating, superimposing, stratifying frequencies. Only then does a figure emerge from the tones. At the start of the film MOSES UND ARON the sound forms a space of its own, obliterating the traces of its unfolding, and turns out to be far more complex and dynamic than the simultaneous cinematic image. All that can be seen on screen is the lowered head of an elderly man, shot in close-up from behind and over his shoulder, against light-brown sand; sand-colored gown, unkempt hair and beard, the outline of his head therefore unclear. But the head lies in the image's area of focus. The face can't be seen, nor can the eyes or mouth. The relationship between image and sound is ambiguous. Should the sound be imagined as inside this man's head? It certainly isn't his own voice, as many voices can be heard. But what is voice at all in this sound? Should it be conceived as coming from the surroundings? Which? Those on screen, of the body, of the auditorium? What is the law that connects sound and image to one another? How does the sound relate to these sandy surroundings? How does the sound in the theater expand into the viewers' bodies? What is the relationship

1 John Cage, "The Future of Music. Credo," in *Silence*, Cambridge 1971, pp. 3–7: 5.
2 Schönberg, *Moses und Aron*, score I, act I, bars 1–7.

of one's own hearing to the image? What space are we in when we hear and see this? What kind of order from undefined space is this, which no recipient, and certainly not Moses, claims to have heard? The sound doesn't belong to him, and he doesn't want to obey it. The old man rejects the call, the calling. He doesn't want to be a law-giver; he wants to remain a shepherd. Nomad. "Laß mich in Ruhe meine Schafe weiden [Let me tend my sheep in silence]."[3]

Even in the first shot of MOSES UND ARON the film's elements—image and sound—are irreversibly torn apart. The rift in the world goes through the film.[4] The filming of Schoenberg's opera *Moses und Aron* by Jean-Marie Straub and Danièle Huillet is also its analysis, the dissolution of the opera by cinematic means. In 1974 it was furthermore a provocation, and exhortation to analyze the prevailing order, to dissolution. Preceding the call, after the television titles, is the filmed Bible text, Exodus 32:25–28, spoken by Danièle Huillet, Luther's translation of Moses' ire and retribution, as unannounced battering violence, to which "vom volck drey tausent man"[5] fell, and then the dedication "Für Holger Meins," handwritten in red ink by J-M.S and D.H. A little red star. A black leader, a title referring to the production conditions and rights of the opera and the film. Then comes that appeal from the realm of cinema in which a new order and a new law should become conceivable—but not imaginable. Thus only sound, only vowels. The film MOSES UND ARON issues a furious challenge to legalism, to scriptural law, to all written knowledge that considers itself more solid than images and sounds. Just as the new music did in the early twentieth century, this film deals with possible spaces as real experience, with what art can and may imagine, depict, portray, and represent: Straub/Huillet's MOSES UND ARON examines the prohibition of depiction, but does so without relating this to figures, forms, or objects but to space, ground, and field. It conveys a history of spaces and spatiality in the visible and audible. The art of migration becomes a politics of space.

3 Schönberg, *Moses und Aron*, score I, act I, bars 21–22.

4 Siegfried Kracauer's paraphrase of Heinrich Heine for the experience of all exiles: "The rift of the world goes through me too," reads the correspondence between Theodor W. Adorno and Siegfried Kracauer; translated from Theodor W. Adorno and Siegfried Kracauer, *Briefwechsel 1923–1966. "Der Riss der Welt geht auch durch mich"*, ed. Wolfgang Schopf, Frankfurt/Main 2008, p. 13.

5 Luther Bible 1523, quoted from Huillet, "Moses und Aron. Das Drehbuch. Beschreibungen – Texte – Photogramme," in *Filmkritik 221/222*, 1975, pp. 203–252: 203. The King James version reads "... and there fell of the people that day about three thousand men."

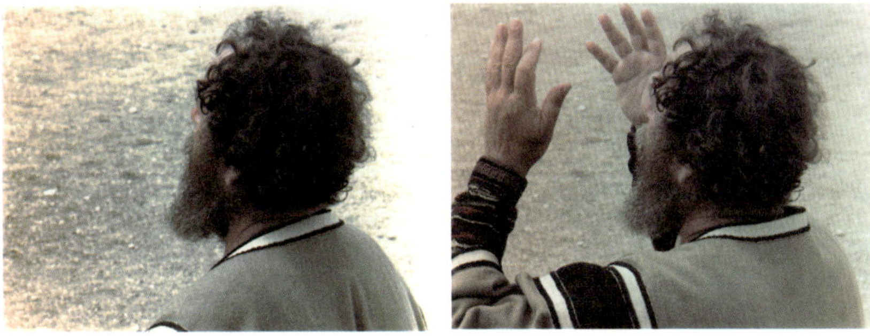

The first shot: Günter Reich as Moses.

With this beginning the film of the opera systematically explores diversely layered cinematic audial and visual spaces before every action and before all acting persons. Even the first image, that long "O______" from wherever, refers to an insistent acousmatics and its apparent founder, Pythagoras,[6] whose world view based on harmonies in pure intervals is dismantled in the film's first sound: slapping Pythagoras.[7] The old harmony of the world is disturbed by new tonal relationships that can no longer be grasped in the logic of consonance

6 Acousmatic sounds are those whose source is unknown. Pierre Schaeffer derived the term for his *musique concrète* from the listening arrangements for Pythagoras's lectures. See Pierre Schaeffer, *Traité des objets musicaux. Essai interdisciplines*, Paris 2002. Commented in Michel Chion, *Sound. An Acoulogical Treatise*. Edited and Introduced by James A. Steintrager, Duke University Press 2016, p. 120 ff. On its Pythagorean origins see *The Life of Pythagoras by Iamblichus of Syrian Chacis*, English version translated and edited by Sylvan Guthrie, New York, 1919. Pythagoras's listeners were divided into two groups: a smaller one, the "philosophers," who had combined into a community of property according to Pythagoras's requirements, but "the greater part of his followers were called hearers, [Acusmatici], of whom, according to Nicomachus, there were two thousand that had been captivated by a single oration on his arrival in Italy." Iamblichos, *Pythogaras*, p. 13. The students were divided into mathematicians and *akousmatikoi*. During their probation, "the property of each man was disposed of in common, being committed to trustees, who were called politicians, economizers, or legislators. Of these probationers, after the quinquennial silence, those who by modest dignity had won his approval as worthy to share in his doctrines, then became esoterics, and within the veil both heard and saw Pythagoras. Prior to this, they participated in his words through the hearing alone, without seeing him who remained within the veil, and themselves offering to him a specimen of their manners." Ibid., p. 34. In this John Mowitt not only discerns, like Chion, a power *dispositif* of the voice but also the element of disturbed transmissions nonetheless broadcast. John Mowitt, *Radio: Essays in Bad Reception*, Berkeley 2011, p. 15.

7 See Tony Conrad, *Slapping Pythagoras*, Table of Elements 1995 (audio CD).

and dissonance. "Via sensory perception,"[8] as intended by Pythagoras, the film initiates us hearers and listeners into the perception of a space that appears as something unconceivable in the ephemeral logic of cinematic sound and image. In this first image Straub und Huillet plant a resistance into the film, which confronts the figure of Moses in Schoenberg's opera with a perception of the world in Western music that was formed in Greek antiquity. In their exploration of the acoustic and visual spaces between opera and film, Straub and Huillet will continually return to this confrontation, as contentious as this seems for an opera called *Moses und Aron* that creates its own space from twelve tones. However, staging an opera as a cultural history and announcement of a new, complex, elementally enumerated sound space was in fact Arnold Schoenberg's concept.

The score of the opera requires a long "O ______ O ______O______O" vocalise to resound *pianissimo* through the complete darkness of the auditorium before the curtain rises. It emerges from the orchestra pit, where six solo voices sit next to six solo instruments, which play "in unison with them."[9] The vocal and instrumental sound should mix indistinguishably: first the soprano and flute, together with mezzo and clarinet and alto with English horn, then, a bar later, tenor, baritone, and bass "in unison" with bassoon, bass clarinet, and cello: a sound, an accord, an acoustic buzzing and booming in the dark at the opening of the opera *Moses und Aron*. So it can be felt that the order is given in a

8 See Iamblichos, *Pythagoras*, p. 29: "Pythagoras conceived that the first attention that should be given to men should be addressed to the senses, as when one perceives beautiful figures and forms, or hears beautiful rhythms and melodies. Consequently he laid down that the first erudition was that which subsists through music's melodies and rhythms, and from these he obtained remedies of human manners and passions, and restored the pristine harmony of the faculties of the soul."

9 Schoenberg, *Moses und Aron*, miniature score, p.1. The form of the vocalise, a piece of music sung in vowels only, goes back to the middle of the 19th century, and was essentially used for teaching purposes before establishing itself as a genre of its own in the early 20th century. Louis Spohr, Gabriel Fauré, Igor Stravinsky, Sergei Rachmaninoff, and Mauricio Kagel are the best known exponents of vocalise composition. Hans Heinz Stuckenschmidt mentions that in 1927 Schoenberg was asked by the publishers Leduc to write a twelve-tone piece for a collection of modern vocalises. This remained unrealized. See Stuckenschmidt, *Schoenberg – His Life, World and Works*, p. 317. For the musical-analytical scansion of the opera and the question of whether the vocalise belongs to Moses' call or not see Marc M. Kerling, "*O Wort, du Wort, das mir fehlt*": *die Gottesfrage in Arnold Schönbergs Oper "Moses und Aron". Zur Theologie eines musikalischen Kunst-Werkes des 20. Jahrhunderts*, Mainz 2004, pp. 57ff.

O ______, the vocalise.

space prior to the law in which the fusion and confusion of instrument and body prevail.[10] Moses' provocation is a lawless space.

What fills the space as an omnipresent, unperceived, and unconceivable sound is given as pure, symmetrical, and conceivable by the score: augmented and perfect fourth in the first and last chords, augmented fifth and minor third in the two middle ones. But such musical symmetry only exists on paper, only in the symbolism of notation. The listeners, following the sound of the opera, will have to enter a space of pitch relations that have no harmonic foothold in fourths, fifths, and octaves, where there is no equivalence to the spheres, to vibrating strings, or the human being. In the relationship of the sounds to one another they will also be confronted with the acoustics of the opera house, the materiality of its space, the presence of bodies. In Straub and Huillet's film things are even more complex. Recorded in the ORF studios in Vienna, shot in the amphitheater of Alba Fucense in Abruzzo, its sound space is composed of the acoustics of each individual thing in its own space, before the camera, in front of the microphones, in the bodies, in the arena. It will be seen that the film thus exactly realizes Schoenberg's concept.

Arnold Schoenberg's opera *Moses und Aron* begins as a pillar of air, an undirected architecture of vibrations, some of which come from bodies, some from instruments, indistinguishable. For Schoenberg this mixing of human and instrumental timbres was extremely important:

> That the six solo voices should always be accompanied by six instruments arose for practical reasons; the intention was to give them some security. But I would ask, that the six solo instruments should not be abandoned even if one believes that the singers can do without them. Their sound is worked into the fabric and should not be lost. NB: in places where singers and instruments should differ (in particular as regards dynamics), the markings are clear. Otherwise the sounds should blend with one another as thoroughly as possible.[11]

10 In his systematic examination of the relationship between twelve-tone method and law, harmonic theory, and legalism in Schoenberg's music, Matthias Schmidt has made the connection to Franz Kafka's text "Before the Law." Matthias Schmidt, "Vor dem Gesetz. Zur religiösen Dimension eines musikalischen Begriffs bei Schönberg," in Christian Meyer (ed.), *Arnold Schönberg und sein Gott: Bericht zum Symposium Juni 26.–29. Juni 2002*, Vienna 2003, pp. 299–310.

11 Schoenberg, *Moses und Aron, Oper in drei Akten*, vocal score, p. 4.

Moses und Aron begins with a mixture of tone colors. A vowel resounds as an inhuman polyphony, a hybrid voice of superimposed frequencies and overtones whose source can no longer be attributed to a particular body. It refers to the emptiness before every audible tone, to the mystery of the origin of sound. The opera begins with a sound of indistinguishability. An aspiration in a space. Only a few bars later do language and text introduce a distinction, which by no means interrupts the overall accord. And a new sound emerges, sung by an unusually polarized choir of soprano, treble, baritone, and bass voices, which will then signify the "Voice from the Burning Bush."[12] Just as a gradual differentiation between reverberation, sound, and noise occurs—for the consonants that interrupt the sound space of the long "O ______ O ______O______O" are nothing other than this—a voice from a burning bush will have reached Moses' ear, or as the sound of the burning bush, while he drives his stepfather Jethro's sheep across the familiar plain. Everything plays out before the law, including acoustic law. But now a distinction has to be made, so that "the infinite unification purifies itself through infinite separation," as Hölderlin comments on the "fearful enormity of God and man uniting."[13] Distinction here becomes hearing in the desert, in the opera, in the cinema.

The decision to distinguish is initially only an aesthetic one, a media-aesthetic one, if you like: Moses decides to perceive a signal in the murmuring and rustling of the thorn bush, decides to distinguish between signal and noise instead of simply carrying on grazing his sheep. By answering somebody, someone or other alien and different, in the middle of the desert, alone with his sheep, signal logic turns into responsibility. Media that cause people to answer embroil them *nolens volens*, unconsciously, in the logic of their new principles. The aesthetic tips into the ethical. Along this sight line Hölderlin's political poetology, to which Straub and Huillet will intensively devote themselves after filming the opera, can be read as a break that compels speech.

In terms of the history of sound, the first vocalise of Schoenberg's opera is a historical reprise, a re-synthesis of the overtone relationships that determine the timbre of human voices when they speak or sing vowels. Or to put it the other way round: when we spontaneously speak and make sounds, overtones

12 Ibid.
13 Translated by Jeremy Adler and Charles Louth, Friedrich Hölderlin, "Notes on the *Oedipus*" in: F. Hölderlin, *Essays and Letters*, pp. 317–324: 323.

form in our bodies. Hermann von Helmholtz first made this visible with the aid of resonating piano strings: "Raise the damper of a well-tuned piano and at one of the instrument's pitches powerfully sing the vowels a, e, i, o, u, ä, ö, ü against the sound board, and these vowels clearly echo on the strings."[14] Later, in *On the Sensations of Tone as a Physiological Basis for the Theory of Music*, Helmholtz systematized this domestic physiology of sound as psychophysiology, found "the same resonances [...] in men, women, and children" with the aid of a series of tuning forks, tested the resonance characteristics of the vowels, investigated frequency and overtone relationships "in coincidence with a proper tone of the cavity of the mouth" and the presence of an "energetic, joyful" or "indifferent and obscure" mood.[15] "The position of the mouth from O to Oa appears to be that which is most favourable for the length of its proper tone and the production of a resonance limited to a very narrow range of pitch."[16]

If we sing "O ______ O ______O," we hear our own physical tone. Psychophysics shows this proper tone from outside, as a resonance with the things of the world and as their interruption, but not as the expression of a psyche. Something different sounds within the self. Je est un O____, un Oa. Moi. Moise. Moïse.

"O ______ O ______O______O." In his vocalise, Schoenberg returns such an analysis of oral sound organization to the indistinguishability of the dynamics of a musical and acoustic materiality that nevertheless remains audible and perceptible in its odd mixture of tone colors. Although such mixtures can indeed be imagined and calculated by composers at their desks or pianos, their acoustic realization in different architectural spaces, climates, times of day, the sound in a movie theater or stadium, only manifests its quality when it is there. Schoenberg treats the "question of God"[17] in *Moses und Aron*, and hence also the question of the law and legalism, not as a matter of writing, intellect, or progress but as the realization of a new, unknown space. In the film by Straub

14 Hermann von Helmholtz to Frans Cornelius Donders, translated from Wolfgang Scherer, *Klavier-Spiele: die Psychotechnik der Klaviere im 18. und 19. Jahrhundert*, Munich 1989, p. 175.

15 Hermann von Helmholtz, *On the Sensation of Tone as a Physiological Basis for the Theory of Music*, trans. Alexander J. Ellis, London 1896, pp. 105ff.

16 Ibid., p. 113.

17 See Kerling, *Die Gottesfrage*, p. 62.

and Huillet this space will encompass much more than can be imagined in the writability of tones.

Arnold Schoenberg addresses the question of God and the law psychophysically from the outset. While the hearers of these first vocalized sounds can't know what they mean or promise—also because the law of the twelve-note row behind the specific sound forms can't yet be discerned—while the audience doesn't yet know who is being summoned or invoked, the Moses figure in the opera answers this sound. In *Sprechstimme* Moses calls back into the complexly unfolding sound space that is entirely unfamiliar to him: "Einziger, ewiger, allgegenwärtiger, unsichtbarer und unvorstellbarer Gott [Only one, infinite, thou omnipresent one, unperceived and inconceivable God]." Straub and Huillet visibly direct this answer to the sand, in an image in which the figure of the singer is not in clear contrast to the background, the floor of an arena.

This interweaving of figure and background is connected to Schoenberg's stage directions, which for the first two acts suggest dividing the stage with "a sand-colored veil" into a frontal and sloping rear area, whose hilly terrain remains connected to the foreground but can disappear into a haze like a panorama. This would form a screen "which is capable of capturing a blurred *picture of the desert landscape.*"[18]

Moses' *Sprechstimme* emphasizes the vocalization of language, the provision of vowels necessary to the enunciation of written language or even a thought. But his reply doesn't only make the vocalization of the voice in language audible; the vowel sequence of his sentence ([a] ei, i, e, a, ä, u, o) topographically marks the places where the vowels are formed within the oral cavity from "high, front" to "low, back,"[19] literally sounding out the sites of physiological linguistic realization. Vocalises had originally fulfilled teaching purposes in the same way,

18 Schoenberg, *Moses und Aron*, vocal score, pp. 2, 3.

19 See Michael Cherlin, "Schoenberg's Representation of the Divine in Moses und Aron," in *Journal of the Arnold Schoenberg Institute*, vol. IX, 1986, no. 2, p. 212: "The musical setting stresses the first vowel of each attribute. The accented vowels form a progression that gradually moves from a relatively 'high, front' vowel toward a 'low, back' one, precisely towards the open 'O' that had been sung by the Divine Voice. [...] The vowel progression in Schoenberg's setting has an interesting relation to Wagner's fanciful theories of speech." Helmholtz sounds out the characteristic physiology of vowels, whose models for him are "bottle-shaped spaces," and then experiments by Bois-Reymond, in three groups: (A, Ä, E, I,), (A, Ö, Ü), (A, O, U). See Helmholtz, *On the Sensation of Tone*, p. 105. The three groups taken from Bois-Reymond are different in the English edition. They are (A), (E, Ö, O), (I, Ü, U).

before becoming an art form of their own. From the very beginning Schoenberg not only links the motif of a physical staging of music, the "O_____" intoned from the musical space, to the listeners' ears; he also connects the human body, via the physiology of speech—lips, mouth, tongue, throat—to the larger sound in the space. The opera *Moses und Aron* begins with music that joins the body with a not yet comprehended exterior, and subjugates it to an unimaginable other. In the "new-fallen snow" of new music "the subject [has] not yet left any tracks," nor can any man, a monotheism, a single God be heard.[20] Language first has to be distinguished by vocalization in the rustling and hissing of the burning bush. Just as, conversely, the space of the vocalise is first distinguished by consonants. Reverberation, sound, and noise, exactly link body, voice, and text, which differentiate themselves against one another.

In Kabbalism the ritual dictate of vocalizing texts written in consonants is identified as an instrument of power, while always disguised as a token of love.[21] Friedrich Kittler, from the perspective of his research into Ancient Greek culture, has formulated this as the difference between vocalic and consonantal alphabets: "So Semitic vocalization is always 'poetry' in itself: a tongue whose free action gives the consonantal sequences voice, sense, and sentential meaning."[22] This tongue is not free in the divine realm. The regulated utterance of holy texts corresponds to the prohibition of pronouncing the Tetragrammaton. The tether of pronunciation, that is the practiced, unwritten vocalization of holy texts, was impressively formulated in the 16th century by the kabalist Elija de Vidas as a kind of micropolitics of divine love:

> Out of his love for man God has fixed these letters in the mouths of man, in order to enable him to cleave to his Creator, by the very pronunciation of the sounds here below, when he studies Torah or prays, he shakes and stirs up the roots above. The meaning of the verb "fixed" is similar to sticking the end of a chain in one place, and the other end in another place; the

20 Theodor W. Adorno, "Music, Language and Composition," in *The Musical Quarterly*, vol. 77, no. 3, pp. 401–414: 407. For the interpretation of the vocalise as the voice of God see Peter Fischer-Appelt, "Die 'göttlichen Stimmen' in Schönbergs Oper 'Moses und Aron'," in Meyer (ed.) *Arnold Schönberg und sein Gott*, pp. 373–383.

21 See Moshe Idel, *Hasidism: Between Ecstasy and Magic*, Albany 1995, pp. 163ff.

22 Translated from Friedrich Kittler, *Musik und Mathematik I*, vol. 1. *Hellas 1: Aphrodite*, Munich 2006, p. 107.

Regieanweisungen

In einigen Szenen soll unbedingt der Schauplatz wechseln. Ich habe nichts dagegen, wenn der Regisseur manchen Szenenteilen eigene Räume schafft, sofern er das mit Takt, Geschmack und Maß tut. Alles, was den Gedanken hervorhebt, ist wohlgetan. Aber ich will den Regisseur auch nicht daran hindern, wo es nötig ist, etwas mehr Abwechslung hineinzubringen. Nur bedenke er: Es könnte sein, daß Abwechslung zum Schluß monotoner wirkt als der Stil, der hier angezeigt ist.

I. Akt, 2. Szene

Die Begegnung ARONS mit MOSES ist szenisch so zu lösen, daß das „Aneinandervorbeireden" (trivial gesagt) der beiden auffällt. Z. B.: ARON steht links vorn, MOSES rechts Mitte, sie sehen einander nicht an.

I. Akt, 3. Szene

Der Auftritt MOSES' und ARONS vor der 4. Szene muß so wirken, wie der CHOR es beschreibt. Das Näherkommen beider muß unwirklich aussehen. Das Schweben und Gleiten, das Unbestimmte, ob sie nebeneinander gehen oder wer vorn oder hinten geht. – Der Weg muß außerordentlich lang wirken.

I. Akt, 4. Szene

Der CHOR bei dem Text: *Bleib uns fern mit deinem Gott* . . . (T. 566–620) ist in steter Bewegung. Die Stellung ist ungefähr so:

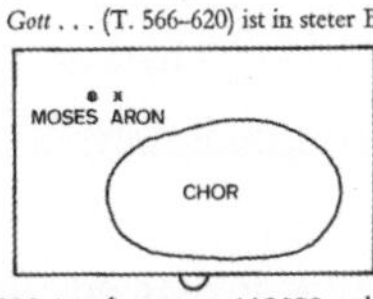

Am Schluß dieser Stelle macht ein Teil des CHORES Anstalten, gegen MOSES und ARON vorzudringen, der andere Teil scheint – links vorn – weggehen zu wollen; dabei ändern die beiden Teile bis zu einem gewissen Grade (soweit es die Musik zuläßt) ihr gegenseitiges Stellungsverhältnis.

In dieser ganzen Szene ist der CHOR immer ganz vorn; MOSES und ARON mehr im Hintergrund, aber sichtbar, also höher stehend. Wenn ARON oder MOSES sich mehr dem Vordergrund nähern, so kommen sie dabei zunächst nicht nach ganz vorn. Erst bei den Wundern stehen sie immer mehr vorne!

Bei dem dritten Wunder (T. 868 ff) muß das Wasser beim Ausgießen anfangs klar sein und sich erst röten, nachdem man wahrnehmen konnte, daß es Wasser ist. Jedenfalls muß der Krug ziemlich groß sein und ARON muß ihn sehr hoch heben, so daß man oben klares Wasser, unten rotes sieht.

II. Akt, 1. und 2. Szene

Die 1. Szene hat auf einer „kurzen" Bühne gespielt: etwa die Hälfte der Vorderbühne; nach hinten ansteigend, aber sonst ohne Aufbau.

Gegen den Hintergrund (wo alles für die 3. Szene Erforderliche aufgebaut ist) ist die Vorderbühne folgendermaßen abgeschlossen:

Etwa von der Mitte der Vorderbühne an bis etwa zum Beginn der Hinterbühne sind Schleiervorhänge (möglichst viele, möglichst dichte, sandfarbene Schleier in möglichst großen Abständen: 2–3 Meter) heruntergelassen (hier in Figur 1 sind z. B. fünf Schleier angenommen), deren untere Enden nicht den gewissen „Kettelabschluß", sondern, womöglich beschwerende, Metallfranzen (sandfarben?) besitzen sollen und die dort also nicht geradlinig, sondern zackig verlaufen sollen (Figur 2). Der Zweck: Die Schleierenden sollen im hügeligen Terrain der Hinterbühne bis zu einem gewissen Grad verschwinden können. Die Zahl und Dichtigkeit und der Abstand der Schleier voneinander soll von der Absicht bestimmt werden: 1. den Bühnenrest gut zu verbergen; 2. aber: einen Schirm zu bilden, der geeignet ist, ein verschwommenes Bild der Wüstenlandschaft aufzufangen, in der die 3. Szene spielt, welches durch Skioptikon auf diesen Schirm projiziert wird. Das auf den Schleierschirm geworfene Bild soll keineswegs bis an den Bühnenboden reichen, sondern, um nicht auf die Darsteller zu fallen und dem hügeligen Charakter des Wüstenbildes zu entsprechen, erst in z. B. zwei Meter Abstand vom Bühnenboden beginnen. Wenn bei der Verwandlung die Schleier hochgezogen werden, erblaßt dieses Bild bis zum Verschwinden. Das Bild wird eine hügelige Wüstenlandschaft von verschwimmender Kontur andeuten, auf welchem vielleicht das Grün und die Umrisse einer Oase und der Berg der Offenbarung geahnt werden können.

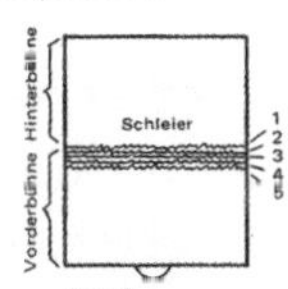

Figur 1

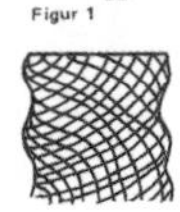

Figur 2

Auf dem bis zur 3. Szene abgedeckten Teil der Bühne wird nach der Verwandlung der Berg der Offenbarung deutlich zu sehen sein. Auch befindet sich dann dort das goldene Kalb nebst allem sonst Erforderlichen.

Schoenberg's set design for act I: "numerous sand-coloured gauzes and veils."

> distance between the places notwithstanding, when a man shakes the end of the chain, which is in his hand, he shakes the whole chain ... and so we can understand the virtue of our ancestors whose prayers were answered immediately, since they were careful not to defile the twenty-two letters that are [pronounced by] the five places in the mouth.[23]

The cultural technique of vocalization places controls on people. There is no question that this fascination with legalism is also seen as a precondition for the possibility of freedom in the name of God, and more concretely as freedom from the state of impurity and the yoke of exile.[24]

Vowels make space, allow distinctions to be anticipated, but they aren't conducive to unambiguous distinction: in order to identify and "smite" the foreign, other, Ephraimite warriors and migrants who wanted to cross the Jordan, the men of Gilead invented a binary consonant opposition, distinguishability, S contra Sh, the shibboleth.[25] Speak how you speak and we know who you are. While consonantal difference became disastrous for the refugees at the fords of the Jordan, for a long time vowels, which are not written in Arabic and Semitic scripts, did not admit of overriding or governmental knowledge. Until the frequency research by Leonhard Euler and later Hermann von Helmholtz their tone quality could only be described, not determined.[26] In the tone quality of vocalization we instinctively recognize the other under the yoke, in exile—in the A and the O we detect the Viennese in Hollywood, the Frankfurter in New York, the Hanoverian in Princeton, or the Berliner in Ann Arbor: Schoenberg, Kracauer, Panofsky, Arnheim. The variability of tone quality, a brighter or darker

23 R. Elija de Vidas, *Sefer Reshith Hokhma*, Jerusalem 1984, quoted from Moshe Idel, *Hasidism*, p. 161.

24 See ibid., p. 50.

25 See Judges 12.

26 Vowels remained among those things whose sound could not be written down or described. Responding to a question apparently posed by Leonhard Euler from the St. Petersburg Academy of Sciences in 1779, Christian Gottlieb Kratzenstein, professor of experimental physics and medicine in Copenhagen, determined the problem of vowels as one of tone quality, in contrast to pitch or frequency, and as the specific character of wave oscillation. Proceeding from Euler's researches, Wolfgang von Kempelen built a speaking machine. Translation from Bernhard Siegert, *Passage des Digitalen. Zeichenpraktiken der neuzeitlichen Wissenschaften 1500–1900*, Berlin 2003, p. 222: "The media experiment is preconditioned by the deconstruction of an analytical order of signs in which everything that exists must be able to be represented by Leibniz's expressions. Calculation ceases to be the model of an analytical art of inventing truth and instead begins to design signal generators."

pronunciation, locates the body in biographical topologies of the sound space. But it is only with the aid of frequency-based instruments and apparatuses that a, e, i, o, u, ei, and ä can be measured, synthesized, and distinctly classified.[27] Arnold Schoenberg, in removing tone quality from the human body, the exiled body, the desert-dweller's body, and indistinguishably mixing it with instrumental sounds, thus obtains his own asylum. Or, more combatively, a "deployment zone."[28] He composes for himself a space of liberation, creates surroundings, history, relationships that are not *völkisch* and conceives—this is what *Moses und Aron* is about—a willful structure of legalism.

Although Schoenberg followed the undertakings of the Zionist movement of the 1920s with interest and sympathy, his composition of the "Moses" opera introduced something quite different: the perspective of a complex sound space that would be capable of making an acoustic exodus possible not *from* Europe but initially within the unavailable regions of Austria, Germany, Italy, or Spain; a space of breaks and ruptures, generated by bodies and sound bodies (orchestras).[29] Schoenberg doesn't therefore engage in geopolitics but in psychophysical topology, proximity strategies. When in twelve-tone music, in musical forms derived from the symbolization and enumerability of written pitches, Schoenberg turns, reverses, and mirrors these forms in permutations, combinations, and inversions, then returning them to the reality of a sound space and its colors, he composes a space in which the sounds no longer have their foothold in symbolization, and perception is subject to a new and undirected space: "*The unity of musical space demands an absolute unitary perception.*"[30]

The opera *Moses und Aron* doesn't belong to the early "genesis" phase of composing with twelve tones, whose tonal expansions Glenn Gould admired in their

27 Hermann von Helmholtz, *On the Sensation of Tone*, p. 105: "The pitch of strongest resonance of the oral cavity depends solely upon the vowel for pronouncing which the mouth has been arranged, and alters considerably for even slight alterations in the vowel quality, such, for example, as occur in different dialects of the same language."

28 See Alfred Bodenheimer, "Biblische Wege. Jüdisches Wandern in Werken Arnold Schönbergs und Franz Werfels," in Ekkehard John, Heidy Zimmermann (eds.), *Jüdische Musik? Fremdbilder, Eigenbilder*, Cologne 2004, pp. 149–156: 150.

29 For Schoenberg's relationship to the Zionist movement of the 1920s see Salome Schöll, "'Der biblische Weg' und der Zionismus in den 1920er Jahren," in Meyer (ed.), *Arnold Schönberg und sein Gott*, pp. 239–246.

30 Arnold Schoenberg, "Composition with Twelve Tones," in Arnold Schoenberg, *Style and Idea*, ed. Leonard Stein, London 1975, pp. 214–245: 223 (italics in original).

burning-bush logic as "flamboyant chromaticism."[31] For Schoenberg, however, the concept of twelve-tone composition always belonged to the logic of genesis, as he emphasized in a programmatic lecture in 1935: "To understand the very nature of creation one must acknowledge that there was no light before the Lord said: 'Let there be light'."[32] This too should be seen as aesthetically recursive, for as another Viennese cleverly suggested in media-theoretical terms, light as a medium may have been there already, but no one perceived it before God pointed it out.[33]

Moses und Aron, the opera that Schoenberg was able to base "solely on one set,"[34] poses the question of the law of that space which an artist or rebel, a leader or someone in despair, Moses, only realizes through initially taking possession of a regime of signs—or is taken possession of by it out of nowhere, and is ultimately expelled to the emptiness between the letters: "O Wort, Du Wort, das mir fehlt [O word, thou word, that I lack]."[35] From the perspective of space as an effect of signs, techniques, and cultural media, the topos of the opera shifts from the problem of a prohibition of images that clings to the mimetic similarities of the figures to the question of emerging media relationships. Aniconism is politically applied to the question of the constitution of an undirected space and a people without a leader. The opera ends with the call to understanding equal distribution as equal status in acoustic and visual space and as political strength: "In der Wüste seid ihr unüberwindlich [In the wasteland you shall be victorious]."[36]

While working on the opera Schoenberg will not only leave Austria, then Germany, and finally Europe; he will also, in 1933 in the Paris synagogue and witnessed by Marc Chagall, ceremoniously return to the Jewish community he had left in his youth. "As you have doubtless realized," he wrote to Alban Berg on October 16, 1933, "my return to the Jewish religion took place long ago and is

31 Glenn Gould, "Arnold Schönberg – A Perspective", in *The Glenn Gould Reader*, edited and with an introduction by Tim Page, New York, 1984, pp. 107–122: 118.

32 Arnold Schoenberg, "Composition with Twelve Tones," p. 223.

33 Heinz von Foerster, "Perception of the Future and the Future of Perception," in Heinz von Foerster, *Understanding Understanding: Essays on Cybernetics and Cognition*, New York 2003, pp. 199–210.

34 Arnold Schoenberg, "Composition with Twelve Tones," p.224 ["set" refers to the tone row, *trans.*].

35 Schönberg, *Moses und Aron*, score II, act II, bars 1133–1136.

36 Schoenberg, *Moses und Aron*, vocal score, act III, unpaginated.

indeed demonstrated in some of my published work ('Thou shalt not ... Thou shalt') and in 'Moses and Aaron,' of which you have known since 1928, but which dates from at least five years earlier."[37]

Jean-Marie Straub and Danièle Huillet, who meandered through Europe from the early 1950s onward under less precarious conditions but for nonetheless explicitly political reasons, began working on the MOSES UND ARON film after seeing a performance of the opera conducted by Hermann Scherchen in 1959 in Berlin. In 1951 Scherchen had organized a concert performance of the "Dance around the Golden Calf" at the Darmstadt International Summer Course for New Music.[38] Straub and Huillet found the Berlin production by Gustav Rudolf Sellner atrocious, "épouvantable," a German post-war "abstraction théâtrale," a kind of "faux Living Theater," and they described the "épidémie" of productions that began at the same time as their filmed version, namely fifteen years later at the hundredth anniversary of Schoenberg's birth, as "en partie ou totalement épouvantables."[39] The start of their production, which was followed by a latency of almost fifteen years between 1959 and 1974, largely due to the difficulty of obtaining funds for such a project from the public-sector broadcasters, therefore marks a resistance against false aesthetics. MOSES UND

37 Arnold Schoenberg, *Letters*, p. 184.

38 See the correspondence between Schoenberg and Scherchen in Arnold Schönberg, *Sämtliche Werke*, section III, stage works, series A, vol. 8, parts 1 and 2, *Moses und Aron. Oper in drei Akten, Entstehungsgeschichte. Texte und Textentwürfe zum Oratorium und zur Oper*, ed. Christian Martin Schmidt, Mainz, Vienna 1998 (referred to in the following as *Moses und Aron, Entstehungsgeschichte*), pp. 26–33. Performances of the opera or parts of it took place on July 2, 1951 in Darmstadt: first performance of the "Dance around the Golden Calf" [act II, scene 3] as part of the Darmstadt Summer Course for New Music, Landestheater-Orchester Darmstadt, conducted by Hermann Scherchen. A concert performance was given on March 12, 1954 with the NWDR Orchestra and Choir in the Hamburg Musikhalle, conducted by Hans Rosbaud (the singers were Hans Herbert Fiedler, Moses; Helmut Krebs, Aron; Ilona Steingruber-Wildgans, Young Girl; Helmut Kretschmar, Young Man; Horst Günter, Another Man; Hermann Rieth, Priest and Ephraimite; Ursula Zollenkopf, Invalid Woman, Choir of NWDR Cologne, Choir of NWDR Hamburg, Symphony Orchestra of NWDR Hamburg). The first staged performance took place on June 6, 1957 at the Stadttheater Zurich, also conducted by Hans Rosbaud (singers: Hans Herbert Fiedler, Moses; Helmut Melchert, Aron; Charles Gillig, Heathen Priest and Israelite Priest; Ingeborg Friedrich, Young Girl; Hans-Bert Dick, Young Man; Nikolaus Toth, Another Man; Mary Davenport, Invalid Woman; Rudolf Fiebelkorn, Youth; Willi Ferenz, Ephraimite, Choir of the Stadttheater Zurich, Choir of the Stadttheater Luzern, members of the Zurich Radio Choir and the Zurich Chamber Chorus. The director was Karl Heinz Krahl).

39 Jean-Marie Straub and Danièle Huillet, "Conversation avec Jean-Marie Straub et Danièle Huillet (Moïse et Aaron). Par Jacques Bontemps, Pascal Bonitzer et Serge Daney," in *Cahiers du Cinéma* 258/259, 1975 (referred to in the following as Straub/Huillet, "Conversation"), p. 6.

Aron, which was in the end co-produced by the Austrian Broadcasting Corporation, ORF, and largely managed and realized by Hessischer Rundfunk for the German Association of Public Broadcasters, ARD, then censored, blocked, and postponed because of its dedication to Holger Meins, and finally, in time for the Christian Easter festival, transmitted by the "regional broadcasters of the Federal Republic, combining forces like at Christmas,"[40] comprises a criticism of German post-war culture from the 1950s to the 70s, but refers this precisely to the time of the opera's composition. Straub and Huillet's superimposition of historical times not only corresponds to Schoenberg's aestheticism and musical procedure but also indicates the debate with monotheism, that is with the complex of power and legalism in the twentieth century that runs through texts from Sigmund Freud to Jacob Taubes. In Moses und Aron Straub and Huillet develop new filmic forms in which, taking up the trail of classical texts, they open up uncharted territory.

The film was conceived as a color film from the very beginning, Danièle Huillet explains, and as a film that would be shot outdoors, that is not on the stage or in the studio—in contrast to their first great music film about Bach in 1968,[41] which also presented complicated acoustic problems and was realized in interiors. "It was clear to us from the beginning that we would shoot in color and not in the studio. The rest was a question of work. You have to see how and why."[42] After traveling almost 7,000 miles in search of a location the choice was finally made for a place near Rome, Straub and Huillet's neighboring surroundings,

40 Translated from Brigitte Jeremias, "Ein sakraler Monolith, mitten in die Landschaft gestellt. Jean-Marie Straubs *Moses und Aron*-Verfilmung," in *Frankfurter Allgemeine Zeitung* no. 49, February 27, 1975, p. 21. Jeremias consistently names Straub as the film's director, but once mentions that his assistant Danièle Huillot (sic.) reads the Lutheran text. Jeremias is clearly opposed to the censorship of the dedication. Not so Gerd Bucerius, "Zensur! Zensur?," in *Die Zeit*, no. 16, April 11, 1975, p. 20. The journalistic rift also divides the editors of the journal *Filmkritik*, which published a resolution in which international and very renowned filmmakers protested against the "unconstitutionality and self-censorship of the German film industry" in its May/June edition of 1975, and in the following September issue minuted the discussion on the "coquetry of such resistance." *See* Gerhard Theuring, "Tagebucheintragungen," in *Filmkritik* 9, 1975, pp. 394–397: 395. The International Forum of New Cinema in Berlin didn't show the film because of its dedication. See Gerd Conradt, "Eine Widmung. Begegnung mit Jean-Marie Straub und Danièle Huillet, Rom, August 1999," in Conradt, Gerd (ed.), *Starbuck Holger Meins. Ein Porträt als Zeitbild*, Berlin 2001, pp. 182–185: 183.

41 Chronik der Anna Magdalena Bach, FRG/I 1967, dir. Jean-Marie Straub, Danièle Huillet, b/w, 94'.

42 Straub/Huillet, "Conversation," p. 6.

the Roman theater of Alba Fucense[43] in the Abruzzo mountains, which features a particular optical form and particular acoustic qualities that correspond to the opera. "At first I was less enthusiastic than Jean-Marie, who immediately fell in love with the wonderful elliptical form and the unusually good acoustics."[44]

Straub and Huillet transfer Schoenberg's layering of spaces of—not only acoustic—perception into cinematic spatial constructions. However precisely our seeing and hearing may understand the cultural-historical contexts, an analysis of the film nonetheless requires a systematic reconstruction of the complex space, assembled from multilayered media configurations, that was distilled from Arnold Schoenberg's sketches and stage directions, and his ideas about acoustic realization. In his texts Schoenberg responds, on various cultural-historical, media, and aesthetic levels, to the challenge of the great "Mosaic distinction," which had created the space of "Western monotheism" through separation and division.[45] Once such a distinction is drawn, according to Jan Assmann, "there is no end of reentries or subdistinctions."[46] Straub and Huillet's film shows that the opera *Moses und Aron* is not simply a return to the endless iterations of a Jewish-Christian-Islamic catastrophe but a break that allows the distinction to turn into responsibility, as a response to an unclear call, and then a transition into a new space. In this sense the story of the film links to a presence of the 1930s, the 70s, and disturbingly accurately to our own time. In his project of constructing an acoustic space that programs its own musical program, heautonomously regulating its own differentiation, Schoenberg dissolved the apparent hierarchical structure of Mosaic monotheism into the possible equal distribution, equal probability, and equal validity of an unprecedented new space. Straub and Huillet, for their part, confront this musical heautonomy with the materiality of media structures and cinematically visible and audible things: bodies, landscapes, and buildings. With Schoenberg they

43 While the Latin Alba Fucen denotes the historical excavation site in a narrow sense, Alba Fucense is the common Italian name of the place near Avezzano. It is called Alba Fucense in the screenplays, reports, and protocols of the film, as well as in its first reviews. For this reason the name has been adopted in this text.

44 Danièle Huillet, "Appunti sul giornale di lavorazione di Gregory," in *Filmkritik* 221/222, 1975, p. 401. Huillet's remarks form a shooting protocol of their own, and were written as a correction and supplementation of the working journal by Gregory Woods, one of the assistants. See Gregory Woods, "Ein Arbeitsjournal," in *Filmkritik* 221/222, 1974, pp. 254–273.

45 Assmann, *Moses the Egyptian*, p. 2.

46 Ibid., p. 1.

set the logic of the signs and sign regimes and spatial constructions underlying his opera to work in order to turn cinema into an experiential space of resistance between calculation and imagination. Because they don't simply stage, but constellate optic and acoustic circumstances, Straub and Huillet can return in 1974 to Schoenberg's experiment, which in 1933 asked about the emergence of a people in a non-ethnic, even non-rasict, namely differentiated sense: in the here and now of media-pervaded space. The political question remains less that of monotheism than the transition into a new media state—for the biblical Moses of vocation and legislation still one and the same.

2.2. VOWELS AND SCARS: GRECOPHILIA, ORIENTALISM

> Abraham, Jacob, or even Moses produces a more concrete, direct, and historical impression than the figures of the Homeric world—not because they are better described in terms of the sense (the contrary is the case) but because of the confused, contradictory multiplicity of events, the psychological and factual cross-purposes, which true history reveals have not disappeared in the representation but still remain clearly perceptible.
> *Erich Auerbach*[47]

When Schoenberg begins his opera with a complex and resistant vocalization, he deliberately and provocatively positions himself at a cultural-historical boundary that has been dealt with epistemologically, and that in terms of cultural studies returns as a collision of script cultures, as a gap between vocalic and consonantal alphabets, between Greece and the Orient, between Greco-centrism and orientalism, but always as a question of linguistic and media power. This cultural crash recurrently occurs as a rift in European thought and art criti-

47 Erich Auerbach, *Mimesis: The Representation of Reality in Western Literature*, trans. Willard Trask, Princeton 2003, p. 20. In the original German publication Auerbach added another sentence that doesn't appear in the English translation: "This initially lies in the Jewish view of people, but more in the fact that the editors were not writers of sagas but of history, and their idea of the structure of human life was derived from the historical." Translated from *Mimesis. Dargestellte Wirklichkeit in der abendländischen Kultur*, Bern 1942, 8th edition 1988.

cism, quite in the sense of Freud's diagnosis that old historical schisms insist on reappearing for as long as they still contain undigested matter. In Schoenberg's opera this cultural difference also foments the conflict between Moses and Aron, between truth and imaginability, thought and the senses. When Aron sings "glückliches Volk [happy is this folk]," Moses angrily interrupts him: "Volk, auserwählt, den Unsichtbaren zu wissen, den Unvorstellbaren zu denken [Folk set apart to know the ever unseen one, to reflect on greatness unimaged]."[48] It is not a coincidental dispute that Schoenberg constructs here but one that, while he writes and composes, polemically intervenes into politics: Greek unconcealment versus the unconceivable God of the Old Testament.

In Germany, when Schoenberg had long since fled to the US, Martin Heidegger discovered in Hellenism the preservation of a form of speech that made the beginning of thought. Heidegger emphasizes the human possibility of reacting to existence itself through unconcealing language. In the Parmenides lectures of winter 1942/43—the same winter in which, in New York, Roman Jakobson delivered his famous six lectures on the link between sound and meaning[49]—Heidegger shows in his translation of the didactic poem that the goddess is not actually a personification but the essence of a conflict, a struggle that brings thought into word, "whose purity and rigor" mark the beginning "and have never recurred since"[50] in this form. Heidegger characterizes Hellenism as being "claimed" and "encompassed" by unconcealment, by ἀλήθεια itself."[51] The Old Testament God, in contrast, as Schoenberg's composition also emphasizes, calls from concealment, from a wasteland nothingness against which language shatters, in the face of which words fail. Hellenism, however, wrests unconcealment from the empty ληθη through the word. In the same Parmenides commentary, in order to convey the imminent threat to the Western world, Heidegger not only refers to the Romanization of the Greeks by people like Friedrich Nietzsche but in particular to the mechanization of writing, from the printing press at the beginning of the modern era to the rotary press, that

48 Act I, scene 2, bars 155–162.

49 See Jakobson, *Six leçons sur le son et le sens.*

50 Martin Heidegger, *Parmenides*, trans. André Schuwer and Richard Rojcewicz, Bloomington 1992, p. 5.

51 Ibid., p. 87 "The Greeks think and poetize and 'deal' with the essence of ἀλήθεια and of ληθη, but they do not think and poetize about this essence and they do not 'deal' with it. For the Greeks it suffices to be claimed by ἀλήθεια itself and to be encompassed by it."

contemporary "triumph of the machine," with which people were deprived of the relationship to being that language contains, without being able to experience this in their accordingly nebulized state: "The typewriter is a signless cloud," he declares after Pindar.[52] According to Heidegger, history around 1942 was determined by a complete and simultaneously concealed mechanization, and Western people were threatened either by the "triumph of the machine" or a dismal metaphysics of technology, not least overtly shown in the a priori of electrification in the Bolshevik vision of a technically totally organized world.[53] In 1942 Heidegger wages his world war of truth against such gloom in the light of Greece.

Friedrich Kittler resumed this war again around sixty years later, as part of his discovery of the alphanumerical, which again makes ontological existence possible, as singing and saying to being, which in turn is threatened by American source-code politics and exclusive consonantal alphabets. Kittler's book on music and mathematics once again celebrates the invention of the vocalic alphabet, in which numbers, signs, bodies, and technologies are openly available to all: "Everyone can speak Greek who merely knows the letters, but not Egyptian and Semitic."[54] He rightly holds the result of this linguistic accessibility up to all administrators of knowledge: "AEIOU, contrived in a single night. No team, no committee, no office, no spelling commission could specify five and later seven vowels one after the other in extended argument. It sings the way it does because it sings."[55] The Greek vocalic alphabet doesn't serve, like consonantal notation, as an exclusive aide-mémoire for scholars and bachelors, but can phonetically incorporate every language and all people, however conventionalized their fixation may later appear. According to this argument, which Kittler's book proposes even as song, vocalic alphabets are not only more efficient than consonantal scripts but are non-exclusive and open-minded, as historians of writing confirm.[56] They open up the world: "A pure miracle, as the world comes forth,"[57] making the same use of opening up as *physis* as Heidegger in his definition of the Greeks: "According to this determination man is τό ζωον

52 Ibid., p. 85.
53 Ibid., p. 84.
54 Translated from Kittler, *Musik und Mathematik I*, pp.108–109.
55 Ibid., p. 108.
56 Barry B. Powell, *Homer and the Origin of the Greek Alphabet*, Cambridge 1991, p. 3.
57 Translated from Kittler, *Musik und Mathematik I*, p. 108.

λόγον εχον—the being that emerges from itself, emerges in such a way that in this emerging (φύσις), and for it, it has the word."[58] Language available to everyone as an opening onto the world is without doubt a consistent model, but one that perhaps overlooks the discipline that connects language in speech with bodies in both the classical and technological periods. This is equally an issue in the procedure of vocalization and the pedagogical alphabetization that Kittler identifies around 1800 as the training of obedient and productive officials. Kittler extends the metaphor of openness in the sense of open-source politics even as far as to understand copy-protected algorithms and industrial software as the concealment of a pure code. However, to celebrate the alphanumerical as the revival of or even return to Greek ontological dispensations is annoying from a philologist who has undertaken painstaking research into historical experiments in which the interfaces of bodies and machines, also calculators, were tested and implemented in data-processing systems. The fact that the unconscious effects of data processing were misunderstood or ignored by philosophy as mental phenomena belongs to the very theories with which Kittler justifies media theory against the humanities.[59] In the light of a Greek openness or not, Kittler shows that power in the twentieth century became a thing of media, codes, and channels. A people of users can be ruled more effectively than troupes of hackers in their clubs. The complex of media, power, and multitudes has migrated into the twenty-first century.

For Kittler, consonantal scripts, like restrictive source-code politics, mark one and the same strategy of regulating thought to which the European universities have recently subjugated themselves. "Every reading that does not remain slavishly faithful should go straight to hell. And that is written by someone who like us can barely write Greek"—or whose computer complicates it—and he continues: "Europe's universities caved in from the start. We don't think about it because we are standing in an open battlefield. So merciless is the domination of writing in which no one is allowed to delete or augment a single letter, while the *Iliad* and *Odyssey* have come down to us in thousands of free variations. Despots crave for the locking of their own signs, so that Christianity, which

58 Heidegger, *Parmenides*, p. 68.

59 See Friedrich Kittler (ed.), *Austreibung des Geistes aus den Geisteswissenschaften: Programme des Poststrukturalismus*, Paderborn 1980, and ibid., *Aufschreibesysteme 1800/1900*, Munich 1985, and finally ibid., *Musik und Mathematik I*.

promises to repeal the law, paradoxically remains the law; only, thankfully, to no avail."[60]

In his extension of Heidegger's deliberations in 1942, Kittler again formulates the problem of European truth as the availability of an unambiguous alphabet, unambiguously described as a conflict with Semitic scripts and regimes of truth. Through this the Moses complex becomes virulent once again, and with it the long history of a European phantasm spanning vocalic and consonantal script, song, and voice, knowledge and thought, and leaders and followers of signs. The law as media power only emerged under the signature of Moses.

Kittler's song is not least the reprise of a conflict that became the prologue to a new theory of media in the 1960s in the context of a first boom in technical media. Grammatology, as advocated by Ignace J. Gelb in the discussion of a natural script,[61] was taken up by Jacques Derrida in the sense of an agency of difference that takes account, through writing, of the principal gap between meaning and being, and thus of a deferral of presence. In Arabic or Semitic cultures this is realized through the recognition of a suspended or delayed linkage of the written language with the body of speech. Speakers of Arabic or Hebrew are not only reliant on the script itself or the code as the basis of all speaking; they are not only dependent but also self-determined in positing meaning with every utterance. This was made clear by the philologist and musicologist Johannes Lohmann, who emphasizes that "at each moment, as it were, Arabic speakers [...] build their word forms themselves from 'consonants' and 'vowels.' Hence there is a lack of that semantic blackout that with us can be only remedied with recourse to the history of word forms (termed 'etymology'). For this reason too the Arabic philosopher, with his concept of the 'articulating being,' was able to provide not only the most universal and prejudice-free but [...] also the most useful definition of the human being."[62] Articulation means making linguistic history oneself, while the post-Hellenistic remains dependent on knowledge after the fact, on having to discern in every meaning the truth of the spoken entity with outstretched ears. Only beneath the cloud of technical media will the

60 Translated from Kittler, *Musik und Mathematik I*, p. 113.

61 Ignace Jay Gelb, *A Study of Writing: The Foundation of Grammatology*, Chicago 1974.

62 Translated from Johannes Lohmann, "Die Geburt der Tragödie aus dem Geiste der Musik," in *Archiv für Musikwissenschaft*, no. 37, 1980, pp. 167–186: 181.

sun and shadow of being give occasion to examine language and script, speaking and writing, under the conditions of their oblivion.[63]

The intellectual involvement with writing, language, and speaking, which goes directly back to the Enlightenment and indirectly to an initial distinction, called "Mosaic"[64] by Jan Assmann, grew into a veritable world war of words during the 1960s, of all times. Jacques Derrida told the European philosophy of being that in its script-forgetting phonocentrism it can't stop hallucinating a "determination of being as presence," and alleged that it was "in the process of imposing itself upon the world."[65] Against this he promised a "liberation all over the world"[66] through grammatological deconstruction, through an unyielding, fundamental opening of the metaphysical gelatinization of sound and script, through revealing the submerged breaks between voices and phenomena. The Old Testament relationship between writing, body, and law was suspended in this promise.

Maurice Olender has systematically followed the battle over signs and scripts, which was reassumed under the conditions of technical media, back to the history of philology. Using historical texts he reconstructs the attempt to distinguish Semitic and Aryan languages in particular through alphabets and linguistic signs. In doing so Olender makes out a background to German racial theory in philology. He refers to the mythologizing, blindfolding and deflection of Greek, Indo-European, and Semitic mythologems that is necessary to maintain this "great divide," and among seventeenth-century texts he discovers some that understand vocalization not as an instrument of power but of vitalization: "The Hebrew word is described as mute, an opaque substance whose occult meaning emerges only when it is voiced. In order to be read, the text must be chanted, infused with the animating breath according to rules distilled from centuries of

63 See Heidegger, *Parmenides*, p. 85: "The typewriter is a signless cloud."

64 Assmann, *Moses the Egyptian*, p. 1. In his reading of William Warburton, Assmann assesses the invention of the alphabet as an economic and a grammatological coup: "The decisive discovery of the inventor of the letters lay in interpolating language as an interface between sign and signed. This enabled a quite decisive reduction of the inventory of signs, but it cut the band between world and writing." [This passage is not in the English version of the book. Translated by MT]

65 Jacques Derrida, *Of Grammatology*, trans. Gayatri Chakravorty Spivak, Baltimore 1976, p. 3.

66 Ibid., p. 4.

vocalization."[67] In differential terms, vocalization has to do with taking meaning from elsewhere, with knowing and overstepping one's own boundaries. When Derrida declares that phonocentrism, as an assertion of naturalness in spoken, vocalized language, succumbs to the hallucination of a presence[68] that annuls the break between sign and thing, word and world, he places the beginning with Rousseau and his idea of pure articulation, of sung or singing aspiration. Derrida gives this the Rousseauist name of the Western phantasm of presence: "With this exemplary model of pure breath (*pneuma*) and of an intact life, of a song and an inarticulate language, of speech without spacing, we have, even if it is placeless [*atopique*] or utopian, a paradigm suitable to our measure. We can name and define it. It is the *neume*: pure vocalization, form of an inarticulate song without speech, whose name means breath, which is in-spired in us by God and may address only Him."[69] But neumes are primarily also the signs that regulated the vocalization of texts from the ninth century onward.[70] These medieval lines and dots weren't simply notation that helped to aspirate a text and vocalize it at the prescribed pitches; they were also a physical disciplinary regime that served to enforce a unified liturgy within the space of the Roman church.[71] In this script the chosen ones are brought into song, and could claim to be linked to a divine channel, while incorporating it, that is simultaneously forgetting it. Michel Foucault will insert the history of sign regimes into the concept of discourse in order to point out the mutually transformative relationship between body, speaking, and subjectivization. In the course of the discussion about his research on madness, he not only charges Derrida with a "reduction of discursive practices to textual traces"[72] but also diagnoses his refusal to accept that subjectivization is itself subject to discursive procedures. Foucault takes up the thread of Enlightenment discourse when he accuses his

67 Maurice Olender, *The Languages of Paradise. Race, Religon and Philology in the Nineteenth Century*, trans. Arthur Goldhammer, Cambridge 1992, p. 24.

68 See Derrida, *Of Grammatology*, p. 18f.

69 Ibid., p. 249.

70 Ibid. Here Derrida quotes the *Dictionnaire de musique*, but only on the practice of singing: "The neume is a kind of short recapitulation of the air in the mode, which is made at the end of the antiphon, by a simple variety of sounds, and without joining them to any words."

71 For an extensive discussion see Wolfgang Scherer, *Hildegard von Bingen: Musik und Minnemystik*, Freiburg 1987.

72 Michel Foucault, "My Body, This Paper, This Fire," in Michel Foucault, *Aesthetics, Method, and Epistemology*, ed. James D. Faubion, New York 1998, pp. 393–417: 416.

former student of proposing a pedagogy "that teaches the pupil that there is nothing outside the text, but that in it, in its gaps its blanks and its silences, there reigns the reserve of the origin."[73] He links this polemic, in which, according to Derrida, the "'sense of being' is said in its grid," with Heidegger's Greek-oriented philosophy of saying. In it Foucault identifies a "pedagogy that gives conversely to the master's voice the limitless sovereignty that allows it to restate the text indefinitely."[74] But with Foucault at the latest the French debate about language, sign regimes, and bodies goes beyond a simple opposition of consonantal or vocalic alphabet, and calls for the observation of procedures of transformation and power in discursive practices outside of the textual as well, in order to examine historical interfaces of articulation, ability to speak, having to be silent, and physical bodies, where subjectivity emerges. The German debate, as insistently shown in Olender's book, was happy to exaggerate the opposition between vocalic and consonantal alphabets under various antecedents. In this constellation it becomes clear how precisely Arnold Schoenberg opens his opera *Moses und Aron*, in his use of a sung vocalize and then consonant-saturated reply in the new, twentieth-century form of *Sprechstimme*. As in the vocalise, signs are materialized in tone colors and breath. He doesn't counter the then virulent Aryanization of a Hellenistic discourse with an originally Semitic or Hebrew one, but through marking lacking structures, languages, and forms of percep tion, and in the modernism of a vocal art that seeks transition, not boundaries.

The rhythm and physiology of the voice form the basis of the twentieth-century vocal arts to which Schoenberg will align himself. But the mediatization of language and the technical history of the voice are not linear processes. We will have to return to Friedrich Schiller's staging of the chorus as rhythmic, in the modern tragedy of the *Bride of Messina*, in order to find someone taking the liberty of employing "the Christian religion and the Greek gods together."[75] With Schiller it becomes clear that language, where poetically composed and spoken, introduces history and makes the boundary to the alien permeable. Messina, where the migrants entered, was the location of a syncretic language: "I have employed the Christian religion and the Greek gods together, and even recalled

73 Ibid.

74 Ibid.

75 Friedrich Schiller, "On the Employment of the Chorus in Tragedy," trans. George Gregory, *Fidelio*, vol. 2, no. 1, 1993, pp. 60–64: 64.

the faith of the Moors. But the location of the play is Messina, where these three religions still express themselves, partly in living form, partly in monuments, and they speak to the senses. And I hold it to be a right of poetry to treat the different religions as a collective whole for the power of imagination, in which everything which has its own character, expresses its own sensibility, has its place."[76] This institutional and pedagogical return to the primate of vocalization of language at the end of the eighteenth century can't be understood as a return to the paradise of the preliterate, and by no means as a par force run into unconcealment. It is, as formulated by Michel Foucault on the shores of the Arabian Maghreb, where he drafted the critical manifesto *The Archaeology of Knowledge*, the entry into a new *episteme*, which locates knowledge in the gap between words and things, introduces temporality and suspension as breach relationships that cause the autonomous human being to appear where he or she is dedicated to language and has to become a philologist in order, and always with a delay, to comprehend the continually flowing flow of speech as discourse. Foucault makes a less fundamentalist diagnosis, and is seeking proximity, when he writes: "Language is sought in its most authentic state: in the spoken word – the word that is dried up and frozen into immobility by writing. A whole mystique is being born: that of the verb, of pure poetic flash that disappears without trace, leaving nothing behind it but a vibration suspended in the air for one brief moment. By means of the ephemeral and profound sound it produces, the spoken word accedes to sovereignty. And its secret powers, drawing new life from the breath of the prophets. rise up in fundamental opposition (even though they do tolerate some overlapping) to the esoteric nature of writing, which, on the other hand, presupposes some secret permanently lurking at the center of its visible labyrinths."[77] The phantasm of an autonomous and natural speech, which still inspired literary Romanticism, is not solely due to the failure to recognize the violent linkage of speaking and writing but also to a complete misapprehension of the media realm. Human language is visualized, made visible in its effects, in the empirical and experimental, but has to be transferred into writing.[78] Media practice atomizes esotericism.

76 Ibid.

77 Michel Foucault, *The Order of Things*, London 1989, p. 311f.

78 See, for example, Brigitte Felderer, "Stimm-Maschinen. Zur Konstruktion und Sichtbarmachung menschlicher Sprache im 18. Jahrhundert," in Kittler and others (eds.), *Zwischen Rauschen und Offenbarung*, pp. 257–278.

In 1942, when Schoenberg was struggling with setting to music the last act, which would remain music-less language but certainly sonorous poetry, the schism between Hellenism and Judaism also affected the work of other exiles, "those whose love for our Western history has serenely persevered,"[79] against all resistance. When Erich Auerbach, exiled in Istanbul without access to the actually necessary specialist libraries, reconstructs a realist theory of Western literature, he does so in the irreconcilable confrontation between the Homeric and the Old Testament styles, which for him equally mark the beginnings of Western poetry, although he does concede a totalitarian aspect of the Old Testament language: "The Bible's claim to truth is not only far more urgent than Homer's, it is tyrannical—it excludes all other claims."[80] Auerbach contrasts Homer's sensuous and open, evenly illuminated, and syntactically sophisticated descriptions with the complex and enigmatic Old Testament figures and stories. Called by their "earlier God of the desert"[81] who speaks from a "lack of form, lack of local habitation, his singleness,"[82] the people have either to obey this "hidden God who yet shows himself"[83] or take the risk of resistance. "The Scripture stories do not, like Homer's, court our favor, they do not flatter us, that they may please and enchant us—they seek to subject us, and if we refuse to be subjected we are rebels."[84] Slave or rebel are the alternatives here, not university teacher or poet. Auerbach discerns the origins of the political in the West in precisely this polarization of obedience and autonomous thinking, in the remorseless challenge to decide. This kind of politics is due to the "irrepressible politico-religious spontaneity of the people"[85] as it emerged in the Exodus, not with the later logic of the polis. But conversely, when he unexpectedly begins his book with the "Odysseus Scar," Auerbach discovers the sign of a sutured thought in Greece too. Even with Homer, *nostos* didn't simply mean coming home, but being recognized and recalled from the marks of previous wounds. In Greece too, *nostos* refers to a past and recovered time. It isn't only Jewish thought that begins with an indication

79 Auerbach, *Mimesis*, p. 557.
80 Ibid., p. 14.
81 Ibid., p. 8.
82 Ibid.
83 Ibid., p. 17.
84 Ibid., p. 15.
85 Ibid., p. 21.

Experimenting with symmetries.

of "thoughts which remain unexpressed."[86] Seen from Istanbul and its alien libraries, the boundary between Hellenism and Judaism becomes recognizable as anachronistic, and Europe itself is nothing more than a scar in the collective memory of truth and reality in mimesis. Here Auerbach's reconstruction of the conflict as scar and symptom corresponds to Freud's in his book on Moses.

In 1942 the motif of purity of thought as the competition of truths is an issue. Arnold Schoenberg makes it central to his libretto, depriving it of its contemporary Grecism, but he knows about the scar that opens at the difference between the cultures of Greece and the Old Testament. At the start of the opera, following the vocalise, in the first encounter with Aron, Schoenberg leaves it to the discretion of the Moses performer to change at one point from *Sprechgesang* to the singing voice, and thus, as Straub/Huillet's film makes audible, suddenly to overcome all the halting and hesitation of speech in a direct embodiment of the voice. At this point Moses challenges Aron, who wishes to make the idea of God conceivable. "Reinige dein Denken, lös es von Wertlosem, weihe es Wahrem [Purify your thinking. Free it from worthless things. Let it be righteous]."[87] Only against the background of the German Hellenist discourse does the line reveal its demand and mark a central conflict in the opera. In direct confrontation with a Germanic Hellenism, Schoenberg doesn't simply insist on a vocalizing speech but experiments with new musical relationships, conceptions of the body, ways of articulating, and their resulting spatialization. He provokes

86 Ibid., p. 11.

87 Schönberg, *Moses und Aron*, score I, act I, bars 208–214.

the question of truth in the field of performance and the political. Schoenberg had experimented with musical notations and symmetries, and long since with typewriters. The fact that notation and the possibilities of its technical production and reproducibility were a central concern of Schoenberg's compositional concepts is shown in his design for a music typewriter, patented in 1909 but never realized, which would have been operated via a keyboard, a type-bearing lever, and a ribbon. 120 characters on forty trapezoid heads enable the notes to be assembled. The writing surface could be moved up and down, back and forth, and in a circle beneath the mechanism.[88] Retrograde and inversion could be scored mechanically in this way, along with all kinds of oddities that don't at first appear in twelve-tone music. The music typewriter is a plotter of sound clouds.

Schoenberg deliberately pushes the difference between technically handled script culture and Greek legend to the edge of divine visitation, in order to blur the boundaries of Grecophilia and Old Testament. As at the same time with Erich Auerbach, Siegfried Kracauer, or Erwin Panofsky, and like them in exile, he was interested in the complexity of the collision of script cultures as constitutive of modernism. Hybrid media constellations are explored in exile.

Both aspects, controlled speech and the availability of linguistic spaces, are interlocked in the first image of Straub and Huillet's film. With it they introduce an evident disjointedness in the figure of Moses, but they also address

88 Christian Meyer and Therese Muxeneder (eds.), *Arnold Schönberg. Catalogue raisonné*, 2 vols., Vienna 2005, vol. 1, p. 218.

the various senses of the cinemagoers in such a way that they are confused and divided as to the connection between image and sound, so that they have to decide how to put them together. This poses the question of whether an Other, as gap or bracket, holds perception and thinking together, or whether the distinction between message and rustling, call and responsibility, is left to the pleasure and provision of the audience, at the beginning of opera and film.

While the opera, as the composer wished, opens up the new experience of space with a call into the dark of the auditorium—thus linking it directly to the bodies—the film, bright and in close-up, shows that recordings of sounds and people in media are always assembled. Hence they first and foremost produce new audial and visual experiences of what people, languages, and bodies are. In experimenting with media all sensory events initially and in equal measure become data relationships, which then, rematerialized instrumentally or mechanically, ally with other sensory constellations into sounds and movies, and generate chimerical, hybrid media people. The transition through sound and space alters what a person is. The sound space, in turn, is the result of complex arrangements of notation systems, buildings, a long history of psychoacoustics, and not least of bodies, which realize what was prescribed and transform it in doing so. In this way, listening to sound is conceived as a non-linear feedback space: "Before studying music, men are men, and sounds are sounds. When studying music, things are not so clear. After studying music, men are men and sounds are sounds."[89] A consistently Hellenistic joining of sound and body, as may still perhaps appear in the score, is disturbed and differentiated in the encounter with concrete surroundings in both the realized opera and in Straub and Huillet's film. The confrontation of writing down and prescription, on the one hand, and the materialitiy of musical dispositions, bodies, and spaces, on the other, is conceived as a material process from the start. Opera and film examine this as a political question about the possibilities of community and dissent in heterogeneous perceptual spaces.

The film by Jean-Marie Straub and Danièle Huillet opens with the observation of a language in which a system of signs is realized in vocalization and incorporation. The first image of the film shows this process as resistant, even torturous. Moses is reluctant. Here the film positions itself precisely between Hellenism and grammatology. The vowels and a vocalic alphabet are presented as the

89 John Cage, *A Year from Monday, New Lectures and Writings*, Middletown 1970, p. 85.

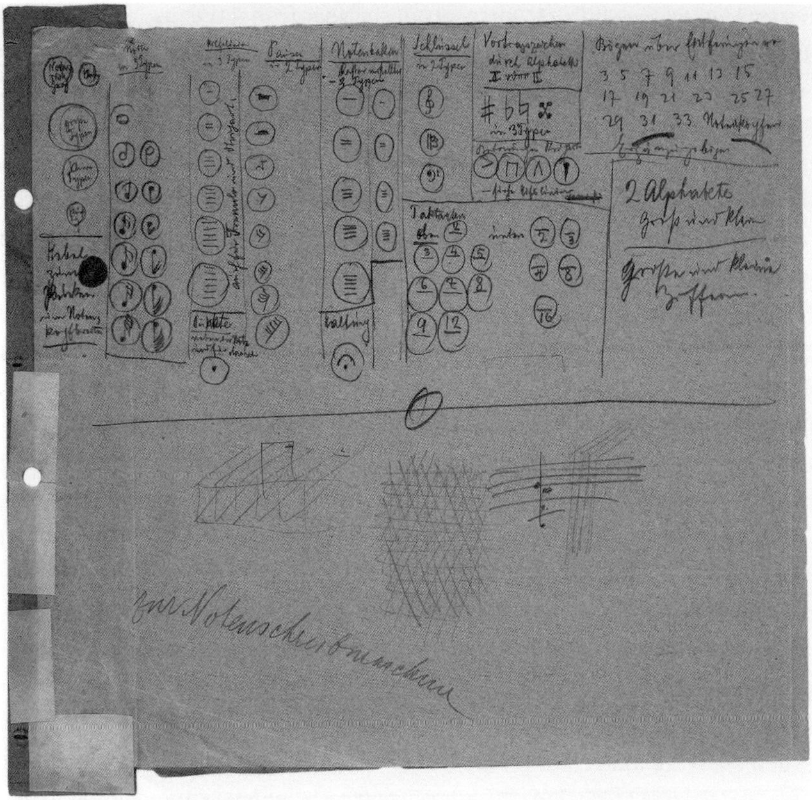

Sketch by Arnold Schoenberg for a music typewriter

evocation of a voice, and thus of a particular and historical physicality. Straub and Huillet show the seizure of the body through the dynamic of language, as long as the scene appears in the light of evocation. In the speaking body of the performer, language and vocalization demonstrate the extent to which writing becomes a prescription for physical constraint, repression, or even castigation. At the same time the scene refers to an operability of letters that only becomes effective in sound, in language, and as relation.

The opposition of vocalic and consonantal alphabets becomes more complex in a historical superimposition of realities. Attention shifts from the embodiment of writing to the inscription of language into bodies. But only when it is focused on media and differences do even biblical heroes appear as rebels. This particularly applies to the figure of Moses, whom writers and scholars have seen as notoriously obedient *and* tyrannical,[90] while for singers and musicians, radio people, rappers, and revolutionaries he has always been a rebel and a role model: someone who has to justify the law himself, who doesn't or can't speak the standard language, who stutters and stammers before speaking up to the pharaoh, a nomad who receives a mandate for land appropriation, someone who doesn't know the ropes and is supposed to open up an unknown media space.

At the moment in which language is spoken, is sounded from a written trace, it no longer stands in relation to a despot, a god, or a leader, but makes its own incisions, expands its relationships into a network, becomes material, and makes the connections between things, elements, and particles perceptible to all. The availability of a script and its vocalization becomes the starting point for a possible culture. But on the other hand everyone must decide for himself to embrace and vocalize the script, if need be against the force-feed of the reading schools and against the authority of teachers. This is the core of the Moses story, and it can be made relevant to today. Where new media open up new spaces, circumstances are established against and before the law. They need to be negotiated, so that new and hybrid cultures come about.

In his study of Moses, Sigmund Freud acknowledges, without referring it explicitly to writing and law, that only the penetration of the Greek into art permits the fusion of intellect and *physis*: "The harmonious development of spiritual and bodily activity as achieved by the Greeks was denied to the Jews." But as to the culture clash and the Grecophile body culture of the German militias in 1936, Freud consoles himself that the Jewish option was the more progressive: "In this conflict their decision was at least made in favour of what is culturally the more important."[91] With Arnold Schoenberg this also includes the overtones that reach beyond the Pythagorean harmonic system. Schoenberg, too, knew about the cultural-technically organized decision he faced: between *physis* and

90 See Yosef Hayim Yerushalmi, "Le Moïse de Freud et le Moïse de Schönberg," in Pierre Nora (ed.), *Le Débat* (1993), no. 73, p. 112; Jacques Derrida, "Archive Fever. A Freudian Impression," trans. Eric Prenowitz, *Diacritics*, vol. 25, no. 2 (summer 1995), pp. 9–63; in relation to Freud see Ulla Haselstein, *Entziffernde Hermeneutik: Studie zum Begriff der Lektüre in der psychoanalytischen Theorie des Unbewußten*, Munich 1991.

91 Sigmund Freud, *Moses and Monotheism*, ed. Katherine Jones, London 1939, p. 182.

psyche and their analysis. In the opera he realizes this in the libretto and in the harmonies themselves, that is musically: in the night of the orgy around the Golden Calf, a naked youth sings "Eurem Vorbild, Götter, leben wir die Liebe nach! [In your godly image we shall let our passions live]"[92] in the variations via fifths and fourth, relationships of 3:2 and 4:3, which form the Greek cosmos as subdivisions of the octave, the cosmos, which doesn't simply mean divine order but, media-theoretically updated, an "open diversity of possible operations."[93] At this point the Israelite calf becomes Greek, although no bull, and not Egyptian, as Jan Assmann has argued in the sense of a counter-history. And Schoenberg is working through the acoustic tradition of a Europe he is about to leave: firstly into the space of twelve mutually relativizing tones—and then, via France to America, into a space of different signs and sounds.

2.3. TONE COLORS: MOOD, NOTATION

When at the beginning of the opera Arnold Schoenberg stages pure vocalization as non-human, or in the hybridization with instrumental sounds as distinctly un-human, he marks the tension between an unmediated, primordial articulation and a speaking constrained by writing or media through emphasizing the superimposition of tone colors. Since his *Theory of Harmony*, from 1911, he had been working on a new way of composing and listening to tone-color melodies in an awareness of overtones and their interferences. With the vocalise he doesn't position himself in the Enlightenment debate around a reconciliation of nature and world, sounds and things, thinking and being, but points instead to the omnipresent, invisible, unconceivable, and ultimately immeasurable abyss from which the "concept and self-presence of the subject" has always been engendered and suspended by a "strange privilege of sound":[94] from a space that Freud will describe around 1933 as traumatic, in his examination of a Jewish origin of his discipline in the light of the figure of Moses. For Schoenberg this space is initially simply the alternative to the prevailing

92 Schönberg, *Moses und Aron*, score II, act II, bars 912–914.

93 Translated from Kittler, *Musik und Mathematik I*, p. 279.

94 Derrida's paraphrase of Hegel, see Derrida, *Of Grammatology*, p. 26.

Western tradition of listening and musical meaningfulness. Through musical and media-technical stagings of the voices and instruments, Schoenberg bases the opera's sound space, which emerges with the vocalise, in a hitherto unheard presence of tremendous sonorities. Something is both absolutely there and absolutely alien. In this way Schoenberg brings back the call of the thornbush's voice from metaphysics into the materiality of sound worlds and illumined profanity. In sound every object bears its own message. In *Moses und Aron* Schoenberg's way of countering the dichotomy of *techné* and naturalness in the age of technical media with a complex layering and mutual determination of materiality and music is neither biblical nor Homeric, neither Hebrew nor Greek, neither despotic nor freely available. Like any cultural technique it has to be historically extrapolated, interlinked with other approaches, practiced, and then willfully utilized. Schoenberg's music constructs force fields and spaces such as the media and sign regimes of the twentieth century permit, but simultaneously indicates their boundaries.

The opposition of presence generated in *logoi* and intervals on the one hand and imagined absence on the other is literally relativized in other models in which textuality and vocality are correlated. As Bettine Menke expounds, the figure of classical and agonal rhetoric, Prosopopoiia, for example, as the media effect of a figure of oration or a text, evokes the appearance of an explicitly artificially produced face. "The *fictio personae* institutes a face of oration, which it conversely declares to be a *necessary fiction*. The figurativity of *prosopon* identifies the 'speaking face' as something not of nature but of language and its *techné*."[95] In this process, dead people, absentees, or imagined opponents and perhaps gods are brought forward through texts or media and hallucinated as faces. Going beyond the Romantic formulas of natural hallucination "between book and lamp,"[96] Bettine Menke develops for literature a process of understanding that anchors the text in a speaker, but that in return has to accept an irritation by paradoxical temporal structures of anticipation and retrospection.[97] In the course of this fictionalization, the *techné* that sets everything going is itself

95 Translated from Bettine Menke, "Die Stimme der Rhetorik – die Rhetorik der Stimme," in Kittler and others (eds.), *Zwischen Rauschen und Offenbarung*, pp. 115–132: 120.

96 Although here this applies to Flaubert: "The imaginary now resides between the book and the lamp," in Michel Foucault, *Language, Counter-Memory, Practice. Selected Essays and Interviews by Michel Foucault*, Donald F. Bouchard (ed.), New York 1977, pp. 87–113: 90.

97 Translated from Menke, "Die Stimme der Rhetorik," p. 124.

forgotten. The first of ten movements or sequences of one of the first compositions of *musique concrète*, Pierre Schaeffer's *Symphonie pour un homme seule* (1949–1950), is also quite logically entitled "Prosopopée." "Prosopopée, voici ce qu'en dit le dictionnaire; 'figure de rhétorique consistant à prêter la vie à des choses inanimées'," [98] writes Schaeffer, explaining his wish to eliminate representation from music and to give a life of its own to every sound object. At the beginning of his opera Schoenberg explicitly proceeds the other way around. He denaturalizes, eliminates naturally seeming life, emphasizes the unnatural, the media aspects, systematically triggers the process of *prosopon-poiein* when in the vocalise he mixes un-human voices from human and instrumental superimpositions of tone colors without text. This does not, as in the Greek theater, evoke a dead person, an absentee, or a god, who appears on stage through the rhetorical effect of an additionally masked voice. Schoenberg instead generates a listener, who is at first confused and then makes a distinction, who has to authorize him- or herself to hear what he or she hears, from the effect of the music. Orienting oneself in tone colors and their possible reproducibility means entering a new sound space without an imaginable god. Schoenberg develops this new space programmatically in *Moses und Aron*. While the figure of Prosopopoiia consigns to oblivion the productivity of the medium from which it results, the *Moses* opera demonstrates and performs the media operations underlying all faceless voices and acousmatically vocalized words.

In their film of the opera, Straub and Huillet here find an initial approach to their development of the concept of visibility and seeing into a media-based knowledge: with them the vocalise doesn't resound from the darkness but in the light of the first lengthy shot. This is at first a close-up, filmed over the shoulder of the Moses figure, in a profile that conceals his mouth and eyes, before the sandy ground. Indications of synchrony are eliminated. The indistinctness of this figure is contrasted by the exposure of the singer's body, head, breath, and breathing. This corresponds to the music: tone colors, as Helmholtz showed, make the particularity of every body, its specific vocalic consistency, audible. The physical presence of this Moses is not due to a script, not to a rhetorical figure masked as a human image, but to a cinematic and acousmatic recording of this body in its specific reality. Straub and Huillet are not concerned with the realization or rescue of fictive constructions of reality, but with the visualization

98 Schaeffer, *Traité des objets musicaux*, p. 64.

and recollection of the media procedures that bring all film figures about. When at the beginning of their film, before the actual Schoenberg opera begins, they call to mind Martin Luther in his Peasants' War translation of the Bible and the director Holger Meins, the vocalise is intoned as if through two death masks into the non-fictional truth of media processes. Straub and Huillet thus make clear that media voices are not a matter of individuals but remain bound to historical constellations.

In having the Moses performer speak with his singing voice, Schoenberg brings biblical and Greek vocal practices into operation as media practices. If *Sprechgesang* has its origin in the delivery of sacred texts, this applies equally to the recitation of the Torah and of the Dionysia and Greek tragedies.[99] Just as in Greek culture the taut body and taut strings were termed *tonos*, Schoenberg develops his intoning speech from the taut vocal chords of the singing voice. This technique, for which Schoenberg adapted a notation from Engelbert Humperdinck,[100] but which can be ascribed, as Matthias Schmidt has shown, to Schoenberg's impression of the ironic speaking practice of Karl Kraus,[101] was initially committed to the tonality of pitches, and referred all eccentricity of song back to the extreme intensity of vocal tension. Theodor W. Adorno described the *Sprechgesang* in *Moses und Aron* as "a kind of alienation effect." In a radio interview with Pierre Boulez he remarked: "It suddenly dawned on me, first in *Moses und Aron*, where Moses, through whom the voice of the spirit speaks, the transcendent voice, as it were, doesn't sing but speaks amidst the music. [...] The speech is not naturalistic, but through the very inappropriateness of the spoken to the musical sound something of the strangeness of the music comes out much more intensively than if it had been left, in itself, to itself."[102] So *Sprechgesang* can be described not as a return to recitation but more as a kind of vocal progress in spirituality (*Geistigkeit*)—to paraphrase a formulation in Freud's Moses book. But Schoenberg stages this progress with regard to the acoustic possibilities of modernism, that is as an advance into the complex-

99 See Juan Allende-Blin, "Über Sprechgesang. Auf Spurensuche," in Heinz-Klaus Metzger and Rainer Riehn (eds.), *Schoenberg und der Sprechgesang. Musik-Konzepte* 112/113, 2001, VII, p. 57.

100 See Ulrich Krämer, "Zur Notation der Sprechstimme bei Schönberg," in Metzger, Riehn (ed.), *Schoenberg und der Sprechgesang*, ibid., p. 12.

101 Translated from Matthias Schmidt, "Musik ohne Noten. Arnold Schönbergs 'Pierrot lunaire' und Karl Kraus," in *Studien zur Musikwissenschaft*, vol. 47, 1999, pp. 365–393.

102 Translated from Theodor W. Adorno and Pierre Boulez, "Gespräche über den Pierrot lunaire," in Metzger, Riehn (ed.), *Schoenberg und der Sprechgesang*, pp. 82–96: 84/85.

ity of calculated frequencies and their tone colors, and into the media spaces they bring about. In this context, Adorno's assumption that "the voice of the spirit [...], the transcendent voice" speaks through Moses is perhaps an ahistorical interpretation. With Schoenberg alienation is an experience very much of this world, and his stage directions are guided by vocal-historical immanence.

Long before the *Moses* opera, Schoenberg outlined the *Sprechstimme* as a means of purifying words or semantic material from all emotionality, and of transferring the control not only of the voices but particularly of the mood to the music. The foreword to *Pierrot lunaire*, from 1912, states: "The performers never have the task of creating the mood and character of the individual pieces from the meaning of the words, but solely from the music. In as much as the tone painting of the events and feelings in the text was important to the author, this will in any case be found in the music. Where the performer cannot find this, he should refrain from giving something that the author did not want. He would not give here but take."[103] Mood is media effect and media art. It would be wrong to think of Herder's linguistic philosophy when Schoenberg's Berlin diary says: "Here the sounds become an almost animal-like expression of sensual and emotional agitation."[104] Schoenberg's score doesn't intend naturalness but a radical denaturalization, a de-anthropomorphizing of the sound in its vibration and tension. For a revival of *Pierrot lunaire* in 1923 Schoenberg insisted in this very sense to his assistant Josef Rufer: "The speaking register is of course inadequate. The lady must learn to speak with the 'head voice'; every voice has it [...]. The most important thing is to achieve the 'speech melody'."[105] Such melody is obtained through various techniques of tone-color articulation. With the *Sprechstimme* Schoenberg also operates in between sign cultures, in between bodies and medium, at the juncture of speaking and singing, law of thought and speech rhythm, between the poles that are equally formulated in the text of *Moses und Aron*.

As Reinhart Meyer-Kalkus has elaborately shown,[106] in the 1910s and 20s various artistic and theatrical avant-gardes, especially on the periphery of bourgeois culture, in cabarets, bars, and salons, experimented with the relations of tension to which bodies are subjected by *Sprechgesang*. Among the most famous

103 Translated from Allende-Blin, "Über Sprechgesang," p. 46.

104 Schoenberg, "Berliner Tagebuch", translated from Allende-Blin, ibid., p. 55, who also suggests the comparison with Herder.

105 Translated from Krämer, "Notation der Sprechstimme," p. 22.

106 Reinhart Meyer-Kalkus, *Stimme und Sprechkünste im 20. Jahrhundert*, Berlin 2001.

speech artists were Rudolf Blümner, who primarily recited the poetry of August Stramm; Lothar Schreyer or Kurt Schwitters, from the Berlin circle known as Sturm; Hugo Ball imported futuristic linguistic experiments into the Zurich Cabaret Voltaire with his sound-poetry, before later, as a "strict Byzantinist,"[107] working through the relationship between words and reality precisely at the boundary between late antiquity and Christianity. Emil Frantisek Burian and of course Raoul Hausmann developed their own concepts of vocal articulation in order to mark their positions acoustically outside of literature itself. Most important to Schoenberg, however, were the readings given by Karl Kraus, with whom he shared the experience of the satirical Viennese popular theater, and whose ironic distance and work with linguistic material decisively influenced Schoenberg's concept of *Sprechgesang*.[108] In contrast to pure singing, *Sprechgesang* stages the physicality of the voice, frequency combinations, and mixing of tone colors, albeit along with disruptive elements and all kinds of side effects of physical materialization. The reproducibility of the voice is reliant on technical media: "Not only can the speech melody not be as adequately fixed as the music, it also cannot be reproduced exactly. There is no repetition in acting and recitation."[109] All the more does *Sprechgesang* seem to call for storage on records or sound film. The arts of the 1910s drew on the experiments and inventions of the nineteenth century. The history of the perception and scripting of speech melodies goes back to the prehistory of the technical media, to the physical and physiological acoustics founded by Hermann von Helmholtz as the study of frequencies and tone colors and the extension of the measurable sound spectrum. Linguists such as Eduard Sievers transferred this sound analysis to the relationship between language, intonation, mind, and body. In his experiments Sievers charted what regulates the reciprocity of spoken artwork and speaking body.[110]

107 Taubes, *The Political Theology of Paul*, p. 64.

108 See the detailed study by Matthias Schmidt, "Musik ohne Noten," p. 365–393.

109 Translated from Meyer-Kalkus, *Stimme und Sprechkünste, p.* 274.

110 Translation from Eduard Sievers, *Ziele und Wege der Schallanalyse. Zwei Vorträge*, Heidelberg 1924, pp. 69–70: "Sound analysis is the attempt to establish, with the aid of methodically executed psycho-physiological reactive experiments, the psycho-physiological conditions under which formed speech comes about, and the unwritten specific qualities they correspondingly possess. Whether we have to do with orally produced, and thus heard speech, or with speech only existing in written form, which has to be sonically reproduced before one can undertake the actual investigation, is irrelevant."

He referred to Wilhelm Wundt's parallel postulate of psychophysics[111] in showing, on the basis of recitations, that poems function like interfaces of body and psyche, or, to take up Herder's concept, like "door hinges": every motion of an utterance is followed by a psychic reaction; every psychic stir manifests itself in movement. Thus the emotional life can be read from perceptible expressions, which differentiate themselves as physical tension in the vibrations of language and its vowels.[112] At this point Sievers' text is important for the cinema in media-archaeological terms because it introduces the psycho-technical concept of *Einstellung* [in the cinematic context "shot," but more widely also "setting," in its active sense, or "attitude," *trans.*], here as "regulation of the continuous sound quality as a whole."[113] For Sievers spoken language forms a "complex system that one cannot dismantle or destroy without damaging the overall effect of the complex."[114] When Sievers sonically examines poetry as well as prose, the prosodies of German folksongs along with the Homeric hexameter and of all things the Pauline epistles, he defines the voice as the materialization of historical and contemporary acoustic spaces, so that he can propose a new philology not only of the ears but also of the soft palate as a philology of sound formation.[115] He measures what evades musical prescription and theatrical staging as the difference between the singing and speaking voice.[116] In his analysis Sievers distinguishes

111 Translation from Wilhelm Wundt, *Völkerpsychologie. Eine Untersuchung der Entwicklungsgesetze von Sprache, Mythus und Sitte*, vol. 1: *Die Sprache*, Leipzig 1900, p. 65: "However an expression is primarily correlated to a particular psychic affect, secondarily these sensations of tension and touch are firmly associated with particular expressions." With reference to the context of the cinema see also Ute Holl, *Cinema, Trance and Cybernetics*, Amsterdam 2016.

112 See Meyer-Kalkus, *Stimme und Sprechkünste*, p. 99ff.

113 Translation from Sievers, *Schallanalyse*, p. 72: "The physical occurrences can partially be covered by the concept of setting, partially by the concept of movement [...]. It stands to reason that setting, as the lasting factor, is an element of permanence, while movement, as an arranged transitory factor, is a source of controlled gradation. Looking at this more closely, 'setting' amounts to the regulation of the continuous sound quality as a whole, while 'movement' signifies the gradation of the sound in detail, within the constant overall framework given by the setting."

114 Ibid., p. 77.

115 See Meyer-Kalkus, *Stimme und Sprechkünste*, p. 73ff.

116 Eduard Sievers, "Über Sprachmelodisches in der deutschen Dichtung," translated from Eduard Sievers, *Rhythmisch-melodische Studien: Vorträge und Aufsätze*, Heidelberg 1912, p. 57: "In song we need the singing voice, in speech the speaking voice, which is in itself characterized by a lesser degree of musical qualities. Music principally works with fixed tones of steady pitch; speech moves largely in gliding tones that ascend or descend from one pitch to another within one and the same syllable. But language is not bound to the specified pitches and intervals of musical melodies: it knows only approximately determined pitches, and although the direction of its sound progressions (whether ascending of descending) is generally predetermined, this

between and measures pitch, size of interval, direction of sound, specific tonal progressions, and the bearers of melody, elements in which the intention of the poet and the realization of the speaker are indistinguishably united.[117] In the winter of 1915/16 a student of Wilhelm Wundt, W. E. Peters, recorded Sievers' practical analyses of reading aloud laryngologically and phonographically, transferring the movements of the larynx onto a kymograph and then onto manuscript paper, and at the same time the sound onto wax discs with a phonograph: so the voice recorded itself in its vibration like a double Dictaphone.[118] The scientific experiments and psychophysical models of voice research were taken up by the arts, on the one hand; on the other they generate social practices that applied vocal physiology for administrative purposes. Scarcely having left the phonetic laboratories, linguistic methods were used in the colonies and in the prison camps of the First World War, for example in the Halbmondlager in Wünsdorf, near Berlin, where soldiers from around the world were obliged to speak into phonographs and microphones.[119] This didn't simply make acoustic fingerprints available to the Wilhelmine administrators; it was the basis of phonetic research into mentality. Indian or North African dialects were noted and analyzed in order to specify governmentality in the relationship between bodies and complexes of signs, and a hundred years later, in a filmic media archaeology of the Berlin phonogram archive undertaken by Philip Scheffner, to dismantle it.[120] In the light of this swift transfer of sound analysis into administration, the unpredictable performances of speech artists in the cabarets turn out not only to be aesthetic but also political experiments. Karl Kraus, in his texts, above all in his contemptuous *Last Days of Mankind*, can be heard in the inflections of Optimist and Begrudger.[121] Schoenberg ties in with this phonetic knowledge in his introduction into vocal music of the physical voice as a mixture of frequencies, a

is not so of their magnitude, which can change according to very different considerations. So throughout the investigation one should only expect to find relative tonal relationships—in poetry too—not the fixed relationships of music."

117 See ibid., p. 66.

118 See Meyer-Kalkus, *Stimme und Sprechkünste*, p. 102.

119 Britta Lange, "Ein Archiv von Stimmen. Kriegsgefangene unter ethnografischer Beobachtung," in Nikolaus Wegmann, Harun Maye, Cornelius Reiber (eds.), *Original/Ton. Zur Mediengeschichte des O-Tons*, Konstanz 2007, pp. 317–341.

120 See the film HALFMOON FILES, D 2007, book/dir. Philip Scheffner, b/w, color, 87'.

121 Karl Kraus, *The Last Days of Mankind*, trans. Alexander Gode and Sue E. Wright, New York 2000, act 1, scene 29.

musical-linguistic vehicle, and in his distinction between the singing voice and the *Sprechstimme*.[122] He is not only concerned with exploring the possibilities of an increasingly complex acquisition of new acoustic spaces through technical media and the superimposition of sounds, but also with a media-differentiated transformation of voices. As a reader and listener of Kraus, Schoenberg was well aware that this would have to occur in contradiction to procedures of political and geopolitical identification.

Schoenberg's notation system for *Sprechgesang* had continually changed from the *Gurre-Lieder*, 1900/1901, to the score of *Moses und Aron*. He gives up the specification of pitches, which applied until the *Jakobsleiter*, 1917, and experiments with various forms.[123] For the *Sprechstimme*[124] Schoenberg sometimes entirely abandons the parameters that can be exactly written down as pitch, duration, and dynamics, releasing the voices into the realm of noise.[125] Finally, in the *Ode to Napoleon Buonaparte (Lord Byron)*, 1942, and *A Survivor from Warsaw*, 1947, the recitative is notated around a single line.

The fact that the relationship between musical notation and realized sound not only continually changes but is also linked to the opera's major theme of the prohibition of images is shown in the trace that Moses' struggle with Aron leaves in the notation: after experimenting with adiastematic forms of notation, that is with headless notes that don't indicate a pitch, firstly in *Pierrot lunaire*, Schoenberg "only uses them again in the final scene of act II of *Moses und Aron*,

122 See Schmidt, "Musik ohne Noten," pp. 365–393.

123 In the *Gurre-Lieder* and the *Glückliche Hand* Schoenberg specifies the pitches exactly, and in a highly differentiated notation. Later he abandons the adherence to pitch, and in *Sprechgesang* writes not a law but the transfer of an attitude or an "abstract gesture of declamation." See Rudolf Stephan, "Wege zur neuen Musik," in Helga de la Motte-Haber (ed.), *Edgard Varèse: Die Befreiung des Klangs. Symposium Edgard Varèse Hamburg 1991*, Hofheim 1992, pp. 11–16: 13. I thank Matthias Schmidt for the information that this was not a linear development, but that the notation varied according to historical subject and type of work.

124 Translation from Krämer, "Notation der Sprechstimme," p. 25: "The decisive step within Schönberg's description of the *Sprechstimme* was the transition from diastematically precise to diastematically imprecise notation. The most important form here is the one-line notation extended by several auxiliary lines, and it most clearly reflects Schönberg's changed opinion about the use of the *Sprechstimme*. [...] Schönberg was obviously only concerned with a relative rendition of the speech melody (in the sense of a 'speech gesture') resulting from the length and direction of the note stems."

125 Translation from Stephan, "Wege zur neuen Musik," p. 13: "A melody becomes a noise curve. This change becomes even more clear with polyphonic speaking ensembles and choruses. Notes become noises."

significantly to Moses' words 'Dein Bild verblich vor meinem Wort [Your image faded at my word]'."[126] While up to this point Moses' *Sprechgesang* has been notated diastematically, that is as crosses that specify the pitch instead of noteheads, Schoenberg revokes this specification at the very point where the tension between the word and its phonetic realization, *sens et son*, is about to burst. Here Schoenberg releases the voice of Moses into the emptiness of its own provision. The singer has to decide.

In view of the question of sign regimes and their power over bodies, the Moses singer's speaking could hence be understood as a space of "ironic displacement" and the staging of aporia, of artistically dealing with the prohibition of images.[127] However, the opera is also pervaded by references to an in-between, a gap, an unimaginable authority from which every idea should be determined. From these fissures we can assume the punishing force of a prohibition on the depiction of divine power. A form of negation at the core of artistic and media thinking operates as a productive difference in Schoenberg's work. Just as at the start of the opera, the act of listening subjects one to an oscillation between vocality and alterity from which the text and context of the call then develop, Schoenberg's vocal dramaturgy calls for the decision to assume the origin of the sounds either in *physis* or in *psyche*, in strict notation or in orchestration, in writing or in images. Conversely, doubt remains as to whether writings and scores subjugate bodies to or rather liberate them from conventional spaces. For the twentieth century Schoenberg suspended the prohibition of images, so instead of explaining obvious metaphors he exposed the operations of armies of flexible signs. Rather than working on the meaning of music he revealed the construction of musical spaces. As Allende-Blin wrote, his requirement was "never [to create] the mood and character of the individual pieces from the meaning of the words, but solely from the music."[128]

This is not only a musical-aesthetic gesture. Schoenberg subjects his imagined audience in this way to a tension that bothered him particularly at the time of the opera's composition: the relationship between law and media as one of regimes of signs that take possession of the body. Through the example of

126 Translated from Krämer, "Notation der Sprechstimme," p. 25.

127 See Gertrud Koch, "*Moses und Aron*, Musik, Text, Film und andere Fallen der Rezeption," in Gertrud Koch, *Die Einstellung ist die Einstellung*, p. 34.

128 Translated from Allende-Blin, "Über Sprechgesang," p. 46.

Adiastematic form of notation: "Your image faded at my word."

fearing the effect of the Tetragrammaton, whose utterance among all words is absolutely forbidden, Schoenberg examines the possibilities of refusing the order of writing. Hence he opens his opera with an unknown space in the ears of the listeners and singers that doesn't, and can't, appear in script culture: the regulation of the *Einstellung*, the setting, in the double sense of the physical direction of perception through modern media on the one hand and psychic mood on the other, as Gertrud Koch makes central to her critique of the film MOSES UND ARON.[129] It is this interlocking space that the *Sprechstimme* of Moses explores and adopts as the new space of exile, less land appropriation than a prospect to which Moses' position will always be restricted: he can only see the Promised Land from afar, never enter it physically. A "progress in spirituality," which Freud will call for,[130] is for Schoenberg no longer to be attained only in the renunciation of a Greek, vocalized "harmonious development of spiritual and bodily activity,"[131] but in the discovery that the materiality of sound goes much further, into the world of frequencies and their complex instrumental, vocal, or synthetic hybrid relationships, that is, into the world of un-human aesthetics. This has the advantage of being radically historical and collective in its mediality. No sovereign people comes about without having experienced and recognized the logic of its media preconditions. Indeed Schoenberg owes this discovery not least to his early interest in the compositions of Richard Wagner, whose triumphal *Gesamtkunst* at Bayreuth is about how new acoustic spaces are founded in new relationships between *physis* and *psyche*. So too does his attempt to have the German spirit emanate from figures thought of as Greek, to fuse the two cultures in heroism, rely on musical psychophysics.[132] But acoustic space suitable for asylum sounds different.

129 See Koch, "*Moses und Aron«*," p. 34.

130 Freud, *Moses and Monotheism*, p. 176.

131 Ibid., p. 223.

132 See Maurice Olender, *The Languages of Paradise*, p. 140: "Imbued with a Christianity from which he had just escaped, Wagner dreamed of Germanizing the Greek miracle."

2.4. OPTICS: LIGHT PATHS, FANTASY

Fortunately for those critics who can't simply see how eye and gaze are modulated in film, in her protocol of the filming of Schoenberg's *Moses und Aron* Danièle Huillet notes for every shot not only the frame size and the length of shot but also the exact focal length of the various lenses used by the cameraman Ugo Piccone: a light telephoto of 75 mm in the long first shot, which turns through a pan from a close-up into a wide-angle; a 44-mm lens for the long shot of Moses and Aron in the second scene, a larger telephoto of 100 mm for the close-up of Aron in the third, and so on.[133] The lenses, which—in the central-perspective *dispositif* of the Renaissance[134]—regulate the relationship between eye point and vanishing point, the relationships between the visible elements of the image, and hence those between the viewers and their relationship to the world, objectively, technically, and non-anthropomorphically, tend like all media-technical setups to be obvious to filmmakers. Film scholars, on the other hand, tend to underrate the basic photographic order of things in film. In film-theoretical or film-analytical studies an image is rarely described in terms of the functions of its focal-length qualities, which don't merely have to do with technical perspectives and angles of vision but with the seeing subject and a world view. For "with the variability of the lens [...] the standpoint of the camera can no longer be concluded directly from what is shown, as the lenses produce quite different depictions of an object from a single standpoint";[135] and film viewing furthermore enters a field of behavior understood by phenomenological film theory, after the famous lecture "The Film and the New Psychology," given in 1945 by Maurice Merleau-Ponty at the Paris film school IDHEC.[136] Regarding the optical modification of the world through cinema, Merleau-Ponty says: "I do not even notice the distortions of perspective, much less correct them; *I am at the cube*

133 See Huillet, "Moses und Aron. Das Drehbuch," op. cit., pp. 203–252. This is not unusual for Straub und Huillet's shooting protocols, while focal length otherwise remains a matter for camerapeople, is rarely disclosed and barely mentioned in film analysis.

134 See Hubert Damisch, *The Origin of Perspective*, trans. John Goodman, Cambridge 1995; Samuel Y. Edgerton, *The Renaissance Rediscovery of Linear Perspective*, New York 1975, p. 124ff (chapter IX, "The Discovery of the Vanishing Point").

135 Translated from Knut Hickethier, *Film- und Fernsehanalyse*, 3. überarbeitete Auflage, Stuttgart, Weimar 2001, S. 66.

136 Maurice Merleau-Ponty, "The Film and the New Psychology", in Maurice Merleau-Ponty, *Sense and Non-Sense*, trans. H. Dreyfus and P. Dreyfus, Evanston 1964, pp. 48–59.

All vectors are related to an invisible center.

itself in its manifestness through what I see."[137] In this text he reflects on seeing in regard to the space and the in-between-ness of an other, which he will later define more precisely as the split between eye and gaze. Here an element comes into play that links the "new psychology," which Merleau-Ponty will identify as film theory, to the research and findings of gestalt theory: perception always organizes itself among things and in the space so as to "re-establish the field's homogeneity."[138] In cinema the optics change the field character of the image—the relationships between near and far, figure and background, movement and light as the imperceptible basis of all semiotic and iconological filmic forms. In film shots this skew, which phenomenologically is an organization of the world before the eye, is essentially structured by the lens, which changes the relationships between things and thus what appears as cinematic space. The setting of the setting is primarily a fixing of intermediate spaces and relationships, and not a depiction of things.

The effective regulation of the relationships within the image through focal lengths that correlate light, movement, and framing in dependencies and differences is one of the elementary factors that modulate space in Straub and

137 Ibid. p. 70 (italics U.H.). Original: "Loin que je les corrige, je ne remarque pas même les déformations perceptives, à travers ce que je vois je suis au cube lui-même dans son évidence."

138 Ibid., p. 65.

Huillet's invention of new cinematic forms. MOSES UND ARON re-radicalizes the element of optics in that the entire first act is filmed from the same camera standpoint in the central axis of the amphitheater of Alba Fucense, although only the first shots are taken from a raised structure, the *toretta*, in the center of the arena.[139] The rule of the game in act I is that all the film vectors are oriented to an invisible center, from which their differences are geometrically developed. Afterwards the shots and lenses follow the combinatory logic of tone row and variation.[140] In this non-illustrative filmic strictness the spaces of the Exodus are staged according to Schoenberg's principles.

For example, the normal lens with a 50 mm focal length is used by Jean-Marie Straub and Danièle Huillet to shoot the scene in which the chorus seeks to measure a space from which Moses and Aron are expected back by the people after their first meeting: the immeasurable space of the desert. In the English translation of the libretto, by the way, this isn't translated as "desert" but, more modern, as "wasteland," as depleted land or, for Thomas Stearns Eliot, to whom we owe the fame of the word, as an American, also as a land of waste, of garbage. This very much corresponds to one meaning of the desert in pharaonic Egypt, in which "T3-mrj" means beloved country, which is contrasted with "h3s.t," foreign land, mountain land, the desert.[141] The desert space is not always one of sand. In the texts of T. S. Eliot, London fog, rain, and water in general disperse the perception into which he places his words. The desert doesn't only pervade the poetry of this time; in the films of Joseph von Sternberg, for example, it is a white radiance that dissolves perspective structures and marks disconcertion, mainly between the sexes, with Joris Ivens it is the wind; and ever since films have been described it has been the light diffused by rustling leaves, "the ripple of leaves stirred by the wind," the motif that since Münsterberg's and Kracauer's reading of an early Lumière critique has haunted cinema history as

139 This becomes clear for the first time in act I, bar 254, when the camera films a "Young Girl" with a 40 mm lens, slightly from below, then pans left to a "Young Man," a shot that becomes more concentrated because he is standing closer to the camera, and the pan continues to a close-up of another man. The three shots are linked to three accounts: "Ich habe ihn gesehen [I saw him from afar]." Only at the end of the sequence does it become clear that Aron is the person in question.

140 See Huillet, "Appunti sul giornale," p. 403.

141 See Beate Hofmann, "Zur Bedeutung der Wüste im pharaonischen Ägypten," in Uwe Lindemann and Monika Schmitz-Emans (eds.), *Was ist eine Wüste? Interdisziplinäre Annäherungen an einen interkulturellen Topos*, Würzburg 2000, p. 17.

an indication of filmic perception.[142] Straub and Huillet also used it as an image for the opening of another film to Schoenberg's music.[143] What Schoenberg undertook in *Moses und Aron* with the restructuring of the sound space, with the equality of all tones for a new sound, is carried out by Straub und Huillet for the visual space as a very artificial equalization of all elements. The visualization strategy is a systematic de-systemization of spaces in a precise historicizing of spatial forms that ceaselessly responds to power relationships in cultural topologies. In Straub/Huillet's films spaces don't illustrate but envision history.

The visible elements of the image aren't only correlated by the layout of the amphitheater, which is never shown in full view; within this scenography the camera lens organizes the concentration and distance that structure the image. Here too Straub and Huillet flout the Ten Commandments of classical, domesticized montage, which only permits sequences of particular frame sizes in the economy of the unity of narrative space.[144] After the intertitle "Moses begegnet Aron in der Wüste [Moses meets Aron in the Wasteland]," which follows the first, approximately ten-minute uninterrupted pan of the mountains and the orchestral music after a long black leader, there is a cut that according to conventional wisdom defies the continuity of a coherent cinematic space, because it not only jumps without transition from a long shot to a close-up but also because the first shot is filmed at a slight wide-angle of 40 mm, the next with a 100-mm telephoto that palpably condenses the world.[145] A cut like this doesn't connect images according to the imperative of similarity between figure and space, in order to secure the identity and identification of the figures within the

142 Kracauer, *Theory of Film*, op. cit., p. 31. "It was inevitable that, in the comments on Lumière, 'the ripple of leaves stirred by the wind' should be referred to enthusiastically. The Paris journalist Henri de Parville, who used the image of the trembling leaves, also identified Lumière's over-all theme as 'nature caught in the act'." Hugo Münsterberg, *The Photoplay. A Psychological Study*, New York 1916, p. 52: "... like the streaming of the water in the brook or the movements of the leaves in the wind." Straub for instance quotes Griffith, 1947: "What the modern movie lacks is beauty—the beauty of moving wind in the trees, the little movement in a beautiful blowing on the blossoms of the trees, that they have forgotten entirely"; as told by Barton Byg, *Landscapes of Resistance. The German Films of Danièle Huillet and Jean-Marie Straub*, Berkeley 1995, p. 21. Another film by Straub/Huillet after an opera by Schoenberg begins with the long shot of a leafy tree in the wind, FROM TODAY UNTIL TOMORROW, D 1997, and their television film EUROPA 2005 – 27 OCTOBRE (2006) is an entire meditation on violence and the fall.

143 INTRODUCTION TO ARNOLD SCHOENBERG'S ACCOMPANIMENT TO A CINEMATIC SCENE, F/I/FRG 1972, book/dir. Jean-Marie Straub and Danièle Huillet, b/w, color, 15' 43''.

144 See Karel Reisz, Gavin Millar, *The Technique of Film Editing*, London 1953, p. 216.

145 Lens change from shot 12 to 13.

image; on the contrary, it confuses this relationship in favor of what the image is intended to show as the specificity of the non-similar: while the first lightly high-angled shot observes the sand, and left and right on the visual periphery the full figures of Aron and Moses with their black shadows, as if doubled in form, the next shot shows Aron's left profile in close-up, with the telephoto, and from a different camera angle. According to conventional spatial logic such a cut either signalizes a jump in time—which in this case is suspended by the continual inherent time of the opera—or a new and unknown point of view, which here, as there is no optically produced basis of subjectivity and no subjective points of view, can also have no significance. The telephoto shot instead shows what the interlocking of optics and architecture always induces perceptually: telephoto lenses, which only focus on a small area of the image space, produce a condensation of figure and background, or—after a word by the photographer in a novel by Hubert Fichte—an "adhesion" and mutual affectation of the objects in the image, while a wide-angle lens emphasizes the relationships between things.[146] Wide-angle lenses open up a deep focus, which can range from objects in direct proximity to the furthest distance; they connect everything to everything else and therefore require extreme strictness of composition and resulting narrative procedure.[147] This corresponds to the different entanglements of Aron and Moses with the world and image worlds, and the brothers' conflict about this. At the same time the optics organize the attitude of the viewers to the image space, as Maurice Merleau-Ponty noticed in himself. Watching films is thus not passive, but becomes a particularized attitude in media spaces, more exactly in respectively historical media spaces.

The basic visual connections through which cinematic space and spatiality arise are demonstrated in the film's first cuts, and linked at the same time to the opera's motif of imagery. These connections are firstly the relationship of image to image, secondly the relationship between the objects within the images, thirdly the visible relationship between the figures, and fourthly their visibility

146 Translated from Hubert Fichte, *Eine glückliche Liebe. Die Geschichte der Empfindlichkeit*, vol 4, Frankfurt/Main 1988, p. 29.

147 See Jean Mitry, *The Aesthetics and Psychology of the Cinema*, Indiana 2000, p. 191. Mitry doesn't emphasize the distances but the composition, that is, the relationships: "Thus we can see that keeping focus on the whole field of view, by the very fact that it brings out the homogeneity of the spatial content, accentuates the association between the compositional elements, thereby giving them character and power of unity."

to the viewers, the visual relationship between *on*, *off*, and *hors-champ*.[148] All these relationships structure the images and imagination of the viewers. With Straub and Huillet they systematically disrupt perception as unpredictable connections. The optical space organizes the prime dispute in the iconoclastic controversy between Moses and Aron, while at the same time the optical organization of the images is superimposed by an opposing, musical scansion. In the 40-mm wide-angle shot from above showing Moses and Aron together for the first time Louis Devos sings in cheerful tenor of the sovereignty promised by the new god, who has proven himself superior to other gods:

> Aron:
> Glückliches Volk, einem einzigen Gott
> zu gehören,
> den zu bekämpfen kein andrer Macht besitzt.
> [Oh happy folk to have one mighty god
> to belong to,
> against whose forces no other pow'r prevails.]
> (act I, bars 139–145)

Günter Reich, in Moses' *Sprechstimme*, responds to Aron's "one god," telling him that alterity has no place in the concept of a single god, and that the Kingdom of God is fundamentally different from the realm of human ideas. The last word, *Raum* (space), is noticeably separated by a caesura:

> Moses:
> Andre gibt es nur im Menschen,
> nur in der Vorstellung.
> In ihr hat der Allgegenwärtige nicht
> Raum.
> [Others live within a people,
> only in fantasy;
> but God the almighty exists apart from
> men.]
> (act I, bars 142–145)

148 See chapter 4.1.

A countershot is unconceivable.

This shot is followed by the—in the conventional sense—inappropriate close-up of Louis Devos as Aron, who in the extreme 100-mm telephoto presence of his face sings a short ode to the back coupling of fantasy and its formations, a sentence that is difficult to follow even for trained listeners of opera:

Aron:
Gebilde der höchsten Phantasie,
wie dankt sie dir's, daß du
sie reizest zu bilden!
[O vision of highest fantasy,
how glad it is that you've
enticed it to form you.]
(act I, bars 148–152)

Once deciphered, this sentence can immediately be linked to the sensuous presence of the image, the shot of Aron's physiognomy. Moses' idea of an impossible "fantasy" shifts to Aron's question of possible "enticement," which can certainly be applied to the perception of cinema itself: in the Mosaic and psychophysical sense enticement is cinematic devilry, which meaninglessly locks the gaze, just as in the Torah the vowels bind the body to divine law.

Aron: "O happy folk."

* Diese Stelle kann eventuell gesungen werden.

Moses: "Purify your thinking."

The cut to this close-up simultaneously places Moses off screen, in an invisible somewhere or other: we have to "imagine" him outside the frame, just as the visible, rhetorically eloquent Aron prophesies. Moses' *Sprechstimme* objections, hurled at Aron to interrupt his praise of enticement, thus issue from a space that suspends visual perception, all the more to entice it. This stimulus, which indeed moves the viewers in the movie theater to continual "imaging" and "imagination," is both criticized and further displaced by Moses.

> Moses:
> Kein Bild kann dir ein Bild geben
> vom Unvorstellbaren.
> [How can fantasy thus picture
> the unimaginable?]
> (act I, bars 150–152)

Not only is the main theme of the opera introduced here, the prohibition of images; Straub and Huillet also project it onto the perception of film, onto the optics as decisive structure, onto the montage as visual caesura. Moreover, the psychophysical problem of the relationship between stimulus and imagination is executed by the shots themselves, and ultimately subjected to the intricate organization of cinematic spatial structures. The prohibition of images in the cinema relates to much more than what becomes visible on screen. It addresses the routines and conventions of connecting the cinematic image to the world. Film is montage in sequences, not a window on the world.

With the next cut Moses stands in close-up, "de face," and, stepping towards the camera, he takes his *Sprechstimme* through all registers in a furious and redundant hammering home of dogmas:

> Moses:
> Unvorstellbar
> weil unsichtbar; weil unüberblickbar;
> weil unendlich; weil ewig; weil allgegenwärtig;
> weil allmächtig.
> Nur einer ist allmächtig.
> [Not conceived
> because unseen, can never be measured,

everlasting, eternal, because ever present,
and almighty.
The one God
is almighty.]
(act I, bars 183–186)

It is apparent that the medium is still new to its man. Moses meanders from one concept to the next, and at this point Schoenberg's score provides, once only, the option of singing: "It is possible for this passage to be sung."[149] Here, at the point which has already proved to be resistance to a Germanic Hellenism, Moses unpredictably switches to a fine song with the frightening and frightfully angry words that link both truth and purity, as well as pragmatically articulating the Jewish credo of possessing nothing superfluous:

Moses:
Reinige dein Denken,
lös es von Wertlosem,
weihe es Wahren;
kein andrer Gewinn dankt deinem Opfer.
[Purify you thinking.
Free it from worthless things.
Let it be righteous.
No other reward is giv'n your off'rings.]
(act I, bars 208–217)

When in the first sequences of the opera, from an indistinct noise, a call and commission is issued to save a people and assemble it under a new law ruled by something unconceivable and concealed, Schoenberg realizes this motif in musical structure, and Straub/Huillet transfer it into cinematic forms. In both works of art, center and orientation are initially abolished. Both put their audiences in the position of being abandoned in an aesthetic desert, of having to take responsibility for what they perceive and wish to perceive. Conduct is required in unknown media spaces, where people become unfamiliar to themselves while hearing and seeing. Acoustic and optical spaces are detached from

149 Schönberg,, *Moses and Aron*, score I, act I, bar 208.

given cultural conventions and contexts, and purified by a logic of counting and enumeration that brings about new relationships. And yet both works are situated in exact historical discourses when they establish and then disestablish differences. Both works are situated as political when they explore the relationship between language, signs, architecture, acoustic and image worlds as subjectivization. The opera's opening already conveys the state of abandonment and aridity as a form of perception that creates resistance.

3. FIELD AND DISTRIBUTION

3.1. MURMURINGS IN THE DESERT

Arnold Schoenberg at first wrote the text and music of *Moses und Aron* in parallel, then, in the Catalonian resort of Bajada de Briz, shortly before departing for America, completed the libretto of the last act, but was at odds with its music until the end.[1] His libretto is closer to contemporary cinema aesthetics than he was perhaps prepared to admit, and its style points to expressionist models, screenplays and their optical modulations, the translation by Murnau and his cameraman Karl Freund of Carl Mayer's screenplays into film images.[2] With Schoenberg, too, not only verse and rhythm but also setting and score, in which the voices are written down for a sound space, organize a dramaturgical distribution of the elements within space. What looks on paper like equal distribution interferes as sound with space, and is differently dispersed again in the images of the film. Decisive to shot, staging, and montage is the topos, or more exactly the condition, of the desert.

In her research and preparation for the film, Danièle Huillet initially researched the desert historically, describing, for the Semitic nomads in the Middle East, a hybrid space of different cultures.[3] In the film the desert won't take on a metaphoric value but an aesthetic one, which contains a political one: in the unstructured equal distribution of possibilities lies the liberation of the people. Straub and Huillet transfer the logic of a space consisting only of mutually related equal elements to the cinema.

This becomes clear in the scene in which Moses and Aron return from their first meeting in the desert, where, as we know, they have argued about the visibility and experienceability of the new, one God, his signs and legalism. In the

1 "...the libretto being definitely finished only during the composing, some of it even afterwards" (letter to Alban Berg, in Schoenberg, *Letters*, p. 151). The opera developed from the concept of an oratorio in 1922 to the project of a cantata until 1926, and was conceived as an opera in 1930. See Kerling, *Die Gottesfrage*, p. 24ff and Schönberg *Moses und Aron, Entstehungsgeschichte.*

2 See Fred Gehler and Ulrich Kasten, *Friedrich Wilhelm Murnau,* Berlin 1990, p. 68ff.

3 Danièle Huillet, "Kleiner historischer Exkurs," in *Filmkritik* 221/222, 1975, pp. 194–202: 197.

libretto this scene is devised as a composition and image of liberation: after the Young Girl sings "Er wird uns befrein! [He shall make us free!]" solo and pianissimo (G-sharp–A–C–D) in bar 397, the following text, beginning with a call to see what can't be seen exactly, is sung by the chorus, which at this point is doubled or also divided. The difference is decisive here:

2nd Chorus	1st Chorus
Seht Aron und Moses!	Seht Aron!
Seht Aron und Moses!	Seht Moses!
	Moses' mächtiges Haupt
	Moses, den Stab in der Hand,
Steht Moses oder geht er?	schreitet langsam, bedächtig, scheint fast zu stehen,
Moses steht! Nein, er schreitet	bewegt sich kaum.
langsam.	Steht Moses oder geht er?
Moses steht! Nein, er geht!	
Mächtig sein weißes Haupt.	Mächtig sein weißes Haupt,
	gewaltig sein Arm! Seht!
Gewaltig sein Haupt!	
[See Aaron and Moses!	[See Aaron!
See Aaron and Moses!	See Moses!
	Moses' powerful head!
	Moses, his rod in his hand,
He's waiting. Is he moving?	moving slowly, reflective, seems to stand still,
Moses waits! No he's walking	now moves somewhat.
slowly.	Does he wait?
Moses waits! No, he moves!	Is he moving?
Mighty his whitened head.	Mighty his whitened head,
	and strong is his arm! See!]
And strong is his mien!]	
Aron, gewiß nicht mehr jung,	
eilt beschwingt, leichten Schrittes	Steht Aron jetzt bei Moses?

weit vor ihm her und
steht doch nah bei ihm!
Vor oder hinter ihm?
An Moses' Seite?
Sind näher, sind ferner,
sie bewegen sich nicht im Raum!
Sind näher, sind ferner, sind höher,
sind tiefer,
verschwinden gänzlich!
Seht Moses!
Seht Aron! Seht Moses!
Sie sind jetzt da!

Nein, er eilt voran!
Geht Aron an Moses' Seite?
Vor oder hinter ihm?
Sie bewegen sich nicht im Raum!

Sind näher, sind ferner,
sind höher, sind tiefer,
verschwinden gänzlich!
Seht Aron!
Seht Moses! Seht Aron!
Sie sind jetzt da!

[Aaron, a young man no more,
moves along with a light step
far before him,
and yet stands close to him!
Front or in back of him?
At Moses' side now?
Are nearer, are farther.
They are moving, but not in space!
Are nearer, are farther, are higher,
are deeper,
have vanished wholly!
See Moses!
See Aaron! See Moses!
They have arrived!]

[Is Aaron close to Moses?

No, he goes before!
Is Aaron at Moses' side now?
Front or in back of him?
They are moving, but not in space!

Are nearer, are farther,
are higher, are deeper,
have vanished wholly!
See Aaron!
See Moses! See Aaron!
They have arrived!]

Although the lines are structured according to a rhythmical meter, the text is a classically cinematic protocol that describes the seeing and recognition of forms and their types of movement. A distinction is made between "moving," "walking," and "moving along lightly," gaits that were measured through chronometry and raster graphics after the first cinematic experiments.[4] At the same

4 See Emilie de Brigard, "The History of Ethnographic Film," in Paul Hockings (ed.), *Principles of Anthropology*, Berlin 1995, pp. 13–43.

TC17 [Beiblatt 5r]

Der Entwurf wird zeilengetreu abgedruckt. Die Klammern vor 3–11 bzw. 12–20 zielen wohl auf simultanen Vortrag. Die Längezeichen für 4 stehen doppelt, beim zweiten Mal aber ohne den Akzent bei der ersten Silbe; die zu 5 sind hinsichtlich der letzten Silbe inhaltlich unstimmig, und das falsche Kürzezeichen am Ende ist oberhalb nochmals notiert.
4: Das Komma am Ende ist KE für Semikolon. 5: *scheint fast* ist KE für *fast scheint er*, was allerdings auch nicht mit den danach notierten Längezeichen in Übereinstimmung gebracht werden kann. 13: *beschwingt leichten* ist KE für *beschwingten*. 14: *weit* ist KE für *leicht*. 15: Vor *und* ist *Ar* gestrichen.

Seht Moses und Aron!
Moses mächtiges Haupt!
Moses den Stab in der Hand
schreitet langsam, bedächtig, –́ ⏑ | – ⏑ ⏑ | – ⏑
scheint fast zu stehn; – ⏑ ⏑ | ⏑
bewegt sich kaum
Steht Moses oder geht er? –́ | –́ ⏑ | ⏑ ⏑ | –́ ⏑ |
Moses steht! –́ ⏑ | –́
Nein er geht –́ ⏑ | –
Mächtig sein weißes Haupt –́ ⏑ ⏑ | –́ ⏑ | –
Gewaltig sein Arm! ⏑ | –́ ⏑ ⏑ | –́
Aron, gewiß nicht mehr jung
eilt beschwingt leichten Schrittes
weit vor ihm her –
und steht doch nah bei ihm!
Steht Aron jetzt bei Moses?
Aron steht!
Nein er läuft!
Geht Aron an Moses Seite ⏑ | – ⏑ ⏑ | –́ ⏑ | –́ ⏑
Vor oder hinter ihm? – ⏑ ⏑ | – ⏑ ⏑
Sie bewegen
sich nicht im Raum.
Sind näher,
sind ferner,
sind tiefer,
sind höher
Verschwinden gänzlich –
– – – und sind jetzt da – – –!

TI126 [8r[1]]

Dazu Abschnittsnumerierungen in TI128 und TI129.
Vor 1: *Seht* gestrichen. 19: *eilt voraus?* ist KE für *läuft!*. 20–21: *Seite?* | *Vor* ist KE für *Seite,* | *vor*.

Chor (in vielen Gruppen) | *Seht Moses und Aron!* | *Moses mächtiges Haupt!* | *Moses, den Stab in der Hand,* | *schreitet langsam, bedächtig,* | *scheint fast zu stehn,* | *bewegt sich kaum.* | *Steht Moses oder geht er?* | *Moses steht!* | *Nein er geht!* | *Mächtig sein weißes Haupt,* | *gewaltig sein Arm!* | *Aron, gewiß nicht mehr jung,* | *eilt beschwingt, leichten Schrittes* | *weit vor ihm her –* | *und steht doch nah bei ihm!* | *Steht Aron jetzt bei Moses?* | *Aron steht* | *Nein er eilt voraus?* | *Geht Aron an Moses Seite?* | *Vor oder hinter ihm?* | *Sie bewegen* | *sich nicht im Raum.* | *Sind näher,* | *sind ferner,* | *sind tiefer,* | *sind höher –* | *Verschwinden gänzlich –* | *– – – und sind jetzt da – !* | */:Moses und Aron sind nun auf der Bühne:/*

TI128 [8r[1]]
Links neben dem Anfang von TI126.

9b

TI129 [8r[1]]
Rechts unter TI126.

folgt 10

Sketch for a rhythmic double chorus.

"Now moves somewhat, walking slowly."

"Does he wait? Is he moving?"

"Far in the distance Moses and Aaron suddenly appear. They approach in the manner described by the choruses."

time the text questions this distinction. In the face of the desert, whose expanse of heat and uniformity allows no visual coordinates, no coordination or collectivization of an objective point of view, but only an agitated and heterogeneous description of subjective perception of the visual field, geometrical space, which makes measurable differentiation possible, dissolves. The desert produces nothing but dazzlement, deception, heat haze, perhaps the occasional mirage. No orientation is available, not even directions, only sight-line vectors.

This same perspectiveless space, which Gilles Deleuze and Félix Guattari describe as the "smooth space"[5] of nomads and war machines in *A Thousand Plateaus*, is also developed musically by Schoenberg. This can admittedly only be sensed in the symbolic record of the score, but even here it can be seen that a heterogeneous, amorphous space is conceived, without a center or central organizing law, and without much reliable meter under which its elements could be counted, despite the bar lines, which conduct the conductor.

Following Pierre Boulez, from whom they take the differentiation between smooth and striated, *lisse* and *strié*,[6] Deleuze and Guattari examine the specific qualities of both these spatial forms. In music, like Boulez, they discern the possibility of making cuts in the metrical or non-metrical space. Boulez, however, who examines the time of music, laying down a band of metrical differentiation maintained by the symbolic code of the score, refers in his description of smooth spaces to a more recent, post-Schoenberg music, which, like John Cage's *Music of Changes*, resembles "throwing sound into silence,"[7] beyond temporal meter, beyond pitches and harmonies. The unpredictable speed with which musicians like David Tudor, for whom Cage wrote the composition, traverse this smooth space on the basis of such notations turns metronomic meter into incalculable duration. Schoenberg doesn't yet have this gliding within duration, and the pitches, apart from Moses's *Sprechgesang*, which permits a certain modulation, are exactly determined. Straub and Huillet's film, in contrast, takes Schoen-

5 See Gilles Deleuze and Félix Guattari, "1440: The Smooth and the Striated," in *A Thousand Plateaus*, pp. 474 – 501.

6 Boulez makes the distinction in the context of time: *temps strié* and *temps lisse*. See Julia Kursell and Armin Schäfer, "Das Band, das die Zeit macht," in Lorenz Engell and others (eds.), *Archiv für Mediengeschichte – 1950*, Weimar 2004, pp. 45–57: 46: "Music organized according to a consistent pulsation creates striated time, and music characterized more by events, sound surfaces or sound blocks, smooth time."

7 John Cage, letter to Boulez, December 18, 1950, in *The Boulez-Cage Correspondence*, ed. by Jean-Jacques Nattiez, trans. and ed. Robert Samuels, Cambridge 1993, p. 78.

berg's work into the wastelands of "espace lisse," and shows that the apparent "congruences"[8] between Schoenberg's opera and Richard Wagner's spatial concepts are pseudomorphic. The decisive difference is whether the concept of an opera develops a through-composed space in overtone effects, as Wagner does,[9] or whether a composition expects the differentiation of the sound space in the constellation of equally distributed tones in unfamiliar surroundings.[10]

The emphasis on vocalization at the beginning of the opera is something in which Schoenberg makes Boulez's smoothness—avant la lettre—the basic theme of the Moses complex, a vocalization that indistinguishably synthesizes the tone colors of voices and instruments, that blurs and smoothes out differences to the benefit of a new experience of sound. Deleuze and Guattari also comment on this:

> When there is no module, the distribution of frequencies is without break: it is "statistical," however small the segment of space may be [...] Can we say that in the kind of smooth space that is without break or module there is no interval? Or, on the contrary, has everything become interval, intermezzo?[11]

Schoenberg's vocalise and choral parts have already given an answer to this question, and Straub/Huillet expedite it: the film constructs a space of materialization of "infinite, omnipresent, unperceived and inconceivable" relationships that can only be experienced beyond a metronomic space-time continuum.

8 See Constantin Grun, *Arnold Schönberg und Richard Wagner: Spuren einer außergewöhnlichen Beziehung*, vol. 1: *Werke*, Göttingen 2006, p. 612.

9 See Friedrich Kittler, "Weltatem," in Friedrich Kittler and others (eds.), *Diskursanalysen*, vol. 1: *Medien*, Opladen 1987, pp. 94–107.

10 The musical-historical context is not important to Constantin Grun, who meticulously compares parallel points in operas by Schoenberg and Wagner. He emphasizes that as a teichoscopy, which he understands this choral sequence to be, it has a model in Richard Wagner's *Parsival*, but only applies the argument to the libretto. In bars 1099–1105 of part one, act one, Parsifal sings: "Ich schreite kaum, doch wähn' ich mich schon weit [I hardly move, yet I have seem to come]," to which Gurnemanz replies, "Du siehst, mein Sohn, zum Raum wird hier die Zeit [You see my son, time changes here to space]" (translation www.impresario.ch, accessed March 22, 2016). The similarities may certainly be established, but only their difference gives some indication of Schoenberg's treatment of his Wagnerian models. See Grun, *Schönberg und Wagner*, pp. 612–613.

11 Deleuze/Guattari, *A Thousand Plateaus*, p. 478.

It must be considered that smooth and striated spaces, as described by Deleuze and Guattari, never exist in pure form, but that the distinction of spatial types allows the observation of their continual merging. The smooth nomadic space is repeatedly converted into the striated and set space of administrative sedentariness, and vice versa. For Deleuze and Guattari this realizes the continual transition from state apparatus to war machine and back. Among other things this movement very well describes Schoenberg's relationship to his project of a Jewish spatial politics, which is at one time concretely bound to a country and territory, then to an ideal, infinite, and unconceivable space, and always to forms of transition. This transformative movement not only determines the composition phases of *Moses und Aron* but also its compositional technique, which sometimes sets the voices in strict counterpoint, sometimes in the superimposition of tone colors. Counting comes up again here, as according to Deleuze and Guattari "in a smooth space-time one occupies without counting, whereas in a striated space-time one counts in order to occupy."[12]

Just as Schoenberg links the question of legalism and its renewal in an interval plateau of the twelve tones, Deleuze and Guattari also connect musical form and its relationality with the Greek formation of legalism: "The smooth is a nomos, whereas the striated always has a logos, the octave, for example."[13] This doesn't correspond at all to Carl Schmitt's concept of nomos, which he understands as "the initial measure and division of pasture land,"[14] but the ambiguous and also active "pasturing" as movement, which he also cites in the genealogy of the term, subsumes the constant transition from smooth to striated spaces envisaged by Deleuze and Guattari. Moses' fine phrase before the burning bush, "Laß mich in Ruhe meine Schafe weiden [I ask thee, let me tend my sheep in silence]," which Schoenberg inserts into the biblical narrative, means traversing the land as a nomadic shepherd without marking or owning it, or, following Deleuze and Guattari's observations, traversing more of "a space of affects, [...] than one of properties."[15] The ambivalence is also an effect of translation. Inexpediently Germanizing nomos as "law"[16] is quite false, according to Schmitt,

12 Ibid.
13 Ibid.
14 Carl Schmitt, *The Nomos of the Earth in the International Law of the Jus Publicum Europaeum*, trans. G.L. Ulmen, New York 2006, p. 70.
15 Deleuze/Guattari, *A Thousand Plateaus*, pp. 663–664.
16 See Schmitt, *The Nomos of the Earth*, p. 71.

and again shows that the German language "is largely one of theologians—the language of Luther's bible translation—and as well a language of craftsmen and technicians,"[17] which acquired the concept of law from the interconnection of the "theological distinctions between (Jewish) law and (Christian) grace."[18] Even though Schmitt holds up legislation as an energetic and space-constituting action of mere settlement against the decadent Christian "mere will to compliance,"[19] it is notable that he, like Deleuze and Guattari, points out a further meaning of the nomos concept: "It surely is significant that nomos can refer also to a scale or succession of notes, i.e. to a musical order."[20] And this is a Greek order. In Schoenberg's opera and Straub/Huillet's film it is returned to a desert space of expansion.

Straub and Huillet will transfer the nomos structure of the desert into the visual, and not in the name of the confusing sham of eccentric liberation that the text of the chorus repeatedly invokes. In their willful de-metricalization and intensification of the spatial, both opera and film draw the attention to how very much conventional cinema is bound to a metrical logos and its order. And how confounding the unleashing of images from this space can be.

The optical, in Boulez's sense of a smooth space, moves towards the fractal, to the periphery, which at the same time it makes porous: lays waste. Schoenberg constructs both his text and his music in this way. Nomads like Moses and Aron disappear into a wasteland and suddenly reappear on the visual field, but not where we would have expected them according to the laws of geometry. In walking through the desert the two establish a hodological space with its own qualities of the visible. In the smooth space of seeing, visual intensities appear as an excessive white, which powerfully catches the eye, seemingly not belonging to any organized body but more to the structure of power itself, which diffusely pervades the bodies and dissolves their organization. The unpredictable intensities of a smooth space create political tumult and turbulence, esprit de corps or esprit de chœur; in Schoenberg's libretto they even divide the chorus into two aggregates continually singing across one another, simulating chaos, the sound of desolation and emptiness, which can finally perhaps be described

17 Ibid., p. 70.
18 Ibid.
19 Ibid.
20 Ibid., p. 71.

as a sound that defies description. At this point, in 1974, Straub and Huillet will extend the sound far beyond Schoenberg's composition with noises recorded in synch on set and mixed with the studio sounds of the orchestra. Only in the nomos of smooth space do the heterogeneous sound effects become recognizable: the various noises, the rattle of equipment, the mooing and bleating of animals, which coalesce into a complex harmony.

A smooth space, whether visual or acoustic, doesn't allow depiction but is only produced from the contingency of events, as they arise through visual and acoustic coincidences of light, sound, and material. According to Deleuze and Guattari, its points are subordinate to the dynamics of lines, alignments, and pathways. This exactly corresponds to Schoenberg's scheme: only when the tones, as required by the method of dodecaphonic composition, "are related only with one another"[21] does a new, heterogeneous sound space emerge. Schoenberg makes this clear in his notes:

> Music is not merely another kind of amusement, but a musical poet's, a musical thinker's representation of musical ideas; these musical ideas must correspond to the laws of human logic; they are a part of what man can apperceive, reason and express. Proceeding from these assumptions, I arrived at the following conclusion: THE TWO-OR-MORE-DIMENSIONAL SPACE IN WHICH MUSICAL IDEAS ARE REPRESENTED IS A UNIT. Though the elements of these ideas appear separate and independent to the eye and the ear, they reveal their true meaning only through their co-operation, even as no single word alone can express a thought without relation to other words. All that happens at any point of this musical space has more than a local effect. It functions not only in its own plane, but also in all other directions and planes, and is not without influence even at remote points.[22]

From Schoenberg's notes it becomes clear how much his concept not only dissolves the metrical and coordinative system but also challenges every form-theoretical aesthetic of the field as the relationship between ground and form. In this sound space, perception crisscrosses surfaces, pulling thought along with

21 Schoenberg, "Composition with Twelve Tones," p. 110.

22 Ibid., p. 112.

it. Such dashing and pulling is not something that moves through space but that permanently creates it. For Gilles Deleuze this spatial production is antagonistically linked to the nomadic: "I was struck by a sentence of Toynbee's: 'The nomads are the ones who don't move on, they become nomads because they refuse to disappear'."[23]

With Schoenberg and Deleuze the insistence of the nomads is a resistance against legalism, or rather an avoidance of the law, which is Moses' theme from the start; he finds excuse after excuse in order to carry on following his herd, to pasture instead of moving forward into a different, unknown but delineated land, be it intellectual or of milk and honey. This resistance, as hesitation, procrastination, faltering, and murmuring, amplifies the continual oscillation between smooth and striated space. In political terms, according to Deleuze and Guattari, every apparatus of state faces at all times its dissolution as a war machine by the nomadic, while the nomads on their flight lines continually get caught up in coordinates of state legalism. Outside of morals or historical epochs, the dynamic of the war machine, which is propelled by countless, uncounted nomadic or migrating people, has its cycles. It corresponds to the political dynamics around both 1930 and 1970 in Germany and, as we now understand, those of Europe and the Mediterranean region in 2014. Territories are involved in both movements. Belligerently or in rivalry, "in a smooth space-time one occupies without counting, whereas in a striated space-time one counts in order to occupy."[24]

Schoenberg also knew that the war machine was starting up in the choral people he was describing, who were up in arms with a new leader, "he who murdered the guard," against the pharaoh and his repressive apparatus of state. Schoenberg's composition undermines the leader principle, expressing great mistrust of a people that wishes to "give worship" and "make off'rings" even of its organic body, and has just cried "Continue working, lest it become harder!" to the desert winds[25] (act I, bars 395–397). This people too obtains a new space. That these various productions of historical and political space in the visual and the acoustic realize a politics of sounds and images as governmentality and

23 Gilles Deleuze, *Negotiations*, New York 1995, p. 138.
24 Deleuze/Guattari, *A Thousand Plateaus*, p. 477.
25 See Deleuze/Guattari, *A Thousand Plateaus*, p. 474–501. Their description of a war machine corresponds exactly to Schoenberg's construction.

control of bodies is then clearly shown in the film by Jean-Marie Straub and Danièle Huillet.

In the light of the spatialization of political conditions and relationships, the film MOSES UND ARON not only aligns the 1970s to the 1930s but also to an exodus movement in the sense of permanent revolution. In an interview with journalists from the *Cahiers du Cinéma* Straub explains: "The idea of Moses is that traversing the desert has no aim, is endless. It is quite simply the idea of the nomadic existence."[26] During the 1970s the idea of the nomadic existence appeared to open up a new space that promised a life on sight lines outside the apparatus of state.

Straub and Huillet were by no means the only ones who rediscovered the desert for a critique of civilization and capitalism at this time. In the "political wastelands" archaic, ethnological-indigenous, and futuristic utopias influenced by science fiction encountered a revolutionary "erstwhile": "The dogs bark, the caravan moves on,"[27] as it was said. However, Straub and Huillet don't link these views of the desert to an ethnographically saturated nostalgia, but expose precise historical layers of a two-thousand-year history of the motif. Hence their journeys through Egypt and their unrelenting search for objects in which the nomadic and rural way of life were deposited, and which could be transferred to the movements of the actors. Danièle Huillet writes about the journey to Egypt: "We didn't only want to find the setting (the settings!) to shoot our scenes, but also to see how people lived: to study behavior, clothing, everyday objects—also to take such objects with us that were indispensable to the film, and about which we knew that if we hired them from 'specialists' in Rome, their falsity and tastelessness would be immediately obvious."[28] The objects weren't used historically in the film, but as aggregates of forms of perception and behavior. These historical layers allowed Straub and Huillet to burglarize German history and historiography with Arnold Schoenberg's opera, which not

26 Translated from Straub/Huillet, "Conversation," p. 8.

27 *Die Hunde bellen, die Karawane zieht weiter* was the title of a then popular urban-guerilla pamphlet, which appeared without publication place or date and cost three marks: one for the material, one as a reserve for the printer, and one for the imprisoned comrades. On the return of the desert in the cinema of the 1960s and 70s, see the detailed article by Tom Holert, "Strudel und Wüsten des Politischen. Michelangelo Antonioni, Robert Smithson und Michael Snow," in *MedienKunstNetz*, http://www.medienkunstnetz.de/themen/kunst_und_kinematographie/wuesten_des_politischen/ (accessed April 16, 2014).

28 Translated from Huillet, "Appunti sul giornale," p. 407.

only makes an issue of resistance to pharaonic power, and to obedience and allegiance in German history, but also of the resistance of becoming a people independent of the leader.

This is shown in the film as the people's "murmuring,"[29] not a civic but a nomadic articulation of a people who refuse to be regulated. The constitutional lawyer Carl Schmitt juxtaposes murmuring and surliness, that maneuvering at the edge of symbolizations and concepts, with the acclamation made possible by regulated constitutional forms: murmuring is the refusal of acclamation by the people.[30] The exposure of such murmuring as the willfully constructive establishment of a new field corresponds to the artistic procedure of integrating recorded or electro-acoustically produced noises into the music. Straub and Huillet take Schoenberg's experiments further in recording these many sounds on location. They transpose the musical procedures into the film, into its acoustic and visual fields. These include the images of the chorus, whose ordered lineup is repeatedly dissolved in the fluttering of the robes in the wind, and is even more clear in the shot visualizing the view of the desert.

Schoenberg's libretto for *Moses und Aron* is infected in many ways, optically as well, by the cinema of the time. The images of the desert he conceives in the text can readily be translated into camera coordinates, or rather camera intensities. This can easily be imagined for bars 399ff of act I, in which the people

29 Michael Walzer describes murmuring as the prime articulation of the slaves in the desert. See Michael Walzer, *Exodus and Revolution*, New York 1985, p. 51. But it also corresponds to the King James translation, Exodus 16.2: "And the whole congregation of the children of Israel murmured against Moses and Aaron in the wilderness." Or Numbers 14.2; "And all the children of Israel murmured against Moses and against Aaron." The continual murmuring, "wherefore has the Lord brought us unto this land?" really gets going in Numbers, where God himself says "How long shall I bear with this evil congregation which murmurs against me? I have heard the murmurings of the children of Israel, which murmur against me" (Numbers 14.27). In the chapter "The Murmurers" of his Moses book, Martin Buber closely associates murmuring with the "stiff-neckedness" of the people of Israel, and links it to a political motif: "The other motive, which I have already indicated, and which will yet engage us, is rather more difficult to grasp genetically. It is the passionate wish to make a serious political issue of the faith in the earthly dominion of the god, such as is met with in varied forms and situations in the Ancient Orient, including Southern Arabia." Buber, *Moses*, p. 87.

30 See Carl Schmitt, *Constitutional Theory*, Durham, London 2008, p. 272: "The genuinely assembled people are first a people and only the genuinely assembled people can do that which pertains distinctly to the activity of this people. They can acclaim in that they express their consent or disapproval by simply calling out, calling higher or lower, celebrating a leader or a suggestion, honoring the king or some other person, or denying acclamation by silence or complaining."

wait for Moses and Aron to return from the desert: very long focal lengths, for example, just like the heat above desert sand, absorb the perception of proximity and remoteness, annul the perception of moving forward, dissolve pathway, distance, and the relationships between people nearby or far away: "They are farther, they are nearer, they are moving, but not in space" (act I, bar 429ff). Framing can similarly cause the relativization of above and below, of height and depth. Focal lengths can cause figures to disappear into perspective contraction and then reappear. The radiant white of Moses' head, on the other hand, which should stand out against the desert surroundings, could also be modeled through shading and contrast, and separated or "liberated" from uniform spatial coordinates by lighting. The camera-technical replacement of the prophet aura as a natural, "unique apparition of a distance, however near it may be,"[31] through pans and soft focus, in a processing of technical seeing, in which it is "impossible to assign to the spectator a single viewpoint,"[32] seems at first glance to be the most appropriate transfer of the libretto, the score, and the sound of the opera into an intensity of cinematic parameters. But Danièle Huillet and Jean-Marie Straub resist such obviousness.

Their film images don't simply illustrate or visualize Schoenberg's opera, but translate its musical and dramaturgical relationships and spaces, the substitution of conventional intervalic harmony with vibration ratios, into cinematic form. The filmic distribution of layers and breaks transfers the rules of the score, as the creation of new laws, to the cinema, and thus rejects all conventional means of filmic concentration that proceed from the homogeneous and straightforward space underlying all cinematic illusion. The so-called classic style, which dominated the spatial logic of both cinema and television until well into the 1980s since asserting itself in the Hollywood system of the 1930s, is primarily characterized by the staged and imaginary clarity of a hermetic space, which nevertheless first has to be set up by "establishing shots" and the notorious "continuity," which literally hallucinates of the old space of an all-containing cosmos.[33] Within its 180° gaze this space, which produces a coordination

31 Walter Benjamin, *The Work of Art in the Age of Mechanical Reproduction*, second version, ed. Michael W. Jennings, Brigid Doherty, and Thomas Y. Levin, trans. Edmund Jephcott, Rodney Livingstone, Howard Eiland, and others, Cambridge 2008, pp. 19–55: 23.

32 Ibid., p. 34.

33 The basic methods of achieving this clarity in "continuity" can best be understood from professional instructions, such as Reisz/Millar, *Technique of Film Editing*. For the construction

of sight lines and vanishing points, guarantees a view of the world in which identity and presence become calculable and above all imaginable in a grid of coordinates. "One will always find the same characters in the same parts of the screen."[34]

This perspectively organized overall space of classical cinema has long since been challenged by topological spatial concepts in experimental film, the Nouvelle Vague, and differently again in the New German Cinema. But the issue is by no means specific to cinema. While Straub and Huillet were exploring the desert space, the mathematically constructed topological space of neighborhood and intention even became important to the official politics of the Federal Republic of Germany. Space was reorganized, by the apparatus of state, of all things, as one of statistics and distribution. The Federal Office of Criminal Investigation (BKA) under Horst Herold began to use the newly available computers to statistically account for the population according to data on their habits, to screen and calculate in order to automate crime fighting, and especially the hunt for terrorists, through cybernetic identification procedures. Herold the visionary imagined introducing a system of "de-hierarchized knowledge transfer" into a German government agency: "In the course of such deliberations the police has become aware that insofar as it fights crime it actually represents a huge data-processing enterprise. Whether we collect evidence at a crime scene, conduct investigations, or examine witnesses, this always has to do with the acquisition, investigation, storage, processing, and combination of information and data."[35] Herold's search engines and algorithms were, as David Gugerli remarks, "an important precondition for the de-subjectivization of constitutional procedures."[36] But then de-subjectivization also means re-subjectivization. It wasn't only revolutionary guys with the Bedouin scarves then popular who turned up in Herold's grid-like parameters of the

of "lucid continuity" they recommend "Matching Consecutive Actions; Extent of Change in Image Size and Angle; Preserving the Sense of Direction; Preserving a Clear Continuity; Matching Tone; Making Sound Flow over a Cut," i.e. precisely the techniques that Straub/Huillet systematically repudiate. See ibid. p. 216ff. See also David Bordwell and Kristin Thompson, *Film Art. An Introduction*, New York 2008, p. 231; Noel Burch, *Theory of Film Practice*, Princeton 1981, p. 8ff., and Stephen Heath, *Questions of Cinema*, Bloomington 1981, pp. 41–42.

34 Stephen Heath, ibid., p. 41.

35 Translated from Herold, *Kriminalität und Gesellschaft.*

36 David Gugerli, "Die Suche nach dem Muster: Horst Herold," in David Gugerli, *Suchmaschinen. Die Welt als Datenbank*, Frankfurt/Main 2009, pp. 52–69.

non-sedentary and recalcitrant; inconspicuous and unexpectedly staid people also got caught in Herold's net through their living habits. Because he fetched differentiated patterns of behavior, not of sympathies, onto his screen, Herold too could speculate: "One will always find the same characters in the same parts of the screen." And so cybernetics constructs new images of people that are unconcerned with continuity or psychology, but take place and regularity of appearance: topological images of people. Under these media conditions, how might it be possible to think with intention and empathy about the emergence of a people?

Cinema, even the classical style, has always featured topological human relationships, but exclusively for the movements of nomads. This applies as much to Murnau's South Sea fable as the Western or David Lean's LAWRENCE OF ARABIA: the indigenous, the others, the "natives," the "redskins" appear suddenly and unexpectedly in the landscape, and not usually in the expected place on the screen. They are not characters in the literal sense, but follow a logic of positional relationships. Straub/Huillet stage Moses and Aron's appearance in the desert in the sense of these intensities. From here their enthusiasm for the films of John Ford becomes more clear, and also explains why Danièle Huillet continually refers to the aesthetic of the Western in her shooting report, even ending it with an image of "frontier":[37] the Western also endlessly repeats the story of legal land appropriation. The images of the Western also show ruins, and are deciphered in a retrospectively allegorical and symptomatic historiography.

The classically straightforward space of Hollywood studio productions defines only a fragment of all film productions of the past 120 years, as early cinema, Soviet cinema, like the antagonists of Hollywood, African or Indian cinema and all the avant-gardes, all developed new forms not derived from the predictable Renaissance space of geometrical ray optics but from the respective cultural possibility of visibilities.[38] In the early 1970s this spatial form was subject, from

37 See Huillet, "Appunti sul giornale," p. 419.

38 See above all Tom Gunning, "An Unseen Energy Swallows Space. The Space in Early Film and Its Relation to American Avant-Garde Film," in John L. Fell (ed.), *Film Before Griffith*, Berkeley 1983, pp. 355–366; Thomas Elsaesser, "Early Film Form: Articulations of Space and Time. Introduction," in Thomas Elsaesser (ed.), *Early Cinema: Space – Frame – Narrative*, London 1990, pp. 11–31. On the replacement of an earlier cinematics by the classical film space see also Burch, *Theory of Film Practice*. And for the results of this spatial organization for montage see Heath, *Questions of Cinema*, p. 40: "In the late 1930s and early 40s, the average shot length of a

apparatus theory[39] above all, to more or less the same accusation leveled by Derrida at logocentric philosophy, namely that it was "in the process of imposing itself upon the world."[40] In their spatial organization, Straub and Huillet's aloof, desert-like staging of Schoenberg's opera systematically dissolves the means and procedures with which the classical American film style developed the art of constructing a continual world view.[41] Putting together topological spaces from crossroads and bridges, knots and angles is one of the strategies of nomadic image production. The images in Straub/Huillet's film also insistently persist, like Moses and the migrants, before an overarching law, but they recursively, neither presenting nor establishing, show up the rules of the game.

The space of the entire film, not only that of the "anticipation sequence," has to remain unclear and unimaginable, although it is the result of an extremely simple plan. At first only two visual spatial forms are depicted sequentially: the architectural space of the Roman amphitheater, setting and stage of the opera production, describable to some extent as pro-cinematic; and those spaces that the camera can produce with its various lenses, settings, and basic possibilities for rotation and tracking. It becomes apparent that this simple combination no longer makes an autonomous observer or gaze conceivable, but rather puts the viewer into new relationships to the events, actions, and places in the image. So the cinema people is the first to find itself where it hadn't expected itself.

3.2. ARCHITECTURE: ARCHAEOLOGY AND MEMORY

The spaces in the film Moses und Aron aren't alogical, and don't follow any constructions from montage or surrealism. In act I they depict the "film set," the amphitheater of Alba Fucense in the topological sense, that is as a logic of

full-length Hollywood film has been estimated at about 9–10 seconds, but that fragmentation is the condition of a fundamental continuity."

39 Teresa de Lauretis, Stephen Heath (eds.), *The Cinematic Apparatus*, New York 1980.

40 Derrida, *Of Grammatology*, p. 3.

41 Barton Byg also describes the film of the opera as "spatial drama," and begins his discussion of Moses und Aron with an analysis of the spaces: "...my main focus is here the relation to cinematic space. The themes of the opera's narrative are located by Straub/Huillet in separate planes of cinematic space, allowing the spectator to move with the camera within and between these planes." Byg, *Landscapes of Resistance*, p. 142.

knots and angles, places and their connections. If film history could be written in classical chapters as the transformation of a nomadic early cinematics into an apparently straightforward, homogeneous geometrical film space of the classical studio system, which at the same time reanimates a specific fixation of the viewing subject and a concept of reality determined by central perspective, Straub and Huillet's spatialization makes the withdrawal, and therefore the means and provisions, of this great illusionizing visible, palpable, and audible—even if this is initially only a visual murmuring in the eyes of the viewers.

The choice of location already shows the work of Straub and Huillet as media archaeology. The camera movements, organized according to simple rules, exhibit the spatial structures of Alba Fucense, an excavation site in the actual sense, in its historicity. The camera stratifies the compound. The amphitheater, which was donated to the city in the year 31 by the opportunely scheming Tiberian prefect Naevius Cordus Sutorius Macro, lies a short way from the theater, which was built in the first pre-Christian century and is considered a typical example of the transition from Hellenistic to Roman theater architecture. Excavations have shown that the cults in ancient Alba Fucense were centered on oriental gods and customs.[42] Whereas the amphitheater, with its 64 by 37 meter oval arena was used as stadium in the Roman sense for horribly spectacular games with slaves and animals attended by around a thousand spectators—a people entirely missing from the film. The amphitheater belongs to a wider archaeologically accessed ensemble that includes the Roman Christian Basilica of San Pietro, erected over the floor plan of a Greek temple to Apollo, and which as a palimpsest of historical buildings depicts the history and encounter of European cultural spheres. This occurs in a kind of iconoclasm of memory: "The most efficient way of erasing a memory is by superimposing on it a counter-memory."[43]

What Straub and Huillet deconstruct is a specter that, as a peaceful Europe, haunts the continent's understanding of its history. At its base—so the film shows as a continual uneasiness—lie layers of manifest violence as conquest and spectacle. In regard to the motif of the legalism in the opera, it is revealing that theater architecture, as Cornelia Vismann expounds in her study on the media of judicature,[44] stands as a *dispositif* in a direct relationship to questions

42 See Joseph Mertens, *Alba Fucens*, Brussels 1981, p. 47ff.

43 Assmann, *Moses the Egyptian*, p. 58ff.

44 Vismann, *Medien der Rechtsprechung*.

of law. As Paul Virilio has emphasized, the Greek theater interrupts the frantic progress or course of events, *dromos*, and becomes an apparatus of sedentariness that allows the spectators, as immobile witnesses from a superior position of an agonal process, to observe, to decide, and to judge.[45] In the transition from an agonal to a theatrical process, tragedy becomes a period of deferral in order to rehearse a decision of the *demos* and the negotiation of democracy. So the viewing arrangements of the theater become the "master pattern of democratic decision-making"[46] but corrupted in form and function in the Roman adaptation of the amphitheater, as in Alba Fucense, being transformed once more into the agonal *corsa* or *dromos* of undistanced spectacle. Furthermore, the spaces of the opera cinematically realized in the theater of Alba Fucense reveal the extent to which, in Foucault's sense, three dominant layers of European discursive history are materially superimposed here: the Greek space of a polis obtaining divine justice in the theater, the space of Roman sovereignty, and, when the biblical story of slavery and exile is performed in this syncretistic space, the justification of a chosen or self-determined people as the zero point of all insurgent speech.[47] "As a result of – or despite – this interaction," says Michel Foucault, summarizing his history or revolutionary discourse, "the revolutionary discourse of seventeenth-century England, and that of nineteenth-century France and Europe, was on the side of – I almost said biblical history – on the side of history-as-demand, of history-as-insurrection."[48] All these historical layers of architecture are actualized in MOSES UND ARON in that each of their elements is exhibited through the calculatedly limited movement axis of the camera. The camera, which opens up the events for the eyes of a different audience, also determines what is seen, and refers in its radicalism to the process of exclusion that is a part of every procedure.

45 See Paul Virilio, "Desert Screen," in *The Paul Virilio Reader*, trans. Michael Degener, London 2002, pp. 156–164.

46 Translated from Vismann, *Medien der Rechtsprechung*, p. 80: "The architectural fact that the seating in an amphitheater is so arranged that from all places, without distinction or privileged positions it permits an uninterrupted view of the events to be judged all around (amphi), this kind of building conventionalizes an ur-model of democratic decision-making. Amphitheaters have stood for a democratic mode of decision since then, and are imitated with roofing under other climatic conditions."

47 See Michel Foucault, *"Society Must Be Defended." Lectures at the Collège de France, 1975–76*, ed. Mauro Bertani and Alessandro Fontana, trans. David Macey, New York 1997, p. 77.

48 Ibid., p. 78.

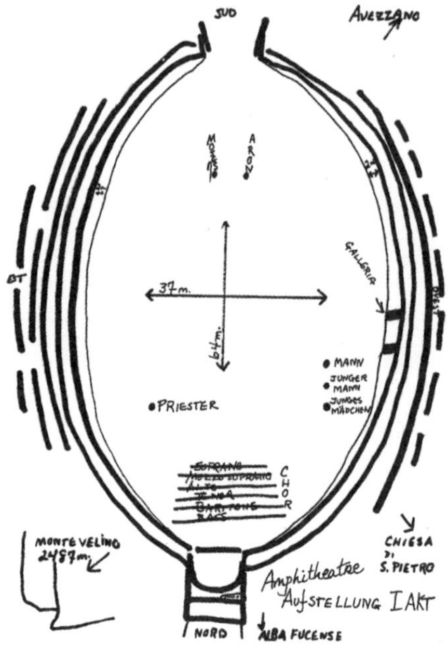

The rules of the game of the visible.

The sequence in which the voices of the chorus stage the oppressed people waiting for Moses and Aron to return from the desert with divine council and social solutions, is the most prominent example of the staging of seeing itself. As we know from Danièle Huillet's shooting record, the famous shot 22,[49] which comprises bars 397–442, "See Aaron and Moses!" was the first to be filmed, along with shot 19, in which the chorus also appears, on August 20, 1974 in the amphitheater of Alba Fucense.[50] During the previous days Jean-Marie Straub, together with his cameraman and assistants, had measured the main axes of the elliptical arena in order to determine camera angles and locations for performers and chorus, who were then placed in geometrical relationships with one another.

49 See Huillet, "Moses und Aron. Das Drehbuch," p. 203ff.
50 See Huillet, "Appunti sul giornale," p. 403.

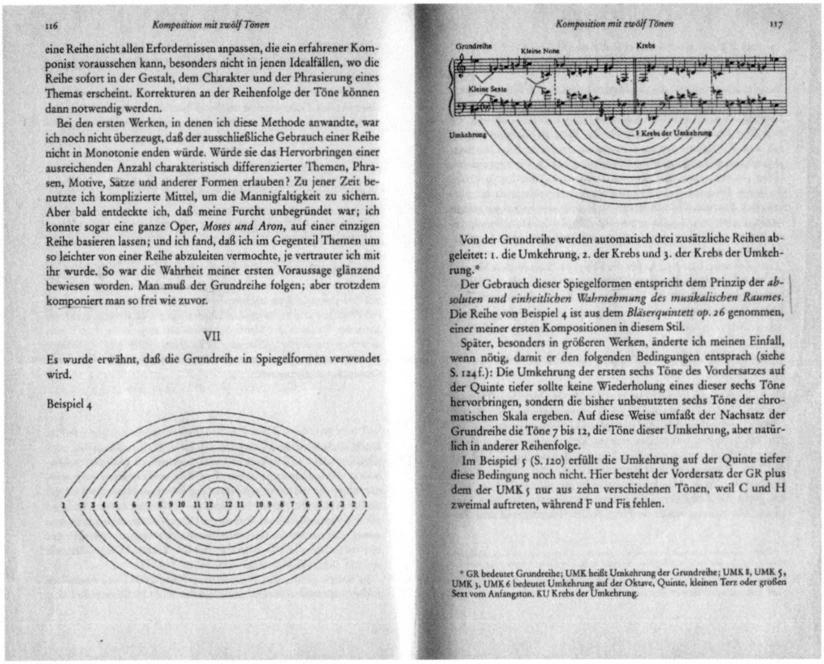

116 *Komposition mit zwölf Tönen*

eine Reihe nicht allen Erfordernissen anpassen, die ein erfahrener Komponist voraussehen kann, besonders nicht in jenen Idealfällen, wo die Reihe sofort in der Gestalt, dem Charakter und der Phrasierung eines Themas erscheint. Korrekturen an der Reihenfolge der Töne können dann notwendig werden.

Bei den ersten Werken, in denen ich diese Methode anwandte, war ich noch nicht überzeugt, daß der ausschließliche Gebrauch einer Reihe nicht in Monotonie enden würde. Würde sie das Hervorbringen einer ausreichenden Anzahl charakteristisch differenzierter Themen, Phrasen, Motive, Sätze und anderer Formen erlauben? Zu jener Zeit benutzte ich komplizierte Mittel, um die Mannigfaltigkeit zu sichern. Aber bald entdeckte ich, daß meine Furcht unbegründet war; ich konnte sogar eine ganze Oper, *Moses und Aron*, auf einer einzigen Reihe basieren lassen; und ich fand, daß ich im Gegenteil Themen um so leichter von einer Reihe abzuleiten vermochte, je vertrauter ich mit ihr wurde. So war die Wahrheit meiner ersten Voraussage glänzend bewiesen worden. Man muß der Grundreihe folgen; aber trotzdem komponiert man so frei wie zuvor.

VII

Es wurde erwähnt, daß die Grundreihe in Spiegelformen verwendet wird.

Beispiel 4

Komposition mit zwölf Tönen 117

Von der Grundreihe werden automatisch drei zusätzliche Reihen abgeleitet: 1. die Umkehrung, 2. der Krebs und 3. der Krebs der Umkehrung.*

Der Gebrauch dieser Spiegelformen entspricht dem Prinzip der *absoluten und einheitlichen Wahrnehmung des musikalischen Raumes.* Die Reihe von Beispiel 4 ist aus dem *Bläserquintett op. 26* genommen, einer meiner ersten Kompositionen in diesem Stil.

Später, besonders in größeren Werken, änderte ich meinen Einfall, wenn nötig, damit er den folgenden Bedingungen entsprach (siehe S. 124 f.): Die Umkehrung der ersten sechs Töne des Vordersatzes auf der Quinte tiefer sollte keine Wiederholung eines dieser sechs Töne hervorbringen, sondern die bisher unbenutzten sechs Töne der chromatischen Skala ergeben. Auf diese Weise umfaßt der Nachsatz der Grundreihe die Töne 7 bis 12, die Töne dieser Umkehrung, aber natürlich in anderer Reihenfolge.

Im Beispiel 5 (S. 120) erfüllt die Umkehrung auf der Quinte tiefer diese Bedingung noch nicht. Hier besteht der Vordersatz der GR plus dem der UMK 5 nur aus zehn verschiedenen Tönen, weil C und H zweimal auftreten, während F und Fis fehlen.

* GR bedeutet Grundreihe; UMK heißt Umkehrung der Grundreihe; UMK 8, UMK 5, UMK 3, UMK 6 bedeutet Umkehrung auf der Oktave, Quinte, kleinen Terz oder großen Sext vom Anfangston. KU Krebs der Umkehrung.

The rules of the game of the composition.

Instead of following Walter Benjamin's suggestion of multiplying the observer's standpoints over and above all anthropomorphic possibilities through the mobility of the camera-eye in Vertov's sense, through a rise and fall of tangents and resultants, Straub and Huillet radically reduce the film's camera axes, and for act I set the middle of the arena as its central standpoint. From here they also organize the protagonists' relationships according to a plan that correlates camera optics and theater space with one another.

The organization of the space in act I of the film replaces the psychology and dramaturgy of the characters, and their resulting viewpoints, with the simple work of "surveyors," who have "apportioned the terrain, marked the center, measured the depths."[51] This organization of measurement, of counting out the relations, is principally distinct from the theatrical idea of an insight

51 Ibid., p. 404.

into a constructed reality, as provided by the model of the theater, a stage with and an imaginary or punctured fourth wall. The surveyed set of the shoot in Alba Fucense counts through the relationships between people and things, but doesn't show the zero point of the network from which all relationships proceed. Without the retrospective overview of the assistant's sketch, every image remains a knot in the large network of seeing, which hasn't a subject or center. This, as Danièle Huillet describes, determines the "rules of the game" for the film and its movements:

> Shots 19 and 22 are like the fixed points of a rule of the game, from which all other shots of the first act develop: hence the necessity of exactly determining the location of the performers (chorus, trio: Young Girl, Young Man, Man; the Priest, and finally Moses and Aron): in relation to the center of the ellipse, a group in relation to others, and every soloist in relation to his or her neighbor. In the case of the three young people, or in the case of Moses and Aron: there has to be enough space between the Young Girl and the chorus, and between her and the Young Man, so that in shot 22, with the 50 mm lens, we can film her first without having her neighbor's arm or the nose of a chorister in view on the extreme left [...]."[52]

The antagonists of the first act, "the opposing forces"[53]—as Straub called them, according to his assistant—themselves form the new space that emerges between the poles of theater space and camera. In order to visualize the smooth space of the desert, the space is at first counted through according to the numerical relationships of the architecture and optics. This is an initially perplexing strategy, as Straub and Huillet adapt a pharaonic practice with this spatial organization: the priests of the pharaoh first surveyed and made calculable the land of the Nile in order to secure their imperial economy in the flood plain. But in order to de-metricalize the elliptical space of the amphitheater into a heterogeneous and smooth space, so as to develop a flatness for vanishing points from the hallucinated three-dimensionality of a stage space, the technical gaze (between conductor, soloists, chorus, and camera) and the dramatic gaze (between the chorus/people and Moses and Aron) had to be connected to a

52 Ibid., p. 403.

53 Woods, "Ein Arbeitsjournal," p. 255.

third, cinematic level of seeing and its relationships, namely as a link between the material, optical and architectural conditions of the arena. Only then can the imagined spectral relationships be purified: "This was also the reason why we played the surveyor, apportioned the terrain, marked the center, measured the depths."[54] The "rules of the game" open up the cinematography as nomadic; Straub's production machine becomes a war machine.

Because of the archaeological "rules of the game," the first long pan can enumerate what comes into view: first architecture, second culture, third biology, without activating the phantasms of vitalism. These relationships are then combined in every shot of the film: geological and historical stone strata in the ruins of the amphitheater structure the shots there; the rampant shrubland around the theater shows signs of the cultivated landscape of the Roman Campania and its typical vegetation—albeit in decline, the stages of which again make history visible, forms of agriculturalization and rural depopulation. The architecture of the ruins, as with the props brought by Straub and Huillet from Egypt, form the movements and postures of the performers, and organize the film in a light that had illuminated spectacles there 1,500 years previously. The costumes, moreover, hired from Cantini in Rome and remodeled, make a film-historical scenographic space visible that has its origins in the Cinecittà of the 1970s.[55]

54 See Huillet, "Appunti sul giornale," p. 404: "The final problem that we had to solve before starting, because once the rules of the game are set there is no further escape, in as much as we also wanted to adhere to them (which was all the more necessary as for economic reasons—not being able to keep the chorus for the entire shoot, having to shoot all the scenes with the chorus first, then those with the soloists, in the end without singers—Jean-Marie couldn't shoot in the prescribed order, which made the tightrope walk even more dangerous): so the position of Gielen, who conducted the chorus and soloists, had to be clearly visible to them, but of course not in the angle of the camera, and also not in the panorama pans, which capture the 300° degrees of the ellipse, as in shot 24, and who in relation to the camera has to take up a horizontal *and* vertical (height) position in which he is clearly visible to the singers (chorus and soloists), who have to be able to look at him without this look—which actually had to be oriented to the chorus (or the soloists)—being 'false', only slightly displaced, so that a third pole can still be felt, but no more than that, so that the displacement doesn't destroy the relationships (also the dramatic ones)."

55 Here too it is enumeration and equalization that links individual things and preserves them from being visualized as historical mass merchandise. The film obtains its authentic materiality from these procedures. See Huillet, "Appunti sul giornale," p. 402: "As for the costumes, we chose them from 3,000 of this kind at Cantini (one of the better-working gears of the Italian film industry, if one knows how to avoid the trap of the decorative element in the Italian talent. Jean-Marie hates having new costumes made; we prefer to choose from those already available), took them home, spread them out on the floor, sorted them (the robes, veils, shoes

But the first rifts and breaks are shown by the materiality of the architectural elements. The actors and their roles fall almost unbearably apart when the camera picks out the sunburned, unmade-up skin of a Viennese singer. But the materiality of the things primarily reveals itself as filmic when the wind not only ruffles the robes of the singers but also the wool of the sheep, the sand of the arena, when it rustles the leaves of the bushes and trees, showing "nature caught in the act,"[56] as Siegfried Kracauer said. Finally, the acoustic space replaces an imagined unity with an audible superimposition of natural, studio, and theater sounds, as well as the background noise, the acoustic atmosphere of the cinema.

Thanks to the archaeological work of surveying, the sequence in which the people wait for Moses and Aron to return from the desert (shot 22) is dynamized by a dramaturgy that differs from a possible expressionist realization. Regulated by the logic of its relationships, the scene is robbed of any hallucinatory subjective gaze and phantasmal effect. The calculated setting de-psychologizes the scene; tension doesn't arise between the protagonists in an illusionized enclosed stage space, but develops as vectors of energy and intensity between the optically constructed film image and the space's no longer unified field. The desert space that expands in this sequence doesn't orientalize and isn't oriental, but like Nietzche's growing desert is a reality of equally distributed cultural stratifications in the Europe of the 1970s, and appears as a space surveyed by Straub and Huillet on its cultural-historical and geopolitical axes.[57] Were it Arabic, it would have more to do with the confinement of the Palestinians in the aridity of their reserves and camps than with the Egypt of overseers and pharaohs. And in our time we would see the wastes of water in which the migrant boats sink on their way to Fortress Europe.

according to color and the sizes that Ms. Kapak, the representative of the chorus, had sent us), and some we washed, mended, and ironed."

56 See Kracauer, *Theory of Film*, p. 58.

57 See Huillet, "Appunti sul giornale," pp. 401–402: "Why did we want Italy from the very beginning? Because Schoenberg was Viennese, his music eminently European, but at the same time pervaded by the vision of an astonishing realism that you can discover in the Orient—in Africa (for us Egypt)—which is why we wanted a European country that represented a bridge between Europe and Africa/Asia. Spain and Greece were out of the question, and Italy, apart from its geography, geology, its climate, its political situation, had the advantage (?) of a film industry that, although it doesn't function as a whole, is still efficient in part, if you are able to muster a great deal of energy, stubbornness, and time."

At the same time these means of cinematic staging lead straight to the crisis in which Moses will find himself as the founder of a space and as law-giver: having to start a process of anarchic disintegration and one of legislation. The tension between rebellion and new legalism in a revolutionary process, the tension between measurement and presumption for which the Moses complex stands, is an aesthetic aspect of the film from the very beginning. In it can be seen the way in which Straub and Huillet don't adapt or actualize historical spaces and transfer them to the year 1974 but record and frustrate the process of spatial formation itself under the discursive and media conditions of contemporary film production. In this way they don't film historical spaces but the differences under which they are formed.

Straub and Huillet are avant-garde among political filmmakers because they direct these differences towards seeing and hearing in themselves. Their procedure can initially be understood as a commentary on the relationship between rebellion and legalism, as resistance against a classical cinematic space. When in the course of cinema history a varied haptic and material space, which determined early films and was repeatedly taken up by all the avant-gardes,[58] gradually and more exclusively had to yield to a homogeneous space and its confident stagings of viewer subjectivity, Straub/Huillet's space-staging precision appears as a kind of back projection of the cinema onto its own "classical" space-producing practices. It shouldn't be thought of as the simple detonation or transgression of central-perspective geometrical order, however.

Straub and Huillet develop cinematic space from relationships between the technical and the dramatic gaze. So it isn't simply the intermediate spaces between the figures and things that become visible but rather the fields, in Merleau-Ponty's sense, in which perception becomes an image of the world. At the same time this dissolves the connection between seeing and knowledge with which classical cinema came into the inheritance of the Renaissance space. Straub and Huillet record distances, intermediate spaces, relationships in their images, but deny an overview. The "rules of the game" of MOSES UND ARON visualize a reality that is arithmetically and numerically depicted; they give a meticulous account of every depictive relationship, but revoke the availability of a subjective view. This always leads to much murmuring at the films of Straub

58 See Noel Burch, "Building a Haptic Space," in Noel Burch, *Life to Those Shadows*, Berkeley 1990, pp. 162–185.

and Huillet, a disinclination to lose oneself, to see the knowledge of self and others continually compromised.[59] Such procedures also lead to the frequent description of these films as not "really" filmic,[60] because the narcissistic element of Platonic cave machinery is demolished.[61]

The work on the film of the opera begins with metrical surveying in the image, in order to transform an established film-historical "imperial spatium" and a "political extension"[62] into visual relationships. Conditions and distributions are shown instead of figures and actions: conditions as lines of force between the exposed points recorded on the plan of the amphitheater, and distributions of figures in a space that the camera only forms through their movements. In turn, the optics of the camera, their focal lengths, determine the visibility of the respective relationships within the images. Not the "absolute" but an "infinite succession of local operations" comes into focus.[63] At times also off screen. On this axis the film borrows a mirror structure from Schoenberg's music.

The technique of serial composition, which sets an absolutely equal distribution of the tone relationships against listening in intervals of the Pythagorean octave relation, corresponds first to the staging of pure relationalities in the visual; and second this principle is cinematically transposed in the surveying of the spatial distances and relay points of the Roman amphitheater.

59 Deleuze and Guattari described the procedure in *A Thousand Plateaus*: "It would seem that the war machine is projected into an abstract knowledge formally different from the one that doubles the State apparatus. It would seem that a whole nomad science develops eccentrically, one that is very different from the royal or imperial sciences. Furthermore, this nomad science is continually 'barred,' inhibited, or banned by the demands and conditions of State science. [...] The fact is that the two kinds of science have different modes of formalization, and State science continually imposes its form of sovereignty on the inventions of nomad science. State science retains of nomad science only what it can appropriate." Deleuze/Guattari, *A Thousand Plateaus*, p. 362.

60 For the description of this lack of understanding in the context of German film criticism see Peter Nau, *Zur Kritik des politischen Films. 6 analysierende Beschreibungen und ein Vorwort "Über Filmkritik,"* Cologne 1978, p. 103ff.

61 In contrast see the theory of Jean-Louis Baudry, who detects a "metaphysical" continuity from the *dispositif* of Plato's allegory of the cave to the sound film: "As we have seen, Plato constructs an apparatus very much like sound cinema. [...] It is the apparatus that creates the illusion, and not the degree of fidelity with the Real." Jean-Louis Baudry, "The Apparatus: Metapsychological Approaches to the Impression of Reality in Cinema," in Leo Braudy and Marshall Cohen (eds.), *Film Theory and Criticism: Introductory Readings*, New York 1999, pp. 690—707: 695.

62 Deleuze/Guattari, *A Thousand Plateaus*, p. 388.

63 Ibid., p. 527.

The transformation of the architectural space of the film into an "absolute and unitary perception,"[64] such as Schoenberg brings about with the twelve-tone rows, is not simply undertaken as a coordination and enumeration of the visual elements following Schoenberg's acoustic model: such numerical, arithmetical coordination smoothes the space, transforms it into a desert. The surveyors of Alba Fucense are pursuing not Greek geometrization but Indian-Arabic arithmetification, looking not in cardinal but in ordinal numbers for a nomos that opens up a processual and musical law that initially opposes the logos as the cosmic order of relationships.[65] Deleuze and Guattari read Exodus and Numbers as war strategies: "... and when Moses applied it to his people in exodus, it was on the advice of his nomad father-in-law, Jethro the Kenite, and was done in such a way as to constitute a war machine."[66] This is indeed a nomadic and somewhat newfangled interpretation, as Jethro's advice to Moses was first to establish a reliable hierarchy of judges. Jethro was not concerned with an authority but with the enumeration of actions, the determination of emergency rule, and a decentralized administration, and "Moses chose able men out of all Israel, and made them heads over the people, rulers of thousands, rulers of hundreds, rulers of fifties, and rulers of tens. And they judged the people at all seasons: the hard causes they brought unto Moses, but every small matter they judged themselves."[67] The visit from father-in-law Jethro, who makes a hydra fit for war out of the warlord system, occurs before the ascent of Mount Sinai, before the giving of the law and the judgment and execution of 3,000 men.

In the hybrid, architecturally and archaeologically stratified space opened up by the filmmakers' arithmetic, the famous shot 22, the reception of the brothers returning from the desert, obtains its significance only in sequence and through

64 Schoenberg, "Composition with Twelve Tones," p. 223.

65 See Deleuze/Guattari, *A Thousand Plateaus*, p. 388: "When Greek geometrism is contrasted with Indo-Arab arithmetism, it becomes clear that the latter implies a nomos opposable to the logos: not that the nomads 'do' arithmetic or algebra, but because arithmetic and algebra arise in a strongly nomad influenced world." Kittler has the wolfman Lykurgos from the "wilderness of Arcadia" travel to Crete to listen to Homer and ask him to Sparta, "so that a state structure will arise for harmony and rhythm. The nomos itself is music." Translated from Kittler, *Musik und Mathematik I*, p. 142. The logos rules "not only as speech and factual reason" but also in all "numerically regulated relationships." Against Kittler's assumption, however, it is thus clear that harmonies were and are not less imperially deployed than other tonal systems. Ibid., p. 253.

66 Deleuze und Guattari, *A Thousand Plateaus*, p. 388.

67 Exodus 18:25–26.

Singers, singly in the wind and at the same time a desert-colored ensemble.

Straub and Huillet's strictly aligned space from which the shots develop. If Schoenberg's text contains more of an expressionist cinema aesthetic, here the entire logic of the cinematic dissolution of space in relationship to shot, camera movement, and optics is shown in regard to the architecture of the theater. The scene begins with a medium shot[68] of the Young Girl. The camera turns to the right in a swift pan and captures the chorus, who are standing in front of the amphitheater's north entrance, one of the two *parodoi*. The pan ends at the line "See Moses! See Aaron!" so as to now show, instead of the camera movement, the movement in the image itself, many and also arhythmic micro-movements of the breathing singers, and the fluttering of their headdresses in the wind. Because this shot of the chorus is filmed from a high angle, in the agitation of the following sequence all the singers—who are arranged, differently from the operatic stage, according to voices in six rows one behind the other as a "trapezoid"[69]—are well visible, both as individuals and, through the color composition of the costumes, as the impression of a desert-colored overall body.

It is enough to see the chorus looking into the sun, in their fluttering yellow-brown colors like a Cézanne painting, in order to understand that here the light orders the space differently from mathematical-geometrical rays. While they sing of the diffuse and unpredictable space of the desert, in which Moses and his brother move relationally—"They are nearer, are farther, are higher, are deeper, have vanished wholly!"—we see the diverse movements of the actors, who produce this space as a confusing composite in the visible of the film. The welds of the cinematic space, its "sutures," open up before our very eyes.[70]

In the course of shot 22 the camera strongly frames the chorus, while the desert space expands acoustically in the dissonant sounds of the two choral halves,

68 "HALBTOTAL bis TOTAL/HALBTOTAL" [MEDIUM SHOT to LONG/MEDIUM SHOT] is the description in Huillet, "Moses und Aron. Das Drehbuch," p. 216. It is a medium shot in as much as the sand and amphitheater walls around the chorus appear as a frame and not like a wide surrounding. The next shot of the chorus is in fact wider. But it is noteworthy that Huillet's terms for the shot size differ from the usual American classification in that they don't proceed from the size of the figures in the image but from the field of the visible surroundings.

69 Woods, "Ein Arbeitsjournal," p. 255. But this arrangement isn't althogether unusual: it corresponds to that of the Bach cantatas. Thanks to Julia Kursell for pointing this out.

70 See Heath, *Questions of Cinema*, p. 43: "[...] terms of a constant welding together: screen and frame, ground and background, surface and depth, the whole setting of movements and transitions, the implication of space and spectator in the taking place of film as narrative. The *classical economy* of film is its organization thus as organic unity and the *form* of that economy is narrative, the *narrativization* of film."

who alternately adopt the *Sprechstimme* in addition to the singing voice. Rapid strings and piano and harp arpeggios introduce extremes of pitch, and changing rhythms defy the ear. With these elements Straub and Huillet subvert cinematic convention: a final polyphonic call of "See!" from the first chorus (bar 418) clearly articulates what must remain paradoxical as an appeal to sight: the arithmetically constructed field of vision doesn't allow a collective view. The people should not be hallucinated as one, but has to form from individuals.

In the end, after the score has demanded a continual musical acceleration and increase in complexity, and after a group of women (which Schoenberg's score would like to have "in the background [...] distributed on higher situated places"[71]) can be heard distinctly from the web of voices, calling "See Moses!" and "See Aaron!" in *Sprechstimme*, the singing finally merges into the orchestral *fortissimo*. "*Poco pesante*," says the score, "only as much as the voices need in order to sound through" (act I, bar 442), when the voices, alto and mezzo still divided, synchronously sing "They have arrived!"

The announcement of the presence of the prophet brothers is an indistinguishable resounding of chorus and instruments, a single yet superhumanly stratified sound space into which the chorus musically dissolves, like Moses and Aron had done in the desert. The camera observing this disappearance does so in impassive framing.

In the general pause that then follows, Ugo Piccone's heavy Mitchell camera hurtles further to the right as if charged, past the Priest, who is barely noticeable, in order to show Moses and Aron in the sand, in front of the far-off southern *parodos* of the amphitheater, which unlike the northern one is unroofed and allows a view into the open. For a fraction of a second the two men stand simply framed in the three-quarter profile of a medium shot, have "arrived" (act I, bar 442) where they hadn't been expected, because the schematic topography of the theater is not yet familiar. For a short moment the physical relationships of the space and the denial of an overview become palpable. There is an immediate cut back to the chorus, who continue to sing in trapezoid form in the ellipse of the theater, filmed now from a much higher angle than before, from now on as a block and tableau, as a choir and corpus in only four parts. The agitated disorientation is over.

71 Schönberg, *Moses und Aron*, score I, act I, bar 440, p. 96.

What these images show is not a continual action, but tension composed of elements that can't be coordinated. In the end there is a transition accomplished simultaneously in the acoustic and the visual: the two rebellious nomads have left the space of the desert for the space of the sedentary, of the state, in which they are consequently welcomed as leaders. Moses, the *máximo líder*, and his brother occupy the transition from war machine to apparatus of state, from nomos to polis. At this point we should further differentiate Gilles Deleuze's classification from his book on the cinema: "Moses is the new nomad, the one who wants no other earth than the always wandering word of God, but Aaron wants a territory."[72] In this film both Moses and Aron appear as figures of the smooth or striated space from which they emerge scene by scene. The same applies to Deleuze's clear distinction between Moses, whom he sees as a pure act of speech, an acoustic image, and Aron as a visual image. However, in certain visual or acoustic constellations both figures monopolize acts of speech, visual acts, or song acts, and are torn apart by this. The type of connection established by the voices to God and the world articulates the respective constellations of power and the law.[73]

Following this scene the chorus is placed into the architecture of the amphitheater by a wide-angle lens with a focal length of 18.5 mm. When they ask "Bringt ihr Erhörung, Botschaft des neuen Gottes? Schickt er als Führer euch uns zu neuer Hoffnung? Gern wollen wir ihm Geld, Gut und Leben opfern! [Bring you good tidings, word from the mighty new god? Come you to lead us, once more to make us hopeful? We yearn to give him gold, goods, and living off'rings!]," they confuse, just as theater and amphitheater can be confused, the public theatricality of the Greek polis with Roman politics of bread and circuses: they are eager to rush into the cruel rituals of sacrifice (act I, bars 443–473), instead of suspending divine judgment in the sense of tragedy and performing a human drama. Schoenberg and Straub/Huillet bring in a third aspect here. What for Schoenberg, in Walter Benjamin's sense, could still be appraised as the legislative power of a Jewish law becomes, with Straub and Huillet, the observation of the dynamics of shifting fields of power under media conditions. Media, of course, in solidarity with capitalism.

72 Gilles Deleuze, *Cinema 2. The Time-Image*, trans. Hugh Tomlinson and Robert Galeta, Minneapolis 1989, p. 255.

73 For the act of speech see chapter 4.2.

3.3. ELECTRO-ACOUSTICS: CONSERVED VIBRATIONS

when eisler urges him to complete
his two great works, one of them an opera,
he says, "it won't be performed anyway,
so long as handicraft continues
to be the order of the day in music here."
and he does a comic imitation
of the struggles of a wind-player and a cellist.
Bertolt Brecht on Schoenberg, July 29, 1942[74]

Like all other spaces, the acoustic space of MOSES UND ARON first emerges with the film, in the movie theater. Jean-Marie Straub, as he says, had long "dreamed" of this sound space, a superimposition of tonal layers and noises. Complementarily to the architectural space, the acoustic space also concentrates historical and cultural forms of audibility, to which it exposes its protagonists and viewers. This space is a unique technical experiment in the history of the opera film. Straub commented on this in an interview with journalists from the *Cahiers du Cinéma*:

> *Moses und Aron* is a technical adventure on the level of sound recording that no one had previously dared—we can say this with pride (everyone was terrified, the musicians, above all the sound engineer). We discussed it for two years, until we made a concrete decision for it in Vienna in the presence of the singers. During the six weeks that had taken place four months before the five-week shoot we excluded all other solutions and came back to those I had dreamed of from the very beginning, and which the sound engineer also thought were right. But we had our doubts, as most of his experience was with jazz; still, it was the most sensible idea to record the orchestra alone first and then have the singers sing over it.[75]

In the movie theater, in the projection of MOSES UND ARON, a sound space can thus be heard in which the acoustics of the large studio of ORF, the Austrian

74 Bertolt Brecht, *Journals 1934–1955*, New York 1995, p. 251.
75 Translated from Straub/Huillet, "Conversation," p. 23.

Broadcasting Corporation, are superimposed onto those of a Roman amphitheater. This wasn't only possible for technical reasons but "because the Straubs and their sound engineer had found out through experiment that the natural reverberation of the studio in Vienna more or less corresponded to that of the arena in Alba Fucense, where the shoot took place."[76] This surprising analogy in a systematic but quite unhistorical media archaeology of acoustics points to an unwritten history of sensuousness, particularly of the sounds of spaces, that Straub and Huillet put into their film. The synthetic acoustic of the film sound is the product on the one hand of Greek and Roman architecture, and on the other of a media acoustic assembled around 1974, an electro-acoustic that now seems as far away from today's digital procedures as cuneiform from the typewriter.

The synthetic acoustic space that Straub and Huillet devised with the musical director Michael Gielen and the sound engineer Louis Hochet is very much not based on fancy electro-acoustic effects but on the radical reduction of acoustic parameters—similar to the visual dramaturgy—in order to produce new layers of sound fields in the mix and acoustic montage. While Arnold Schoenberg's overture, the vocalise, requires the concordant superimposition of voices and instruments, Straub and Huillet take this exactly and systematically apart: with Gielen they developed the recording-technical preconditions for the separation of sound levels, and the separation of the orchestra from the human voices.

All the tracks were synchronized in a then usual clocked electronic procedure, using a quartz piezoelectric pilot-reference system. Both the orchestral parts and the off-screen choral sequences were pre-produced in Vienna. During the shoot these studio recordings were combined with the live recordings of the singers and chorus in the amphitheater of Alba Fucense. All of this required an unusual positioning of the musicians, who don't orient themselves to the acoustics of a concert hall but to one that is unconceivable, because it is only constituted in the mix of all elements.

First a dry, reverb-free, four-channel mono version was produced for the film[77] and then copied onto a narrow strip with two Nagra-IV devices. In this

76 Translated from Michael Gielen, "'Aus einem Gespräch mit Michael Gielen.' Wolfram Schütte spricht mit Michael Gielen," in *Filmkritik* 221/222, 1975, pp. 280–283: 281.

77 At the same time, in order to finance the recording, an eight-track stereo version was produced by Philips for a broadcast tape and an LP edition, which was later given artificial reverb for the "usual audience taste." See Michael Gielen, *Unbedingt Musik. Erinnerungen*, Leipzig 2005, p. 180.

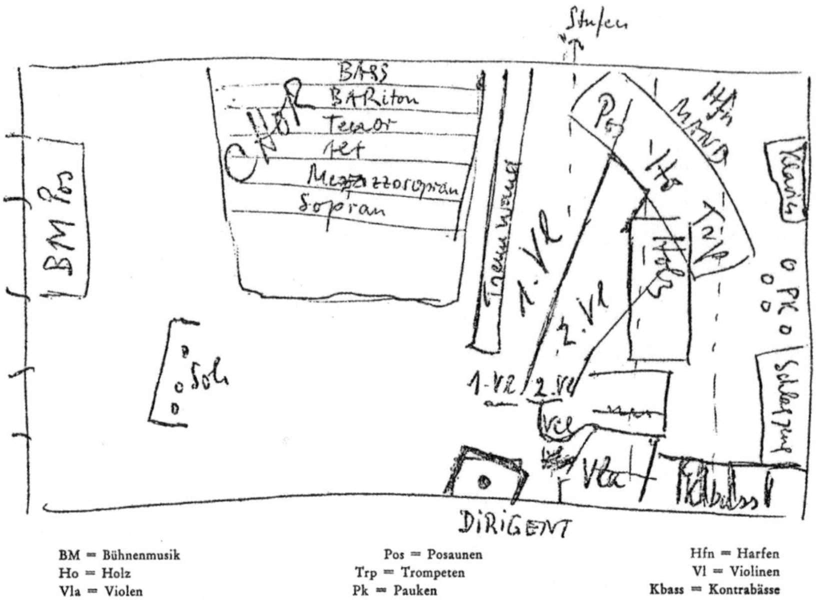

Michael Gielen: sketch of the line-up of the chorus in the ORF sound studio.

form it supported the singers during their open-air appearances via small speakers installed among the choristers. Their emissions could of course not enter the sensitivity range of the microphones. The soloists sang with small earplugs, so as to be able to orient themselves to the orchestral sounds. Michael Gielen, who stood on a mobile pedestal, wore headphones "and beat time almost without hearing what was being sung,"[78] while the acoustic supervisor Bernhard Rubenstein controlled the tone quality. So complementarily to the many interruptions of a collective acoustic space by the technical isolation of the individual participants, recording and mix on set represent, on the one hand, a continual artificial sound space. The singing of the chorus and the soloists in the arena, with all its reverberation effects and ambient noises, was angled with several microphones.[79] During the shoot in the amphitheater the sound engineer Louis Hochet

78 Ibid.

79 I.e. "sound angles" were recorded with extended elastic and mobile brackets, not yet transmitted by radio or clip-on microphones, whose cables would have been visible and whose quality is much worse.

added the Vienna studio recordings—as a *live* synchronization—to those of the singers, whose voices were thus brought together again on tape. At the same time he distributed them onto the different tracks of the Nagra. After the shoot it only remained to mix the already synchronized material dynamically.[80] The fact that in an amphitheater ruin in the Italy of the mid-1970s the regularity of the electricity frequency conveyed via copper cable had to be continually monitored is an indication of the fragile and volatile situation in which a "temporal basis" was established. It's not only for this reason that such temporal basis is a long way from a strict metricalization of the music as synchronization.

In 1974 the recording procedure involved various technical difficulties, when for example the recording properties of the studio microphones—similarly to the optics in the visual—had to separate certain acoustic fields from one another. In the acoustic, differently from the visual, such "framings" can't be exactly sealed. This meant that both the spatial positioning of chorus and orchestra in the ORF sound studio and the placing of the microphones on set were oriented towards a future space that was still to be created, not towards the actual sound in the studio or amphitheater. Quite differently from what Arnold Schoenberg had imagined when he hoped that "in a distant future [...] electronically produced tones and sounds could make a performance of this powerful unfinished work possible,"[81] Straub and Huillet create a synthetic sound space in which not electronically produced tones but reverb-free, recorded sounds of instruments and voices, together with the voices on location, natural, and other atmospheric sounds in the cultural space of the amphitheater resound together. The entire atmosphere of the surroundings was not recorded, however, only what Straub and Huillet felt corresponded to the image: "Discontinuation with every airplane, even with birdsong."[82] The montage is not the decisive thing here but the superimposition of the sound layers.

Since the end of the 1940s, at the latest, sound artists had been experimenting with magnetic audiotape, whose technical improvement—similarly to that of 16 mm film—had made much progress because of its strategic importance during the Second World War. New procedures and practices were put to the

80 A third Nagra on site monitored the synchronicity of the "canned" music of the orchestral and choral recording in Vienna and the "live" recording of the singing in the amphitheater. See Huillet, "Appunti sul giornale," p. 405.

81 Stuckenschmidt, *Schoenberg—His Life, World and Works*, p. 500.

82 Translated from Gielen, *Unbedingt Musik*, p. 180.

test, against the grain of its designers, in experimental studios, radios, universities, and by amateurs.[83] These included the Office de radiodiffusion-télévision française, RTF, where Pierre Schaeffer, Pierre Henry, and Michel Chion, worked, the BBC Radiophonic Workshop, and many other contemporary experimental radio studios. The Project of Music for Magnetic Tape, founded in New York in 1951 on the initiative of John Cage, [84] or Bebe and Louis Barron with their own studio, influenced compositional procedures well beyond electronic music. On the one hand they explore cut-up techniques of editing of montaging fragments of sound and noise, primarily according to aleatoric principles, on the other the superimposition or merger of sound material through varying tape speeds, for example, or two tapes running in opposite directions. In the relativity and variability of these techniques a time structure is experienced that can no longer be reduced to a chronometrical measure.[85] It was not technology that opened up aesthetic forms but experimental practice.

In his *Music of Changes*, for example, John Cage uses what looks at first like a classical notation, but it doesn't refer to metricalized time, nor to a basic pulse; it simply marks the beginning and end of a sound, which unfurls depending on the acoustics of the space and the musician's physique: "The tones pass [...] like a tape, whose playback device is called David Tudor."[86] This no longer metricalized time, found in the compositions of John Cage, Morton Feldman, or Edgar Varèse, which in performance becomes indeterminate duration or, as in one of Varèse's titles, Déserts, temporal wastelands of "vibrating

83 For the history of magnetic tape see André Ruschkowski, *Elektronische Klänge und musikalische Entdeckungen*, Stuttgart 1998, pp. 184–207.

84 Founded by John Cage, Earle Brown, Morton Feldman, David Tudor, and Christian Wolff. See ibid., p. 193. For more detail on their experiments see David Revill, *Roaring Silence. John Cage: A Life*, New York 1992.

85 John Cage reminds us that audiotape changed all musical practice, both of composing and of hearing: "Whether one uses tape or writes for conventional instruments, the present musical situation has changed from what it was before tape came into being." He particularly goes into altered time structure: "But several effects of the tape on experimental music may be mentioned. Since so many inches of tape equal so many seconds of time, it has become more and more usual that notation is in space rather than in symbols of quarter, half and sixteenth notes and so on. Thus where on a page a note appears will correspond to when in a time it is to occur. A stop watch is used to facilitate a performance; and a rhythm results which is a far cry from horse's hoofs and other regular beats." Cage, "Experimental Music," in *Silence*, Cambridge 1971, pp. 7–13: 11.

86 Translated from Kursell/Schäfer, "Das Band, das die Zeit macht," p. 55.

mixtures,"[87] prompted Pierre Boulez to distinguish between a temps lisse and a temps strié, concepts that Deleuze and Guattari would later apply to space in order to describe its smoothness in nomadic movement and all de-metricalized cultural techniques.[88] And Jean-Marie Straub projects the difference onto *Moses and Aron:* "L'idée d'Aaron, c'est celle d'une traversée pour arriver dans le pays. L'idée de Moïse, c'est que la traversée du désert est sans fin. C'est l'idée du nomadisme, tout simplement."[89] Aron stands for traversing the desert in order to arrive at a country. Moses stands for the endless traversing of the desert. That is quite simply the idea of the nomadic existence.

In the light of this distinction, film becomes a very complicated procedure. Because the recording of MOSES UND ARON required a tireless analysis and repetition of pieces and sequences,[90] *temps lisse* in Boulez's sense initially seems not to apply. For the moment the tape has the function of transporting a piezoelectrically clocked *temps strié* to Italy in order to minutely maintain the metrical time between the Vienna studio and the amphitheater in Abruzzo. The meter allows the recordings to be fragmented, repeated, and re-cut.

With this procedure Straub/Huillet and Gielen found themselves, in 1974, in a discussion about the authentic performance of music under media conditions. This arose from the question of whether faithfulness to the original also demands the uninterrupted duration of the performance, which respects

87 In *Déserts* Varèse combines orchestra (winds, piano, percussion) and tape recordings, and the open piano serves as resonance chamber as in Helmholtz's home laboratory. Varèse writes the music in sound blocks and static elements. The two-track tape was compiled in the RTF Studio de la recherche under the direction of Pierre Schaeffer from "real sounds" recorded in the US (factories, steel mills, saw mills in Philadelphia) that were put together and superimposed according to tone colors, as Ruttmann did in *Weekend*, for example. "In the music of Varèse the musically created vibrations and the summation and difference frequencies between them are what count concretely. It seems to be a small conceptual step, yet it went far into the future, to proceed from this thinking in concrete sound structures and put together completely new sounds from traditionally created tones. Tones are joined into vibrating mixtures and should not longer be thought of as something to be noted abstractly." Helga de la Motte-Haber, "Aufbruch in das Klanguniversum," in Helga de la Motte-Haber (ed.), *Edgar Varèse: Die Befreiung des Klangs*, pp. 41–55: 43. "Tone-color melody is not intended," unlike Schoenberg's wish, rather the production of layered tone-color surfaces that bring to mind the "paintings of Robert Delaunay." Ibid., p. 47.

88 Deleuze/Guattari, *A Thousand Plateaus*, p. 657ff.

89 Straub/Huillet, "Conversation," p. 8.

90 See Gielen, *Unbedingt Musik*: "Some scenes were filmed up to twelve times, although we always thought about the very low budget and economized on the expensive film material." Translated from p. 181.

the continual sound but also needs to take in processes of fatigue or breathing movements, possibly even the resonance of the audience, as is usual for opera performances in Italian ruins, as alien or disruptive elements. The idea of such a coherent temporal space of musical authenticity is admittedly an anachronism, as editing and splicing have been a part of new music, both electronic and acoustic, since the 1950s, and the studio practice of the record industry privileges temporal and spatial montage.[91] The recording procedure in Moses und Aron takes advantage of the "blessings of technology," upheld by a musician like Glenn Gould, in regard to editing and montage.[92] However, entirely in the tradition of sound-concentrating tape compositions, it pursues the transformation into a duration through multiple sound superimpositions.[93]

91 Glenn Gould, who withdrew from concert activities in order to tinker in the studio, was among the few to celebrate—and no less idealistically than his detractors—the now possible electronic intervention into artistic procedures. "[Technology's] capacity for dissection, for analysis—above all, perhaps, for its idealization of an impression—must be exploited, and no area with which it is currently occupied better demonstrates the philosophical conflicts with which its practitioners and theorists have been too long preoccupied than the aims and techniques of recording." Glenn Gould, "Music and Technology", in *The Glenn Gould Reader*, pp. 353–357. In the 1970s a "re-authentication" took place among "younger" musicians. In 1975 Gould could still make fun of Daniel Barenboim, who was "fond of the conceit that recording technique should involve two takes per work, take them or leave them." At the same time he was able to prove in a small experiment that even a musically educated audience was unable to hear the splices in music productions. See Gould, "The Grass is Always Greener in the Outtakes: An Experiment in Listening," in *The Glenn Gould Reader*, pp. 357–368: 362ff.

92 Glenn Gould writes: "But like Bishop, Watts and Barenboim, other younger artists have begun to assert the artificiality of the recording, to insist that it be placed within precisely the sort of snapshot context that immunizes the music at hand against the benefactions of technology." Gould, "The Grass is Always Greener," p. 358. The fact that Gould, in order to mock the phantasm of the "candid" reality of a recording, uses the metaphor of the snapshot— which in photography requires short exposure time and thus would be more suitable as a metaphor for splicing—shows that a piano player who interprets Bach masterfully is allowed relative immunity to the problem of duration. Splicing in recordings of music only exists in the imaginary of the LP, which, differently from film, can simulate continuity and uninterruptedness in its grooves, particularly when the usual reverb is mixed in.

93 Again it is John Cage who introduces a new differentiation into tape music in his text "Experimental Music," in which, proceeding from the technical impossibility of exactly synchronizing audiotapes, he refers to metrical and non-metrical procedures: "Also it has been impossible with the playing of several separate tapes at once to achieve perfect synchronization. This fact has led some towards the manufacture of multiple-tracked tapes and machines with a corresponding number of heads; while others—those who have accepted the sounds they do not intend—now realize that the score, the requiring that many parts be played in a particular togetherness, is not an accurate representation of how things are. These now compose parts but not scores, and the parts may be combined in any unthought ways. This means that each performance of such a piece of music is unique, as interesting to its composer as to others

Although the film recordings were interrupted shot for shot and edited together, sound editor Hochet, who on set didn't bring the two sound spaces together according to the strict law of metronome and score, but according to musical considerations, introduced a de-metricalization into the mix. The singers, who only heard the Vienna studio recordings through ear plugs and loudspeakers, run side by side like the tape players in Cage's setups. On the one hand they are connected to the transmission of the recorded music, "to give them some security," but on the other they are physically exposed to the noises, movements, and acoustics of the arena and their surroundings, and react to them as well: with their breath, in their movements, through their clothing. The film documents this process in every frame. The singing is therefore, recording after recording and layer after layer, always simultaneously a physical resistance to the metricalized time of the quartz tapes, on which for their part the individual times, that is every individual tone quality, every breath and rustle of the studio performance is conserved. The mechanical synchronicity of a forcible coordination is therefore not the aim of the re-recording and simultaneous mixing on location, but on the contrary the documentation of the indifferent distribution of the smallest differences of all manner of acoustic parameters. The varied spatial ensemble of radio concert hall, sound studio, audiotape, arena architecture, cinema apparatus, and movie theater puts its own layering of the audible events into the opera as authentic sound. Thus the tape from Vienna is not only an aid but an instrument that uses the bodies of the singers as playback devices, who nevertheless add their own tone qualities, their own relationship to the surroundings, heat, wind, landscape, and the people on site as physiological modulations.

The technical aids themselves become a decisive part of the sound production, and the arrangement that Schoenberg devised for the beginning of the vocalise is unexpectedly repeated: "That the six solo voices should always be accompanied by six instruments arose for practical reasons; the intention was to give

listening. It is easy to see again the parallel with nature, for even with leaves of the same tree, no two are exactly alike." Cage, "Experimental Music," p. 11. While he builds increasingly large machines with integrated synchronized tape heads in his studios, in *Variations V*, for example, he has ten tape players run side by side in their slightly shifted times. This nomadic, patchwork wasteland and new territory merges with an admiration of the beauty of leaves on a tree—for Straub and Huillet also the beginning of an aesthetics of film.

them some security. But I would ask, that the six solo instruments should not be abandoned even if one believes that the singers can do without them. Their sound is worked into the fabric and should not be lost."[94] The fact that an electro-acoustic bond was established between Vienna and Alba Fucense had practical reasons, but then the sound is worked into the film and should not be lost. The mix, which is ultimately transferred onto the soundtrack of the film copy and amplified in the movie theater, thus renders an authentic space.[95] Authenticity is a media effect, the analysis of which will reveal the elements of the media-technical and psycho-physical perception of a historical spatial reality.

In their integration of media into the musical aesthetic, Straub and Huillet follow Schoenberg's concept, which allows for all kinds of frameworks in his acoustic organization of the operatic space. These can be stages, recording studios, or even the unavoidable bodies of the listeners, as Schoenberg remarked in 1918 to Alexander von Zemlinsky in reply to a reminder to give the necessary "consideration for the listener": "I have exactly as little of this as he has for me. All I know is that he exists, and in so far as he isn't 'indispensable' for acoustic reasons (since music doesn't sound well in an empty hall), he's only a nuisance."[96] Schoenberg himself had imagined integrating media-technical devices into his compositions. In the score of *Moses and Aron* he says of the voice from the burning bush:

> These parts (at first 4, later 6; at the beginning only a few voices) speak in the same rhythm, very clearly accentuate, approximately to the given registers as closely as possible (not sung!). One might consider having them speak over telephones from behind the scenes, separated aurally and only in visual contact with one another, each voice being carried to the front on

94 Schoenberg, *Moses und Aron*, vocal score, p 4.

95 Straub remarks: "Filming with direct sound you can't fool with space, you have to respect it, and in doing so offer the viewer the chance to reconstruct it, because film is made up of 'extracts' of time and space. It's possible not to respect the space you are filming, but then you have to give the viewer the possibility of understanding why it has not been respected and not, as is done in dubbed films, transform the real space into a confused labyrinth and put the viewer into the confusion, from which he can no longer escape." See Jean-Marie Straub and Danièle Huillet, "Direct Sound: An Interview with Jean-Marie Straub and Danièle Huillet," in Elisabeth Weis and John Belton (eds.), *Theory and Practice of Film Sound*, New York 1985, pp. 150–153: 152.

96 Letter to Alexander Zemlinsky, March 20, 1918, in Schoenberg, *Letters*, p. 54.

> its own line to different points and broadcast over a loudspeaker so that it is only in the concert hall that they become unified.[97]

On the one hand this technical arrangement also corresponds to the model of having the singers sing separately and only establishing the overall sound space in the opera house, just as Straub and Huillet did later for the movie theater, where the sound space of Moses und Aron is finally completed. Straub and Huillet are thus probably the last—and perhaps also the first—for whom a classical cinema *dispositif* is constitutive of film perception. The theater becomes the actual sound space of the filmed opera. On the other hand, in his production note, and as in other works, it is clear that Schoenberg doesn't simply use the telephone to proclaim a message from the far side of the curtain—acousmatic in the exact historical sense—but equally for its acoustic qualities as a communication medium, which always limits frequency bandwidths and alters tone colors. In this way Schoenberg both changes the sound of his music, that is the acoustically and electro-acoustically produced qualities that can't be notated in the score, and introduces media history into the art form of opera.

This occurs in recourse to a media history of opera itself, as around the turn of the century concerts and operas were broadcast to private homes in Paris, London, or Budapest via the telephone network. In the swift and exact information transmission of the time the telephone seemed to be inferior to the telegraph, and its strength appeared to lie in relaying the slow, old arts.[98] This form of telephonic transmission anticipates an aesthetic-receptive destruction of the false collectivity of opera-like cultic perception, as Adorno detected in the friends of classical music on the radio: "No one listening to a symphony in a private home can misjudge himself to be physically contained in the community; in this respect the destruction of the symphony on the radio is also an elaboration of the truth."[99] In this sense technology emancipates music from bourgeois reception, which forgets the technical basis for the possibility of community formation in operas and theatrical performances and hence subscribes to them.

97 Schoenberg, Arnold, *Moses und Aron. Oper in drei Akten, miniature score,* Mainz 1958, p. Xf.

98 See Ruschkowski, *Elektronische Klänge,* p. 20.

99 Translated from Theodor W. Adorno, "Über die musikalische Verwendung des Radios," in Theodor W. Adorno, *Gesammelte Schriften*, ed. Rolf Tiedemann and others, vol. 15: *Kompositionen für den Film. Der getreue Korrepetitor,* Frankfurt/Main 2003, pp. 369–401: 377.

With the telephone, however, Schoenberg primarily integrates a media history of the voice itself into opera. Telephonic communication is technically a systematic alienation of the voice, which is dissected into a discrete code and reaches our ear as a reconstruction.[100] The calculation of voice frequencies by telephone services is an early form of signal processing that affects the human body. On the equipment side, and in order to support the phone companies' decisive interest in economizing on material, in the late 1940s communication was quantified and the signals to be transmitted reduced to a minimum that only just made the information distinguishable from the noise of the channel. On the physiological side of the body, the more or less continual flow of air in human speech was divided into a sequence of discrete units that could be processed as signals. During transmission the spoken phonematics of the voice were allowed only enough redundancy for the voice to remain recognizable as human and language as language.[101] In the technical sense voices were made discrete, statistically calculated, and held at an interval of 69 dB from the noise of the channel.[102] At the beginning of his opera, Schoenberg takes up the distinction between signal and noise as a musical and media issue, which at the same time must prove to be a theological and moral issue—a question of response and responsibility. The fact that the telephone, as a medium that mathematizes voices, doesn't make meaning but calculated data the basis of the transmission exactly corresponds to Schoenberg's strategy of voices and *Sprechstimmen*, which are intended to realize musical relations and not their own emotionality.

Extending the operatic space through complex electro-acoustical spaces, and privileging the medium above the musical figure, is Schoenberg's declared aim, and corresponds to the "mathematical" means of composition with twelve

100 For more detail see Annette Bitsch, *"Always Crashing in the Same Car." Jacques Lacans Mathematik des Unbewußten*, Weimar 2001, particularly pp. 162–177.

101 As an engineer at Bell Laboratories, Claude E. Shannon also calculated this redundancy, on the basis of his crypto-analytical calculations of discrete signal transmission via noisy or enemy-impaired channels during the Second World War, for continual analogue sources, for "speech or music transmission," for example. He calculated the transmission probabilities of their elements, from which possible reductions in the data flow could be ascertained. See Claude E. Shannon, "A Mathematical Theory of Communication," in *The Bell System Technical Journal*, vol. 27, no. 3, 1948, pp. 379–423.

102 See Friedrich Kittler, "Signal-Rausch-Abstand," in Friedrich Kittler, *Draculas Vermächtnis: Technische Schriften*, Leipzig 1993, pp. 161–181: 169.

tones.[103] Mathematization is the rule of the game under which relationships are made. "Every musical configuration, every movement of tones has to be comprehended primarily as a mutual relation of sounds, of oscillatory vibrations, appearing at different places and times."[104] In *Moses und Aron* it is consistent, but risky from the religious point of view, that the voice from the burning bush, of all things, is put together by a projected arrangement of telephonic voices, an alienation of the voice by a technical medium or, psychoanalytically, the great Other. Following the first vocalise, this sound, conceived as an ensemble of telephone voices, issues as a synthesized *Sprechstimme* mix of various voices—initially soprano, treble, baritone, and bass, later supplemented by alto and tenor—and adds a further contrast to the vocal coloration of the first six solo voices. At this point in the score, however, the ensemble is expressly identified as the voice of God.[105] The prohibition of images also structures the acoustic. The electro-technical *dispositif* suggests the conception of a divine principle in the relay of individual, human, and technical aspects as an experience that isn't collective or unified but rather a stratification of many individual vibratory spaces, or a back coupling in time. Gregory Bateson called such apparently supernatural, imaginary unities of feedback, "entities, being fictitious persons, more or less endowed with cybernetic and circuit characteristics," which help people to translate short-term intentions into long-term cultural processes, gods.[106]

The musical synthesis of oscillating vibrations at the beginning of the opera confront the thought of God—in double genitive—with the sensory perception of the shepherd Moses, who responds with a long formula that declines the name of God through all the vowels. Schoenberg only allows Him the One to be realized in manifoldness: God is one, but only perceivable in the variety of

103 See Wolfgang Hagen, "Silencetechno: Cage und das Radio," in Helmut Rösing (ed.), *Step across the Border. Neue musikalische Trends – neue massenmediale Kontexte: musikalische Aufbrüche und die Medien*, Karben 1997, pp. 73–91. "Schoenberg [makes] mathematical relationships between the 12 tones the starting point of his structural considerations." Translated from p. 83.

104 Schoenberg, "Composition with Twelve Tones," p. 223.

105 The media staging makes it problematic to speak of the "direct word of God," as Kerling does, instead of, like Jakob Ullmann, the "word of God crossing the operatic boundary." See Jakob Ullmann, "zwei sprachen," in Heinz-Klaus Metzger and Rainer Riehn (eds.), *Schönberg und der Sprechgesang, Musik-Konzepte* 112/113, 2001, and Kerling, *Die Gottesfrage*, p. 66, and particularly Peter Fischer-Appelt, "Die 'göttlichen Stimmen' in Schönbergs Oper 'Moses und Aron'," in Meyer (ed.), *Arnold Schönberg und sein Gott*, pp. 373–383.

106 Bateson, "Letter to Warren McCulloch," December 20, 1967, p. 65.

his sound structure; God is infinite, but only audible in the endlessness of His articulation in the pitch, color, and strength of a sound; God is omnipresent, but in order to make Himself felt has to resort to specific, material, human, and technical channels in all their limitations, to the crackle of a pillar of fire and to the noise of a telephone wire; God is unperceived, but His existence materializes itself in vibrations, visual or acoustic, waves of light or sound, which unite all presences, also those of the indispensable listeners, into a single sound space.[107] The idea of God appears in difference. A decision is required here: religion or media analysis.

Although it isn't clear at the beginning of the film whether the first sounds are noise, a signal, or music, the opera, which despite its strictness of composition, can suggest an unpredictability of all parameters, develops an oscillating vibratory space that shows the coherence of all these aspects and media conditions. Only the differentiation of space can prevent the message of God from simply becoming a modern telecommunication relay, for the Ten Commandments would be understood as such by 1950s communications engineers and probably even teachers: "Because [...] communication systems that transmit a single message (such as the number π, a particular sinus wave, or a Decalogue as well) would be superfluous and replaceable by two separate signal generators, information theory is so indifferent to the messages themselves that only their statistics count."[108] This differentiation of sounds and noises is thus medium and re-medium against forcible moral coordination.

The fact that Straub emphasizes having "dreamed" from the very beginning of the electro-acoustic synthesis of music according to tone colors and sound spaces[109] establishes a further relationship to Schoenberg's compositional method, and shows how precisely the film of the opera proceeds in both an aesthetic and a political sense. In his *Theory of Harmony*, written in 1911, Schoenberg dreamed of composing in tone colors—it was then still a long way off—as a sublime ecological ambition. Here it can again be seen that in the early phase of all media art the effects of technology are still undifferentiated and unclear:

107 Michael Cherlin similarly differentiates between "God" and "His messenger": "This reading makes an important connection between God and His messenger, a connection resonant in the narrative to come, which concerns the reporting of God's messages through other agents, Moses and Aron in particular." Cherlin, "Schoenberg's Representation of the Divine," p. 212.

108 Translated from Kittler, "Signal-Rausch-Abstand,", pp. 161–162.

109 See Straub/Huillet, "Conversation," p. 23.

their unconscious is described as subtle, occult, and at the same time as ecological. Schoenberg surprisingly ends his early theoretical work with this dream of the yet undifferentiated:

> Now, if it is possible to create patterns out of tone colors that are differentiated according to pitch, patterns we call 'melodies,' progressions, whose coherence [*Zusammenhang*] evokes an effect analogous of thought processes, then it must be possible to make such progressions out of the tone colors of other dimensions, out of that which we call simply 'tone color,' progressions whose relation with one another work with a kind of logic entirely equivalent to that logic which satisfies us in the melody of pitches. That has the appearance of a futuristic fantasy and is probably just that. But it is one which, I firmly believe, will be realized. [...] I firmly believe that it will bring us close to the illusory stuff of our dreams; that it will expand our relationships to that which seems to us today inanimate as we give life from our life to that which is temporarily dead for us, but dead only by virtue of the slight connection we have with it. Tone-color melodies! How acute the senses that would be able to perceive them! How high the development of spirit that could find pleasure in such subtle things.[110]

Schoenberg ends the last paragraph of the book with a bold (for theorists) exclamation: "In such a domain, who dares ask for theory!"[111]

Straub and Huillet have heard the exclamation, and naturally dare to ask for a theory of this musically ecological dream, from which they distill the aesthetic of their film, explicitly as a critique of capitalism. Free movement in the desert of smooth space, the nomadic existence, will remain a dream or historical utopia until capitalism has ruined the planet: "[...] c'est une utopie. À moins qu'on arrive à un point où le capitalisme ruine la planète."[112] Then the dream will become the nightmare of ubiquitous migration. The musicological, theological, and ethical questions raised by the opera are thus asked in the political field.

110 Arnold Schoenberg, *Theory of Harmony*, translated by Roy. E Carter, Berkeley 1978, p. 421f.

111 Ibid.

112 See Straub/Huillet, "Conversation," p. 8.

3.4. NOISES: GOD AND ENVIRONS

In Schoenberg's dramaturgy, noises—first of all the burning bush—operate before the law. But as the composition proceeds he increasingly maneuvers noisy elements onto the side of the doubters, the barbarians, the drug-takers, and raw-meat-eaters, onto the side of the cultic dancers and nomads. A change occurs in the optical and acoustic organization of the spaces between the opera's first and second acts. It is the change from the regime of Moses to that of Aron. In the still vague "disposition plans and sketches for stage directions" suggested by Arnold Schoenberg the scene in which the ceremony around the Golden Calf reaches its high point of polytheistic eccentricity (act II, bar 371ff) is referred to as follows:

> TD 66
> 1. Processions march in |
> a) unload, | b) livestock is decorated | c)
> butchers appear | (5) dances of the butchers.
>
> TE 23 (17r)
> From various sides | Pro-
> cessions:| [left column:] laden
> camels | carts| riders | bear-
> ers [right column:] wine |
> grain | oil | gold | livestock.
>
> TD4 (1r)
> Slaughter | preparations:
> livestock is dragged in | gar-
> landed ... | (5) butchers dance around
> it | the livestock is slaughtered; in
> several places | the butchers throw
> pieces of meat into the crowd |
> crowd scuffles for the pieces | a
> few run around with bloody
> pieces of meat, devouring them | (10)

(roasting, boiling [kettle] | fuel
is – | dragged in – | fires
are lit.[113]

This vision, even abstracted and projected into ballet, promises a great deal of noisy clatter. What can be heard as the noise of a caravan or an oriental market can simply be described as a frequency mix of non-integral relationships, as particularly found in the alarming, tinny paraphernalia of oriental music, military marches, and carnival rattles.

The fact that the "[kettle]" is marked as a part of the rattling ritual and as an instrument, the kettle drum—whose overtones don't have integral frequency relations—and finally as a word [*Kessel*] that itself rattles onomatopoeically, shows Schoenberg's intention to defy the boundaries between music, noise, and text in opera, and to realize a sound space of undecidability. This applies to both the cultic acts of the nomads and to the confrontation with the monotheistic god, whose order from the thornbush also occurs as an ambivalently rustling mixture, put together from instruments, voices, and human bodies, probably also telephonic technical devices. But with Schoenberg this voice isn't acousmatic in the simple sense, as Mladen Dolar describes that of God, and not only in the Old Testament.[114] Schoenberg's calling voice is composed of concrete sound sources, instruments and human voices, but the sound mix can't be retraced or dissolved; it isn't reversible. In the process of the opera the music subjects the ears of the listeners to the same undecidability that challenges Moses in the decree of voice and word when compelled in the name of freedom to use violence, in the name of obedience to break the law, in the name of the people to regiment and chastise the people. In this sense it is *exercitatio* and oratorio in one. But Schoenberg, like all systematic thinkers, knows that only

113 Translated from Schönberg, *Moses und Aron, Entstehungsgeschichte*, pp. 143–144.

114 "One only needs to think of the extremely significant circumstance that in the Old Testament God regularly appears in the form of an acousmatic voice—a quality that he admittedly shares with numerous other deities, as if there were a direct mysterious link between acousmatic voice and deification. The voice whose source is invisible, because it cannot be localized, seems to come from nowhere and everywhere: it becomes omnipotent. Could we go so far as to say that the hidden voice results in 'divine effects'?" Translated from Mladen Dolar, *His Master's Voice: Eine Theorie der Stimme*, Frankfurt/Main 2007, pp. 84–85.

Zum Ende der 2. Szene:

TI369 [15r^{1}]
2: *Schleier-* ist Einfügung.

/: Während des Nach- und Zwischenspiels hat sich die Chor-Gruppe abgelöst, die den | folgenden Chor während der Verwandlung vor dem Schleier-Vorhang singt:) | *VERWANDLUNG*

Zur 3. Szene:

TI377 [15v]

Ein Blutopfer | vorführen

TI378 [15v]

Vielleicht könnte das Mädchen bei den nackten Jungfrauen | vorkommen und ein paar Solotakte geben | Etwa so der Jüngling bei den Jgl. | Der Mann bei keiner Gruppe

TI400 [15v^{5}]

Nach den Jungfrauen | Stammesfürsten

TD83 [17r]

Nachlassen [?] *bei den | „Scenen" | andre Gruppen nach vorn bringen*

TI431 [16r=*17*]
Schräg von unten nach oben laufend und weite Teile des Haupttextes überschreibend. Nur teilweise mit Sicherheit zu entziffern.

Diese Gruppen bereits[?] *in den Tanz | verteilt*[?]

TI468 [16v^{2}]

Die Gruppen | (Greise, | Bettler | Stammesfürsten | [5] *Eine Kranke | 4 Jünglinge | 4 Jungfrauen) | sind zwischen die | „Tänze" | einzuteilen*

Die Dispositionspläne der Quellen **TD** und **TE**.

Einheit			
1156	**TD1** [1r] *Aron erklärt und übergibt d gold Kalb*		**TE24** [18r] Unten links durch *P1* signiert. *I Aron	erklärt und übergiebt	das goldene Kalb*
1163	**TD2** [1r] *1 Aufzüge beladene Kameele, Esel, Pferde	Wagen,	Reiter* **TD3** [1r] Rechts neben TD2. Zwischen *Schläuche* in 1 und *Oel* doppelt gerichteter Pfeilverweis. *Wein, Fässer, Schläuche	Getreide	Schläuche Oel, Gold,	Vieh*	**TD66** [16r] 5: Ist rechts durch einen Querstrich markiert (d. h. 1. Tanz). *1. Züge marschieren auf	a) laden ab,	b) Vieh wird geschmückt	c) Schlächter treten auf |* [5] *Tänze der Schlächter*	**TE23** [17r] Unten links durch *A1* signiert. *IIa) Von verschiedenen Seiten	Aufzüge: |* [linke Spalte:] *beladene Kamele	Wagen	Reiter	Lastträger |* [rechte Spalte:] *Wein	Getreide	Öl,	Gold	Vieh*

Reconstruction of the development of the text "Aron explains and hands over the gold calf."

Einheit			
	TD4 [1r] Vom Ende Pfeilverweis zum Anfang von TD6. *2 Schlachten | Vorbereitungen: Vieh wird herbei geschleppt | bekränzt … | [5] Schlächter umtanzen es | Das Vieh wird geschlachtet: an mehreren Stellen | die Schlächter werfen Fleischstücke in die Menge | Menge balgt sich um die Stücke | Einzelne laufen mit blutigen Fleischstükken | herum, daran fressend | [10] (braten –, sieden [Kessel] | Brennstoff wird – | hergeschleppt – | Feuer werden entzündet*	**TD67** [16r] 5: Rechts Markierung durch zwei Querstriche (d. h. 2. Tanz). *2. Vieh wird geschlachtet | a) Kessel werden gebracht, aufgehängt | b) Brennmaterial aufgeschichtet | c) Verteilung der Fleischstücke | [5] d) Menge balgt sich etc Tänze | e) Brandopfer | Kranke wird gebracht*	**TE21** [16r] Unten links durch *T1* signiert. *2) Vieh wird geschlachtet | 1) Schlächter tanzen | vorher | 3) werfen Fleischstücke | [5] in die Menge | 4) Menge balgt sich darum | 5) Einzelne laufen mit | blutigen Fleischstücken | herum, | fressen davon*
1167	**TD5** [1r] 1–2: Rechts in marg. durch dicke eckige Klammer markiert. *3 Eine Kranke wird hereingetragen, | zum gold Kalb | Menge weicht zurück | s. Text*	**TD68** [16r] *3. Kranke*	**TE1** [1r] Unten links durch *P2* signiert. *Eine Kranke*
1169	**TD6** [1r] Zum Anfang Pfeilverweis vom Ende von TD4. *4 Feuer werden überall angezündet | (man kocht [Kessel] und brät. | Weinschläuche, Oelschläuche werden | gebracht. | Fackeln werden [allmählich] gebracht.* **TD7** [1r] Links in marg. neben dem Ende von TD6. *es dämmert | (wird langsam | dunkler)*	**TD69** [16r] Außer der Ordnungszahl alles gestrichen. 1: Rechts Markierung durch drei Querstriche (d. h. 3. Tanz). 2–3: Sind nicht zu entziffern. *IV. Feuer – Tänze | [?] | [?]* **TD70** [16r] Rechts Markierung durch vier Querstriche (d. h. – wie TD69 zeigt, irrtümlich – 4. statt 3. Tanz). *4. Feuer Tänze*	**TE2** [2r] Unten links durch *E1* signiert. *Feuer | anzünden | Wein | Lichter | Fackeln | Wasser*
1170	**TD8** [1r] Rechts in marg. durch dicke eckige Klammer markiert; die *2)* mit Pfeil nach unten fordert die Vertauschung mit TD9. *5 2) Bettler zum gold. Kalb | s. Text*	**TD71** [16r] *5* ist KE für *4*. *5. Bettler – – –*	**TE3** [3r] Unten links durch *Chgr. 2* signiert. *Bettler*
1172	**TD9** [1r] Die *1)* mit Pfeil nach oben fordert die Vertauschung mit TD8. *6 1) Greise (s. Text*	**TD72** [16r] *6. Greise – – – | Älteste*	**TE4** [4r] Unten links durch *Chgr. 1* signiert. *II^te^ | Greise | siehe Text*

Reconstruction of the development of the text “Slaughter, preparations, livestock is dragged in.”

people can and must decide the undecidable. The rest is undertaken by God, logic, and world spirit.[115]

Straub and Huillet will make acoustic boundary-breaking a matter of their adaptation, and allow noises to break in not only at the two poles of overwhelmingness, the mythical cult on the one hand, the monotheistic call on the other. They principally destabilize a space of designated perception and legalism by letting the surrounding noises into the music: animal sounds, the sounds of actions, the crunching of the sand beneath the dancers' feet, the rustling of the wind in costumes, buildings, and leaves.[116] Thus they adapt natural sounds and the varied sounds of objects as studio-adequate instruments that integrate the rumbling of reality into the work. This also includes the "gasping of the singers,"[117] which usually annoys listeners and is suppressed in opera. Making the breath into operatic material was already part of the Wagnerian tradition, in which Schoenberg places himself, albeit critically. But Schoenberg doesn't demand the sound of breathing at all costs, only in the sense "that, everything done which the *idea* demands, the external appearance will be adequate."[118] By integrating environment and transmission into the outer manifestation of the music, through adding the media-technical and acoustic conditions to the pure

115 See Heinz von Foerster, "Ethics and Second-Order Cybernetics," in *SEHR*, vol. 4., no. 2, *Constructions of the Mind*, 1995 and http://web.stanford.edu/group/SHR/4-2/text/foerster.html (accessed July 13, 2016). According to von Foerster, this decision makes metaphysicians of us.

116 Michael Gielen recalls how "purist sound engineers and music critics in West German newspapers were bothered by this, but he remarks that the noises in the film are always integrated into the composition, and don't interfere with it: "Particular 'ingenuity' can be seen in the sacrifice of the four virgins: you hear the cicadas, which lay a soundtrack of very high frequencies over the entire music. This was difficult in the mix; namely establishing the relationship between the noises and the music so that the noises are present but don't disturb the music." Translated from Gielen, "'Aus einem Gespräch mit Michael Gielen.' Wolfram Schütte spricht mit Michael Gielen," in *Filmkritik* 221/222, 1975, pp. 280–283.

117 Ibid., p. 281.

118 Arnold Schoenberg, "New Music, Outmoded Music, Style and Idea," in Arnold Schönberg, *Style and Idea*, pp. 113–124: 121 (italics U.H.). Schoenberg is not a materialist in regard to noises and disturbances in the way of John Cage, who certainly counted Schoenberg among his teachers. "While Schoenberg makes mathematical relationships between the 12 tones the starting point of his structural considerations, Cage develops mathematical relationships between the duration of sounds and non-sounds. Before the horizon of a philosophy of physics [...] it could be said that Cage changed from Schönberg's absolute-spatial, Galilean inertial system to a relative-temporal, Einsteinian inertial system of sound." Hagen "Silencetechno," p. 83. Schoenberg, however, is a meticulous materialist in regard to media, and in particular in regard to the technical media of acoustics.

idea of the form, Straub and Huillet radicalize Schoenberg's idea of the materiality of music.

In profiling the media aspects of Schoenberg's opera, which they strengthen in its own tradition, Straub and Huillet not only bring their own political questions into their film. They also counter various reservations about the work, such as those expressed by Theodor W. Adorno. Adorno firstly criticizes a false cult value, saying that Schoenberg "must have grasped the fact that its absolute metaphysical content would prevent it from becoming an aesthetic tonality."[119] Secondly, and probably a more serious accusation, in the musical form and performance of the opera, particularly in the culminating confrontation between Moses and Aron and the bloody orgy of the people, Adorno objects to the indistinguishability of myth and monotheism: "The pathos of the music is identical in both."[120] He sees Schoenberg, not least in the closeness of the work to oratorio, getting caught up in an impossible project, aiming, in evident anachronism, for a sacralization beyond religion and a cultic music without cult value. Non-intentionality, over-subjectivity, and the cultic, Adorno warns, "cannot [...] be willed."[121] Schoenberg risks submerging, and thus damaging, "the idea of the One Spirit"[122] in an adaptation of the false totalization of the Wagnerian tradition. *Moses und Aron* "relates to the biblical narrative in just the same way as the music of the *Ring* or *Parsifal* relate to their underlying texts."[123] In a further discussion of the opera in the 1960s Adorno again takes up his extensive criticism of the work of Schoenberg, developed in 1940/41 in the *Philosophy of New Music*[124] on the periphery of the *Dialectic of Enlightenment*. Here he primarily criticizes the process of fundamental rationalization, which he discerns in Schoenberg's music, the purification of musical form in the sense of, as he puts it, the "musical domination of nature"[125] and a compulsive organization of musical idiosyncrasy. In short, Schoenberg appears to him as Odysseus on the high

119 Theodor W. Adorno, "Sacred Fragment. Schoenberg's Moses und Aron," in Theodor W. Adorno, *Quasi una Fantasia. Essays on Modern Music*, trans. Rodney Livingstone, London 1998, pp. 225–249: 226.

120 Ibid., p. 241.

121 Ibid., p. 228.

122 Ibid., p. 236.

123 Ibid., p. 239.

124 Theodor W. Adorno, *Philosophy of New Music*, trans., ed. Robert Hullot-Kentor, Minneapolis 2006.

125 Ibid., p. 52.

Letting environmental sounds into the music.

seas, rigidly trying to structure the wastes of water in the era of mass-media capitalism, yet formulaically and ultimately "without depth."[126] In Schoenberg, so Adorno, resistive individuality in the face of social law merely comes about in the dynamic of chance.[127]

In as much as Adorno's analysis ignores all the detailed instrumental and particularly media configurations of Schoenberg's aesthetic method, it represents a brilliant music-historical study that misses the decisive point. In all Schoenberg's techniques, in tone-color composition, atonality, and seriality, forms that Adorno can precisely ascribe to music-historical procedures, he acknowledges the principle gesture in which Schoenberg refuses to mediate or reconcile antagonistic forces on the social or conceptual levels. But for Adorno the basic question of the organization of the musical material in which the work confronts reality as an aesthetic phenomenon is decisive.[128] For him the concept of material is not material in the sense of physicality or sound psychology: "From this, however, the compositional material is as different as is speech from the inventory of its sounds."[129] Adorno understands material as the historically available tonal relationships and conditions that have to be realized in the work so that art isn't simply a depiction of reality but generates perceptible contradictions to the production process. Only in aesthetic form and mimeti-

126 Ibid., p. 76
127 See ibid., p. 43.
128 Ibid., p. 54f.
129 Ibid., p. 31.

cally can the historical truth of a work be measured that liberates the intention of the composer in the objective demands of the material. "Not only does it [the material, U.H.] contract and expand in the course of history. All of its specific traits are marks of the historical process."[130]

Adorno's understanding of music remains bound to a dialectic historical process, from which perspective he criticizes the twelve-tone technique. He works through Schoenberg's music, and particularly the twelve-tone opera, in a kind of purification procedure. The rules of twelve-tone music, writes Adorno, are not freely chosen but a submission to music-historical compulsion. "They are configurations of historical constraint in the material. They are at the same time schemata of adaptation to this constraint. In them, consciousness undertakes to purify music of the residues of a lapsed organicity. Cruelly, they combat musical semblance."[131]

Adorno's ruthless accusation of rationalization continually breaks down in observations that don't fit in with the strategy of dialectical authority. The "incessant permutations" in which twelve-tone music operates are unable, according to Adorno, to lay a symmetrical foundation: "Clearly the demand for symmetry in twelve-tone technique is raised just as it is inexorably denied."[132] Adorno won't hear or admit that even in its first sound the opera makes a

130 Ibid.
131 Ibid., p. 52.
132 Ibid., p. 76.

constitutive issue of the incompatibility of notated symmetry and originating sound. Neither does he consider that the core of Schoenberg's opera is perhaps not a purification of the musical material, in the sense of a rigid mathematicization of the music, but rather the possible distinction between calculated and sensorially perceptible, psycho-acoustically formed sound. In this very sense the opera addresses acoustic crises in which contemporary media and propaganda machines generate an ethnic people as *faux peuple*. For Schoenberg, as is shown not only in his letters and notes but also in his compositions, which always require decisive new distinctions, the theological question is a systematic one about the interference, the vibratory relationship, between God and environs, not that of a dialectic of God and world.

Wherever Adorno fails to drive Schoenberg into the trap of the bourgeois hero, he signalizes incomprehension. In a criticism of *Moses und Aron* in 1941, that is, from London exile to Californian, he writes that "the need to finish works was unknown to him."[133]

In 1941, with regard to commercialized mass art and the "listener trained to the sound of radio,"[134] Adorno not only questions the possible experience of music altogther but in particular the aspect of collectivity, which for Schoenberg is central. In gaging the aesthetic of the opera with a dialectic process whose task is to lead out of a sacral epoch towards the horizon of bourgeois art

133 Ibid., p. 94.
134 Ibid., p. 12.

and criticism, he requires modern artworks to be at once autonomous and *fait social*. With Schoenberg, however, he discerns only "the ideal collectivity that music still carries in itself, though separated from the empirical collectivity,"[135] which at the same time leads to its social isolation. What Adorno can't or won't hear in his precise formal analysis is that Schoenberg realizes modernity, as the opera's *fait social*, in the negotiation of the openness and closedness of the sound space. At this point Schoenberg allows a media aspect into his music, on the one hand as a concrete techno-acoustic setup, on the other as the integration of a differential. This involves both the technical media of his historical present and the rhythms, physicality, doubling, and multiplying of the chorus, in which, as Schiller did for the people of Messina, Schoenberg strengthens the sensory in a superimposition and merging of musical cultures. He isn't interested in the historical process in its correct dialectical direction but in the resistance between concrete material arrangements that causes disturbances and thus noises, sounds, visibility, and visions. In the confrontation of these elements, in the unpredictable, unimaginable, yet not in the unintentional, Schoenberg poses the question of a possible revelation, which he incidentally expects more as catastrophe than Promised Land.

From the perspective of the philosopher of music, Adorno articulates very justified misgivings about the aspiration to transcend the subjective through artistic form. "A cultic action is one which obeys a law that goes beyond the mental capacity of those involved in the cult, in accordance with the idea of something which is not just surmised, but is actually revealed in the language of truth. In the same way the musical construction, for which the subject requires nothing but its own powers and preformed material, shall transcend the spere of the subject from its own impetus."[136] This argument, too, only applies when the law of music is postulated as antecendent. Only then can a higher knowledge be thought of, a musical legalism, to which the subject is subjugated. However, the ordering of the twelve tones is not a law but, as with Straub and Huillet, a rule of the game. It structures the notion of the world. Schoenberg's stage and playing directions show that on the basis of this rule the equality of all sounds and tone colors, the rustling of the world and the rattle of the breath can be taken as

135 Ibid., p. 18.
136 Adorno, "Sacred Fragment," p. 229.

non-prejudicial into the experimental system of the composition. Adorno and Schoenberg have a fundamentally different concept of the work. Adorno argues within well-defined musical boundaries; Schoenberg subjects these boundaries to negotiation as an area of experience and decision.

Adorno only grants Schoenberg that the failure of his opera can be shown not as expected enlightenment but as fragmentariness. Here Adorno insists on an element that Straub and Huillet will meticulously work out in their film: "the caesura was to be decisive."[137] For Adorno the caesura shows the quality of aesthetic law in which an artwork has to become similar to its objective ideal, not its empirical ideal, in order to be true. Mimetics may only become operative as the similarity of the work of art to *itself*; its appearance must distinguish it from the empirical world. In Adorno's posthumously published *Aesthetic Theory* there is a reference at this systematic point to the prohibition of images: "By the autonomy of their form, artworks forbid the incorporation of the absolute as if they were symbols. Aesthetic images stand under the prohibition on graven images. To this extent aesthetic semblance, even its ultimate form in the hermetic artwork, is truth."[138] In his criticism of the opera *Moses und Aron* the idea of the appearance, which should vouch for the autonomy of the artwork and must visibly break open in antagonistic reality, is applied to music. Adorno suspects that in Schoenberg's music, where caesura shows appearance, all that can be perceived is fracture, a thing made in handiwork and ratio that lacks all resistance: "This is achieved technically by an unprecedented art of disposition which distributes the complex sonorities so as to eliminate any friction between them." In plain terms, Schoenberg overreaches himself. In the sense of imageless aesthetics Adorno only accepts the concentration of the form itself in composition, which permits a radical decentralization "so that the distinction between consonance and dissonance is deprived of its raison d'être."[139] "The sheer density of the construction becomes the medium in which the ineffable can manifest itself without usurpation. For it is this that can be wholly and convincingly created in the material by Schoenberg's own musical

137 Ibid., p. 241.

138 See Theodor W. Adormo, *Aesthetic Theory*, trans., ed. Robert Hullot-Kentor, London 2013, p. 144.

139 Adorno, "Sacred Fragment," p. 237.

consciousness."[140] But he sees the opera as threatened by excessive complexity[141] and his suspicion confirmed that *Moses und Aron* can barely be differentiated from melodrama or the operas of Richard Wagner. Straub and Huillet respond to this argument by crystalizing the constrained programmatic Adorno objects to in Schoenberg's technique onto an overall space of perception, by dissecting the acoustic space through sound on vision into its individual elements, noises, and vibrations, and by opening up the caesuras of the opera from the texture, in this case the exact opposite of the fracture. Straub/Huillet's film critique—or filmed critique—of Schoenberg's opera causes his composition to break open in a media reality—and not only that of technical media but also of the transmitting third party as difference—in order to bring Schoenberg's debate with the question of the collective, of the people, to the surface. With Schoenberg this topos is clearly arranged in the implementation of media acoustics in the Moses motif, but it was apparently not realized or not perceived in the productions of the 1950s. Both the aesthetic of a "faux Living Theater,"[142] as Straub puts it, and to a greater degree the suppression of an effective and operative ethnic space in Germany in the 1950s become the political reason for making the film.

A further debate Straub and Huillet take up is that of the impossibility of articulating history artistically, as claimed by Adorno for the time after the annihilation of the European Jews.[143] In their film Straub and Huillet show that

140 Ibid., p. 245. Adorno's text is itself divided into three "movements": an introduction of the motif, namely the question of the sacral and the cultic under the conditions of modernity (ibid., pp. 225–232); then a second movement ruthlessly accusing Schoenberg of failure, as he doesn't put the fragmentary into his composition decisively but loses himself in false form through the density of an intended totality (ibid., pp. 232–243); and a third that self-satisfactorily works through the aesthetic possibilities of the piece (ibid., pp. 243–248).

141 Ibid., p. 248.

142 Straub/Huillet, "Conversation," p. 6.

143 See Theodor W. Adorno, *Prisms*, trans. Samuel and Shierry Weber, Cambridge 1983, p. 34, and *Negative Dialectics*, trans. E.B. Ashton, London 1973, p. 362 f.: "Perennial suffering has as much right to expression as a tortured man has to scream; hence it may have been wrong to say that after Auschwitz you could no longer write poems. But it is not wrong to raise the less cultural question whether after Auschwitz you can go on living—especially whether one who escaped by accident, one who by rights should have been killed, may go on living. His mere survival calls for the coldness, the basic principle of bourgeois subjectivity [...]." See also Theodor W. Adorno, "Is Art Lighthearted?" in Adorno, *Notes to Literature*, vol. 2, ed. Rolf Tiedemann, New York 1992, pp. 247–253:251: "The statement that it is not possible to write poetry after Auschwitz does not hold absolutely, but it is certain that after Auschwitz, because Auschwitz was possible and remains possible for the foreseeable future, lighthearted art is no longer conceivable."

Schoenberg deals with realism as a question of the frame, the periphery, and the openings of an acoustic space. They emphasize that Schoenberg's idea can only be realized in an archaeology of sounds and images, anachronistically and not in some kind of contemporary adaptation. In this they reconstruct the artistic decisions Schoenberg took in the light of political developments during the 1930s. While in the *Theory of Harmony*, from 1911, Schoenberg had proposed composing with tone colors, during the 1930s he began to undermine and fragment such tone-color spaces, to have them shatter against non-musical realities. As Adorno rightly discerns, Schoenberg links this with cultic, fascist media politics.[144]

Adorno can only criticize media as more or less destructive of culture. In his aesthetic theory a critique *through* media, as Schoenberg enacted politically in and through his compositions, has no role to play. But the frequency-reduced sound of a telephone voice, the rattling of kettles, animal voices, animal noises marks a new field in the sound space of opera, and responds to contemporary technical media and *dispositifs*. It can be understood as the breaking down of an older perceptive space of art. Within Adorno's concept of the culture industry, however, it represents nothing more than an extension of the capitalist zone of mass-aesthetic conformity. In his critique of the radio, Adorno distinguishes, similarly to Brecht, the mutilated use of the device in capitalism from the problem of technology, whose availability is socially regulated: "Technology itself, as a socially produced medium of social experience, can only be dogmatically isolated from its social location. The technology as such bears no blame for its effects, which people in their naivety and consciousness of being left behind it believe they observe everywhere, but only by virtue of its social status:"[145] In his concentration on abstraction in aesthetic perception, Adorno states, in an attitude similar to Schoenberg's towards the interference factor of the audience: "What is technically conveyed obtains a physical closeness that often denies precisely those seeking concentrated perception the immediacy of the living performance."[146] For Adorno perceptive truth lies in what is purified of all media fusion and confusion. He is uninterested in perception as an equation between technical, instrumental, and organic sound bodies. So he underesti-

144 See Adorno, "Sacred Fragment," p. 325.

145 Translated from Adorno, "Musikalische Verwendung des Radios," pp. 374–375.

146 Ibid., p. 369.

mates the constitutive disturbances that media add to all intellectual and sensory art concepts, and equally the interferences and caesuras produced in the body and the social body that refer to the surrounding system: the autonomy of the work of art is compromised.[147]

Straub and Huillet pursue these very caesuras in the listening realm by emphasizing the fragmentation and artificial consolidation of the perceptive space, by showing every collective as something conveyed through media and whose conveyance should be clearly audible. It's true, Adorno is right, a unified and indistinguishable sound space for Christian congregations in the same way as for fantasies of medieval leagues, for fascist communities, and for democratized societies—but it only lasts as long as these groups don't want to know anything about the media organization of their voices. The emphasis on media conveyance as amplification or caesura shows the led people its leader. In artistic media analysis, such as those of Schoenberg and Straub/Huillet, perception of the conditions of communization competes with critical theory, which has been polished by the concepts of production relationships, commodity aesthetics, and the culture industry.

Straub and Huillet's transfer of acoustic forms into cinematic and media ones underlines the difference between Schoenberg's composition of a reality and the sound space that Richard Wagner realizes in his operas with the architectural division of space at Bayreuth. Wagner anticipated the electro-acoustic formation of space in building the effect of electronic feedback through the staging of musical overtone relations into the architectural space of his opera house. As a technical anachronism the space simulates these effects through the sound of the composition in the logic of vibratory relationships, not yet as electronic interference and no longer within the laws of harmony.[148] The physical aspect, which Straub and Huillet also emphasize in their version of *Moses und Aron*, in their recording of the breath or even the criticized "gasping" of the singers, has a certain recourse to the Wagnerian tradition, to which Schoenberg oriented himself early on.[149] But where Wagner imperceptibly fuses instruments and

147 In the context of the radio and the Princeton Radio Research Project see Wolfgang Hagen, *Gegenwartsvergessenheit. Studien zu Lazarsfeld, Adorno, Innis und Luhmann*, Berlin 2003.

148 See Kittler, "Weltatem," p. 94.

149 For biographical and aesthetic reasons there is a consensus among researchers to understand Schoenberg as a successor to Wagner, as Herbert Lindenberger does in *Opera in History. From Monteverdi to Cage*, Stanford 1998, or as an anti-Wagner, as Hartmut Zelinsky does in "Arnold

singers into divine worlds or world breath in the semi-darkness of the opera house, Straub and Huillet analyze, with Schoenberg, the hard landing of these voices onto historical ground, in the heat and aridity of the world, and in the resistance in the bodies of the singers. They don't do this in order to obtain authenticity from simple positivity, but because the sound relationships noticeably alter under the influence of technology and environs, and thus the musical material in Adorno's sense. Things and their effects are brought into play against any insinuation of transcendence.

The comparison between Wagner and Schoenberg can't therefore be made on the basis of motif, proceeding from fable and libretto to interpret *Moses und Aron* as *Anti-Parsifal*,[150] but on the basis of the organization of sound. Adorno emphasized this in reference to the orchestration, the "timbre, which is integrated into the construction of *Moses and Aaron* to a greater degree than almost any other of his works,"[151] only to criticize it harshly elsewhere: "Nowhere is this more striking than in Schoenberg's relation to musical drama. It was determined directly by Wagnerian aesthetics, despite the extreme expressionism of the first two dramatic works. As late as *Moses und Aaron*, the relation of music to text is scarcely different from any post-Wagnerian opera no matter how little attention is paid to the music-dramatic scores. In Schoenberg different historical moments collide. The composer who, in immanent-musical terms, was light-years ahead of his epoch, remained a child of the nineteenth century where its *terminus ad quem*, its function, was concerned."[152] Schoenberg takes the debate with the media aspects of the constitution of aesthetic space in

Schönberg – der Wagner Gottes. Anmerkungen zum Lebensweg eines deutschen Juden aus Wien," in *Neue Zeitschrift für Musik* 04/1986, pp. 7–19, and Constantin Grun, *Schönberg und Wagner*, p. 559ff, who says on p. 628: "It must by now have become clear how strongly Schönberg links to Wagner, not only in Wagner's overall conception, from which Schönberg distances himself in ideological terms, but also in musical detail: in the ('virtual') chromaticism of his dodecaphony, in the tendency towards traditional form, in the leitmotivic melody in particular, and not least in certain aspects of orchestration and treatment of the voice. Even the choice of Wagner's publishers Schott fits into the picture, and may possibly be more than a coincidence." From the perspective of film analysis, however, these music-historically enlightening gestures of succession show continual attacks on the boundaries of a musical sound space that can no longer be perceived in a unified or collective manner because of such disturbances.

150 See Grun, *Schönberg und Wagner*, p. 610ff.

151 Adorno, "Sakrales Fragment," p. 324.

152 Adorno, *Prisms*, p. 167.

Wagner's compositions further than tone color.[153] The difference between the old arts and the new media arts, whose constitutive effect takes place below the threshold of consciousness, couldn't interest Adorno the music theoretician. But it does interest media studies.

The Wagnerian form of opera is held to be the first media form of the genre, in as much as the two "data flows," the verbal—libretto and words—and the acoustic—score and sounds—which opera had hitherto strictly distinguished, are brought together to become indistinguishable. The boundaries that symbolic order such as letters or notation draw around the arts are thus aggressively broken down to an imaginary that feeds off the physical, but thus off the unconscious, and even off a reality of the singers' bodies. Opera not only enters the stage but, politically conceived, the perceptive space of media.[154] Friedrich Kittler has shown that in this case the breath is the channel in which the two data flows are made indistinguishable and "processed" together, creating the context that simulates world breath and world stage above and beyond every individual subject in the overall media space of Bayreuth.[155] This relocates the basis for the noise of opera to the physical bodies, and operatic rapture to a body that can be historically defined in psycho-physical discourse. What according to Adorno's verdict against Schoenberg's procedure "cannot be willed" was and is most certainly willed and realized on the level of staged sound. With Wagner this sound anticipates what could later be installed electro-acoustically as the positive feedback of circuits. In Wagner's compositions this acoustic practice also initiates an erotically charged (if this can be "willed") process of dissolution or self-dissolution in the vibrating sound space of Bayreuth.[156] For this reason it's possible to speak of a Wagner "sound," even before the term entered musicology as the description of electro-acoustically produced audibilities: via strategies of musical vibration in the wooden paneling and seats of the Bayreuth opera house, it anticipates, *quasi una fantasia*, what will later grow loud through voices in public address systems, both in political cults and pop music. It is

153 Grun only elaborates on this in regard to the stage space: "Certain tendencies in the composition of space, that is certain attempts on the side of the composer to extrapolate the stage space in a musically evident way, also refer to Wagner." Translated from Grun, *Schönberg und Wagner*, pp. 674–675.

154 Kittler, "Weltatem," p. 95.

155 See ibid., pp. 94–107.

156 From which the German Bundestag profits in the meantime.

primarily "vocal noises, spatial sounds, and reverberation effects"[157] that bind individual desire to the global sound space—paradigmatically with Wagner in acoustic wordplays such as "Weia" and "Wehe" [both approximately "woe" in its double sense, *trans.*]—because, as Kittler writes, "they can only interconnect in voices and instrument, text and score."[158] At the beginning of his opera, Schoenberg also fuses voices and instruments, not on the basis of phonemes but of vowels as linguistic elements of a regime of signs that, following both the Torah and late nineteenth-century psycho-physiological, phonetic knowledge, implement and regulate power relationships as physical. What can only be detected retrospectively in Wagner's sound space,[159] namely the relationship between governmentality and acoustic notation, is Schoenberg's intrinsic theme in *Moses und Aron* from the start: regimes of signs, bodies, and legalism are indivisible and must therefore be differentiated. Historically and in media terms Straub/Huillet made this complex cinematic.

The singers' breathing and gasping, clearly audible in the film MOSES UND ARON, allows the appearance, artistically irrelevant but constitutive in relation to media, of a channel of transmission in its materiality. So when Straub and Huillet dismantle the undifferentiated "O ______ O ______ O" of the vocalise, with which Schoenberg follows Wagner onto the world stage, into its media elements, this should be understood as a political analysis of a space that since Wagner has inhabited the "drilled" ears of listeners as a neo-cultic aspect of electro-acoustics. The decisions that Schoenberg expects of the ears and intellect of his audience are those of analytical distinction within artistic worlds. Around 1930 the constitution of acoustic overall spaces became a significant political strategy. Their differentiation is therefore the first step on the way to a political critique.

157 Translated from Kittler, "Weltatem," p. 98.

158 Ibid., p. 100.

159 See ibid., p. 97f.

The Dance of the Butchers.

3.5. TABLEAUS: EXCHANGE VALUE, ECSTASY VALUE

In its very precise acoustics, strictness of musical micro-dynamics, openness to environmental noises, and its porous mixture and superimposition of sound realities, the film of the opera *Moses und Aron* clearly shows the degree to which Schoenberg's work is a project against Bayreuth, an anti-Wagner piece.[160] This in no way only refers to Adorno's somewhat derisive imputation of Schoenberg's misogyny and "sexual hostility" when he "intensifies monotheism against polygamy."[161] The so-called orgy in the camp before the law is in fact a difficult element of the opera. In the course of the vitalistic exultation with which the people welcome the security and lust for life brought by the Golden Calf the general offerings first become mutual sacrifice, but then turn into murder and offering in the name of gods now visible once more. This is aesthetically handled as a juxtaposition of visibility and audibility.

The awkward thing about these scenes, which essentially make up the second act, is that Schoenberg completely breaks out of the historical dialectic and presents the behavior of the people, who aren't yet in fact a people, in their lawless state. The link between the aesthetic and the political becomes ambivalent, as Adorno accurately identified. Schoenberg conceptualizes violence, despotism, and the abuse of bodies in the lawless structure of equal distribution—of the tones, spaces, and voices. What Adorno doesn't perceive is that the drama or tragedy of the opera consists exactly in the question of how a society established in violence and murder can ever, with or according to the law, become a sustainable community again. Menace, murder, and genocide extinguish the possibility of reconciliation. Freud also states this in his book on Moses in 1938. This is the condition of the camp, which Schoenberg understands in the 1930s. But for this reason the opera also addresses the war-dominated present, whether that of the 1970s or of the twenty-first century.

In their film, Straub and Huillet don't give in to the temptation to show the orgy as wild goings-on and wish fulfillment. They persist in showing the disenfranchised and lawless people as individuals trying to cope with the problem of living together among an antagonistic many. The interesting thing about

160 See Adorno, "Sacred Fragment," p. 325.

161 Ibid., p. 320. Here Adorno comments on the Murnau commune: "He who early on celebrated free love later showed sexual hostility."

Tableaus staged in very fine lighting.

the opera is that it refuses to become utopian, and instead develops contradictions, resistance, and intractability from the detail. The film by Straub/Huillet explicitly resists the dynamic of the composition in the orgy sequences, however. Straub and Huillet don't stage Schoenberg's imagery as a grotesque, but observe singers, actors, and the many extras from the district of Alba Fucense embodying the frenzy and Schoenberg's wild exchange of offerings.

Schoenberg opens the Feast of the Golden Calf musically with forced rhythmic passages in which the strings are required to make wide *glissandi* "very well audible; down the whole string" (act II, bars 330–333). The Dance of the Butchers can be heard as the connection and confrontation between archaism and modernity.

After the people's first ecstasy, an outbreak of lust for life that is still today associated with festive slaughter and consumption of animals, Schoenberg writes murder, violence, and sacrifice into the composition before, and as its reverse side, a boundless giving of presents. But this is interrupted by an "orgy of destruction and suicide." Schoenberg again seems to fantasize filmic scenes:

> The TRIBAL LEADERS slay the YOUTH, then mount their horses, mingle with the people individually and in disorder, then disappear, riding off unobtrusively. Among the people a wish to offer one another gifts follows on what is gone before. Women give one another jewelry, scarves, etc., the men weapons, equipments, etc., and food and drink is exchanged, also gifts of flowers. Everybody helps everybody else with their tasks.[162]

Straub and Huillet film the orgy of exchange in soberly framed tableaus with fine lighting. The logic of the film images at first seems to go over to Aron's side: the "rules of the game" in act I have been abandoned; the scenes of the night of ecstasy extensively show the vivid sensuality that Aron promised the people in the camp. The sculptural light of the night shots, in which everything white stands out, makes the bodies appear more beautiful, but also more forlorn. Individual hand movements in contact with objects and equipment are singled out, forcing the chiaroscuro into genre painting. But at the same time they point to the use of the objects, fabrics, wine jugs, conspicuously exhibiting the historicity of the movements and again allowing historical thinking into the images.

162 Schoenberg, *Moses und Aron*, vocal score, act II, bar 592ff.

Symmetrical arrangement, ascetic ritual.

The acting follows Brecht's logic of the gesture, which requires the portrayal of a fable in a form of portrayal that points out this contradiction: "The actor masters his character by paying critical attention to its manifold utterances, as also to those of his counterparts and of all the other characters involved."[163] But film is distinct from the stage in that things and noises, in their singularity and pertinacity, split this dialectical contradiction into varied references, which as bodies, robes, and things, as walls, landscapes, vegetation, and climate all contain their own historicity, and in being recorded by technical media put a new layer of history into the image, and above all onto the soundtrack.

Contradictoriness is also prescribed by Schoenberg as abrupt change, as reversal or cut. At bar 606 of act II, where the rhythm unexpectedly moves into "swaying dance tempo," the composer specifies an "orgy of drunkenness and

163 Bertolt Brecht, "A Short Organum for the Theater" (1948), in Bertolt Brecht, *The Development of an Aesthetic*, trans. John Willet, New York 1977, pp. 179–205: 198.

dance." "Everywhere wine is poured out by the gallon. Everyone gets drunker and drunker. The stone jugs are thrown about and a bacchanalia ensues which leads to quarrels and blows."[164]

In the film version it is striking that no wanton hordes and masses are shown but individuals, differentiated, undecided, small groups of people trying to wear themselves out in their little fears and joys, individuals at the edge of an abyss between reluctance and self-abandonment into the coming society of the Golden Calf. The tableau contrasts the motives of the hangers-on and accomplices, who produce, beyond guilt and innocence, the very catastrophe in which they will perish. But these shots of the muddled cultic proceedings are never denunciative, never condescending, are always unsparingly exact and implacable.

After a series of offerings have been exchanged, once again between individuals, and red wine has been audibly poured by the gallon, Straub and Huillet again resist the temptation of visualizing the acceleration Schoenberg requires, and interrupt the progression into imagery and physicality with a very lengthy shot, encompassing the song of the Elders, of a burning torch and a wall, as a negative teichoscopy, a displaced view from the wall. Then they suddenly cut to the scene of the virginal sacrifice, which even Schoenberg describes in the score as an "orgy of destruction"[165] and doesn't give it an operatic logic. This shot is also a nocturnal tableau. Four virgins, says Schoenberg, "naked to the extent that the rules and necessities of the stage allow and require,"[166] should be paraded in. During the 1970s in Italy this problem turned out to be an inverted one, as nudity was the basis of successful film productions, and feeding this golden Moloch with more of it involved the practice of virginal sacrifice. Again Straub and Huillet carry out a mathematical distribution of the spatial forces when they film the scene as a symmetrical arrangement of the four naked young women with their backs to the camera, directly opposite them four priests in regalia, on either side two almost veiled women, motherly types, holding the offering bowls and flashing knives ready. The figures stand almost immobile in front of the Golden Calf as a reluctant constellation of innocence, calculation, and violence, in contrast to the song of voluntary surrender to the patriarchal

164 Schoenberg, *Moses und Aron*, vocal score, act II, bar 606ff.

165 Translated from Schönberg, *Moses und Aron*, score II, act II, bar 752.

166 Schoenberg, *Moses und Aron*, vocal score, act II, bar 780.

knives of the old men, who have just complacently praised the gods for the gift of sensuality they believe to have received. A reprise of the Dance of the Butchers is suggested in the music.

In this scene the voice of a girl can be heard off screen. To the very nervously fluttering tones of flute, harp, and harpsichord, she sings:

> Du goldener Gott, wie Lust durchströmt mich dein Glanz!
> Was glänzt nur ist gut.
> Unangreifbare Tugend des Golds, unverlierbare Jungfräulichkeit,
> belohnt als Vorbild und Abbild.
>
> [O golden of gods, your glow streams through me with pleasure!
> What gleams must be good.
> Unassailable virtue of gold, its virginity cannot be lost,
> repaid as model and image.][167]

A women's chorus then breaks into the somewhat halting rhythm of a dance without cymbals that continues the grisly metaphor of the teenagers sacrificing themselves to gold: "... das Blut jungfräulicher Unberührtheit, gleich Goldes metallischer Kälte zur Frucht nicht erwärmt [... our blood, virginal and still unblemished, is coldly metallic as gold is, not warmed to bear fruit]."[168]

At least in Straub and Huillet's film there is no doubt that resolution is neither sought here in the name of the camp and its logic of sacrifice, nor in the name of monotheism and its implied violence, but that techniques and gestures of a society in which very young women, now suitable for child-bearing, are used by old men and their displaced procreative strategies. In the film the sudden shift from excessive reciprocal exchange, as shown in the first images of the sequence, to chilling ecstasy, bloodlust, and murder, as Schoenberg dramatizes the society of the Calf, is shown as the reverse side of one and the same capitalist society—no different from George Bataille's analyses of fascism undertaken at the same time.

167 Schönberg, *Moses und Aron*, score II, act II, bars 759–768.
168 Ibid., bar 786 ff.

What Adorno identifies as the opera's "sexual hostility" could just as well be understood as the observation and criticism of a sexual behavior between the generations and sexes that has apparently changed very little. In his link between ritual violence and paternally regulated sexuality, in his relentless portrayal of dynastically, ethnically, or capitalistically oriented bio-politics as a politics of desire, Schoenberg can be credited with postulating, *ex negativo* but clearly, that a future law would have to consist not only in progressive ideas but also in a new and unimaginable sexuality. This also applies to Schoenberg's later experiments with a "twelve-tone family," which horrified his contemporaries.[169]

In the following scenes, however, Straub and Huillet also subordinate earthly love to the prohibition of images. Long dark shots interrupt the actions of the naked lovers. These aren't in fact black spacing but blackish images in which only the moon or the mountains can be seen. The relationship between image prohibition and materiality is dealt with again here in regard to physicality, and differently from the opera's opening sequence, in which this is explored in terms of the voice and vocalization.

Here too Straub and Huillet deal with the prohibition of images not as iconoclasts but in the sense of the Moses complex as a marking of sudden changes, of a resistance that salvages the view of vulnerable bodies. They show the blood, as a countershot to the knives of the sacrificing priests and the naked female bodies, not as a shock effect but as a retarding image and a challenge to actually think about the murder of bodies—and not merely to imagine it, as the cinema generally requires. At this point, after a very slow string *glissando* and the voices of the virgins, who "emit a death cry," as it says at bar 823 of act II, the music is interrupted for almost a minute. The hand of a priest pours blood or red paint into an altar stone. A caesura suspends image, sound, and ritual, marking the unimaginable, death, and withdrawing it from the conventional economy of the cinema.

Perhaps the most striking thing in this scene is the constant sound of the cicadas over the music. It challenges both the indifference of nature and any idea of the natural in regard to the still continuing sacrifice of young girls. "You hear

169 See Hanns Eisler, *Gespräche mit Hans Bunge. Fragen Sie mehr über Brecht*, Leipzig 1975: "Schönberg's house [...] was a private hell. [...] This mixture of disorganization in his private life with small children—Schönberg's eldest daughter was twenty-four years old; the youngest son was six. So this twelve-tone family relationship, where for example the children of the twenty-four-year-old daughter had to greet the little man as uncle, a six-year-old—it was hell." Translated from p. 61.

the cicadas [...] so that the noises are present but don't disturb the music."[170] But what the noises do pierce through is the fiction that such rituals are nothing but imagination. Nowhere in this footage, which reconstructs power relationships, is there a moral gesture, and everywhere the call to perceive violence in the smallest of gestures.

Sacrifice, dance, and sex aren't orgiastic in the film. In the end a naked young man carries a naked girl off screen in such a way that their vulnerable bodies and thin skin can be felt. If Straub and Huillet liberate Schoenberg, then certainly not in regard to sexual morals or practices, rather in view of the volatile relationship between physical individuals in the space of concrete power. This is shown as a relationship of people and voices in the sound space, which Schoenberg, too, thinks of as space breathing. The opera is not about the space of the world but the possibility and impossibility of creating spaces, places, camps in the world. The film fundamentally reorganizes Schoenberg's implied anti-Wagner sound space, and grapples with the problem of sound as an electro-acoustic and media effect among instrumental, technical, human, animal, and vegetable bodies. An effect that can't be symbolically notated and is difficult to imagine from the score. So when Straub and Huillet, in their media-archaeological investigation, disassemble and then reassemble the acoustic space in layers, this also effects the sensuousness of the bodies, which liaise, orientate, or isolate themselves in an acoustic world. The bodies of the performers, like those of the moviegoers, are themselves disassembled and then reassembled in perceptive layers through experiencing this sound space. This corresponds to an unrest in Schoenberg's music, which first had to invent its place in history.

Hearing bodies aren't placed into a historical space and socialized there by audible sounds alone; this also occurs through spatial sound qualities that aren't normally heard. Given the very dry recordings of the Moses opera in Alba Fucense, Michael Gielen mocked the "usual reverb"[171] required by opera audiences for reproductions, as Schoenberg had already done: "Length, to most people, seems to be essential to sound. They observe it only if it lasts for a comparatively long time."[172] The spirit of Wagner is probably also better conserved

170 Translated from Gielen, "Gespräch mit Michael Gielen," pp. 281–282.

171 Translated from Gielen, *Unbedingt Musik*, p. 276.

172 See Schoenberg, "Composition with Twelve Tones," p. 240: "Formerly, sound had been the radiation of an intrinsic quality of ideas, powerful enough to penetrate the hull of the form.

in such standard reverb effects than, as Adorno suspected and Schoenberg's work implies, in the material. Dwelling in reverberation, the spirit of Wagner found a haven in the cinema.

In their cool, dry sound processing, Straub and Huillet ally themselves with a sound politics of "reorganization of noises"[173] by Robert Bresson and the Nouvelle Vague. They put together the audible space on the sound track from a variety of elements, which Bresson says to dig up in situ, then to "play them back one by one in silence" and "adjust the blend."[174] Decisive to this tradition is a temporal and historical differentiation of noises, voices, tones, and spatial acoustics that doesn't institute an overall body but assembles a complex one. Through and also in resistance to this spatial experience, according to the strategy of both opera and film, bodies are realized as sexual, too. This concept can't be located in the simple distinction between polytheism and monotheism, polygamy and monogamy, or sexual hostility and amity.

3.6. TELEVISION AND TELEPHONY

> The telephone had already been dreamed of when Moses and Zoroaster conversed with god. And the radio as an instrument for the transmission of divine messages was well imagined before that.
>
> *R. Murray Schafer*[175]

Arnold Schoenberg had drawn his concept of media, or of a space formed by media, from the cinema and its curious realism very early, during the time of his friendship with Wassily Kandinsky and his contributions to projects by the Blauer Reiter. It was based on discussions on the effects of light and field, about

Nothing could radiate which was not light itself; and here only ideas are light. Today, sound is seldom associated with idea."

173 Robert Bresson, *Notes On Cinematography*, trans. Jonathan Griffin, New York 1977, p. 24: "Reorganize the unorganized noises (what you think you hear is not what you hear) of a street, a railroad station, an airport. [...] Play them back one by one in silence and adjust the blend."

174 Ibid.

175 R. Murray Schafer, *Soundscape. Our Sonic Environment and the Tuning of the World*, Rochester 1995, p. 89.

which Schoenberg had been thinking around 1911 in his *Theory of Harmony* and Kandinsky in *Concerning the Spiritual in Art.*[176] In the fall of 1913 Schoenberg wrote to Emil Hertzka, director of Universal Edition in Vienna, asking about the possibility of a cinematographic—which at the time meant silent film—rendition of his opera *Die glückliche Hand* [The Hand of Fate]. The letter outlines certain artistic spatial concepts that look like a first matrix for the exposition of *Moses und Aron.*

At first Schoenberg develops a lighting concept, particularly for the possibility of a lightless cinematic space that frames the action like a darkened mirror: "Another problem, it seems to me, is that of the opening and concluding scenes, which are to be '*almost entirely in darkness.*' I do not know whether the cinematograph can do this, since there is no such thing as 'dark light.' But I dare say there are solutions even for such problems."[177]

For Schoenberg the colors play a decisive role in the cinematic transfer. He wishes them to be devised in cooperation with an artist, suggesting Oskar Kokoschka, Wassily Kandinsky, and Alfred Roller, the Viennese painter and scenographer. His music-cinema would have derived its coloration from the inking, toning, or tinting of the film strip, while also using colored light.[178] Finally Schoenberg imagined a new form of interlocking visibility and audibility for the film version of *Die glückliche Hand.* Yet here he derived his audio-visions from stage setups, hiding the singers behind curtains or objects, as would have

176 See Werner Haftmann, "Über die Funktion des Musikalischen in der Malerei des 20. Jahrhunderts," in Lucius Grisebach and others (eds.), *Hommage à Schönberg. Der Blaue Reiter und das Musikalische in der Malerei der Zeit* (exhib. cat.), Berlin 1974, pp. 8–41. Haftmann emphasizes the relationship between media, sound, and the construction of space in Schoenberg's work: "But it was the great modern composer Schönberg who, from a compelling inner necessity, took on the idea of the musical formation of space. In 1915—from a deep religious disposition—he began his *Jakobsleiter.* During its composition his imagination was entirely taken up with the idea that a sound structure within the space should itself resound—as a medium for the numinous. From this necessity Schönberg conceived of "tele-choruses" and "tele-orchestras" positioned outside the auditorium that could be transmitted to different parts of the concert hall via technical means—he thought of a system of tubes. This idea was then far ahead of any possible technical realization." Translated from ibid. p. 36. But perhaps the media-technical idea was more obvious than Haftmann knew. See Ruschkowski, *Elektronische Klänge.*

177 Schoenberg, *Letters,* p. 44.

178 See ibid.: "Then, when the scenes are all rehearsed to the exact tempo of the music, the whole thing will be filmed, after which the film shall be coloured by the painter (or possibly only under his supervision) according to my stage-directions. I think however that mere colouring [will] not suffice for the 'Colour Scene' and other passages where strong colour effects are required. In such passages there would also have to be coloured reflectors casting light on the scene."

been possible in spaces for silent-film projection in the sense of an "Expanded Cinema" *avant la lettre:*

> Regarding the music: The 6 men and the 6 women would of course have to be there, just like the Man. I mean: they would have really to sing and speak. Naturally behind the stage or the orchestra, beside the organ, or in some such place. That can be worked out.[179]

Schoenberg develops his specific musical approach in regard to a necessary abstraction of the sensory experience in the cinema in only apparent contradiction to "what cinema generally aspires to":

> My foremost wish is therefore for something the opposite of what the cinema generally aspires to. I want: *The utmost unreality!* The whole thing should have the effect (not of a dream) but of chords. Of music. It must never suggest symbols, or meaning, or thoughts, but simply the play of colours and forms.[180]

The plan to devise constellations of abstract units that could just as easily appear as colors and forms made Schoenberg into a model and combatant for Kandinsky, whose aesthetic theory of the spiritual in art oscillated between avant-garde theories of knowledge and perception and very occult theosophy. Schoenberg's production model anticipates, more materially and concretely, what will become known a few years later as optical sound under the name of Triergon, a procedure for transforming the intensity fluctuations of light into tension fluctuations of electro-acoustic vibrations. Optical sound is one of the fundamental inventions of the cinema, but it was only implemented in the cinema apparatus in the late 1920s.[181] Schoenberg can only dream of possible transformations of vibrancy relationships among and between the senses.

The elements that Schoenberg lists for the cinematographization of *Die glückliche Hand*, lay the foundations for a spatial unity that requires "*an absolute and*

179 Ibid.

180 Ibid.

181 See Ruschkowski, *Elektronische Klänge*, p. 78, and Friedrich Kittler, "Das Werk der Drei. Vom Stummfilm zum Tonfilm," in Kittler and others (eds.), *Zwischen Rauschen und Offenbarung*, pp. 357–370.

unitary perception," not restricted to the acoustic, in which, like "Swedenborg's heaven, [...] there is no absolute down, no right or left, forward or backward."[182] Schoenberg also qualifies the lack of direction as meaninglessness, in the French sense of *pas de sense*, at least in regard to the human senses: "Just as music never drags a meaning around with it, at least not in the form in which it [music] manifests itself, even though meaning is inherent in its nature, so too this should simply be like sounds for the eye, and so far as I am concerned everyone is free to think or feel something similar to what he thinks or feels while hearing music."[183]

The film by Jean-Marie Straub and Danièle Huillet will proceed from these basic concepts of a media space constituted equally from all elements. The primacy of the surface and materiality of the landscapes or things that continually disturb and smooth out the illusion of a homogeneous cinematic three-dimensionality, in order to constitute a space that asserts its dimensions against all conventions of depth and reverberation, is connected to a particular concept of filmic reality. Siegfried Kracauer has described it as a "material aesthetic"—in contrast to the "formal"—of the cinema, which "is conceivably animated by a desire to picture transient material life, life at its most ephemeral. Street crowds, involuntary gestures, and other fleeting impressions are its very meat." At this point Kracauer also recalls the visualization of the wind, which is so noticeable in MOSES UND ARON, as the cinematic principle par excellence.[184]

For the sound film it should be said that the wind, recorded with good microphones and paradoxically with good wind shields, can also make the rustling of the leaves audible, a noise that despite the uniformity with which its sound emerges from the loudspeakers, is not white but very green: it contains the minimal differentiations with which the varied vegetations have reacted to their historical and climatic surroundings. Straub conceives a decidedly material aesthetic that puts resistance into the realm of ideas when he says:

> First there is the idea. Then there is the matter, and then the form. And there is nothing you can do about that. Nobody can change that! The idea, that's what Eisenstein had when he organized his sequences. He had his

182 Schoenberg, "Composition with Twelve Tones," p. 223.
183 Schoenberg, *Letters*, p. 44.
184 Kracauer, *Theory of Film*, p. xlix.

> montage of attractions ... Then there is the matter. He has to determine the duration of the shots he has stringed together. That is the matter. And what we are doing here is the idea that was on paper, the construction of the film, and that is working on the matter. We work with a matter that resists us and you just can't cut anywhere you like between shots. [...] And through this work, the struggle between the idea and the matter [...] gives rise to the form.[185]

From here it becomes clear how Schoenberg's two different heirs, Adorno and Eisler—Teddie and Hanns, just like Moses and Aron—enter into a debate with his media concepts when they write about film music, in collaboration and antagonism, from their experience of 1940s American media projects. In their reckoning with Hollywood's commercial musical forms they not only reject leitmotif, illustrative background music, motivic-cultural clichés, and the prevalent and cheap "stock music," with its standardized orchestration and its "melody in the highest voice," which reduce the acoustic perceptive space of cinema. Music in film, according to Adorno and Eisler, must remain the basis of the cinematic image in a double sense. It has to open up a space without being mere décor, and it needs to give food for thought:

> Melody of this type is a figure, not a background. But in the motion picture the foreground is the scene projected on the screen, and permanent accompaniment of this scene with a melody in the highest voice must of necessity lead to obscurity, blurring, and confusion. The liberation of harmony and the conquest of a genuine, polyphonic freedom, which is not reduced to academic conventional techniques of imitation, permits the music to function as a background in another sense than that of a mere backdrop of noise, and to add the true melody of the picture, namely the action portrayed, meaningful illustrations and genuine contrasts.[186]

In his early drafts Schoenberg develops a correspondingly polyphonous cinematic space in which opposites can be played off against one another. Adorno

185 Subtitles from Jean-Marie Straub interviewed in Ou gît votre sourire enfoui?, F/P 2001, dir. Pedro Costas, color, 109', minute 14:20.

186 Theodor W. Adorno and Hanns Eisler, *Composing for the Films*, London 2007, p. 27.

and Eisler's text on film composition examines, much closer to score and sounds than Adorno's later criticism of *Moses und Aron*, the element of plurality and the collective in regard to film forms of the "false collective" and the "invisible people," which Gilles Deleuze will also take up in reference to Straub and Huillet.[187] In 1944, when *Composing for the Films* was still in progress, the opera had not yet been performed, but had been composed through to the end of act II between Spain and Brentwood, Los Angeles and then discontinued. In Los Angeles Eisler was one of Schoenberg's last confidants, and took an interest in the work. Therefore, what Eisler and Adorno were discussing at the same time as a problem of political dynamics in the acoustic space can certainly be understood as a comment on *Moses und Aron*:

> For this reason acoustical perception preserves comparably more traits of long bygone, pre-individualistic collectivities than optical perception. At least two of the most important elements of occidental music, the harmonic-contrapuntal one and that of its rhythmic articulation, point directly to a group modeled upon the ancient church community as its only possible inherent "subject." This direct relationship to a collectivity, intrinsic in the phenomenon itself, is probably connected with the sensations of spatial depth, inclusiveness, and absorption of individuality, which are common to all music.[188]

The relationship to the collective, the question of whether a people should be sought for, whether the people should be constituted or enlightened in art, or rather whether the problem of the masses as consumers of cultural productions is on the agenda, is also addressed in Adorno and Eisler's analysis of film music. Hanns Eisler is the one who applies the argumentation of the essay more precisely, and from his own research, to the material relationships in the acoustic and the visual. In 1941, as part of a Rockefeller Foundation research project at the New School for Social Research, he had composed *Fourteen Ways to Describe Rain* for the film REGEN, by Joris Ivens (1929), as a base in the acoustic and political sense. The composition is not only "in honor of Arnold Schoenberg's seventieth

187 Straub und Huillet take up the deliberations of the exiles in Hollywood—Brecht, Eisler, Adorno, Schoenberg—which come together again with Deleuze.

188 Adorno/Eisler, *Composing for the Films*, p. 13.

“Rain” in the tone colors of *Pierrot lunaire*.

birthday";[189] Eisler also adopts Schoenberg's instrumentation for *Pierrot lunaire*: flute, clarinet, violin (alternating with viola), cello, and piano. Eisler puts these "advanced resources," in terms of tone color, and a correspondingly "complex composing technique"[190] to the test on Iven's film, which for its part translates the perception of wind, rain, surfaces of water, and bare, swaying tree trunks into the cinematic. About his treatment Eisler notes: "Measures 43 and 44 accompany a panorama showing clouds over the city and a weak wind that is beginning to blow. Measure 45 accompanies the picture of a detail—branches of a tree shaken by the wind. The music intones a recurrent chorale-like phrase recognizable by its triplet ending, to which the flute, clarinet, and cello join, while a violin figure, with thrills almost like a faint noise, reproduces the wind. In measures 45 and 46, the shaking of the boughs is translated into an incidental piano phrase, which is also important for the piece as a whole, and which, from a formal musical point of view, has the significance of the conclusion of a chorale stanza. Thus the form of the picture determined the musical form down to the smallest detail."[191] Eisler places his music with the image in such a way that the spatial—as the collective of the choral form—and the mobile—leaves and rain—create their own perceptive layers that correspond structurally to the visual perceptive layers of Joris Ivens, but nonetheless in counterpoint to them. In this Eisler follows Schoenberg, who wishes his music to be placed in its own space via cinema, and proceeds from a dramaturgy of light, color, and audible presences and absences that reorganize the prevailing time–space coordinates. In this sense Eisler and Adorno conclude their essay with a plea for objectivity in new compositions for film: "In the prevailing practice, the effect on the spectator is planned while the content of the music is planless. The situation should be reversed. The music should be planned without an eye for the effect, and then the public will get its due."[192] So non-intentionality can be intended after all, despite Adorno's dictum.

The film version of Schoenberg's opera proceeds in this exact sense objectively, and translates the variety of the light and sound space Schoenberg conceived into cinematic parameters: these include the dramaturgy and materiality

189 Ibid., p. 108 (appendix).
190 Ibid., p. 101 (appendix).
191 Adorno/Eisler, *Composing for the Films*, p. 102.
192 Ibid., p. 84.

of light and color, as can be determined by camera optics or the choice of film material—the Eastman Color Negative 5254, from Kodak, which needs a long development time in the lab, slowly differentiating a wide range of contrast, and granted Straub and Huillet their sculptural, haptic lighting effects;[193] they include the organization of the arena space in regard to visibility and audibility and their mutual displacement; and finally they include the concept of abstract and concrete, or, since Straub and Huillet understand their work to be in the tradition of Brecht, alienation, in order to cause the form of the artwork to emerge from a treatment of historical materialities, exactly in the sense of Kracauer's film theory of a redemption of physical reality. The fact that both Schoenberg and Straub/Huillet develop events from the aesthetic of an equally differentiated space produces a further proximity to Kracauer: the form of a film-specific historiography, which particularly in the film MOSES UND ARON makes the visual space, which is stratified culturally, historically, and by media, into the basis for an archaeological analysis.

The cinematic staging is striking at the very beginning in foregoing the darkness the opera requires for its first bars, although this darkness, both for Schoenberg and for cinema as a whole, initiates the transition into a specific directionless or meaningless perceptive space and is a kind of montage standard: the fade-in as a substitute curtain. MOSES UND ARON doesn't provide this initiation. Although Straub and Huillet at first wanted to have the vocalise emerge from the darkness of the movie theater, in the end they decided differently. In her commentary on Gregory Wood's protocol of the shoot, Danièle Huillet corrects Wood's observations: "'Bars 1 to 5, black screen': this was envisaged in the screenplay; but while editing we said to ourselves that it would be better to show Moses with the first note, slowly raising his hands into the image: it is difficult for a performer to carry out such a movement perfectly, so why cut the beginning of it? So shot 10 begins with the first note of the opera."[194]

193 EASTMAN Color Negative film, 7/5254. Tungsten, EI 100. Replaced 5251 (EI 50). Image structure equal to 5251. Discontinued March 1977 (E). OSCAR (41st Academy Year) class I: Scientific or Technical Award. From http://motion.kodak.com/motion/About/Chronology_Of_Film/1960–1979/index.htm (accessed January 28, 2013, no longer online). Despite its discontinuation in 1977, Danièle Huillet remarks that the film was taken out of Kodak's program before the start of the shoot because its development processes were too slow and presumably uneconomical. An anachronistic material for an anachronistic film. See Huillet, "Appunti sul giornale," p. 400.

194 Ibid., p. 412.

The dark theater space isn't used analogously to an opera auditorium to produce the transition into a "different reality." Instead, as Kracauer wanted, reality is pictured as "transient material life [:] at its most ephemeral," and "other fleeting impressions are its very meat."[195] It is remarkable that, of all things, the gesture of the Moses performer begins in the *hors-champ*, and can't initially be seen, but comes into view unexpectedly and thus emphatically refers to the "before" and the "outside" of the field of vision. Not only do Straub and Huillet document formations of cultural and historical stratification, such as pervade gestures and scenes; their filmic method further initiates a process of layering or division in the realm of the visible, so that seeing likewise becomes an analysis of the image and describing of the images becomes an archaeology in the media space. The production of the sounds and sound colors, the optics and shots, the architectural, metrical, non-metrical, and electro-acoustic fields show that Straub and Huillet amplify a decisive aspect of the opera: the differentiation of materialities and their particularities in resistance to the perception of a coherent totality. The whole drama of uniqueness, eternity, omnipresence, invisibility, and inconceivability that provokes Moses is cinematically tied back into images of things and people.

Understanding the film space as a conceptual space in all materiality and form, which doesn't depict but construct, would be the *terre promise* to which the Moses complex is headed. Moses and Aron, like the principles of monotheism and polytheism, belong on both sides. They call for the nomadic, and then again for legalism and the constitution of an apparatus of state, oscillate between smoothness and striation, exist in the film's different acts in the transition between one perceptive space and the other. That a process is initiated here which can only dissolve and resolve in the course of hearing and seeing is already suggested in Schoenberg's still confused conceptual sketches:

> TE58 (41r) People demand law | instead of law give them image | destroy image | Our word reflection of inability | image is – reflection of inability – God's presence | God's eternity.[196]

195 Kracauer, *Theory of Film*, p. xlix.
196 Translated from Schönberg, *Moses und Aron, Entstehungsgeschichte*, p. 165.

Where Schoenberg conceives of the single but "two-or-more-dimensional space" in which everything that occurs has "more than a local effect"[197] and eternity and the present interlock before the law, Straub and Huillet dissolve the space into a material plurality, which in 1974 is even anachronistic, too early, too late for prevailing film aesthetics. In this way they radicalize Adorno's speculative correction, "the caesura was to be decisive,"[198] into a way of thinking that isn't solely constituted in interruption, into a cinematic thinking, in a plurality of optics, materialities, and montages, that continually re-finds and reinvents itself. Filmic caesuras, with Straub and Huillet, are set by the *off* or the pan, for example—always in resistance to cinematic conventions of spatial production.

The aesthetic of opera and film follows an epistemology of unrest. The Moses complex can only be grasped recursively. When the works take up the motif of migration and media as exile and camp they experiment with media-archaeological constellations. This applies both to the architecture of the sound spaces, which experiments with electro-acoustic setups, and to the heterogeneously assembled playing area of the film footage. If Schoenberg insists on allowing noises into the opera, deploying technical media in order to draw attention to the periphery of the musical and aesthetic field in his search for a new law of perception, Straub and Huillet translate this into the media and political conditions of their time. All elements and ensembles are directly addressed to the senses and bodies of the moviegoers. In place of psychological or perspectival effects there is the systematic distribution and redistribution of forces through numerical relationships and topological arrangements. In this sense the Moses complex proceeds historically and media-archaeologically, but refers as it does so to the emptiness and noise that can be heard at its point of origin. In regard to film, Straub and Huillet also develop new procedures that expose and lay open the system of classical cinema, opening eyes and ears to real, visible, and audible spaces and times that are nonetheless interwoven with media.

197 Schoenberg, "Composition with Twelve Tones," p. 220.

198 Adorno, "Sacred Fragment," p. 241.

4. CAESURAS: CINEMATIC PROCEDURES

> The space of modern representation beyond political or religious hegemony is riddled with gaps, with temptations from the invisible and concealed, so that the game has become more complicated or obscure, while at the same time more superficial and simpler.
>
> *Pascal Bonitzer*[1]

When in his opera *Moses und Aron* Schoenberg treats the motifs of the people, the law, migration, and the prohibition of images in musical procedures, Straub and Huillet seek filmic solutions. In doing so they confront themselves more radically with the problem of lack and its aesthetic solution, absence. In the Moses story the people are lacking, the law is lacking, the place of exile is lacking—hence the camp—and images are supposed to be eliminated. In filming the opera Straub and Huillet initially transform conventional ideas of space into the logic of fields. Visual forces and conflicts are then no longer generated through editing and montage. In the film MOSES UND ARON Straub/Huillet develop four procedures in order to establish new cinematic topologies: first, a complex arrangement of *hors-champ* and *off* in both the visual and the acoustic; second, the use of panoramic camera movements, of the pan; third, the abrupt and recursive turning of the filmic onto its materiality in white- and black-image sequences; fourth, the reflection of lack and withdrawal as a dynamization of thinking in a politics of the caesura.

4.1. OFF AND HORS-CHAMP

The imposition of the "only one, infinite, thou omnipresent one, unperceived and inconceivable God," which with the opera and the drama of the calling begins, introducing the motif of the prohibition of images, is staged by Straub

1 Translated from Pascal Bonitzer, *Décadrages. Peinture et cinéma*, Paris 1985, p. 80.

and Huillet through a rather complicated organization and confrontation of different qualities of *off*, *hors-champ*, or *hors-cadre*, through purely spatial cinematic policies.[2] This strategy is presupposed by the organization of the filming in the amphitheater, which is quite differently conceived for the first and second acts. In both cases shots and montage are directed against a central-perspective, stage-like perception of space. For the first act, with its challenge of creating a new and monotheistic legal space, a geometrical structure of filming is envisaged in which all the figures are shot from a central camera position, from which a field of 360° is taken into account. Whereas in the second act, in which a polytheistic image space returns under the aegis of the Golden Calf, shots of people, groups, and individuals are put together from a variety of directions; in the night scenes they are tableaus, the figures modeled in chiaroscuro. Between these two cinematic forms the struggle between Moses and Aron over the question of the prohibition of images essentially plays out in control over the *off*.

The geometrizing deployment of the camera, whose shots organize the first scenes of the opera, and the resulting transformation of the cinematic space into a series of topological relationships has three decisive consequences in terms of a traditional organization of the film space. First, the technique of shot/counter-shot, through which, as diagnosed by André Bazin, "a feeling of being totally present" is conveyed in an illusionary spatial totality, is excluded from the configuration in the amphitheater.[3] Harun Farocki identified the essential law of value of classical montage in shot/counter-shot. The predictability of all stage-like shots, which assembly-line production allows to a certain extent on set, guarantees an initial production-economy surplus value. More importantly, this technique conceals all reality between the angles of shot and counter-shot as a matter of course, thus causing the added value or meaning of all constructed relationships to arise precisely from what is hidden. But the concealment of this hidden space isn't seen. "Des champs-contre-champ, il n'y en a jamais chez nous"—we don't do shot/counter–shot.[4] The auteurs' principal

2 For an extensive study of *hors-champ* see Kayo Adachi-Rabe, *Abwesenheit im Film. Zur Theorie und Geschichte des hors-champ*, Münster 2005.

3 André Bazin, "Theater and Cinema, I and II," in André Bazin, *What is Cinema?*, vol I, trans. Hugh Gray, Berkeley 1967, pp. 76–95: 91.

4 Straub/Huillet, "Conversation," p. 14.

methods include the abandonment of predictable spatial relationships, the marking of visual boundaries, camera movements, and the identification of the constructive laws of cinematic spaces. "It is the authors, authors-authors, who are against the shot/countershot technique."[5] Second, the exclusion of this procedure also removes the illusion of a given space that can simply be "filmed off." Cinema, according to auteur strategies, must always construct space first. And third, the relationships between *off* and *hors-champ* multiply with the arithmetic-nomadic organization of space by the camera, which constructs equal fields of visibility in all directions from a central standpoint. The surplus effect, which produces an imaginary fourth wall, is annulled.

Every concept of cinematic space produces a different idea of what can be regarded as *hors-champ*—as related to the effectiveness of the visual field—*hors-cadre*—geometrically related to the shot—or *off*. Moreover, framings and camera movements give rise to different states of excluded space: in the temporary, in the imaginary, in the optical. Straub and Huillet preclude an absolute *off*, however, which indicates interventions from a better informed, all-knowing, eternal, or otherwise transcendent otherworld or narrative level that exists complementarily to the visible realm, through their shots and sequences, but also through the figures and objects. They present what economic film analysis calls diegesis, a compact narrative in a sealed framework,[6] as an ideology: every saddle, every pair of shoes, every stone altar step breaks out of the fictional into the reality of historical things. To put this the other way around, with Straub/Huillet what is announced from the otherworld of the shot always corresponds to real seen or heard things, which become real elements of the film and can relinquish all forms of spook or spirituality. Every shot produces its own relationships to the things and forces out of frame, even though this outside never becomes straightforwardly conceivable. This strategy has originated

5 Harun Farocki, "Shot/Countershot: The Most Important Expression in Filmic Law of Value" in Susanne Gaensheimer, Nikolaus Schaffhausen (eds.), *Nachdruck/Imprint. Texte/Writings*, Berlin 2001, pp. 86–111: 86. Stephen Heath also remarks on the economic aspects of shot–counter-shot: "... the investment is in the process." Heath, *Questions of Cinema*, p. 53. In this context it is immaterial that Barry Salt, for example, can subdivide the fields of the *contre-champ* into three types. See Barry Salt, "The Early Development of Film Form," in *Film Form*, 1976, no. 1, pp. 91–106: 97f.

6 See Etienne Souriau, "La structure de l'univers filmique et le vocabulaire de la filmologie," in *Revue International de Filmologie*, no. 7–8, Paris 1951, pp. 231–241.

the *terminus technicus* of a "Straubian off-screen space,"[7] from which all kinds of references, connections, and contradictions emerge, and not only dialectically.

The acoustic organization of *hors-champ* and *off* play a particular role in the film of the opera *Moses und Aron*, because Straub and Huillet link the different recording spaces as *on* or *off* and transfer them to an artificial acoustic space that can't be traced back to real architectural spaces or identified in the presence or absence of voices: the entire orchestral music from the Vienna studio, together with the chorus parts recorded in advance, marks an acoustic *off* that is fundamentally distinct from an *hors-champ* of the performers, who quite possibly sing during a take but aren't necessarily caught on camera. By the same token this Viennese *off* can be described as a temporary or media *hors-champ* that re-emerges in the *on* of Alba Fucense through the loudspeakers and headphones. Every *off* is thus drawn into the *hors-champ* or even the *on* of the individual singers. In addition, all the sounds are mixed on set and then put on an equal footing in the single undistinguishable sound space of the movie theater. In Straubian space even *off* and *on* become relative. Between the opera and its film version the acoustic *hors-champ* structure of the film puts together contrary movements of archived timescales. The acoustic storage technology anticipates the future sound space of the soundtrack, which has to be realized on location before it can be perceived in the theater. In this respect filming is also archiving here.[8]

André Bazin's fundamental distinction between the image frame on the one hand as *cadre*—analogous to the "contemplative area" of a painting, as an inward space "oriented so to speak in a different direction"[9]—and on the other as cinematic *cache*—a mobile mask or cover that suggests the direct extension of every visible field into its surroundings while simultaneously withdrawing it in order to endow the image with meaning—relies on the organization of the

7 See Byg, *Landscapes of Resistance*, p. 5. Also Heath, *Questions of Cinema*, p. 56: "Where Godard breaks space, fragments and sets up oppositions in the interest of analysis [...], Straub-Huillet film a unity, sound and image, on and off, that will never 'make a scene'; in both cases, the address is complex, in process, no longer the single and central vision but a certain freedom of contradictions."

8 Derrida, *Archive Fever*, p. 18: "This archival technique has commanded that which in the past even instituted and constituted whatever there was as anticipation of the future."

9 André Bazin, "Painting and Cinema," in André Bazin, *What is Cinema?* trans. Hugh Gray, Berkeley 2005, pp. 164–173: 166.

imagination in the space of geometrical ray optics with an above, below, right, and left. Where this space, like Swedenborg's heaven cited by Schoenberg, has no absolute above, below, right, or left but only relative proportions, *cache* and *cadre*, *off* and *hors-champ* begin to oscillate. The question of the unconceivable is materialized cinematically in this sense by Straub and Huillet. The effect of the non-visible is demystified and becomes an operative space. As precisely as Bazin's distinction is drawn between painting, whose image form is centripetal, and the film screen, whose frame appears to be centrifugal, we should concur with Pascal Bonitzer, who remarked on the basis of his study of *décadrage*—the melting of the frame structure in post-war cinema—that in avant-garde works and films that question the spatial aesthetic of their own art these two functions, *cache* and *cadre*, are made permeable and played out against one another.[10] The painters—you could also say the nomads—among the directors are characterized by their systematic questioning of all knowledge about what can't be seen in their works, and of all techniques that assure this knowledge. The construction and deconstruction of the imaginary is the subject matter. Bonitzer has pointed out that such films follow a poetology of absence and create tension from the discontinuity of the perceived space:

> Straub, Duras, Antonioni are painters in as much as they use unusual framings and those that don't fulfill expectations. This brings something like a non-narrative suspense into cinema. Their gap-filled productions don't provide a complete image in which the fragmented elements come together as a whole, as required by Eisenstein. In their films the tension continues from shot to shot, so that the "narrative" doesn't liquefy; a non-narrative tension that owes its existence to the camera angles, the framing, the selection of objects, and the length of shot, which all establish the tenacity of the gaze [...], in which the exercitation of cinema is strengthened and subject to a silent questioning of its function.[11]

10 See Bonitzer, *Décadrages*, p. 85: Bonitzer writes "sidérer le cadre," melting the frame. And he says that nothing needs to be added to Bazin, apart from the fact that the qualities of *off* and *hors-champ* can reciprocally change one another, which Bazin had actually also shown: "Rien à ajouter à cela, sinon que ces deux propriètés peuvent mutuellement se pervertir, comme d'ailleurs montre Bazin."

11 Ibid., pp. 82–83.

So films by Straub/Huillet, Duras, and Antonioni produce a tension that ruptures the total and continual space of cinema, thus questioning and examining it and discovering within it the explosive charge of a narrative. The aesthetic of the shot in such films is insistently reflected, in order to take the conditions of narrative into account. The aim, as Adorno might have put it, is to search for the "broken outlines"[12] in which a work of art takes a stand against the idea of the absolute within the world. The disjointedness of the world is held open. Straub and Huillet primarily open up historical and historiographical rifts in the image of the world. Like historians or psychoanalysts they perceive non-sense and disjointedness and show up what will not comply. Critical films would be those in which the montage exposes the scars in the image of reality. At the same time the scars mark the moments of intervention: here a people can show itself where it hasn't been expected, and here it can appear, beyond the idea of the masses, as a complex of singularities.

When Bonitzer wrote his text for the *Cahiers du Cinéma* in 1978, in regard to Danièle Huillet—whom, like many critics, he doesn't name—and Jean-Marie Straub, he must have had their most recent film MOSES UND ARON in mind, from 1974.[13] He describes its scenography, which is actually a sceno-stratigraphy, not as *lacuneuse*, incomplete or flawed, but as *lacunaire*, that is essentially constructed from gaps. And in fact all the film's speeches, actions, images, and music revolve around the possible lack of knowledge and want of sight in the double sense: Aron establishes nothing but the "stimulation of the imagination"; Moses demands "pure law of thought." Attractive fantasies or radical inconceivability, the chiastic positions of the protagonists, are dealt with cinematically as questions of *off* and *hors-champ*.

In order to underline the difference between the concept of a *central* absence on the one side and the complex, "lacunaire" images of Straub and Huillet on the other, let us return to Deleuze's differentiation of the *cadre*, which he describes as the constitution of a "set which has a great number of parts, that is of elements, which themselves form sub-sets."[14] This ensemble structure,

12 "Broken outlines," writes Adorno of Schoenberg's opera, are "ciphers of a supreme, unnameable truth." See Adorno, "Sacred Fragment," p. 226.

13 The next film, VON DER WOLKE ZUM WIDERSTAND [From the Clouds to the Resistance], was only produced in 1978/1979.

14 Gilles Deleuze, *Cinema 1. The Movement-Image*, trans. Hugh Tomlinson and Barbara Habberjam, Minneapolis 1986, p. 12.. For Deleuze's concept of the ensemble, see the differentiation

which exactly corresponds to the complex visual composition in Moses und Aron, develops its own forms of an *off* and an *hors-champ*, a non-visible field, in correlation with the things and figural constellations that become visible within the image: "This is the first sense of what we call the out-of-field: when a set is framed, therefore seen, there is always a larger set, or another set with which the first forms a larger one, and which can in turn be seen, on condition that it gives rise to a new out-of-field, etc."[15] Every image field organizes its optically selected ensemble, and therefore also the vanishing point of the *hors-champ* it produces. In this context Deleuze sets *hors-champ* more explicitly against an absolute, unconnected *off* indiscriminately produced in the montage. But this difference, as between *cache* and *cadre*, becomes permeable and brings about another system that is its outside—even if, and not only in science fiction, it is the universe.

In accordance with the bond that links the image ensemble and *hors-champ*, Noel Burch's blithe remark that every *off* or *hors-champ* is "purely imaginary"[16] should instead read that in their direct dependency on the visible, *off* and *hors-champ* are "strictly imaginary," compel imaginary relationships according to the laws of the cultural, historical, and material effect of the field. Viewers organize the space beyond the frame of the *cadre* not simply according to the points of view of the ray optics but according to the desire to produce imaginary wholes in the image: the body to the arm holding the jug, or the look that answers another, or the sky above the horizon in the desert. Or, to put it less psychoanalytically

between element, individual, and ensemble as levels of the complexity of technical objects in Gilbert Simondon, *Du mode d'existence des objets techniques*, Paris 1958, p. 15. While the technical object remains subordinate and with the coming of industrialization enters, as *individual*, into competition with human activity, demands the conquest and domination of nature, and encourages technocracies, as technical *ensemble* in the 20th century it can regulate the chaos of the world on the basis of information theory in solidarity with the living: "The machine is the thing through which the human being opposes the death of the universe." The transfer of this concept of the ensemble to cinematic images is probably one of the most important aspects of Gilles Deleuze's film books.

15 See Deleuze, *The Movement Image*, p. 16: In itself, or as such, the out-of-field already has two qualitatively different aspects: a relative aspect by means of which a closed system refers in space to a set which is not seen, and which can in turn be seen, even if this gives rise to a new unseen set, on to infinity; and an absolute aspect by which the closed system opens on to a duration which is immanent to the whole universe, which is no longer a set and does not belang to the order of the visible. *Deframings [decadrages] which are not 'pragmatically' justified refer to precisely this second aspect as their raison d'etre.*"

16 Burch, *Theory of Film Practice*, p. 21.

and rather in the terms of gestalt theory: the *hors-champ* obeys the law of the field, which suggests certain continuities of simple shape and form.[17] When this imaginary or field-logical *hors-champ* is frustrated, we notice, murmuring, that something is missing. *Lacune*. Or specifically in Deleuze's example: the people. In the cinema of Straub/Huillet—but heaven knows not only there—we ourselves have to construct the space in which a people can appear. Straub and Huillet also incidentally allow us to notice that our own subjectivity, the I and we of the viewers, depends on the image and how it is ensembled.[18]

In their organization of the image as field and effect, Straub and Huillet play out the conflict between conceivability and inconceivability cinematically. In contrast to the economics of shot/countershot, where the exactly complementary and calculable counterpart of the visible may be supposed in the non-visible *hors-champ*, the ensemble compositions refer to various elements and qualities of the non-visible. The logic of *hors-champ* can be formed and varied according to figural constellations, lighting conditions, diagonals, horizon lines, camera movements, and focal distances. Always against the background of an emptiness. There are parallels to this in Schoenberg's score, when in Moses' part, although his entry is in no way expected, the composer insistently includes pauses, instead of leaving out the line, as is usual when the singer is *tacet*.[19]

By implication, in reference to Straub/Huillet, we should ask more radically whether the Moses story, as one that poses the question of visibility and inconceivability from the very beginning, should be thought of as a "pure" montage of *off* spaces, a film whose plot can only be assembled from *hors-champ* and *off*, whose action takes place in the negativity of the non-visible, from which the scenes and images of the film as we see it ensue.

17 See Rudolf Arnheim, *Film as Art*, Berkeley 1957, pp. 8–33.

18 At this point it is not even necessary to draw on the American film theory—schooled psychoanalytically by Lacan and structurally and semiologically polished by Christian Metz—which boldly states: "The subject is an effect of the signifier in which it is represented, stood in for, taken place (the signifier is the narration of the subject)". See Heath, *Questions of Cinema*, p. 52. Concise too is Kaja Silverman, *The Acoustic Mirror. The Female Voice in Psychoanalysis*, Bloomington-Indianapolis 1988, pp. 194–236. Silverman writes: "As the preceding discussion indicates, suture is not so much one theory as a group of overlapping theories. Whereas for some theoreticians it can be isolated in the shot/reverse shot formation, for others it is inherent in all of the operations which constitute narrativity. However, the theoreticians of suture agree that it provides the agency whereby the subject emerges within discourse, and (at least ideally) takes up a position congruent with the existing cultural order." Ibid., p. 235f.

19 See Schönberg, *Moses und Aron*, score I, act I, bars 178–180.

The prohibition of images is relocated to the cinema as an *off* debate. Nonetheless this isn't outside of experience. The film MOSES UND ARON tests its viewers' perception right at the start, when Danièle Huillet, reads aloud the report of 3,000 murdered men from the page of the Luther Bible shown on screen. All at once the combination of text, image, and voice examines how the imagination functions, whether this information is used for self-information or self-deception, whether historical memories arise or rather images of current terror, or whether terror can never actually be visualized and must remain trauma.

In this historiographical excavation Straub and Huillet discover their own position not as an overview but as mobile, for one thing. Filming history means filming latencies, shifts, and omissions. Danièle Huillet thinks about this in her historical sketch: "The part of Genesis that tells of the Patriarchs comes from three sources of the Hexateuch, which need to be differentiated: the Jahvist, mainly written between 850 and 760, the Elohist, between 800 and 760, and the Priestly Source, between approximately 550 and 450. Because the history of the Patriarchs took place after the chronology of Genesis around 2000 BC there is a time span of 1,200 to 1,500 years between our documents and the period they describe, i.e. the same time span as between us and the Merovingian epoch."[20] The historicity of the Moses complex crystallizes between times. Historiography, always a medium of some sort, reconstructs relationships and interests that allow an understanding of even one's own epoch as the symptom of past struggles and boundaries. Cinema deals with this between the shots, *on*, *off*, *hors-champ*.

Nowhere in the film is the *on/off* structure merely an illustration of Schoenberg's text and his remarks on conceivability and inconceivability. The montage itself operates as a reflection on the prohibition of images. After Aron's question in bars 180–181: "[…] kannst du lieben, was du dir nicht vorstellen darfst? [can you worship what you dare not even conceive?]" comes Moses' angry *on* reply, in a very close-up shot with a 100 mm lens, shocking in its abrupt frontality, extreme presence, proximity, and exclusivity: "Darfst? Unvorstellbar, weil unsichtbar, weil unüberblickbar, weil unendlich, weil ewig, weil allgegenwärtig, weil allmächtig. Nur einer ist allmächtig [Dare not? Not conceived because unseen, can never be measured, everlasting, eternal, because ever present, and almighty]." Here everything easily imagined ceases to function.

20 Translated from Huillet, "Kleiner historischer Exkurs," p. 194.

But the physiognomic presence of the face in close-up jumps out of the stage-like events in the amphitheater, and the *off* that forms in the imagination is one of faces, human faces, but above all male faces, furious in the face of an all-powerful *off*.

The next shot is exactly complementary; also filmed with a 100 mm lens and in close-up, but of Aron's right profile. Not the shot/countershot of a dialogue but a negotiation before an indeterminate third party. While the Patriarch brothers debate about morality and essentiality as different realms of the mind, Moses once again speaks from the *off*, which, following the previous *off*, is not singular but one of the lacking many, the absent multitude.

Only at bar 208 does Moses become visible once again in a 100 mm telephoto medium shot—and thus finite, present, and powerless, at least in terms of language. His hands are slightly raised; he holds his shepherd's crook in his right hand and for once sings: "Reinige dein Denken, lös es von Wertlosem, weihe es Wahrem [Purify your thinking. Free it from worthless things. Let it be righteous]."[21] Not only as an answer to Hellenism but also after the varied formations of the *off* spaces in the previous sequences, it can be seen that Straub/Huillet's film of the opera transforms this "purification" into a "smoothing" of the space. This is an equal probability of the elements in the ensemble, which allows the opening up of new surroundings, new outside fields, new conceivabilities as soon as thinking has freed itself from conventional structures and automatic associations like shot/countershot as the cinematic Oedipus complex. The "unerbittliches Denkgesetz [law of thought irresistible]," of which Moses speaks, compels the liberation of the imagination.

Straub and Huillet fundamentally question an absolute *off*, that is a space not connected by visual peripheries, elements, or vectors as a utopian aspect of film. They systematically put the *hors-champ* and the relativized *off* to work as heterotopias, as utopias to be actually realized, and cinematically realized, as they press into the image from all sides. It's characteristic that in relation to Moses and Aron *off* and *hors-champ*, utopia and heterotopia, are mutually dependent and so form the basis of their war of images.

This becomes clear in the first act of the fight for image and law as a power struggle between the patriarchal brothers. In shot 26 of act I Moses is first filmed at close range with the very short focal length of an 18.5 mm lens, frontal in

21 Schönberg, *Moses und Aron*, score I, act I, bars 208–214.

his disillusionment, rejected by the entire people, having failed in his mission: “Bleib uns fern mit dem Allmächtigen! [Keep away with this almighty!]” sings the chorus in a long shot, and then stridently calls: “Wir wollen durch ihn nicht befreit sein! [Through him we do not want our freedom!].” Because the people can’t see the god Moses has announced, can’t imagine and certainly can’t and won’t conceive of something as *off*, they suspect deception and threat. At this point of disillusioned utopia Arnold Schoenberg gives clear stage directions: “Chorus in motion: part of them press Moses and Aaron forward; the others press upon them or they leave” (act I, bars 621–622). Straub and Huillet do it differently, showing Moses in a medium-length shot very alone with a lowered gaze. Then he raises his eyes to the distance and addresses the omnipresent and unconceivable *off*: “Allmächtiger,” says Moses in *Sprechstimme*, “meine Kraft ist zu Ende: Mein Gedanke ist machtlos in Arons Wort! [Almighty one, now my strength is exhausted, and my thought become pow’rless in Aaron’s word]” (act I, bars 623–626). In this sequence the caesura between knowing and seeing, thought and language, structure and material opens up in every detail. Moses has renounced all relationships apart from the one with the other world to which he speaks, and in which the viewers are suddenly sitting in their cinema seats. *Off* is there. Here. Cinematic absence.

At this point Schoenberg demands action, a show-down: “Moses more and more in the background. Aron, arms raised and fists clenched, moves menacingly toward Moses” (act I, bars 627–629). In Straub/Huillet’s film nothing happens at first, while six solo voices, in unison with instruments, call “Aron!” up to a single stroke on the edge of a drum. Then Aron, while the camera remains on the still broken face of Moses, sings a downwardly and then upwardly leaping sequence that starts with top A and ends on the high B-flat: “Schweige! Das Wort bin ich und die Tat [Silence! The word is mine and the deed].” When Schoenberg states “He tears the rod from Moses’ hand,” Straub/Huillet translate this into a complementary inversion of *off* and *hors-champ*, utopia and heterotopia: Aron swiftly reaches out of his finite *hors-champ*, out of his other space, into the shot of the abstracted Moses portrait, in which “the word is lacking,” and grabs the rod, while the camera reverses quickly so that now both brothers can be seen in competition for the rod of deed. The people sing in confusion. After an abrupt cut Aron is seen alone, the rod in his fist, but he immediately throws it out of his *cache* box and calls: “Dieser Stab führt euch! Seht, die Schlange! [Moses’ rod leads you. Look, a serpent!].” And indeed cameraman Renato Berta gives a cobra almost two minutes to creep through the next shot.

Aron quite simply ignores all frames and *caches*, intervenes into the empty space of Moses, and, in this series of cuts and violations, opens up a new space of miracles in which proof is given of divine apparition. "Die Schlange wächst! [The serpent grows!]" sings the chorus in horror. In this, although the voices acoustically come from the *off*, one might say that they place themselves in the poison-threatened *hors-champ*, but at the same time comment on the logic of the screen depth and keep the vanishing point into the *off* open. Straub and Huillet underline this when landscape and sky from outside the amphitheater are seen for the first time through the northern *parodos* behind the chorus. Aron, meanwhile, explicitly asserts his control over this incorporated, real—though only visible as filmed—sidling *hors-champ*, which replaces Moses' silent, empty *off*, as his own elastic but all the more compelling form of legalism: "In Moses' Hand ein starrer Stab: Das Gesetz in meiner Hand die bewegliche Schlange: die Klugheit. Stellt euch so, wie sie euch zwingt! [In Moses' hand a rigid rod: this, the law. In my own hand the most supple of serpents: discretion. Now stand so, as it commands!]" (act I, bars 653–665).

The space of Moses, in his wordless world of pure thought, which evidently can't be conveyed or shown to the people, "Not conceived because unseen, can never be measured"—like the rules of the game in Straub/Huillet's staging—and the space of Aron, a cosmos of word and deed, of visions and visible wonders; according to the logic of the laws of thought of the figures, these two different spaces don't share a common *hors-champ* or a common *off*. What the pan or cut visualize as miracle and sign with Aron is nothing but desert and emptiness in the images of Moses. The conflict between Moses and Aron becomes a struggle for control over possible connections, through the heterotopian *hors-champ* and visibility in the film in general: through cuts Aron will transform the rod into a snake, a healthy hand into a leprous hand, water in a jug into blood; before our very eyes he will control the merry magic of illusionary funfair cinema and thus encourage the people to rebel against the pharaoh: "Ein Wunder erfüllt uns mit Schrecken: Der Stab, der sich wandelt zur Schlange, zeigt Aron als Herrn dieses Volkes. Wie groß ist die Macht dieses Aron! [A marvel has filled us with terror. The rod that did change to a serpent shows Aaron as lord of this people. How great is the might of this Aaron!]" sings the chorus. But from the point of view of the space of Moses the colorful heterotopia of Aron's wizardry immediately tips into a dull utopian *off*, into an otherworld, into transcendence, into a trap for the people. The people don't know that the leprosy is not only a sign but the signal of a struggle, that of the image-makers against the image-breakers. Moses is attacked by this magic.[22]

Straub and Huillet allow the series of miracles its comic aspect when, before Aron transforms the Nile water into blood, they have him quit the frame with a decisive step to the left into an *off* that is the shared production sphere of film and wonder: not one that is discredited as hocus-pocus, though, but a culturally and technically based cinematic work on the material of things. For then follows a close-up of a jug and Aron's hands, which hold the handles in such a way as to initiate a pouring movement that has been associated with the jug form for thousands of years. From this jug Aron pours a heavy dark liquid, while he sings: "Nein: Ihr irrt euch nicht: Was ihr jetzt seht, ist Blut! Versteht ihr das? [No, you are not wrong. What you now see is blood. What does this mean?]." A question, incidentally, that was always at the core of cinema ethics as the transubstantiation of light into matter.[23] At the same time a short, mysterious harp interlude can be heard in which overtones sound—Schoenberg calls for "Harmonics (sound as notated)"[24]—the resonation of associated frequencies that produces a new musical space following its own logic. Schoenberg's music, too, operates with a resonant *off*. So for the acoustic we should translate: "No, you are not wrong. What you hear is a new sound space. What does this mean?" But although with acoustic help and in the sense of visual logic Aron invades the space of Moses, he will still be unable to lay a finger on its specific *hors-champ* and *off*.

This is again radicalized in the first scene of act II. Aron stands silently in the *on* for almost two minutes, his gaze lowered, while the chorus pummel and threaten him from the *off*: "Vierzig Tage, wie lange noch? Vierzig Tage warten wir auf Moses und noch immer weiß keiner Recht und Gesetz! [Forty days now! When will this end? Forty days now we have awaited Moses, and still no one

22 See Assmann, *Moses the Egyptian*, p. 42: "Idolatry is conceived of as a mental aberration, not as a bodily disease. Leprosy is the metaphor used by the other side, the iconists, in order to characterize the 'iconoclasts'."

23 See Ute Holl, "'Ich kann beim besten Willen kein Blut sehen.' Gesellschaftsvertrag und rote Farbe in Godards WEEK-END," in Anja Lauper (ed.), *Transfusionen. Blutbilder und Biopolitik in der Neuzeit*, Zurich 2005, pp. 243–266.

24 Schönberg, *Moses und Aron*, score I, act I, bar 877.

knows either law or command!]" (act II, bars 48–59). This doesn't simply come from the *hors-champ*, from outside the frame, but from a "Straubian off-screen space," because in this desert-like film there is no central perspective, no overview of events, and because only the relationship is important, the tension between attitudes. In their insecure state, in their camp, the people demand vivid gods and an effective law.

Straub/Huillet couldn't have expressed more clearly the crises of all contemporary peoples looking for something other than their chains. Aron, alone, must find a solution in this constellation, and he precisely formulates Schoenberg's intellectual concept, which we simultaneously experience in the film or movie theater: "Erwartet die Form nicht vor dem Gedanken! Aber gleichzeitig wird sie da sein [You cannot expect form before idea, for together they'll make their appearance]." Straub and Huillet show that form and idea don't simply appear from anywhere; they have to be thought out first. Concept and images belong to a single resistant and intractable process.

As a counter-image to the cloying jubilation of the people, who are happy to believe Aron's trickster argument that the Egyptians are easy to overcome, and for whom the retransformed water in the jug is pledge enough of freedom—"Doch was Pharao bleibt, seht her, ist wieder das klare Wasser des Nil. Und darin wird er untergehn! [What for Pharaoh remains, look here, is once more the Nile's clear water alone. And therein he is sure to drown!]"—at bar 918 of the opera there is an abrupt cut to the real waters of the Nile, a long pan across the river in 16 mm material,[25] whose grain, coloration and spatiality sets it apart from the rest of the film. As a literal *hors-champ* of the film so far, this pan over the Nile is the film's first image from *outside* the sandy ground of the arena and links the freedom of the people with a shot showing that it can never be a matter of blank demands for freedom, of territory, promises, and occupation, not simply of settlement, but that this freedom requires the knowledge, cultural technologies, and experience of cultivating the land. More than in 1974, the year 2014 has clearly shown that it is water that will and must be fought for, and that people are deprived of it. The region is karstified, dry, and brutal, but it

25 The footage was shot in May 1973 near Luxor, on a mountain that Straub and Huillet reached by bicycle. They filmed without permission, and therefore with a small 16 mm Beaulieu, but the film's surface quality supports the logic of its imagery. See Huillet, "Appunti sul giornale," p. 409.

contains the possibility of settlement through cultivation. Straub and Huillet set this image against state administration; here they juxtapose the smooth space of the desert with the mapped boundaries of the Middle East.

This renewed trap, Moses against Aron, now affects the eye of the viewer: anyone seeing these images of the Nile as a utopian *off* simply proves that they are looking over from the cinema-wonder-Aron space and relegating a rebellion into the realm of the impossible. The Nile images are no mere idea. They observe the real possibilities of settlement and fertility in this region, a post-Six Day War view that isn't illusion but archaeology and disillusionment. In a material way the visible landscape of the Nile delta binds all the promises of happiness and victory given by the liberation discourses, and anchors the Moses story in the concrete cultural and social conditions that Jean-Marie Straub and Danièle Huillet had studied during their journey through Egypt in 1972.[26]

The visible structures at the basis of all struggles over the conceivability or unconceivability of what is to come is linked to tactile, visual, material, and substantive tangibilities in the image. Cultural techniques are interconnected with bodies. The smoothed space, initially geometrically surveyed as an organization of distances in the amphitheater, is compressed in the course of the film's *on*, *off*, and *hors-champ* constructions, and the various spaces and layers are concentrated into an explosive reality. In this filmic texture—which, to use the same metaphor, is not woven from shot and countershot, but from shot and weft—the story of the Exodus and Schoenberg's opera from the 1930s are only particularly bright threads. The tradition of knowledge in things and their use, as Danièle Huillet notes in her report, are as much a part of the film as the migratory movements of the 1970s and their capital flows.[27]

26 See ibid., p. 407.

27 Translated from ibid., p. 408: "We bought the dromedary saddle from a farmer in Luxor for 10,000 lira. The saddle was all that was left to him, as he had been compelled to sell his dromedary months before, and he didn't know whether he would be able to raise the money some day to buy another one. An Egyptian friend helped us with this purchase. He understood a little French because he had worked with French archaeologists (who, in both Luxor and Alba Fucense, only here the archaeologists are Belgian and the farmers Italian, hire farmers for two months for their excavations; when the archaeologists stay away—which is a catastrophe, as it amounts to the drying up of a source of money, and the farmers of Alba Fucense have as little ready money as those in Luxor—30,000 people leave Abruzzo every year in order to look for work in the north or abroad)."

The pan pauses above the wide Nile delta when the chorus sings of the Promised Land flowing with milk and honey. It continues over the karstified mountains beyond the riverbed when the singing invokes the strength of people against the Pharaoh. These images foil anything visionary, all the film's visuality, and form a concentrated, entangled *hors-champ* to the opera, its aesthetic, and the film itself. *Moses und Aron* takes place in the Middle East, that heterotopia of Europe, the *hors-champ* that Europe will have desired. In the early 1970s the liberated colonies launched their countershots; today Europe is experiencing being the heterotopia of the others, to which its own is being played back as a destructive difference. Heterotopia means studying the *hors-champ* as one's own other. "Why did we want Italy from the very beginning? Because Schoenberg was Viennese, his music eminently European, but at the same time pervaded by the vision of an astonishing realism that you can discover in the Orient—in Africa (for us Egypt)."[28] Jewish exile, which Schoenberg in fact planned in Africa, has to become heterotopia, realized utopia, with real people who are already there, not in the *off* of the Mediterranean. Geographical and geopolitical strata are laid over the elliptical arena of Alba Fucense from the realism of the Egyptian material. On the other hand the amphitheater in Abruzzo contains knowledge from the entire Mediterranean region. The politics of the *cadre* as ensemble shows which relationships overshoot the image frame, and how the *hors-champ* looks at us and concerns us: no *off*, nowhere.

4.2. PANORAMA POLITICS: ABOUT THE PAN

The missing people in the film Moses und Aron corresponds in the first scene to a particular cinematic form: the pan. The long pan across the Nile later connects the idea of the people with a view in which its own situation is bound to a responsibility for the settled land. If it initially seems far-fetched to link politics and film techniques, and then a politics of the people to a movement like the pan, of all things, we should remember that cinema was understood as a social machine from the beginning. It was declared the eye of the social by Vertov, and by the theory of the cinematic apparatus a power structure that puts constraints

28 Ibid., p. 401.

Pan across the Nile, scanning the face of the earth.

on our seeing. In MOSES UND ARON Straub and Huillet use extensive pans for the first time in their work. In this they take up the opera's motif of the prohibition of images rather than Schoenberg's music.

After Moses has responded to the call from what the score describes as the "Voice from the Burning Bush" at the beginning of the opera, and after he has rejected, with all available means, the mission to lead the people out of captivity, his final argument in this dialogue of responsibility, "Meine Zunge ist ungelenk, ich kann denken, aber nicht reden [But my tongue is not flexible. Thought is easy; speech is laborious]," is interrupted by the sudden start of a long pan, which according to Danièle Huillet's description encompasses about 300°, a dimension that is inapplicable to any film image, for with the panoramic pan the entire visual space on the screen is transformed.

Proceeding from the close-up of Moses, the image transitions into a physiognomic flatness and scans the "Gesicht der Erde," as described by Balázs,[29] and that of the sky, until 34 bars later the camera movement comes to a standstill in an almost symmetrical shot of the two peaks of Monte Velino. The pan baffles all spatial perception, and stretches the landscape into a long panoramic band. Three-dimensionality is cancelled by the illusionary two-dimensionality of the cinema screen, as Arnheim said,[30] and produces its own intensity. This pan is

29 See Béla Balázs, *Early Film Theory: Visible Man and The Spirit of Film*, trans. Rodney Livingstone, ed. Erica Carter, New York/Oxford 2010: "There are films [...] that do show us the face of the earth," pp. 39–51:41.

30 See Arnheim, *Film as Art*, p. 11ff.

not the moving equivalent of an overview of an Arcadian landscape beyond the amphitheater, which, at least in the imagination of theater scholars, would have tempted the audience of the Greek tragedies to superimpose fiction and reality.[31] Straub and Huillet's filmic pan above and beyond the boundaries of the theater space strings the elements of the landscape together and counts them off, additional to events, letting them pass by. The panorama becomes nomadic here, or, more exactly, transforms the landscape into a nomadic space.

Without cuts, and hence with the same 75 mm lens that filmed the semi-profile of the Moses performer, the pan commences with an image that according to a photographic rhetoric belongs to the convention of the portrait. It can be said, however, that in this pan the landscape, too, is portrayed, is physiognomically photographed. But the shot, whose optics remain unchanged after the close-up, is primarily an extreme example of the production of an "any-space-whatever" in the sense of Gilles Deleuze's classification of the cinematic image. Deleuze updates the connection between affect and close-up as the fundamental transformation of a culture that Béla Balázs described as "the great score of

31 See Bernd Seidensticker, *Das Antike Theater*, Munich 2010, p. 22ff., and Ulf Heuner, *Tragisches Handeln in Raum und Zeit. Raum-zeitliche Tragik und Ästhetik in der sophokleischen Tragödie und im griechischen Theater*, Stuttgart 2001. "In the Greek theater, not only did the audience have the possibility of raising their eyes at any time and looking out at the surroundings, but their attention, as the texts at least suggest, was almost forced onto the background by the drama on the stage, [...] For while the eye is directed to a performance space on which something takes place fictionally but is not shown, the fiction breaks and the real dimension of the space obtrudes. In other words, the openness of the theater causes the theatrical fiction to self-destruct in the perception of the audience." Translated from p. 129.

the polyphony of life,"[32] which film lets us read. When, as Deleuze shows, the close-up of the face produces the "pure building material of the affect," delivering its "hyle,"[33] it takes possession of the world with the dynamic of this affect and its inhuman priming above and beyond all space-time coordinates, but only after it has torn these to pieces: "Although the close-up extracts the face (or its equivalent) from all spatio-temporal co-ordinates, it can carry with it its own space-time a scrap of vision, sky, countryside or background."[34] This tearing out of elements and their renewed constellation in unforeseen ensembles is carried out by Straub/Huillet's slow and steady pan, which establishes new visual contexts with every movement, while knocking down and tearing up old connections.

In Deleuze's systematics an "any space whatever" such as this actually belongs to an earlier form of the moving image, in which the affect absorbs the lost time between action and reaction in order to develop a tremendous heterogeneity of space. Deleuze doesn't relate the formation of such a space to modifications through camera movements, but to the editing, the montage, which draws its potential from this affect structure. When he insists that this any-space-whatever in no way exists beyond space and time but rather as a "singular space," a connection can be made to the strategy of Moses und Aron, in which historicity brings about a particular, peculiar, maverick space-time

32 Balázs, *Early Film Theory*, p. 38.
33 Deleuze, *The Movement-Image*, p. 103.
34 Ibid., p. 108.

stratification of its own that is neither linear nor metrical but relates to historical times and spaces. When Deleuze adds that this space "which has merely lost its homogeneity, that is, the principle of its metric relations or the connection of its own parts, so that the linkages can be made in an infinite number of ways,"[35] he locates it in proximity to smooth space and emphasizes once again that this space of virtual connections is "grasped as pure locus of the possible,"[36] but is singular and qualitatively specific at every point. Deleuze calls this type of space tactile, and his examples relate to forms of distortion through a non-metrical, smoothened surface structure. As an example of a space that exhibits its potential qualities as *particular*, Deleuze incidentally names Joris Iven's film REGEN, for which Hanns Eisler composed *Fourteen Ways to Describe Rain* "in honor of Arnold Schoenberg's seventieth birthday."[37]

The nettlesome thing about putting the pan into the context of "any-space-whatever," however, is that according to Deleuze "the law of this space is fragmentation."[38] This too Straub and Huillet dissolve. The transformation into the tactile, which is accomplished by this first long pan in their film, becomes more plausible against the background of a short history of the cinematic pan. Since the early cinema it has been one of the techniques that incorporates cin-

35 Ibid., p. 109.

36 Ibid.

37 See Adorno/Eisler, *Composing for the Films*, and Ute Holl, "Vierzehn Versuche, eine Oberfläche zu beschreiben," in Doris Kern and Sabine Nessel (eds.), *Unerhörte Erfahrungen. Texte zum Kino. Festschrift für Heide Schlüpmann zum Geburtstag*, Frankfurt/Main 2008, p. 341–366.

38 Deleuze, *The Movement Image*, p. 108.

ematic self-reference.[39] In 1932 Rudolf Arnheim, himself on his way into exile, pointed out that the cinematic eye of camera movements causes a rift in psychophysical perception, palpable even as a rift in the body of the viewer and thus as giddiness: "This giddiness is caused by the eyes participating in a different world from that indicated by the kinesthetic reactions of the body, which is at rest."[40] Arnheim expands on this: "If the camera was rotated while the picture was being shot, the bookcase, table, window, and door will proceed across the screen when the picture is projected; it is they which are moving. For since the camera is not a part of the spectator's body like his head and his eyes, he cannot tell that it has been turned. He can see the objects on the screen being displaced and at first is led to assume that they are in motion."[41] The perception of space in the cinema is particularly distinct from that of everyday perception in that " [f]resh objects are continually appearing within the frame of the picture and then disappearing again, but for the eyes there is an unbroken space-continuum through which the gaze wanders at will."[42] With the pan, says Arnheim, cinema puts two new relativizations into optical space: that of moments, in as much as it can't be distinguished whether the camera, the object, or the background are in motion, and that of spatial coordinates, as the spatial relationships produced by the camera, such as "up and down,"[43] can't be ascertained through physical perception. These two relativizations are admittedly themselves anchored in a cultural history of the pan.

Panoramic seeing, from which in English and French, at least, the pan (or "panoramique") derives its name, is a nineteenth-century transformation of the gaze, a "transformation of landscapes and oceans into panoramas,"[44] which, not least through the experience of train travel, is based on a swift movement that blurs the contours and annuls the depth structure of space. Exactly as Arnheim describes, this seeing relativizes both movement—whether the eye or the landscape is moving is indistinguishable in a train—and attitude to spatial coordinates. The panorama, as with the view from a train carriage, is charac-

39 See Guido Seeber, *Der Trickfilm*, vol. II of the series *Der praktische Kameramann* (1927), *Schriftenreihe des deutschen Filmmuseums*, Frankfurt/Main 1979, pp. 160–161.

40 Arnheim, *Film as Art*, p. 30.

41 Ibid. p. 30f.

42 Ibid., p. 31.

43 Ibid., p. 32.

44 Translated from Dolf Sternberger, *Panorama oder Ansichten vom 19. Jahrhundert*, Hamburg 1946, p. 200.

teristically a sideways movement: the landscape rolls by as if on a long conveyor belt; it becomes a sequence of scenes, in which, according to Gastineau's "synthetic philosophy of the eye" allows the "indiscriminate" assimilation of "the distinguishable,"[45] and thus, parallel to the epoch of the first forms of industrial production, it becomes serial.[46] A perceivable foreground disappears in favor of a gaze placed by the apparatus and before which the landscape and its foreground is transformed into a "geographic space" characterized by sameness.[47] The person seeing panoramically steps out of an "'overall space that connects proximity and remoteness. [...] The panoramic gaze, in contrast to traditional seeing à la Ruskin, no longer belongs to the same space as the perceived objects."[48] The person seeing panoramically from the train carriage has the experience of being separate from his gaze, and instead encounters a gaze that comes from outside, from the open field, as his own. Only on reflection—or escaping back to a book—can he evade this giddiness. Only through a caesura or shock, which is also a part of rail travel, can this seeing be understood as a relationship to oneself, in order to extract from it the meaning that traveling no longer offers.

This structure of a separation of scenery and viewer, in which the gaze expresses a self-relationship, became a general experience in the panoramas that schooled a new way of seeing in the cities of the nineteenth century.[49] This enables the restructuring of seeing and the visible in the early nineteenth century to be understood in the context of the *coup d'œil* of military comprehension, in which at the moment of danger seeing resorts to the sudden "mental" grasp of material contiguities from the fog of a space-time continuum, and at great speed, as *survol*, flyover. For the Flemish School Allan Sekula has described

45 Translated from Wolfgang Schivelbusch, *Geschichte der Eisenbahnreise. Zur Industrialisierung von Raum und Zeit im 19. Jahrhundert*, München 1977, p. 59.

46 See Theweleit's chapters "Stones, Cans and Roses" and "Geist in der Flasche," in Klaus Theweleit, *Buch der Könige*, vol. 2y: *Recording angels' mysteries*, Frankfurt/Main 1994, p. 430ff.

47 See Schivelbusch, *Eisenbahnreise*, p. 51ff. See also Thomas Kleinspehn, *Der flüchtige Blick. Sehen und Identität in der Kultur der Neuzeit*, Hamburg 1989, p. 241ff.

48 Translated from Schivelbusch, *Eisenbahnreise*, p. 61.

49 In this context Lorenz Engell has emphasized that the panorama is the complement, and in no way the equivalent, to the experience of "outside": "The vivid, sensory and odd experience in the panorama contrasts with the concentrated and chaotically fragmented experience of the environment, but at the same time the extension of the gaze into the quasi horizon does not exclude the outside urban world, but concludes it, completes it, and rounds it off." Translated from Lorenz Engell, "Erzählung. Historiographische Technik und kinematographischer Geist," in Eva Hohenberger and others (eds.), *Die Gegenwart der Vergangenheit. Dokumentarfilm, Fernsehen und Geschichte*, Berlin, 2003, pp. 247–275: 261.

the panoramic as related to the martial: "Expansive panoramic space is always haunted by the threat of collapse or counter-expansion. Thus the panorama is always implicitly or explicitly militarized: the net can close in from the other side of the horizon," he writes in a study of seeing at sea or from it.[50]

The seen architectural space and the public structure of the panoramas have always been compared with watching movies, since a remark by Walter Benjamin in his *Arcades Project*,[51] in as much as darkness and a distanced, physically becalmed viewing position is similar in both *dispositifs*. But camera movement on the stand plate, known as the pan or panning shot has not been related to this history of mobilized, industrialized seeing and its corresponding production of space. A standard work on film and television analysis, for example, states: "Camera movements are oriented to possible changes in human viewpoint."[52] Cinema theory has historically claimed the opposite. Dziga Vertov understood camera movements only as mechanically possible motion that could teach the human eye to see: "Now I, a camera, fling myself along their resultant, maneuvering in the chaos of movement, recording movement, starting with movements composed of the most complex combinations. Freed from the rule of sixteen-seventeen frames per second, free of the limits of time and space, I put together any given points in the universe, no matter where I've recorded them."[53] The pan is in fact more oriented to the possible changes in the viewpoint of an ostrich than to the physiognomy of the human neck,[54] an observation that Rudolf Arnheim pursued in reverse in his recognition of the improvement in the pan with the introduction of the tripod head, which he discusses in relation to animal photography[55] and, probably as a reminiscence of Marey's

50 Allan Sekula, *Fish Story*, Rotterdam 2005, p. 47.

51 Walter Benjamin, *The Arcades Project*, trans. Howard Eiland and Kevin McLaughlin, Cambridge 2002, p. 530.

52 Translated from Hickethier, *Film- und Fernsehanalyse*, p. 62/63.

53 Dziga Vertov, *Kino-Eye. The Writings of Dziga Vertov*, ed. Annette Michelson, trans. Kevin O'Brien, Berkeley 1984, pp. 17f.

54 Remark by the filmmaker Nina Rippel, Hamburg.

55 In a passage omitted from *Film as Art*, but in the German original, Arnheim writes: "Incidentally the camera has become much more mobile since the introduction of the fluid head, which was invented, as Dr. Nicholas Kaufmann says, by the American researcher Akeley, the better to keep flying birds and running animals in sight. The tripod head had hitherto only permitted movements from left to right or from above to below. Every other movement was only possible through a combination of the two, which necessitated much complicated work with two winders (apart from the crank to roll the film!)." Translated from Rudolf Arnheim, *Film als Kunst*, Frankfurt/Main 1979 p. 134.

photographic shotgun, describes the camera movement, and the pan in particular, as pursuit, the act of a hunter, and thus as the strengthening of subjectivity in cinematic expression.[56] In the context of the pan the subjective is much more the abrupt relativization of the self in regard to the field of the other, which is attractive and seductive. Sekula described this as a kind of voraciousness of the panoramic view: "The panorama is paradoxical: topographically 'complete' while still signaling an acknowledgement of and desire for a greater extension beyond the frame. The panoramic tableau, however bounded by the limits of a city profile or the enclosure of a harbor, is always potentially unstable: 'If this much, why not more?' The psychology of the panorama is overtly sated and covertly greedy, and thus caught up in the fragile complacency of disavowal."[57]

The filmic legacy of panoramic seeing—which in the early nineteenth century could only be practiced on meter-long bands of urban cityscape[58]—includes, first, the smoothening of the three-dimensional spatial illusion into an almost two-dimensional one, second, the technical separation of space and viewer, the aspect of panoramic seeing emphasized by Dolf Sternberger,[59] and third, a renewed interconnection of these separate positions and thus the division of the viewing subject into a seer and a seen (from the panoramic field): the rift that Foucault called the human *episteme* around 1800.

The fact that a camera movement with or without tracks, called a tracking shot in English and in Babylonian film French "le travelling," is a force and effect of the visual fields, in as much as the viewers—exactly like the travelers in two trains running side by side—can't decide what is moving and what isn't, was emphasized by Jean Mitry—and Jean-Luc Godard realized this paradoxically in his long, sideways tracking shot in WEEKEND, which proceeds like the continuous loop of a bloody breakfast picnic. The traffic has come to a halt, while the camera travels onward: traveling is the exceptional state of camera movement. The tracking shot, says Mitry, has to do with mutually displac-

56 Arnheim, *Film as Art* p. 111f.

57 Sekula, *Fish Story*, p. 43

58 See Bodo von Dewitz und Werner Nekes (eds.), "*Ich sehe was, was Du nicht siehst." Sehmaschinen und Bilderwelten. Die Sammlung Werner Nekes*, Göttingen 2002.

59 See Dolf Sternberger and Joachim Neugroschel, "Panorama of the 19th Century," in *October*, vol. 4 (fall 1977), pp. 3–20: 3f: "The Kaiser had a special treat on opening day, a small heightening of the platform, which, on request, would slowly revolve, 'affording the spectator, with no effort required on his part, a view in the round of the panorama,' a circumstance more likely to ensure his being carried away, or rather detached, from himself."

ing relationships in the visual field, and he refers to back projection, which is only possible as an optical illusion because of this indistinguishability.[60] In this context he questions the possibility of an available field of view, which André Bazin saw as particularly guaranteed in the depth of focus and the sequence shot, and declared the basis of an autonomous arrangement of the elements within a scene and the freedom to autonomous seeing in the cinema.[61] Mitry describes elements through which camera movements draw the act of seeing into the cinematographic field of view. He refers to a physio-psychological update of the represented space in the gaze.[62] The body, like in the train ride, is inserted into the course of things, and appears to abandon itself without resistance or awareness of the process of representation to a "speeding alternation of ideas."[63] While Bazin saw a heightened cinematic realism and the possibility of abstraction ensured in the portrayal of the "real time in which things exist" and the "duration of the action,"[64] which makes watching movies a form of thought, Mitry's diagnosis is that the impression of cinematic reality comes about through the sense of currency: "Presentification is replaced by actualization. [...] For that reason, represented reality appears 'more true'."[65] The rush of the camera movements causes the frame that relates the image to reality to be forgotten: "We shall conclude these observations on the tracking shot by adding that though, in the film image, the characters' movements and continual changes of shot tend to make us forget the 'frame,' this tendency is made all the more pronounced with camera movements."[66] The pan provokes a peering

60 See Mitry, *The Aesthetics and Psychology of Cinema*, p. 183: "We saw the original purpose of the tracking shot was to follow the actors, but we could stretch the point and say that a tracking shot which keeps equal distance and speed with the characters it is following is another form of static shot; it is the background which appears to be moving."

61 André Bazin, "The Evolution of the Language of Cinema," in André Bazin, *What is Cinema?* pp. 23–41.

62 Mitry, *The Aesthetics and Psychology of Cinema*, p. 188: "Indeed, the moving camera has made it possible to 'actualize' the represented space, since the space in which we *effectively* move can only be a space *actually present*. Things are 'in the process of happening,' since we follow them in their very mobility, according to their continuous development. We move *with them* and therefore act (or feel as though we are acting) at the same time as them. The here and now presented to our eyes through editing is presented physically to our perception, our senses through the tracking shot."

63 Hölderlin, "Notes on the Oedipus", p. 318.

64 André Bazin, "The Evolution of Cinematic Language," p. 39.

65 Mitry, *Aesthetics and Psychology of the Cinema*, p. 189.

66 Ibid., p. 190.

loss of self in the field of things, and is poisonous to the subjective. The train travelers' return to self, just like that of the film viewers', only takes place with a break, an unexpected caesura, an accident, cut, or tear in the film—or also in the excess of simultaneous impressions—which returns the attention to the mechanically or technically induced imagination, after Vertov.[67]

With the pan this can occur through a pause, which has to be done slowly in order to preserve an illusion, but is carried out abruptly by those auteurs who take a stand against illusionism in film and place seeing itself in the foreground. Godard, who was interested in breaking down spatial illusion, and in caesuras that expose its artificiality and ideological coherence, and therefore staged the tracking shot as a movement of congestion, accordingly ends the one in WEEKEND with a bloody accident: as a metonymical and metaphorical shock. Whereas with Straub and Huillet, who experiment for the first time with the pan seven years later in MOSES UND ARON, the break must be sought on a different level: the interruption or end of the pan doesn't cause a rift in the space but allows every figure and place in the image to form and transform itself in relation to the space. So, just as a tone in a twelve-tone composition doesn't always have the same value within a harmonic system—such as fourth or fifth, for example—but takes on a differentially constructed position to the previous and following tones, generating other tone colors, the figures and groups alter their significance with regard to spatial relationships, which are essentially established through the liaisons and lesions of the pan.

With Straub and Huillet the camera produces relations between the figures on the one hand, but on the other it is bound to the location allocated to it through the division of the terrain; the measurement of these fields, which Straub calls force fields, in turn goes back to archaeological and historical architectural layers that become visible in this space as a kind of cinematographic excavation.

In an interview conducted with Danièle Huillet and Jean-Marie Straub by Jacques Bontemps, Pascal Bonitzer, and Serge Daney in summer 1975 for the *Cahiers du Cinéma*, the questions about the filmic space and the correlations produced by the camera are posed from the critics' immediate experience of what they had seen on screen. They also document the cahieristes' irritation about the interweaving of technical and theoretical levels, of the materialities

67 See Annette Michelson, "'The Man with a Movie Camera': From Magician to Epistemologist," in *Artforum* X, 1972, no. 7, pp. 60–72.

and thinking of the moving image. The "panoramique" is discussed regarding its status as a technical or technically strengthened view on the one hand and as a rhetorical or theoretical figure on the other. Jean-Marie Straub explains the use of the pan in this context as a re-medium against the idea of a window on the world "in which the theater of the world [could] somehow inscribe itself."[68] He considers the depiction of a *spectaculum mundi*, a view of the world lying open before the technical eye of the camera, to be sheer idealism and bullshit ("C'est de la connerie!"),[69] and instead develops a theory of staging relationships that first and foremost creates the image space, and its construction through camera movements. This construction is due, for example, to different relationships produced by different camera movements. The pan, in contrast to the tracking shot on rails, which also occurs in the film, not only allocates the people in the film to different respective positions but also to their relativized role in the antagonism of forces and power relationships:

> *Straub*: [...] there is never a pan linking Moses with Aron, or Aron with Moses, until the one in the final shot, where we leave Aron after his last sentence ("Für seine Freiheit, daß es ein Volk werde! [For their freedom – so that they would become a nation!]"). We leave him in a pan and see Moses as he will be seen until the end of the film. It's a glaring exception. There's another one previously, but not a glaring exception, more that it's connected to something else, when in the shot with the leprous hand we leave Aron with a pan to the chorus, passing Moses by, in the same way as we pan past the priest standing to the right of the chorus. EVERY TIME A PAN INTERVENES, IT DOES SO IN CONNECTION WITH THE IDEA OF THE CHORUS (AND THE PEOPLE). And every time there's a camera movement towards Moses or Aron, it's a tracking shot, or no movement at all. [...] so something is concealed behind the history of the pan."[70]

In these remarks Straub seems to be surprised about how the "rules of the game" that structured the shoot automatically led to a coherent system of cam-

68 Translated from Straub/Huillet, "Conversation," p. 12.
69 Ibid.
70 Ibid.

era movements and thus also optical relationships between the protagonists in a logic behind every pan and track.

The camera-technically, topologically emergent place of the chorus—which in act I stands in front of the *parodos*, the northern entrance to the arena, but doesn't enter through it, as it would at the start of a Greek tragedy—and its function in the perception of the opera seems to astonish even Straub, particularly in regard to the people, which plays a decisive role in *Moses und Aron*. In Schoenberg's opera the idea of the chorus and the idea of the people are neither clearly separated nor is the chorus part of a genealogy of Greek tragedy. In Straub's comment on the pan the logic of the Greek structure of the amphitheater seems to appear suddenly through the mathematical examination of the space and the formalized camera movements quite apart from any directorial intention, yet in theater-historical terms the chorus in MOSES UND ARON remains a hybrid.[71] It doesn't stand, as in Greek tragedy, for a public sphere of the polis, whose conventional values contrary to the events on stage it more embodies than represents. Even the stage-like lineup in the arena, placing the chorus between spectacle and tragedy, is continually dissolved by camera movements. In act II, above all, the visible and audible spaces are distinguished through the constant displacement of the chorus in regard to *off* and *on*: thus the chorus sings for the Beggars in the first person plural, while the Beggars themselves, played by local farmers, wordlessly pay their respects to the idol and the camera image, adding new metonymic layers to the film. The chorus also sings as a collective for the self-sacrificing Elderly Men. Whereas in act I the chorus corresponds to a plurality arguing about the gods and their usefulness, as conceived and composed by Schoenberg. The composer's text develops Brechtian qualities here. To an objection by the Priest to the new god, "Die alten Götter haben auch beschützt. Tat's der eine nicht, wandte man sich an den andern [The olden gods did also give protection. And if one did fail, prayers were made unto the others]," the chorus replies, "Man kann von den Göttern auch nichts Unmögli-

71 The chorus regularly falls into rhythmic singing and *Sprechgesang*, as Aristotle required of it in tragedy, and comments on events, but it neither dances nor is restricted to the essential "I" of tragedy, which should never be collectivized. In Greek tragedy, in contrast to later theatrical or liturgical forms, the chorus was never mixed, neither in terms of sex, age, nor social affiliation. "Accordingly the tragedy chorus never portrayed the 'people' as a whole." Translated from Siegfried Melchinger, *Das Theater der Tragödie, Aischylos, Sophokles, Euripides auf der Bühne ihrer Zeit*, Munich 1974, p. 65. See also Detlev Baur, *Der Chor im Theater des 20. Jahrhunderts. Typologie des theatralen Mittels Chor*, Tübingen 1999, p. 18.

ches verlangen [O ask not the gods, then, impossibility's fulfillment]" (act I, bars 306–324). In act I people still see themselves as a community with an idea of themselves as a religious or cultic congregation. This strengthens—Adorno's reservation—the oratorio character of the piece.[72] The work on the opera and its filming consisted in materializing these ideas, to put them out into the world, or more exactly to cause them to appear where no one expected them.

The lightness with which Straub outlines the connections between pan, chorus, and people doesn't hide the fact that the relationship between chorus and people in the film is quite complex. This is not only a legacy of Schoenberg's opera, in which the relationship is also ambivalently conceived from the start, but is also connected with the deliberately staged ambiguity between people and ethnicity or nation, which Straub and Huillet survey in the light of historicity and the law. Gilles Deleuze found that along with Resnais "the Straubs" were "the greatest political film-makers in the West, in modern cinema [...] But, oddly, this is not through the presence of the people. On the contrary, it is because they know how to show how the people are what is missing, what is not there."[73] This lack of the people is differently organized in MOSES UND ARON than in the two directors' previous films. While Schoenberg located the complexity of the relationship between chorus and people in the compression and scansion of the biblical text and his corresponding musical organization, Straub and Huillet literally place it in the space. Straub initially states that in MOSES UND ARON the people is represented by the chorus, but he formulates the relationship ambiguously:

> *Cahiers:* Back then, with OTHON, you said that it was a film about the absence of the people, and that MOSES UND ARON would be a film about the people and its presence. Well, it's true that the people is present in the sense that it is on set.
> *Straub:* It is present, represented by the chorus.[74]

The minimal but problematic difference with which Straub says that the people is present but at the same time only represented is one that is itself

72 Adorno, "Sacred Fragment," p. 322.

73 Deleuze, *Cinema 2. The Time-Image* p. 215f.

74 Translated from Straub/Huillet, "Conversation," p. 10.

differentiated in the image or through the visual space. In Straub's words this difference is not only manifested as performative displacement and delay[75] but also as resistance, which the people bring into the progression of the film: "From the very beginning it creates a resistance. At first resistance to a basic principle, that of monotheism, which is the rift and motor of emergence and liberation."[76] Here Straub undertakes a surprising translation of historical or social processes into filmic and dramaturgic categories: monotheism is both the inhibition and impetus of liberation (or, more clearly, the liberation movement), and the people form the resistance to it. In this resistance the actualizing function interlocks with the materiality of the alternating ensembles so as to hold the friction of real things against the pure law of thought of monotheism. The chorus, both the Israelite opera people and its Viennese representatives in the film, and then the cameraman's pan produce a deceleration that counters the assertion of monotheism. The fact that the idea of the people is cinematically linked to the movement of the pan specifies the pan's function as resistance to the linear order of simple historical progress. To vary one of Walter Benjamin's formulations, which described revolutions as historical emergency brakes,[77] it could be said in this case that pans, just like the absent people or the idea of it, are the slow if-and-but of matter that is switched in between the dogmatism of a theoretical philosophy of history and historical practices of liberation.

The pan is already associated with the idea of the people long before the people make their appearance, Straub insists in the interview with the journalists of the *Cahiers du Cinéma*. He explicitly refers here to the first long camera movement, which is panoramic in the strict sense of the word: "For MOSES UND ARON it's true that the pan is always linked to the idea of the people, long before the people can be seen, through the first swerve around the ellipse, which is some-

75 "The chorus always plays a chorus," writes Detlev Baur. Translated from Baur, *Der Chor im Theater*, p. 26.

76 Translated from Straub/Huillet, "Conversation," p. 10.

77 "Marx says that revolutions are the locomotive of world history. But perhaps it is quite different. Perhaps they are the locomotive traveler's reaching for the emergency brake." Translated from Walter Benjamin, "Über den Begriff der Geschichte, Anmerkungen," in Walter Benjamin, *Gesammelte Schriften*, ed. Rolf Tiedemann and Hermann Schweppenhäuser, vol I. 3: *Abhandlungen*, Frankfurt/Main 1980, pp. 1223–1266: 1232. The remark does not appear in the English translation: Walter Benjamin, *On the Concept of History*, trans. Dennis Redmond, New York 2009.

thing that replaces the burning bush. And it's true that we hadn't done this before in a film. It had never occurred to us."[78]

The start of the pan at the beginning of the film therefore marks a double caesura, which at bar 48 goes through the figure of Moses himself when he says "Ich kann denken || aber nicht reden [Thought is easy || speech is laborious]," a caesura that is also repeated in the musical composition: a division of the tone-row progressions in which one of the basic forms of the hexachord of the opening vocalise is taken up again and there is a transposed reprise of bar 11—the one in which spoken language breaks into the opera.[79] The striking thing is that this mirroring in bar 48 cuts through Moses' sentence—"dramatically, the section divides in two at 48"[80]—namely at the breaking point of what he imagines, when he interrupts himself at "My tongue is not flexible," to continue in a new form, *pianissimo*, "Thought is easy; speech is laborious." Speaking, as an articulation in the symbolic system, is thus set against the endless flow of imagined images, but also against the acoustic sphere and the music. Moses, who stutters, stumbles, and stops, seems to bring more resistance into the work than "the people." Complementary to the caesura of Moses' speaking, the pan moves to the left and, from ensemble to ensemble of framings, invites us to see, to retain, what can be seen and what simultaneously and continually disappears on the right edge of the visible, becoming memory. At first the camera pans across the sand, then over stones, which are recognizable as Roman ruins, then diagonally upwards over some stone steps to flat shrubbery, then higher to the thicker vegetation of trees and olives around a strange rock formation, pans on to single, somewhat scrawny trees, and finally over the horizon into the sky, full of cloud formations, which fills the screen at bar 66—the end of the *agon* phase of the first scene. In this shot the directors' almost 7,000-mile search,

78 Translated from Straub/Huillet, "Conversation," p. 12/13.

79 David Lewin, "Moses und Aron: Some General Remarks and Analytic Notes for Act 1 Scene 1," in *Perspectives of New Music,* vol. 6, no. 1, 1967, pp. 1–17:8: "Throughout, the chorus becomes very active in all respects (modulation, new textures, initiative for same). Up to 48 1/2, Moses becomes more and more passive, musically as well as dramatically; here he is not so much raising real problems as offering excuses and evasions. [...] At 48 1/2 though, Moses finally articulates a real insight and problem: 'Ich kann denken, aber nicht reden.' Here, Moses becomes active again, musically also. He returns to the original area A_0 'all by himself') [...] The serial return is supported by a sort of reprise from mm 11ff. This finally gives the chorus some pause."

80 Ibid., p. 8.

as Huillet described their research journey to locations and acoustics, seems to have found its filmic summary, its filmic "abstract," and its own interruption.[81] With the last phase of this first scene of act I, in which the voice from the burning bush announces its blessing and prophecies, rough terrain comes into view and finally the two mountains, on which the pan ends at bar 82. In the calm of this shot all the axes of symmetry that intersect the space vertically, horizontally, and diagonally to the camera lens become visible. The space falls surprisingly back into a fixed form, while our thinking about it makes its presence felt as resistance.

Just as the visual caesuras segment the music, the flow of images is segmented and scanned by the music. During the pan the six solo voices and the small chorus, which according to the score makes up the actual "Voice from the Burning Bush," are heard. Both are juxtaposed with slightly displaced texts, although the difference between spoken and sung language also creates the tension that will become precarious between Moses and Aron. In contrast to Schoenberg, incidentally, who drew on Exodus 3 and 6 for his verses, Straub and Huillet understand the entire group of solo voices and small chorus as a "Voice," implicitly "from the Burning Bush," maintaining the indetermination of its source or origin that requires incision and decision.[82]

THE VOICE sung	spoken
Wie aus dem Dornbusch, finster	Wie aus diesem Dornbusch
Eh das Licht der Wahrheit	finster, eh das Licht der Wahrheit
auf ihn fiel	auf ihn fiel
so vernimmst du meine Stimme	so vernimmst du meine Stimme
aus jedem Ding	aus jedem Ding.
Aron soll dein	Aron will ich erleuchten,
Mund sein.	er soll dein Mund sein!
Aus ihm soll deine Stimme sprechen	Aus ihm soll deine Stimme sprechen
Wie aus dir die meine!	Wie aus dir die meine!
Gesegnet, gesegnet,	Und ihr werdet gesegnet sein.
das gelobe ich dir:	Denn das gelobe ich dir:

81 See Huillet, "Appunti sul giornale," p. 401.
82 See Huillet, "Moses und Aron, Das Drehbuch," p. 206.

Dieses Volk ist auserwählt
vor allen Völkern,
das Volk des einz'gen Gottes zu sein,
daß es ihn erkenne,
sich ihm ganz widme
alle Prüfungen bestehe,
vor allen Völkern auserwählt,
denen der Gedanke ausgesetzt ist.
Und das verheiße ich dir:
Ich will euch dorthin führen,
wo ihr mit dem Ewigen einig
und allen Völkern ein Vorbild werdet:
Und nun
gehe!
Aron!

Erkennen.
Verkünde, verkünde, verkünde!

[E'en as from this bush in darkness
ere the light of truth
fell there upon,
so will you perceive my message
in ev'ry thing.
Aaron shall be
your mouth
From him will your own voice
then issue
As from you comes my voice!
Be blessed, be blessed,
for I promise you this:
Your folk are the chosen ones
before all others,
They are the folk of God alone,
They are thus to know him,
give him their worship.

Dieses Volk ist auserwählt
vor allen Völkern
das Volk des einzigen Gottes zu sein
daß es ihn erkenne
und sich ihm allein ganz widme;
daß es alle Prüfungen bestehe,
denen in Jahrtausenden
der Gedanke ausgesetzt ist.
Und das verheiße ich dir:
Ich will euch dorthin führen,
Wo ihr mit dem Ewigen einig
und allen Völkern ein Vorbild werdet.
Und nun gehe!
Aron triffst du in der Wüste.
Er kommt dir auf deinem Weg
entgegen,
Daran sollst du ihn erkennen.

[E'en as from this bush in darkness,
ere the light of truth
fell there upon,
so will you perceive my message
in ev'ry thing.
Aaron will be enlightened,
He shall be your mouth!
From him will your own voice
then issue,
As from you comes my voice!
And your people will now be blest,
for this I promise to you:
Your folk are the chosen ones
before all others.
They are the folk of the one God alone.
They are thus to know him
and give him alone their worship.

And all trials devised,
in ages past,
will be submitted to this people.
And this I promise to you:
I shall conduct you forward,
to where with the infinite oneness
you'll be a model to ev'ry nation.
Now be
gone hence!
Aaron!

Inform him.
Go forth now, go forth now!]

Also they will undergo all hardships,
that have ever – in millennia –
come to be conceived.
And this I promise to you:
Conduct you from here forward,
to where with the infinite oneness
you'll be a model to ev'ry nation.
Now be gone hence!
Aaron nears you in the wasteland.
You soon will see him approach
and greet him,
Of this you are to inform him.]

This extract shows how much the production by Straub and Huillet, which Gilles Deleuze describes as not only tearing "the speech-act from what is resisting it" but also the "speech-act being made resistant against what is threatening it"[83] conveys Schoenberg's compositional and linguistic compression. From selecting the biblical passages to the first handwritten text for an originally planned oratorio to the final short score that Schoenberg left behind, a microscopic differentiation and distribution takes place of the consonants and vowels, and ultimately of the spoken and sung sounds in a space that in turn changes from canonically striated into alien and smooth. The voice from the burning bush should therefore be imagined as a collected multiplicity, and it declares itself in this way: "So vernimmst du meine Stimme aus jedem Ding [So will you perceive my message in ev'ry thing]." Schoenberg took this for his compositional program in conceiving a space of "oscillatory vibrations, appearing at different places and times,"[84] with which the act of speech must be equally differentiated so as to meet them.

This causing of the rifts in nature to speak, explicitly in and emphatically in all things and all living beings, as is always a part of Jean-Marie Straub and Danièle

83 Deleuze, *Cinema 2. The Time-Image*, p. 254f.
84 Schoenberg, "Composition with Twelve Tones," p. 223.

Huillet's dramaturgy against the "ruination of the planet through capitalism,"[85] was not immediately perceived by the *Cahiers* journalists, however. Instead—thus not passing at the first attempt the test, imposed to a certain extent by every thorn bush, of seeing history in every thing—they heard nature in the pan as silent:

> *Cahiers*: For example, we don't see the burning bush, and the pan that follows, if you relate it to the bush, is a kind of utter muteness of nature.
> *Straub*: Not entirely, because it gradually transforms, in that it is evident from the start that we will make the ascent before Moses. In that moment it has nothing to do with the burning bush. But suddenly we brush past something that people could say: that relates to the damaged trees up there. We leave the trees and say to ourselves: that wasn't the burning bush after all. We reach an empty spot without correcting the horizon line. So this is more than just the sky, because it's as if the ascent has been interrupted. But it continues, and you see a bare rock appear. And in this moment we hear: "Dass es alle Prüfungen bestehe denen in Jahrtausenden der Gedanke ausgesetzt ist" [...]. This rock then begins to function in a particular way. It is now the one who has made a stand for thousands of years, submitted to an idea, a thought. As soon as we have completed the ascent, and as soon as we have re-established the horizontal, which we then won't correct any more, there is something that functions like a burning bush, and at the same time the people is there, demanding something.[86]

From this sentence Deleuze draws his conclusion that "it is now the earth, the tree and the rock which resist the speech-act, resist Moses."[87] However, this should conversely be extended to the observation that Moses' act of speech should also be articulated so resistively that the materiality and historical layers of earth, tree, and stone become visible. That, according to Straub and Huillet, would be the beginning of revolutionary thinking.

85 Interestingly, this aspect of ruination as thought of in the name of nomadism: "C'est l'idée du nomadisme, tout simplement. [...] Historiquement, bien sûr, c'est un utopie. Au moins qu'on arrive à un point où le capitalisme ruine la planète." Straub/Huillet, "Conversation," p. 8.

86 Translated from ibid., p. 14. The literal translation of the line Straub quotes from the libretto is "that it survives all the ordeals to which the idea is subjected down the millennia." The English libretto reads: "And all trials devised in ages past will be submitted to this people."

87 Deleuze, *Cinema 2. The Time-Image*, p. 255.

The materialities, resistances, and appeals give a disintegrating image, not a homogeneous one. In the pan across the trees, plants, and terraces, the beauty and history of exploitation in the mountains, in culture and nature, in the landscape, doesn't appear as utopian but as heterotopia, which of course is linked by Straub and Huillet to the *hors-champ*. The pan is a movement that continuously produces new *hors-champ*. From this perspective the comparison that Deleuze makes between Straub/Huillet's cinematic procedure and a geological process goes far beyond simple image description: "To the question: what is a Straubian shot?, one can reply, as in a manual of stratigraphy, that it is a section comprising the stippled [*pointillees*] lines of vanished *features* and the complete lines of those that are still touched. The visual image, in Straub, is the rock."[88] In the sense of the acoustics of the *Moses* opera we might add: a rock that demands to be struck, so as to ring out its frequencies and resonances.

The images of the shockingly beautiful but culturally ravaged landscape are scanned or chopped up by further caesuras that run through the film, the music, and above all through the text of the opera. Aside from the division of the space into hearing and speaking, into the call and the answer, into visibility and seeing, it is primarily the separation of eye and gaze that marks a rift in the imaginary unity. In a clever turn of phrase the journalists of the *Cahiers du Cinéma* allege that the people—*sit venia verbo*—makes a visual claim: *"Cahiers:* The striking thing in Moses und Aron is that the people is conceived like a gaze. It is a gaze that requires us to satisfy it."[89] Straub replies with the observation that the entire sequence involves a mutual evocation of gaze and people, one that naturally also involves the burning bush and its appeal:

> *Straub*: My thought just now was that the people, despite everything, is the gaze. Okay, so what then suddenly causes the gaze to bring about the pan? It isn't Aron who brings about the pan, and not the connection between Moses and Aron. For Moses is never linked to the people through a pan (apart from the one that passes him by). Moses is never linked to the people through any kind of camera movement—apart from the pan of his "calling," (Burning bush = people in the *hors-champ*.)[90]

88 Ibid., p. 244.

89 Translated from Straub/Huillet, "Conversation," p. 13.

90 Ibid., p. 13f.

The people is outside the field of view and action, or, cinematically, in the *hors-champ*. It is only there in as much as it invokes and demands all movements. Depending on how we look at the film images, we constitute what Straub calls the people.

The metonymical relationship between pan, burning bush, chorus, and people, this bundling of dramaturgical and political conception, the parallelization of photographic realism, as it appears in the "the ripple of leaves stirred by the wind"[91] in the long panoramic landscape shot, connects the film's diverse levels at the very beginning. The pan, which excludes a certain subjective viewpoint and contemplation, which dissolves a metrized or mapped landscape into a leveled, smoothed view, which introduces temporality as deprivation and at the same time a visual murmuring in the face of its long duration, exposes the gaze to a cultivated landscape that is thoroughly pervaded by the cultural techniques of industrialized societies: in this sense it is collective. But it is made up of individual gazes, not a total, overall cinema eye.

> *Cahiers*: So you want to say that the pan is the figure that inscribes the people, and is hence not only a single eye moving fast, and also not the gaze of anyone in the film.
> *Straub*: It's certainly someone's gaze. And in as much as it can't be a single eye moving fast, this means it's somewhere in between the two.[92]

Resistance is inflamed less by antagonisms, poles, or positions than by movements, in transitional spaces, between shots, and beyond the shot, *champ* and *hors-champ*, and between the movement of an image and its interruption: "There's something that could be interesting in what you just said," says Straub to Bonitzer, "When you said: what would happen if the pan *halted*?"[93]

In the interruption, the caesura, seeing becomes thinking. It is this differential relationship between technical set-up and thought process that Straub and Huillet also found in Schoenberg. In the opera the relationship between form and thought, which Schoenberg repeatedly also deals with as style and thought, is sung by Aron: "You cannot expect form before idea, for together they'll make

91 Kracauer's prime example in *Theory of Film*, p. 31.
92 Translated from Straub/Huillet "Conversation," p. 13.
93 Ibid., p. 16.

The idea of the people, cinematically bound to the pan, represented by the chorus.

their appearance." Aron sings this at the beginning of act II, when the chorus, impatiently murmuring because Moses has already been away in the mountains for forty days, begins to cry for the leader, and above all for the law, although for one that is visible and conceivable: "Wo ist Moses? Wo ist der Führer? [...] Vierzig Tage warten wir nun auf Moses, und noch immer weiß keiner Recht und Gesetz! Unvorstellbares Gesetz des unvorstellbaren Gottes [Where is Moses? Where is our leader? (...) Forty days now we have awaited Moses, and still no one knows either law or command. Unperceivable command from one who's yet unperceived]" (act II, bars 1–61).

Schoenberg himself, as writer and composer—perhaps less as painter and portraitist—struggled with this problem of the transformation of the materiality of artistic "material," and in the words of the hard-pressed Aron he anticipates its solution, proposed while working on *Moses und Aron*, in the concept of space. In a text originally delivered as the lecture "Style and Idea: Composition with Twelve Tones" in the summer of 1935 at the University of Southern California he says:

> Music is not merely another kind of amusement, but a musical poet's, a musical thinker's representation of musical ideas; these musical ideas must correspond to the laws of human logic; they are a part of what man can apperceive, reason and express. Proceeding from these assumptions, I arrived at the following conclusions: THE TWO-OR-MORE-DIMENSIONAL SPACE IN WHICH MUSICAL IDEAS ARE PRESENTED IS A UNIT. Though the elements of these ideas appear separate and independent to the eye and the ear, they reveal

> their true meaning only through their co-operation, even as no single word alone can express a thought without relation to other words. All that happens at any point of this musical space has more than a local effect. It functions not only in its own plane, but also in all other directions and planes, and is not without influence even at remote points.[94]

With this concept of space Schoenberg denotes the possibility of a volume whose elements enter into relationships and form interferences over whichever distances, and only become significant in this cooperation. This means that they make a qualitative leap from material data to movements of thought. For Schoenberg a musical space is not an existing one in which previously written music is made to sound; the space only emerges with the vibrations of the music, and like it has an orientation:

> […] the unity of musical space demands an absolute and unitary perception. In this space, as in Swedenborg's heaven (described in Balzac's *Seraphita*) there is no absolute down, no right or left, forward or backward. Every musical configuration, every movement of tones has to be comprehended primarily as a mutual relation of sounds, of oscillatory vibrations, appearing at different places and times.[95]

94 Schoenberg, "Composition with Twelve Tones," p. 220.
95 Ibid., p. 223.

It isn't hard to see the similarity between Swedenborg's heaven and Moses' desert. The lack of an absolute coordination is compensated by the ability, akin to a phenomenological orientation, to recognize forms independently of spatial coordinates, and, with regard to the music, by the possibility of recognizing melodies, even if they are transposed, or appear in inverted or retrograde form. Schoenberg was thus the first to formulate an acoustic field theory, which can be understood as lateral in Merleau-Ponty's sense: "I am at the cube in its manifestness through what I see," he said in a lecture to film students in 1945, and Schoenberg's earlier lecture could be read as "I am at the tone itself and its manifestness through what I hear."[96]

> To the imaginative and creative faculty, relations in the material sphere are as independent from directions or planes as material objects are, in their sphere, to our perceptive faculties. Just as our mind always recognizes, for instance, a knife, a bottle or a watch, regardless of its position, and can reproduce it in the imagination in every possible position, even so a musical creator's mind can operate subconsciously with a row of tones regardless of their direction, regardless of the way in which a mirror might show the mutual relations, which remain a given quality.[97]

96 See Merleau-Ponty, "The Film and the New Psychology", p. 50.

97 Schoenberg, "Composition with Twelve Tones," p. 223. In his manifesto "New Music—My Music" (which he wrote before 1930, and which in its rapid style partly reminds one of Jean-Marie Straub's notoriously harsh reactions to slow audience reactions), Schoenberg says in paragraph IV: "That is how music must proceed, if it sets out from complicated figures, to

In his fragmentary manuscript "Der musikalische Gedanke und die Logik, Technik und Kunst seiner Darstellung" [The Musical Thought and the Logic, Technique, and Art of its Portrayal], which he finally drew up after many preparatory drafts in the summer of 1934,[98] Schoenberg uses the term *Gedanke* (thought) almost synonymously with *Gestalt* (form), which he does in fact apply in reference to gestalt-theoretical experiments he knew about. The so-called "'Gedanke' Manuscript" deals with the organization of wholes and their perception in the space of music. Schoenberg marks them in his drafts as abbreviations: "Fsl (for Faßlichkeit) and Zhg (for Zusammenhang), which reappear in the text."[99] For Schoenberg, too, it is the swaying bridge of the concept of space that is intended to bring about the impossible compatibility of the "technical" and "conceptual" in harmonic relationships, those phenomena that can also be a theoretical model and manifestation of things themselves.

To the same degree that Schoenberg doesn't assume a unified space of sounds, Straub and Huillet's film will not assume a predefined, coherent cinematic space: in music and in film, as the parallel argumentation goes, this space emerges as an act of perception that recognizes the relationships between the tones, tonal progressions, and intervals, or in film between the figures, distances, geometrical and force fields, as a composition. Just as the teacher Schoenberg utterly opposed "that narcotic emanation of music which affects the senses without involving the mind,"[100] Straub and Huillet dismantle the rhetoric of cinematographic spatial construction: "There are pans that participate, you could say, in the rhetoric of the cinema, even if we endeavor never to do anything rhetorical."[101]

arrive at still more complicated ones." Arnold Schoenberg, "New Music: My Music", in Arnold Schoenberg: *Style and Idea*, pp. 99–106: 104.

98 See Alexander Goehr, "Schoenberg's 'Gedanke' Manuscript," in *Journal of the Arnold Schoenberg Institute* II, 1977, no. 1, pp. 4–25: 5f: "The manuscript is as Rufer [Joseph Rufer, who edited a catalogue of Schoenberg's compositions, writings, and paintings, U.H.] describes it. It consists of 199 pages, some of them closely written, others almost blank. There are interruptions, or what seem to be interruptions, for canons are generally unfinished." Goehr organizes the fragments under four headings: *Gedanke (Gestalt), Zusammenhang, Fasslichkeit, Rhythmus* [Idea (Form), Context, Comprehensibility, Rhythm]. See ibid. p. 9.

99 Ibid., p. 7.

100 Arnold Schoenberg, "Eartraining through Composing," in Schoenberg, *Style and Idea*, p. 378. Schoenberg undertakes this with the aim of awakening "only one pleasure: the pleasure of balance between the joy he expects from music and the joy he actually receives" (ibid., p. 382).

101 Translated from Straub/Huillet, "Conversation," p. 12.

So if the people emerges from the function of seeing, although at its technically and emphatically placed caesura or break wrested into the material, these rifts can be discerned on various levels: in the relationship between the technical and the conceptual, at the moment between movement and stasis, in the text itself, in its placement into the musical composition and its sounds, and in the renewed detachment and appropriation that its intonation by the performers signifies. The people is a differential phenomenon, and the chorus trains itself and us in realizing this. In as much as the differential elements become visible as rifts or crises, the journalists of the *Cahiers du Cinéma* ultimately wished to describe the pan as the (camera-technical) equivalent to a dialectic movement, as one of the most inexorable laws of thought of the nineteenth century that has been preserved in the technical functioning of media in the twentieth century:

> *Cahiers*: So the pan would be the movement of the dialectic itself? It won't be the people, because in fact the pan views the people quite differently. And neither is it the viewer's gaze, nor that of power. So could it be what supplements everything else?
> *Straub*: Yes. It was redundant to show the people there once again, because there was no longer any danger for the viewers: at that moment everything was just as evident as for the people.[102]

The people is a form of perception that appears unexpectedly.

When Straub says to the journalists that the people is a gaze brought about by the pan or another cinematic movement, it becomes clear that "the people" stands for a visual constellation that provokes a corresponding state of perception or a decision to resist what is seen. The tone-color constellation in the first scene brings about the necessity to make a decision in the sound space in the same way. Opera and film operate media aesthetically, not illustratively. Constellations that elicit attitudes, stances, and behavior in the visual and audible, and at the same time resistance—as murmuring demand for a halt, as a declaration—against hearing voices where there was noise, generate a political aesthetic out of the absence of the people.

Straub's remark, however, can be related to a much more precarious element that appears explicitly in Schoenberg's opera: where the question of mono-

102 Ibid., p. 16.

theism is linked to the prohibition of images—a structure, as Philippe Lacoue-Labarthe argues, that causes the opera to fail[103]—the panorama politics of Straub and Huillet realizes the absence of the people as a *dispositif* of perception. Here they bring about the collision of Moses' and Aron's attitudes. To show the people is to show only a representation. Hence the fundamental politics of the film consist in the fact that the people "may not" be shown in the cinema. "Darfst? [Dare not?]" responds Moses to the way Aron wants to convey the prohibition of images to the people (act I, bar 175f). Moses declaims the implacable law of thought of radicalism against Aron's aestheticizing diplomacy: "Unvorstellbar, weil unsichtbar, weil unüberblickbar; weil unendlich; weil ewig; weil allgegenwärtig; weil allmächtig [Not conceived because unseen, can never be measured, everlasting, eternal, because ever present, and almighty]." Purify your seeing. Free it from worthless things. Don't imagine the people as a troupe of Bertolucci extras.

4.3. FORBIDDEN IMAGES, IMAGES LAID WASTE

The prohibition of images is not only the central topos of the opera and the film Moses und Aron, it is also a resistance inscribed into the work itself: its own aesthetic procedures have to assert themselves against any simple portrayal, performance, or conveyance. So aniconism causes fundamental rifts in the materiality and fabric of both works. The concept of art itself is challenged from within the work. The audible and visible groundlessness of a Moses opera and its film version shows up the limits of all forms of conventional depiction and representation, and requires the portrayal of the conditions of depiction itself. So it's no wonder that Schoenberg, in his "Gedanke" manuscript, and Straub, in the interview, are constantly grappling with the question of space as a field that needs to be organized through artistic means, and in which differences and relationships form without regard to coordinates and Cartesian order. "Show the idea from all sides," Schoenberg notes on June 5, 1934 on the

103 See Philippe Lacoue-Labarthe, "Die Zäsur der Religion. Zu Schönbergs Moses und Aron," in Christiaan L. Hart Nibbrig (ed.), *Was heißt Darstellen?*, Frankfurt/Main 1974, pp. 451–479: 451.

edge of his manuscript.[104] In both cases the problem of the prohibition of images is detached from the imitative, mimetic context and redeveloped in the field of the topological. Yet every opera requires at least sounds, if not tones, and every film at least projected light, if not images. How far both works triumph or sink in their moral and political aspirations in this question of the substantial or the material is still a matter of critical debate: the discontinuation of Schoenberg's opera after act II and the sequences of white or black screen in Straub and Huillet's film are alternately seen as the death mask or resurrection of the work in the light of its conception. But these procedures could also be seen as an aesthetic of resistance within the work.

The prohibition of images in both opera and film cause the differences between the arts and media to appear at different dramaturgical or strategic points. In relation to *Moses und Aron* Adorno emphasizes that actually, and in particular in Jewish culture, "music is the imageless art and was excluded from that prohibition,"[105] but mentions that expressive music, among which he includes Schoenberg's, is "interwoven with the pictorial arts throughout Europe"[106] not only in its conventions of composition or orchestration but also in its specific sounds, in its *stile rappresentativo*, as *musica ficta*, as shown in Schoenberg's own reference to Claude Debussy's exploitation of F-sharp major as something beautiful because unusual. Schoenberg himself sought a way out of the pictorial aspect of music through tone color as a higher musical mathematics of frequency relationships, which goes beyond categories of dissonance and atonality to produce an unyielding outer space. Frequency relationships are the sight line on which Kandinsky, the Murnauer Kreis before 1914, and subsequently other Bauhaus artists would follow Schoenberg. Experiments with vibrations examined an aesthetically intrinsic problem of portrayal, and should also be seen as the invention of new models of sensuousness, relationships, and sociation away from the indifference of social relationships in the capitalism of the Weimar Republic. But these experiments essentially dealt with the problem of depiction and imagery, *rappresentazione* and *finzione*, as an imminent republic of calves.

Against Adorno's generalizing argument that European music is always oriented to representation it can be said that advanced painting, as far back as the

104 Translated from Goehr, "Schoenberg's 'Gedanke' Manuscript," p. 11.
105 Adorno, "Sacred Fragment," p. 230.
106 Ibid.

Renaissance, defended its strength in the *paragone* in its self-conception not as a poetic visual entity, not as an aesthetic phenomenon, but as indebted to mathematics, as the rebirth of a Pythagorean art of relationship rather than the imitative depiction of gods or men. This was insistently expressed in the spatial theories of the Quattro- and Cinquecento, in which, in the Renaissance, the principle of monotheism was anchored in the abstraction of the arithmeticized world, and not, as in the Middle Ages, through variable and hierarchically ordered ratios within a world view mapped according to the anatomy of *ecce homo.*[107] Giotto's fresco of the Franciscan exorcism of the many devils from Arezzo's architecture into the heaven once reserved for angels stands for such an introduction of a unified space, which creates a place in the sky for monsters, but only to be able to dispose of them more easily.[108] With the early Renaissance, depiction as perspective order becomes a foundation of the bourgeois art of government, but no work of art can be found that doesn't also depict the resistance to such regimentation as spatial disturbance. Light, color, or the distortion of form appear as material waywardness outside of perspective order.

The discovery of corresponding material boundlessness and formlessness in music as well would mean not seeking its beauty but its possible perception in the tradition of the sublime. The topos of the prohibition of images, which Adorno identifies as the actual subject matter of the opera *Moses und Aron*, refers precisely to this tradition. Despite this Adorno specifically *doesn't* mention it, as Philippe Lacoue-Labarthe notes in his careful reading of Adorno's critique of the work.[109] On the one hand Lacoue-Labarthe puts this down to Adorno's discretion: to understand the opera in the tradition of the sublime would have been equal to a devastating criticism, as for Adorno the analysis of the sublime, at least in the tradition of Kant, was always allied to dominance and power.[110]

107 See B. Martin Warnke and others, *EbsKart – Die Ebstorfer Weltkarte in hypermedialer Aufbereitung*, http://www.uni-lueneburg.de/hyperimage/EbsKart/start.html.

108 It's perhaps not by chance that Guido of Arezzo, a Benedictine monk, pushed through musical notation and solmization to unify and discipline liturgical chant. See Scherer, *Hildegard von Bingen*, p. 143ff.

109 See Lacoue-Labarthe, "Zäsur der Religion": "But now everything seems to point to the fact that Adorno would not hear of this." Translated from p. 462.

110 Evidence of this is given in the much-quoted passage from *Aesthetic Theory*: "[...] by situating the sublime in overpowering grandeur and setting up the antithesis of power and powerlessness, Kant directly affirmed his unquestioning complicity with domination." Theodor W. Adorno, *Aesthetic Theory*, trans. Robert Hullot-Kentor, London 2002, p. 199. A different view is offered by Wolfgang Welsch: "The shock in the experience of the sublime is that of subjectivity.

But on the other hand, as Lacoue-Labarthe objects, Adorno obscures a particular salvation of the work, namely the alternative of understanding it not from the perspective of beauty but from one of an unconceivable unaesthetic. Straub and Huilllet take up the tradition of the sublime when, in the case of Schoenberg against Adorno, they put the prohibition of images into their film as aesthetic explosive power and resistance. In this they link three aspects of the opera in which, as their commentaries and notes show, they confront Schoenberg's work with the political constellations at the time of its composition. In the aesthetic of the unconceivable under the sign of the sublime they again expose the historical breaks—1914, 1938, 1974—thus addressing the fundamental political problem of modernity as one of power and the masses. They cinematically radicalize Schoenberg's question of the people as the question of a people able to act politically, that is a people "under the law."

In fact Kant's analysis of the sublime stands more concretely in the context of the social, technical, and political upheavals of the seventeenth and eighteenth centuries than a limitation of the problem to aesthetics wishes to perceive. Speculations about worlds beyond a possible sensory experience make the sublime look like the appropriation of something unknown, and thus the emblem of a "modern imperialism" and its correlate scientific-technical forms of dominating the natural world.[111] Technical instruments and media, which Kant very cautiously lists in this context—microscopes and telescopes—may have provided infinitely large and small scales for imagining the "size of the world," but complementary to this the suspicion remains that not everything can be encompassed by this measurement and presumption, and that the human senses are

It certainly has to do with freedom (as laid down by Kant), although not (as he said) as superiority over nature but conversely in the sense of a liberation from the nature-dominating principle of self and subject." Welsch shows how the sublime, in this reversal to the "matrix of beauty," becomes an "explosive charge [...] on the horizon of reconciliation" and thus the essence of Adorno's aesthetics. See Wolfgang Welsch, "Adornos Ästhetik: eine implizite Ästhetik des Erhabenen," in Christine Pries (ed.), *Das Erhabene: Zwischen Grenzerfahrung und Größenwahn*, Weinheim 1989, pp. 185–213: 194.

111 For a concise discussion of this see Hartmut Böhme, "Das Steinerne. Anmerkung zur Theorie des Erhabenen aus dem Blick des 'Menschenfremdesten'," in Pries, *Das Erhabene*, pp. 119–141: 124: "This is initially the infinite space that results from the consequences of the Copernican revolution and translated from the More/Newton idea of infinity. It is the infinity that arose from the terrestrial spatial revolutions, and which—parallel to the cosmic conquest of space—massively intervened in the consciousness of European humanity in the increasing dominance of the oceans after Columbus."

fundamentally inadequate to the world: the realm of the non-aesthetic extends with every media-initiated aesthetics.[112] To bring this otherworld of the imagination back into the regime of thought, although it "infinitely surpasses all our powers,"[113] would be a function of the sublime, and it enters philosophical consciousness at the very point where the boundaries and peripheries of standard order make themselves felt "in the disposition of the mind" and not in the object, as Kant warns. The sublime should therefore be understood as resistance, which introduces the problem of the materialities, boundaries, and disturbances of perception. Hegel took up this aesthetics, which he delegated to a subject-less spirit.[114] Bringing back such progress into sensibility, into a world of things, and showing that the transference into a realm of heaven and hell is initially nothing but concrete though unperceived media operations, is the achievement of the opera's film version. It corresponds both to the enlightener Kant and to the epistemologist Schoenberg, in that epochal shifts in the field of knowledge require the development of forms of portrayal in which new fields can be revealed and conceived. That, since Kant, is also a political problem.

Similarly as pioneering as Giotto in Arezzo, with the sublime Kant liberates certain overwhelming kinds of perception from their conventional feudal forms of reception, and in the "unleashing of the elemental"[115] formulates a new, ascetic frame of mind for the incomprehensible, particularly in nature. A paradox in Kant's radical strategy emerges here: in the sublime the self should boldly be subjected to what daunts it as an aesthetic that, although putting the

112 See Joseph Vogl, "Medien-Werden: Galileis Fernrohr," in Lorenz Engell, Joseph Vogl (eds.) *Mediale Historiographien. Archive für Mediengeschichte*, Weimar 2001, pp. 115–123.

113 Immanuel Kant, *Critique of Judgement*, trans. James Creed Meredith, ed. Nicholas Walker, Oxford, New York 2007, p. 212.

114 See Georg Wilhelm Friedrich Hegel, *Aesthetics. Lectures on Fine Art*, vol. 1, trans. Tim M. Knox, Oxford, New York 1975, p. 362. Hegel takes up Kant's distinction and transfers it in a dialectic turn to the realm of the artistically beautiful. The section on the "symbolism of sublimity" opens with a formulation which reflects Schoenberg's own about "purifying one's thought": "Now the first decisive purification of the absolute [meaning] and its express separation from the sensuous present, i.e. from the empirical individuality of external things, is to be sought in the sublime. Sublimity lifts the Absolute above every immediate existent and therefore brings about the liberation which, though abstract at first, is at least the foundation of the spirit." Schoenberg's "purify your thinking" would thus be an initial dialectic progress into sensibility. For an analysis of the opera *Moses und Aron* Hegel provides the insistence on the opposition of beauty and sublimity, and that the sublime must be released from subjectivity into absolute substance, into "what is there." (ibid., p. 112).

115 Adorno, *Aesthetic Theory*, p. 196.

imagination in its place, can be processed by reason[116]—Schoenberg calls this its "comprehensibility."[117] Even so, in order to liberate the subject from incomprehensible devils and demons that are monstrous, unlovely, and yet attractive, Kant develops his analysis of the sublime as a procedure of reason, which is not freedom or the law but the capacity for freedom and legalism, and thus puts a progressive intellectuality to the test of a new bourgeois subjectivity.[118] Independence is to be had in recognizing the sublime as the unportrayable, which "must in every case have reference to our way of thinking,"[119] that is "to maxims directed to giving to the intellectual side of our nature and to the ideas of reason supremacy over sensibility."[120] This is also promised by Schoenberg's Moses in his final words of the opera, when he promises "Aber in der Wüste seid ihr unüberwindlich [But even in the wasteland you shall be victorious]."[121] A further aspect of the sublime can be seen here, and is made up of the media upheavals, the dynamic forces that reason is unable to control, and an unconstituted people: it is the fear, so easily instilled, of the threat of inhuman power. The figure of Moses, like his successors, faces this fear by going into the desert. He can thus, like Freud's Moses, be described as the hero of an analysis exploring the fate of desires in the space of collective symbolic fields and orders rather than individual experience. As with Freud, the model for Schoenberg's Moses is the inhuman, which he, like Freud, first discovered in Michelangelo: "My Moses more resembles – of course only in outward aspect – Michelangelo's. He is not human at all."[122] Schoenberg's Moses also assumes a smooth space of the "Wunschlosigkeit der Wüste [wasteland's renunciation]."[123] Schoenberg's Aron

116 See Böhme, "Das Steinerne": "The process of reason exists in this. It serves the comprehensive autonomization of the subject against all other-directedness. The pathos of the Enlightenment can be felt here—a liberation from primordial powers that break in upon human beings largely through the gate of fear, and rob them of the possibility of intellectual or practical self-determination." Translated from p. 121.

117 Schoenberg, "Composition with Twelve Tones," p. 216.

118 See Kant, *Critique of Judgement*, p. 335: "We should properly have to describe this legislation as heautonomy since the power of judgement furnishes the law neither for nature nor for freedom but solely for itself," and also the systematics of the critique of judgement, ibid., p. 347.

119 Kant, *Critique of Judgement*, p. 104.

120 Ibid.

121 Schoenberg, *Moses und Aron*, vocal score, act III, unpaginated.

122 Schoenberg on March 15, 1933 to Walter Eidlitz, who had sent him his own research on the Moses complex, the book "Der Berg in der Wüste," in Schoenberg, *Letters*, p. 172.

123 Schoenberg, *Moses und Aron*, vocal score, act III, unpaginated.

will have to remind him that the desert, like the sleep of reason, produces monsters.

While in regard to Schoenberg's opera the divine name and its pronunciation in a demythologizing prayer would perhaps obtain a partial truth in Adorno's sense, through Straub/Huillet's film it becomes clear that the ideas about the prohibition of images are more radical even in the opera and its libretto.[124] They raise issues about the preconditions of visual, tonal, and sensory perception, which are secularized in classical critical theory as the question of ideology and the fetish character of images.[125] But while it's perhaps premature in the context of critical thought to claim a "visual reception" of Straub and Huillet's film that "seems to shatter" in the conflict between a "radicalized aniconism" and "a downwardly conveyed media culture,"[126] the film's procedures, in reorganizing the visual space not iconoclastically but analytically, show this break and discontinuance as a form of analysis. As a result, and differently from Adorno's claim for the technical medium,[127] it isn't natural beauty—food for the culture industry as desire and pleasure—that is taken into the calculation of the media image construction, but rather sublimity, which distills aversion from the desire to look. According to Kant this occurs "in the event of an absolutely large object – the desert, a mountain, a pyramid – or one that is absolutely powerful – a storm at sea, an erupting volcano – which like all absolutes, can only be

124 Here Verena Lenzen's dictum "In two short commentaries Adorno and Lacoue-Labarthe advance to the quintessence of Schönberg's aniconism, to the essential truth of *Moses und Aron*: the concept of the divine name," is very brief, and in regard to Lacoue-Labarthe, who examines *Moses und Aron* in the tradition of tragedy, not to the point. Translated from Verena Lenzen, "Vom Bilderverbot zum jüdischen Gebet bei Arnold Schönberg," in Michael J. Rainer and Hans-Gerd Janßen (eds.), *Bilderverbot. Jahrbuch politische Theologie 2*, Münster 1997, pp. 239–251: 246.

125 See Koch, "In Sachen Moses gegen Aron": "[...] the suspicion that the essence of the image condenses in its fetish character has continued through into contemporary debates. The fact that the prohibition of images contained in the Second Commandment has an aesthetic aspect (which seems to have arisen from the theological legacy) is one of the key ideas in Theodor W. Adorno's aesthetics; that the prohibition of images became a productive inherent conflict in Judaism, on the one hand in the tendency to the scripting of images, on the other in the focus on word and music as expressive media, is an often-aired cultural-historical supposition." Translated from p. 13.

126 See ibid., pp. 13–14.

127 See Theodor W. Adorno, "Filmtransparente," in Adorno, *Ohne Leitbild. Parva Aesthetica*, Frankfurt/Main 1967: "The technical medium par excellence is deeply akin to natural beauty." Translated from p. 81f.

thought, without any sensible/sensory intuition, as an Idea of reason."[128] When therefore, as Lyotard writes, "the faculty of presentation, the imagination, fails to provide a representation corresponding to this Idea,"[129] a strict media realization of this failure could mean visualizing the unavoidable disturbances of mimesis itself in order to point out to the imagination its dissoluble connection to historical techniques of seeing and hearing. This wouldn't be a critique of ideology but a literal laying waste of the image and its perception.

Explicitly disassociating himself from the Anglo-Saxon tradition, Kant elucidates five aspects of a culture of the sublime that are intended to explain why the imagination so disastrously fails[130] when faced with certain phenomena: first, the formlessness of the sublime; second, the sheer materiality that emerges; third, the palpable enormousness, fourth, resistance in the perception of the sublime; fifth, its emotional charge,[131] which brings home the fact that it has to do with a "disposition of the mind," not with that of the outer world and its waterfalls, and that the sublime thus dwells not "in the things of nature, but only in our own ideas."[132]

The analysis of the sublime particularly suggests itself for cinematic theory and thought because it is exactly in the sight lines of this aesthetic that Gilles Deleuze, in his film books, exposes the tremendous "power-quality"[133] with which the cinema transforms perception and thinking. In his concept of the random space, which unleashes the dynamic of affects and takes affectivity beyond subjectivity, Deleuze draws a line back to sublimity. For he develops the concept in regard to Béla Balázs's remarks about the close-up, in which Balázs precisely follows the qualities of the sublime, as systemized by Kant, as impressions of boundlessness and formlessness. Not only because he sees the close-up as resistance within the space-time continuity of the flow of perception but also in that he observes the correspondence of incomparable phenomena in the dissolution of proportions, Balázs follows Kant's analysis and gives almost the same example: "A raging sea, a glacier above the clouds, a storm-lashed

128 Jean-François Lyotard, *The Inhuman. Reflections on Time*, trans. Geoffrey Bennington and Rachel Bowlby, Cambridge 1991, p. 98.

129 Ibid.

130 See Kant, *Critique of Judgement*, p. 84ff.

131 Böhme, "Das Steinerne," p. 120. He speaks here of "oxymoronal affect form."

132 Kant, *Critique of Judgement*, p. 80.

133 Deleuze, *Cinema 1. The Movement-Image*, p. 110.

forest or the painful expanses of a desert."[134] It suddenly becomes very clear how close Deleuze's deliberations on affect are to the disposition of mind described in the *Critique of Judgement* that is brought about when the boundlessness and formlessness of particular phenomena surpass the faculty of imagination and through this emphasize the material. At the same time it is this state beyond subjectivity that creates perceptual resistance and gives rise to contradictory emotions. But it can primarily be seen that Deleuze, in his adaptation or transformation of the sublime for the cinema, reveals an aspect of Kant's thought that could be productive and liberating for film and media theory: in the function and effects of images that, like those technical media that undermine conscious and intentional reasoning, are "ill-adapted to our faculty of presentation, and do violence, as it were, to the imagination,"[135] it is no longer solely the eeriness of the large single Other that is at work in Hegel's tradition, but diverse elements. Kant's critique can be made productive for a media theory that follows the trail of resistance in order to get the measure of the unperceivable constructions, textures, and operations of media configurations in the blind field of perception. Research into the nature of the affect follows this notion precisely.

1) FORMLESSNESS

With formlessness Kant refers to the attempts of thought to discover the conditions of its possibility beyond the imagination and before all form. His reference to lack of form is a recursive figure of thought. At this point sublimity is directly connected to the absolute nothingness that dictated the Mosaic prohibition of images, a nothingness that Schoenberg extends to the possibility of portrayal and a look into the abyss beyond nature and symbolic systems. Different from sublimity in nature, which incapacitates the imagination because it permits no synthesizing conception in the storm, the flash of lightning, and the wave, the sublime in art—unconceivable for Kant—has first to be produced. Schoenberg frustrates the totalitarian aspect that threatens the absolute in this sense, not only in the "sheer density of the construction" mocked by Adorno, which "becomes the medium in which the ineffable can manifest itself without usurpation,"[136] and not only in his attention to the fragility of language (as

134 Balázs, *Early Film Theory*, p. 41. See also Deleuze, *Cinema 1. The Movement-Image*, p. 91 ff.
135 Kant, *Critique of Judgement*, p. 76.
136 Adorno, "Sacred Fragment," p. 245.

discovered by Philipp Lacoue-Labarthe), but primarily through admitting an otherworld beyond representation into the work as a wealth of non-notatable sounds. In Schoenberg's experiments with tone color, in his media-technical stage directions, and in the noises he requires to be staged, he evokes formlessness as a diversity of differences. Schoenberg opens his opera with an acoustic space from which an absolute, monotheistic God will announce himself, but even this absolute is only realized as concrete sound. This is repeated in the relationship between the score, the symmetrical rows of the first symbolic configurations, and the realized sounds of voices and instruments. What the Moses figure thinks is a constellation and a media-technical effect. What is heard requires a decision that can't be reduced to a symbol, and has to be decided in so far as it is undecidable.

Straub and Huillet strengthen the implicit undecidability with cinematic means when they have the voice from the burning bush sound from an *off* space that can't be clearly assigned to the image. This voice isn't readily attributable to a source, not even of a sound source or tone color, in the conventions of the *off*, the *hors-champ*, or the acousmatic. The correspondence of voice and audibility to the call only comes about through the audiovisual integration operating in the viewer's perception: as an effect of the "disposition of mind" in the age of technical media that "infinitely surpasses all our powers."[137] Call and calling are not imagined or imaginary circumstances but media effects. Such hearing can be sublime or an adherence to a decision, but only so long as the undecidability is kept open.

Schoenberg takes formlessness further in his dissolution of conventional musical forms, in the serial technique, which isn't itself audible as form, and particularly not in the dissolution of individual voices and positions. In the altercation between Moses and Aron this relationship between speaking and singing voices, which makes a difference audible without marking a here of portrayal and a there of the voice as a significate of the said, there is no secured space from which representation and the represented could be related and attributed to one another.

Particularly in the second part of the opera, in the tumult of the people and its bloody rituals in the night of the Golden Calf, the sublime is juxtaposed as the power of the work to the failing imagination of the people, although "the" people oscillates in terms of media and staging between the chorus and the

137 Kant, *Critique of Judgement*, p. 212.

perception of the viewers. Neither Schoenberg's opera nor Straub/Huillet's film cynically direct the sublime, in its ambivalence as both repellent and desirable, against a dull-witted people, but on the contrary to its potential: the desire to see and imagine something that gives the Golden Calf form is foiled by the ecstatic orgy required by the libretto, in which all form is once again dissolved. Schoenberg in particular regarded the orgy scene as the outrageous and monstrous core of his opera: "In the treatment of this scene, which actually represents the very core of my thought, I went pretty much to the limit, and this too is probably where my piece is most *operatic*; as indeed it must be."[138] The ambivalence of unity and plurality, inhumanity and humanity, becomes the core and catastrophe of the performance.[139] The unperformability that the opera and the film enforce on themselves holds them to the law. This division, the portrayal of the unportrayable, is the compositional principle of the music, text, and staging. Schoenberg shows what cannot be shown as a non-place in a complex network of relationships, and even speculates about the intrusion of chance into his thinking: "Composing is basically gambling."[140]

The project of conceiving formlessness as thought and system, and not as the fragment or shard of a Tablet of the Law but as the entirety of an opera that, as Adorno bewilderedly remarks, "no doubt can be permitted to impugn the category of greatness,"[141] was taken by critical theory as sheer delusion, less sublimity than bourgeois megalomania. Schoenberg's opera, however, differently and no less radically, sketches a systematic cultural analysis that traces the origin of forces and relationships back to the elementary units of the audible, written, and visible and their sensory conveyance. When Schoenberg returns the unconceivable whole to signs and sounds, writing and voices, words and tones, and finally to apparatuses and transmission systems, through which such a whole is reflected in the empirical subject, he is above all interested in the genealogy of power and its unconceivable entrenchment in bodies. Class relationships and

138 Letter to Walter Eidlitz on March 15, 1933, in Schoenberg, *Letters*, p. 172.

139 Schoenberg calculated that "at least four to five hundred persons should be on the stage in order to create the impression of the many. This is one of the difficulties of this performance." Letter from Schoenberg to Hermann Scherchen on January 16, 1950. Translated from Schönberg, *Moses und Aron, Entstehungsgeschichte*, p. 17.

140 Translated from Goehr, "Schoenberg's 'Gedanke' Manuscript," p. 6.

141 Adorno, "Sacred Fragment," p. 242.

racism aren't negated but explored in the dynamic of wider relational networks of the visible and audible.

The division of labor between Moses and Aron then appears to negotiate media laws of transformation: "Aron, was hast du getan? [Aaron, o what have you done?]" "Nichts Neues! Nur was stets meine Aufgabe war: Wenn dein Gedanke kein Wort, mein Wort kein Bild ergab, vor ihren Augen, ihren Ohren ein Wunder zu tun [Naught diff'rent, just my task as it ever has been: When your ideas gave forth no word, my word gave forth no image for them, I worked marvels for eyes and ears to witness]" (act II, bars 984–988). What today is critically seen as trivial knowledge about the transformation of media data flows in words, music, or films is not simply bemoaned by Schoenberg as a cultural history and crisis of absolute thought since Moses, but dealt with by means of his opera and its "synthetic" music of the future. The question of when a signal becomes a tone, an image, a form, a voice, and finally a mission had already been posed by Wagner's confusion of noise and tones.[142] But Schoenberg was the first to work through the problem systematically as a social theory and foundation for a genesis of power and morality in *Moses und Aron*.

Straub and Huillet follow him precisely where his analysis concerns the history of the perception of film. They transfer Schoenberg's procedures to cinematic constructs in which Mosaic differentiations are strictly and self-referentially questioned in optics, shots, and camera movements. In this they profess an increasing interest in the figure of Aron, who is compelled in his politics of images and sounds to continually devise new solutions and dissolutions in order to sell the portrayal of the unportrayable in a world of transferences as a political message. Aron analyzes media just as exactly as Moses before the burning bush. In his high, lyric, somewhat truculent song he ironically repeats or simulates the indistinguishability of hearing voices and receiving and understanding a command in order to appear himself as a medium to some extent, while Moses regards himself as the message itself.

Straub and Huillet intensify this antagonism through cinematic means by unambiguously staging it as competing spatial structures. This can clearly be seen, for example, in those shots that are framed and edited in such a way that Moses and Aron each require their own *hors-champ*, their own surroundings, which are no longer merged into an overall space. Straub and Huillet make use

142 See Kittler, "Signal-Rausch-Abstand," p. 175.

of the confusion of *off* or *hors-champ* in the Straubian off-space to put the indistinguishability of hallucination and command, of hearing voices and perceiving behests to the test of the perception of the film audience between sound and semantics:

> Shot 74, Long/Medium, lens 18.5: on Moses and Aron; Moses with the tablets, left, more to the front, Aron right, more to the rear (bar 984ff)
>
> Moses:
> Aron,
> was hast du getan?
>
> [Aaron,
> o what have you done?]
>
> Aron:
> Nichts Neues.
> Nur was stets meine Aufgabe war:
> Wenn dein Gedanke kein Wort, mein Wort kein Bild ergab,
> Vor ihren Ohren, ihren Augen ein Wunder zu tun.
> [Naught diff'rent,
> just my task as it ever has been:
> When your idea gave forth no word, my word gave forth
> no image for them, I worked marvels for eyes and ears to witness.]
>
> Moses:
> Auf wessen Geheiß?
>
> [Commanded by whom?]
>
> Shot 75 Close-up: on Aron
> Aron *on*:
> Wie immer:
> Ich hörte die Stimme in mir.
>
> [As always,

I heeded the voice from within.]

Moses *off*:
Ich habe nicht gesprochen.

[But I did not instruct you.]

Aron *on*:
Aber ich habe dennoch verstanden.

[Nevertheless I comprehended.]

Moses *off*:
Schweig![143]

[Cease!]

In the filmic analysis the problem of the opera is condensed in this interlocking of *off* and *on* voices as apparently inner and outer, as Aron suggests, in the interlocking of call, interpretation, command, and obedience: the overwhelming issue of ubiquitous and omnipotent voices and noises can be diagnosed as an expanding and even imperialist system that, at least media technically, infinitely surpasses human senses. That would be the desert position, which has become media-theoretically productive as critical paranoia. Or we could simply develop its picturesque side: stereotypical thinking that doesn't come to grips with the law and the overall dynamic, and to a certain extent realizes the endless examinations of material studies. It becomes clear that opera and film both go beyond a simple aporia of polytheism and monotheism. With his "Cease!" Moses establishes a caesura, at which he, and with him Schoenberg, puts authority in place of this contradiction. Straub, on the other hand, brings in the authority of the people at this point:

143 Translated from Huillet, "Moses und Aron. Das Drehbuch," p. 242.

Cahiers: What is it that causes you to think today about polytheism with the figure of Aron, after you made this film in 1974, or Schönberg his opera. after two thousand years of monotheism (this monotheism, which incidentally has fostered imperialist civilizations)? Or to put it another way, how can we HISTORICIZE the pair Moses/Aron? Or is it more an eternal, uncrossable pair?

Straub: It isn't entirely true that Aron draws everything from Moses. He also draws something from the people. The two men are compelled to correct things through continual invention. And therefore two elements are necessary in order to understand Aron: the two last shots in which we see him singing. The first, which remains on Aron, in which he is completely stunned, terrorized, and aggrieved at Moses' sentence: "Gottes Ewigkeit vernichtet Götter Gegenwart! Das ist kein Bild, kein Wunder! Das ist das Gesetz! [God's eternity opposes idols' transience! No image this, no marvel! These are the commands!]" The shot is protracted, as the orchestra goes on playing and we stay on Aron. Then we return to Moses, who is showing his tablets. And in the next shot, the last one in which Aron sings, there are these two key sentences about him: Here he explains that he knows very well what to do: to "dissolve" Moses's idea [the German libretto contains the word "auflösen" here, but the English libretto doesn't convey this meaning, trans.]. "Dissolve," which is meant in the exact etymological sense of the chemical term: to analyze.[144]

Straub refers here to the dialogue in which, after Aron wishes to convey the unconceivable idea to the people, Moses asks from the *off* in threatening complex syncopation, *off-off* beat, so to speak: "Ich soll den Gedanken verfälschen? [Am I to debase the idea?]" to which Aron replies in a complex melody "Laß mich ihn auflösen!" [literally, and not in the English libretto "Let me dissolve it," *trans.*], boldly clearing the octave of Pythagorean cosmology by a semitone between the syllables "auf-lö" into a high *pianissimo* (act II, bars 1041–1042).

This is not only the key sentence for Straub and Huillet but also for Schoenberg's compositional procedure of not simply putting the expressionist music

144 Translated from Straub/Huillet, "Conversation," p. 17.

into the space that Adorno wanted to hear in it, but sounds of dissolution: a musical spatial analysis as social analysis.[145]

However, it isn't realized as an idea of simple, zestful humanity, as Aron suggests: "Auch du würdest dieses Volk lieben, hättest du gesehen, wie es lebt, wenn es sehen, fühlen, hoffen darf! [You also would have loved this people, had you only seen how they lived when they dared to see and feel and hope!]" (act II, bars 1023–1028). Such humanity, as Aron well knows, is due to a simple technique of control that doesn't assert the law but instead "umschreibend, ohne auszusprechen: Verbote [describing, without specifying: restrictions]" (act II, bar 1043). Instead of translating legalism with the aid of illustrative images and scenes into concrete instructions of resistance, "furchterregend doch befolgbar [fear-inspiring yet not too harsh]," as Aron advises (act II, bar 1044), Straub and Huillet again put the people as absence at the center of their own analysis and initiate political thought processes in the withdrawal of images.

2) MATERIALITY: CONSONANTS AND BLACK LEADER

Complementarily to the formlessness of an aesthetic of sublimity, Straub and Huillet examine the materiality of media. In this they can rely on Schoenberg in their basic operations—the modulation of movement, light, and vibrations, and recurrently their fundamental withdrawal. Where Schoenberg operates with theater and media techniques, Straub/Huillet use basal cinematic forms: black-screen sequences, which show the unformed aspect of the medium itself as a withdrawal of its materiality, of light, and white-screen phases break into act II, which is constructed conversely to the geometrically staged act I and functions like a series of heterogeneous tableaus. This corresponds to a dissolution of the acoustic form. In the interlude before act II, in a passage in which Schoenberg's music operates almost exactly between Bach and Eisler in its rhythm, setting, and dramaturgy of tone color, the chorus is divided into two sound aggregates, two *Sprechstimme* choirs, a rhythmically whispering one and a hissing one: "Where is Moses?" The opening vocalise now becomes a consonantise. The people expresses itself in sibilants, not as harmony and reverberation and

145 Film criticism is always social criticism—as a variation on Siegfried Kracauer's claim: "The film critic of note is conceivable only as a social critic." Siegfried Kracauer, "The Task of the Film Critic," in Martin Jay, Anton Kaes (eds.), *The Weimar Republic Source Book*, Berkeley 1995, p. 635.

“Auflösen” [dissolve], Schönberg, *Moses und Aron.*

space. The people become rhythmical. "Wo ist Moses? Verlassen sind wir!" [Where is Moses? Abandoned are we!]" Consonants, ejections of breath without vowels, with the sharpest of sounds that can be transmitted, that shibboleth of all choral singers and sound technicians: ss-ss-ss-ss-ss.[146] For this section, in which voices alternately sing a few sequences and then return to *Sprechgesang*, Schoenberg requires a small chorus, "invisible in the darkness," to sing in front of the curtain so that "the different voices will be heard to come from different directions." Once again Schoenberg assembles the people in the constellation of heterogeneous acoustic spaces and small shifts in the choral parts. The voices should sing softly, but "sharply distinguished from one another."[147]

Straub and Huillet follow these instructions in that they simulate this purely acoustic space in the movie theater, and cut it black leader for the more than two minutes of the choral interlude of the—as we know from Freud—attempted murder of Moses.[148] The darkness of a primordial murder suddenly becomes a cinematic experience of liminal perception. Kant's argument of a sheer materiality with which the sublime overwhelms the imagination is transferred to the reflection of a cinematic physical perceptual situation that has to constitutively undermine consciousness, intellect, and understanding. At the same time this withdrawal of the image concentrates the attention onto hearing. While Freud explains that the traumatic moment of the primordial murder, which can't be recollected, is covered over by a symbolic castration, and thus the establishment of a legalism based on a complete proscription of killing,[149] in the black screen in the cinema, that true blackout,[150] the experience of a completely disorganized matter—black leader, darkness, voices—is likewise transformed into the cinematic organization of the senses, while annoyingly recalling the hidden *dispostif* underlying all cinematic perception. For the intermittent movement of the images beneath the threshold of perception must continue on the black

146 Here a connection could be made to Hollywood's legendary tongue twister "Moses supposes ...," from SINGIN' IN THE RAIN, which demonstrates the intrusion of phonetics into the studios as a result of the revolution of sound film. SINGIN' IN THE RAIN, USA 1952, dir. Gene Kelly, Stanley Donen.

147 All quotes from Schoenberg, *Moses und Aron*, vocal score, interlude, bar 1ff.

148 Naturally a considerable and not at all sublime impossibility for any television channel, which today would have to flag up the information "Black screen, no intermission."

149 Freud, *Moses and Monotheism*, p. 192.

150 See Matthias Wittmann, "Am Anfang war das Blackout. Zur Konstruktion des Gedächtnisses in der Erfahrung des Films," in *Zeitschrift für Medienwissenschaft* 2, April 2010, pp. 41–52.

screen, which thus functions differently from simple darkness. But this too can't be perceived in itself. What is perceived is a transformation of the space and the sensory order. In this regard the materiality of the black screen refers to the darkness of the theater; it turns the gaze of the viewer onto itself and transfers the events at a (cymbal) stroke[151] from the arena of Alba Fucense into the movie theater. At the same time the theater is no longer the place of a fictional occurrence but a form of sensory reality.

On the visual level, in this application of the prohibition of images, the dark of the black leader causes gaze and eye to come apart, while on the acoustic level the voices and the auditory space fuse. The sound space is realized in such a way that "Where is Moses?" hisses into the moviegoers' ears, as the burning bush hummed in the beginning, as an "agitation," following Kant, "that characterizes the pathos of the sublime, as opposed to the calm feeling of beauty."[152]

The black-screen phase is followed by a medium shot of the silent Aron in the arena to the right of a deep black field—an exit to the underground foundations of the amphitheater. Alone and isolated in the frame, he is exposed to the *hors-champ* sound of the chorus of the Elders and a Priest, who mockingly demand the production at last of the "unperceivable command from one who's yet unperceived." This is all handled through the provision and withdrawal of the cinematic image. The demand, declaimed by the representatives of the people, directs the interest to Aron, who has to find a solution to the popular petition on his own. At this point he replies with the happy formula "You cannot expect form before idea" (act II, bars 92–96).

Straub and Huillet have the uproar of the people grow loud—for the first time clearly above the music—as indistinct noises of sand and stones on the acoustic level of the soundtrack, as dry, objective, and spaceless as only the Nagra and Hochet's studio microphones could record. Schoenberg, more drastically and in much clearer reference to the space, specifies: "Growing sounds of shouting and raging approach quickly, then in furious agitation the roaring crowd rushes upon the stage from all directions."[153] Straub and Huillet's solution does without ethnic tumult with reverberation and space, and instead places the noise

151 Actually the cymbal F-sharp of the last sound of act I, bar 970.

152 Lyotard, *The Inhuman*, p. 98.

153 Schönberg, *Moses und Aron*, score II, act II, note after bar 113, with the general pause, preceding scene 2.

onto the soundtrack as a disturbance whose extent can't be gauged; it could be an insurrection or a rat nibbling at a cable. As a sensory stimulation of the viewer's ear, and from an invisible and unconceivable *hors-champ*, this disturbance is certainly discomforting. Consistently, from a new *off*, which in this case is insinuated to be the *hors-champ* of the chorus of Elders, the people's chorus continues its sharp consonantal threat: "Wo ist Moses? Daß wir ihn zerreißen! [Where is Moses? We'll tear him assunder!]" (act II bar 114ff). An ejection that would make any lawgiver wish he had brought back a vocalic alphabet from Mount Sinai: no dimension or relation as logos can be had from the sibilants.[154] With this cinematic coup of having the people appear as media disturbance and not as form or formation, Straub and Huillet again transpose Schoenberg's opera into an aesthetics of resistance.

3) BOUNDLESSNESS: LIGHT WITHOUT SUN

For Kant the lack of a suitable gauge distinguishes the sublime as "not merely great, but, without qualification, absolutely, and in every respect (beyond all comparison) great."[155] To have based the material, form, and thought of the opera on such boundlessness is Adorno's implicit criticism when he interprets Schoenberg's opera as a post-Wagnerian attempt to replace polytheistic cultic artistry—postmodernism *ante litteram*—with a coherent work once more. But Straub and Huillet discover something else in this project: Schoenberg's attempt to open up a space of possibility and enumerability through a politics of equal tonal and visual relationships. It's media-historically conspicuous that intensive work on the opera took place around 1930, when the relationship between visual and spatial order became politically virulent, and in which fascist and anti-Semitic nationalism clouded, in Heidegger's sense, the horizon of media politics. Riefenstahl's images of Hitler's landing from a giant cumulus among the gables of Nuremberg were a telling realization of this.

Arnold Schoenberg counters such ideas of clouds with the construction of potent fields. He opposes the cloud of statistics in procedures of enumerability,

154 See Lohmann, "Die Geburt der Tragödie aus dem Geiste der Musik." Lohmann emphasizes the following translation: "It is decisive to the history of the lógos concept that the word was a mathematical term in Greek science from the earliest times, translatable as 'relationship' (from this ana-log-ía, 'analogy' is then derived, a relationship of relationships)." Translated from p. 176.

155 Kant, *Critique of Judgement*, p. 80.

and explores the minutest of relationships. On the one hand Moses' and Aron's programmatic forms of perception encounter one another in the field of post-Romantic aesthetics. At the beginning the voice from the burning bush says "[...] so will you perceive my message in ev'ry thing" (act I, bars 56–58), and Aron will call out before the Golden Calf "Dieses Bild bezeugt, das in allem was ist, ein Gott lebt [This gold image attests that in all things that are, a god lives" (act II, bars 308–310). But Schoenberg seeks to establish a musical relationship to the world that goes beyond such presence and representation, that is liberated from convention and the old imaginative laws. For this he had to create a non-coded space. Hence for twelve-tone music it isn't the mathematical, formal, or calculable aspects that are decisive but the experiment of transcending all familiar forms in enumeration and new cultural techniques.

The danger of madness admittedly looms in this experiment. At the end of act II Moses will declare in despair, when even he is no longer sure of the distinction between bush and call, imagination and thinking, concrete image and abstract law: "So habe ich mir ein Bild gemacht, falsch, wie ein Bild nur sein kann. So bin ich geschlagen. So war alles Wahnsinn was ich gedacht habe [Then I have fashioned an image too, false, as an image must be. Thus am I defeated! Thus, all was but madness that I believed before]" (act II, bars 1121–1127). Once again Schoenberg's treatment of the Moses complex meets the Enlightenment idea of Immanuel Kant. Here too, in the liberation of the imagination, in the extension of the mental faculties beyond familiar bounds, he discovers not only a Promised Land of perception, not only liberation, but also new problems: imagination freed from the image easily leads to excess and enthusiasm in which morality considers itself to be a direct manifestation of the divine. Kant primarily sees this symptom in the monotheistic religions.

In the *Critique of Judgement*, which examines the forms of arresting the synthesizing imagination, Kant introduces the Mosaic prohibition of images as paradigmatic for the sublime in the Old Testament: "Perhaps there is no more sublime passage in the Jewish Law than the commandment: Thou shalt not make unto thee any graven image, or any likeness of any thing that is in heaven or on earth, or under the earth, etc. This commandment can alone explain the enthusiasm which the Jewish people, in their moral period, felt for their religion when comparing themselves with others, or the pride inspired by Mohammedanism. The very same holds good of our representation of the moral law and of our intrinsic capacity for morality."[156] In order to avoid the hubris, enthusiasm, and self-importance of monotheistic holy warriors and priests, Kant expressly uncouples the question of a legal structure in the categorical imperative from the name of the Lord to concentrate instead on general maxims in the face of the other, and also of the stranger. The other must always be thought of as special, that is the risk. In this context Kant brings in a short media-theoretical discourse: when images, as in the case of the sublime, become boundless and unconceivable, the power of the apparatus is shown. A prohibition of images, he argues, in no way leads to a withdrawal of emotionality or empathy that would have to be compensated by particular apparatuses. On the contrary: "For when nothing any longer presents itself to the senses, and the unmistakable and ineffaceable idea of morality is all that now remains, there would be need rather of tempering the ardour of an unbounded imagination to prevent it rising to enthusiasm, than of seeking to lend these ideas the aid of images and childish devices for fear of their lack of power."[157] In government through images and apparatuses of projection—and warned by Athanasius Kircher's Jesuit projection trick—Kant discovers a regulation of thought: "For this reason governments have gladly let religion be fully equipped with these accessories [that is, 'childish devices,' U.H.], seeking in this way to relieve their subjects of the exertion, but to deprive them, at the same time, of the ability, required for expanding their spiritual powers beyond the limits arbitrarily laid down for them, and this makes it all the easier to treat them as though they were merely passive."[158] In the light of Kant's observations, the cinema—which having been seen as morally harmful trash in its early days has always had to put up with the accusation of being a childish device, and which at the time of the opera's composition, under the National Socialists, became a medium of political regulation not only in its images but also in its regulated performance practices—requires an analysis that should not be entirely restricted to the side of images, depictions, and ideas, nor to that of the apparatus and its technical setup. Straub and Huillet take on this challenge at the very point in the opera concerned with the production of an image that should not simply represent but bear witness to the divine essence. In the scenes of the transformation of the people's wealth into a golden calf, and then

156 Ibid., 104.
157 Ibid., pp. 104–105.
158 Ibid., p. 105.

the portrayal of the dance and sacrificial rituals, they decisively no longer follow Schoenberg's instructions. Where Schoenberg hoped to realize his vision "with modern means as suggestions"[159] Straub and Huillet analyze suggestibility itself through cinematic means. In their montage of the film they on the one hand take on the position of Aron against Moses, namely that of making the mediality of images visible under monotheism too, and of showing up Moses' controlling aniconism to the eyes and ears instead of accepting a pure spirit that can't be manifested among people. On the other hand they strengthen Moses' position against Aron, namely that images are never an ersatz, representation, metaphor, or sign of the divine but directly stratifying power structures from which only nomads, victorious in the "wasteland's renunciation,"[160] can escape. In the movie this is realized by a piece of empty film. But exactly what kind of emptiness is difficult to determine. Some radiates before the gold takes on the glittering form of the calf. Something becomes "alltäglich sichtbar [common and visible]" (act II, bars 96–97), as Aron says, before the magic is attributed to the gods. The wind flutters his caftan as he sings.

"Bringt Gold herbei [Bring out your gold]," sings Aron, finally *on*. He takes over the leadership of the desperate people, and gives in to a reliable and dependable idea and conceivability: "Ihr sollt glücklich werden! [You then shall be happy!]" (act II, bar 200ff). Then follows that cut into the blue, which at first sight, and in old copies looks like blank film, white screen, and is so described in Danièle Huillet's protocol of the film: "Shot 50: white film."[161] The transformation from the immaterial to the material and back, from wind in motion, movement in light, from fabric to form[162] is shown while the chorus can be heard from the *off* as an almost three-minute imageless film on the screen. This shot is actually an image of light itself, light filmed in the Italian sunshine that on the new DVD edition shimmers blue like the film's images of the sky. An image without figures, but in the theater still an image of light. Not a nothing, no *off*. Cinema light always seeks a place this side of transcendence.

159 Letter to Hermann Scherchen on January 16, 1950, translated from Schönberg, *Moses und Aron, Entstehungsgeschichte*, p. 17.

160 See Huillet, "Moses und Aron. Das Drehbuch," p. 251.

161 Translated from Huillet, "Moses und Aron. Das Drehbuch," p. 230.

162 See Schönberg, *Moses und Aron*, score II, act II, bars 192–195. Aron: "Ihr spendet diesen Stoff, ich geb ihm solche Form [You shall provide the stuff; I shall give it a form]."

The people forms itself as a social body in this image. It is indeed happy that something should become visible at last. The chorus goes into three-four time, feels its "certainty assured" in the "earthly and visible" and waltzes through its good fortune of contributing to the construction of conceivable gods and worlds. Here Schoenberg causes the beat to flow. It is only striated in a state-supporting four-four time with "Juble Israel [Joyous Israel]," at bar 240, but from bar 246 the time signature varies between three-four, two-four, and four-four, so that it transitions into *lisse*, non-striated, smoothened tonal layers at the point when the chorus proclaims: "Farbig ist diese Gegenwart, düster ist jene Ewigkeit; Lebenslust scheut ihr Ende nicht, furchtlos, furchtlos sucht sie es freiwillig [Bright is this present instant, and dismal is that distant timelessness. Pleasure shuns not its consequence, fearlessly seeks it willingly]" (act II, bar 246ff). Straub and Huillet deprive this exuberance and declared security of the figural image and thus of a base. They let the people float for a while before the law in the smooth space of wishes, until with the final call of "Joyous Israel" (bars 300–307) everything is ordered in striated space in four-four time. Then with a wonderfully open chord and a further cymbal stroke the Golden Calf itself appears, materially, really, unmetaphorically, entirely authentically, though admittedly still an image of light.

While the acoustic element of the film MOSES UND ARON only comes together, and is thus realized, in the movie theater, the visual aspect of the white or sky-blue film takes on a different aspect: with the projection of the bright light, in contrast to black leader, the community of moviegoers becomes visible to itself in a practical analysis of what at least for early cinema theory was invoked, sometimes with pathos, as a collective in the dark of the projection. The sublime implodes into media empiricism. Or empirical materiality. The collective falls back into a multiplicity of individuals; the space becomes an ensemble of potential qualities that first have to be realized. For the time being, the people is still sitting in its cinema seats.

In this sense Straub and Huillet riskily bring together the formation of the Golden Calf, an image of light in the strict sense, and the formation of a people as a process of cinematic spatialization. Left alone, leaderless, sunless, imageless, what happens is what Kant apprehended from the mists of Königsberg: the fantasmatic goes to people's heads, takes up the "the ardour of an unbounded imagination," and sails beyond all reason. This not only questions the cinematic transformation of light-material into image-form; it also challenges the imagination, in "the brightness,"[163] as Deleuze says, to visualize what isn't or can't be portrayed: "das Grenzenlose in ein Bild zu fassen! [to enclose the boundless in an image!]" as Moses irately comments.[164]

When Moses finally returns from the mountain and sees the idol, he calls, from the *off*: "Vergeh, du Abbild des Unvermögens, das Grenzenlose in ein Bild zu fassen! [Be gone, you image of pow'rlessness to enclose the boundless in an image!]" (act II, bars 980–982). While Schoenberg simply notes "The golden calf vanishes. The crowd moves back and quickly disappears from the stage," encompassing the realization of people and depiction in one and the same process, Straub and Huillet apply the instructions cinematically and analytically: exactly at "Be gone!" they have a bright white light appear on the screen through a quick fade-in of the image of the Calf. This transition causes the image of the Calf and its after-image, produced on the retina by the blinding white film, to merge indistinguishably for a short while: a visual call, therefore, which unsparingly foils the division of subject and object, to perceive the shock of the boundless as the precondition of every order of seeing. When they dissolve in this cinematic light and link the optical illusion with the image on the screen, Straub and Huillet enlighteningly refer to the power that media automatically exert on bodies. Enlightenment through blinding; that would be the dialectic of the procedure.[165]

163 Deleuze, *Cinema 1. The Movement-Image* p. 103 (in the context of the construction of a random space of potential qualities).

164 Of course this white film is also a reference to Arnold Schoenberg, who wrote about "Composition with Twelve Tones": "To understand the very nature of creation one must acknowledge that there was no light before the Lord said: 'Let there be Light.' And since there was not yet light, the Lord's omniscience embraced a vision of it which only His omnipotence could call forth. We poor human beings, when we refer to one of the better minds among us as a creator, should never forget what a creator is in reality. A creator has a vision of something which has not existed before this vision. And a creator has the power to bring his vision to life, the power to realize it. In fact, the concept of creator and creation should be formed in harmony with the Divine Model; inspiration and perfection, wish and fulfillment, will and accomplishment coincide spontaneously and simultaneously. In Divine Creation there were no details to be carried out later." Schoenberg, "Composition with Twelve Tones," p. 214f.

165 The embodiment of visual power is an interesting variation on the biblical story in which Moses, after breaking the tablets, melts the Calf in the fire, grinds it to powder, dissolves it in water, and gives it to the Children of Israel to drink. Magical practices appear in the imageless monotheistic world. See Exodus 32.20.

An image of light, this side of transcendence.

4) RESISTANCE: "GIVE LIFE ITS TIME"

Straub and Huillet juxtapose the black leader and white film with the extreme materiality of the things their camera and tape record and transfer. Under the regime of the Golden Calf these are primarily images and sounds of animals. When Aron, filmed from below in a medium shot sings into the camera, "Quasi Recit.," as Schoenberg instructs, "This gold image attests that in all things that are, a god lives" (bars 308–310), the Calf stands behind him, in front of the now vividly azure sky of Abruzzo, demolishing the film's hitherto color dramaturgy and surface structure. Metallic light lies over this scene, turning the gaze against the eye. The word "Bild" (image) is set to two notes, more exactly to an interval, to the downward leap from D to F-sharp, minus eight semitones, and thus initiates an acoustic stratification, a difference and differentiation that then pervades the visual montage. A double or even triple referentiality divides and transforms the perceived image: "This image," of which Aron sings, could be both the Golden Calf and the entire filmic shot, which is so clearly out of line with the color and texture of the film; but the reference to "this image" might also announce the following very lively long shot. Filmed with an extremely short focal length with the high mountains in the background and the arena in the foreground, in which a large herd of animals—donkeys, oxen, and a white camel—show the film as a specific form of reality in their idiosyncratic movements, and the Golden Calf as the depiction of a quite different order, yet both still in the radius of culturally conventionalized forms of representation. Aron's witty reference to the image as an oscillating perception, as a changing attention to the sensuality of things, refers to a disposition of mind in Kant's sense of the sublime—that is, distinguished from the simple facts of things—but also to something that offers decisive resistance from outside, through the cinematographic *dispositif*, through the enhanced hearing and seeing of every

unconsciously synthesizing vision. Aron thus ruptures all simple iconological *and* iconoclastic contexts in order to make the fabric of reality visible. The film insistently replaces the question of what an image is with that of how an image transforms the perception of material, so that historical and social layers come to light.

In Straub and Huillet's film the "density of the construction," which Adorno saw as a merely technical way out of a philosophical crisis, is emphatically intensified. The only apparent ahistoricity of the animal movements, like the rustling of leaves in the wind, thus contributes to a realism that—historically precisely dateable through its cinematic recording and reproduction, and through corresponding archiving and historiography—can be perceived as resistance against homogeneous times and spaces, against the "stoniness" of history. In their montage from the position of Aron, that of media reflection, Straub and Huillet return the theological question to the arena of the historicity of seeing. Danièle Huillet describes this process in reference to the scene with the animals: "We make three very extended shots, because for such shots you only need to film and give life its time. Georges records the sound, and we greatly value the snorting of the animals and the lovely sounds of the harness and the wagon."[166]

The specific reality and historicity of the images is overridden in the next shot by a historical and historicizing stratum. Through the roofless, clear southern *parodos* of the amphitheater, which architecturally calls up a particular Graeco-Roman history, shepherds wearing archaizing costumes drive more animals, herds of sheep and oxen, into the arena, with movements that recall a cultural history of a few thousand years. These historicizing layers show that Straub and Huillet aren't concerned with dating but with surveying historical realities. The

166 Translated from Huillet, "Appunti sul giornale," p. 418.

Giving life its time; life takes its time.

shot brings cultural and natural history together in recorded gestures, traces, and voices.

At this point in the film Schoenberg's music is clearly overlaid for the second time, in this case by many kinds of animal noises, whose tone colors, at the end of a long orchestral section that juxtaposes extreme and outrageous *glissandi* with a quasi-oriental rhythm, mingle with those of the instruments—piano and percussion, wind and string: oxen and contrabassoon merge, in the way that previously the voice from the burning bush was a mix of instruments and voices.

In this scene of driving the herds, in which image and sound, as Huillet writes, waited for the rhythm from the shot,[167] a call synthesized from animal voices and instruments is issued. However, it is no longer heard from the otherworld, from transcendence but as a call from life and its concrete tone-color mix of beings, things, instruments, and probably recording machines: animal and mechanical. In this shot the viewers, we, are challenged to a certain extent to make a distinction: not to think of voices or gods but of living conditions. For this we need time, as this listening distinction is a recursive process that takes a while. To "give life its time," Huillet's neat formulation, exactly describes the lengthy and non-linear processes of knowing, or better of understanding, under media preconditions. In this sense it is the exact opposite of an ontological revelation. Connections with film history are always maintained. In the Golden Calf, which was replicated in plaster by Italian craftsmen from a granite

167 See ibid., p. 419: "We made a second attempt, and it was better. The rhythm came."

 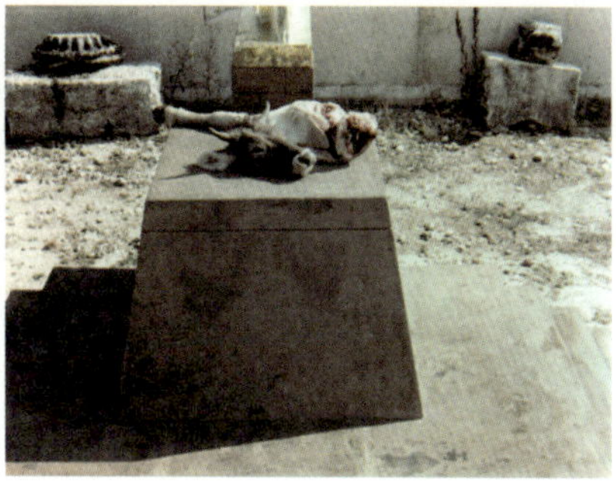

original in the Louvre and gilded in Cinecittà, Straub and Huillet were surprised to discover a "similarity to the little bull in LA LIGNE GÉNÉRAL. But we said to ourselves, it's no longer the general line, it's the right line, *la ligne juste*, and so we called it Justinian-Giustigniano."[168]

In their montage, which sets one image against another, one reality against another, noises against tones, sound against reverberation, and thus material historicity against the sameness of social processes, Straub and Huillet put a cinematic resistance into the opera *Moses und Aron*, not as a prohibition of images but, as Straub emphasizes in the interview, as an analysis of images. This operates with caesura and difference, and ultimately takes the affectivity of the sublime into account as a perverse delight in a "momentary check to the vital forces"[169]—which are then set in motion all the more violently—that "pleases immediately through its resistance to the interest of the senses."[170] Giving life its time means above all that the process of understanding includes the heart standing still, the breath faltering, the jaw dropping, and the words failing. Thus Danièle Huillet's protocol is an observation of her own reactions. When the camel mare had to be transported away at the end of the film she noted: "The sudden freedom, the donkeys, the sand—now she didn't want to go back to the zoo. She had to be forcefully pulled into the truck, and her

168 Ibid. p. 403.
169 Kant, *Critque of Judgement*, p. 76.
170 Ibid., p. 97.

rebellion, which I hear of after I have completed the payments, strangles my heart."[171] Liberation is always a shock for the body. The dusty image of the herds streaming into the arena is a good example of this. Michael Gielen said: "The two big intrusions—the pan over the Nile Valley and the herds streaming into the arena—awaken and convey a feeling of liberation such as I have hardly ever experienced—and certainly not in a film."[172]

The resistive organization of the smallest differences in the visual space corresponds to the distribution and displacement of differing layers of sound in the musical composition. Here the people enters the acoustic and visual image as a plurality. In the following scenes Straub and Huillet develop careful subtleties of camerawork and movement.

This applies, for example, to the lyrical, woodwind-accompanied aria of the Invalid Woman (act II, bars 457–468), which Elfriede Obrowsky sings half reclining, from a stretcher covered with a large cowhide. While the ice-cold Golden Calf, to which she sings, "O Götterbild, du strahlst, du wärmst, du heilst, wie niemals die Sonne heilt [O godly form, your rays give warmth, you heal, as never the sun's rays have healed]," isn't visible in the frame, a possible bovine warmth, the hide, fills almost a third of the screen in solidarity, like the rest of the visible fabrics, with the warm tone of the oboe and English horn against the smooth and hard elements of the monumental structure. At the end of this shot, after the Invalid Woman has been carried off screen and the pedestal of the idol becomes visible, the camera unexpectedly moves across the geometry of its stones to the grass-covered floor of the arena and centers for a long while on old hewn architectural remains, while the strings vary the aria once again. Such shots, which are completely out of line with a narration, and in which, like filmic deliberations on the musical structure of "tones which are related only with one another,"[173] "images are related only with one another" in a single take, are precise methods of constituting a non-hierarchical cinematic space.

Straub and Huillet proceed correspondingly in regard to the people. In the next shot farmers from the environs of Alba Fucense enter the scene one after another and make sacrifices to the Golden Calf. Schoenberg envisaged this as

171 Translated from Huillet, "Appunti sul giornale," p. 419.

172 Translated from Gielen, "Gespräch mit Michael Gielen," p. 283.

173 See Schoenberg, "Composition with Twelve Tones," p. 218.

a spectacle: "[A]s the darkness falls [...] flames arise everywhere"; the actions he thinks up arise from fascination: "Enchanted by the miracle of the Invalid Woman some people have gathered round the Golden Calf and form themselves in two groups, Beggars on one side, a few Old Men on the other."[174] Straub and Huillet, in contrast, show the *contradini* themselves in a disturbing vulnerability, but rather the people themselves in a disturbing vulnerability. When they have laid before the altar their "[letzte] Lumpen, die uns vor Sonnenglut und Wüstenstaub geschützt haben [last tatters, that have protected us from desert sands and sun's blazing],"[175] the naked torsos of the farmers, their arms and necks sunburned and gaunt, can suddenly be seen. The women in their headscarves, who offer fruit and bread, "Und hier die letzten Bissen, die wir uns für morgen erbettelt haben [And here are the last of our morsels, those which we have begged for tomorrow's subsistence],"[176] seem to move no differently than at the Sunday service in Avezzano, and they walk past the camera impassively.

This scene takes a stand against the exclusion of the rural population from the wealth of industrialization and the cities, against their exclusion from the benefits of the 1970s Green Revolution, against the exclusion of people who only appear as "population," statistically recorded for administrative purposes,[177] and finally against the exclusion of people from the cultural-industrial iconology. This is not simply a matter for politics and its stony representation of power; it also concerns the cinema, which reserves such a view of bodies for the documentary. This criticism is not only aimed at Cecil B. DeMille's heroically staged Technicolor extras in THE TEN COMMANDMENTS but also at John Huston's Bible film—whose production-related scorched earth complicated negotiations with the local people, as Huillet never tires of mentioning[178]—and is an

174 Schoenberg, *Moses und Aron*, score II, act II, bar 575.

175 Ibid., act II, bars 478–484.

176 Ibid., act II, bars 485–489.

177 See Michel Foucault, *Security, Territory, Population. Lectures at the Collège de France 1977–1978*, London 2004, pp. 337–358.

178 Huillet, "Appunti sul giornale," p. 409: "After long discussions, in which we make clear that we aren't the Americans (Huston had shot the exteriors for his Bible film about 100 km from here, on the other side of Abruzzo, and the rumor must have got around that money was to be had where a film was shot), although we don't deny that we're on the road with the sound van, Gabriele's van, the camera van, and some private cars, we do agree to remuneration within reasonable limits."

Unprotected: rural population, extras, people.

implicit commentary on the continued staging of the people as fascinated and fascinating, even in Italian neo-realism.

Here too Straub and Huillet follow Schoenberg's radical relativism of having the people emerge solely from a self-empowerment within the complex relationship between visibility and audibility. A monolithic idea like an objective "sphere of interests" is demolished in favor of differentiating thinking, hearing, seeing. The montage of the film OSKAR LANGENFELD. 12 MAL (1967) is a reliable reference here too. In such images, physique is insistently and resistively observed as vulnerability and mortality, that of the protagonist and of the viewers, one's own and that of others. Heide Schlüpmann has described this in contrast to the stony sublimity of the idol: "Humanity consists—entirely contrary to the stony image of the hero—in the ability to perceive oneself as a sensual and transient being, and not only in being one."[179] This needs time. And an art that succeeds, as Friedrich Nietzsche said, in redirecting "those repulsive thoughts about the terrible or absurd nature of existence into representations with which man can live," including those that are "sublime, whereby the terrible is tamed by artistic means."[180]

In this tradition the "analysis" of the prohibition of images in the opera and film MOSES UND ARON, that is Schoenberg's discontinuation of the composition

179 Translated from Heide Schlüpmann, *Abendröthe der Subjektphilosophie. Eine Ästhetik des Kinos*, Frankfurt/Main 1998, p. 52.

180 Friedrich Nietzsche, "The Birth of Tragedy" in Nietzsche, *The Birth of Tragedy and Other Writings* (1999), ed. Raymond Geuss, Ronald Spiers (trans.), Cambridge 2007, pp. 36–40: 40.

after act II and Straub/Huillet's use of white and black screen, would not be a failure but a putting to the test of historical perception, also as showing the time that life needs. Discontinuation and white and black screen are the media caesuras that visualize the process of perception itself. The movements and noises of the animals aren't beautiful in themselves, but it's the moment in which cinema suddenly frees the eye and ear to see and hear them.

4.4. TEARING AWAY, REVERSAL, BREATHING

> ... that the infinite unification
> purifies itself through infinite separation.
> *Friedrich Hölderlin*[181]

Servitude in the context of the Moses complex is the unconscious linkage of body and senses to signs that have the speakers and actors in their power and make media marionettes of them. In such servitude there is an indistinguishability of voice and sound space, of imagery and medium, of mimesis and mission. This indistinguishability comes in the guise of "sorts of supernatural powers, i.e. gods" (Bateson). The liberation movement out of servitude, Exodus, is understood as an appropriation of the power of control over these signs, which

181 Friedrich Hölderlin, "Notes on the Oedipus," p. 323.

thus forms a history of its own and—this is the second aspect of the Exodus—its own forms of collectivity. The Exodus is theologically imagined through the intervention, admission, and appearance of a monotheistic God. Through his revelation, his call, he interrupts the attachment of human subjects to imagery, conceivability, and imagination, and instead mandates a new system of writing, a new space, and, before the new law, a time of tumult, or, as Paolo Virno puts it, the "declaration of the state of emergency on the side of the oppressed."[182]

Hence every portrayal of the Exodus aesthetically requires a transition of power in the regime of signs, or at least artistic procedures that expose the structure of the old order. In the Exodus the uprising of the signs unites with that of the people.[183] In the opera *Moses und Aron*, and in its film version, the Exodus is implemented as the transformation of signs into material. The plan can already be seen in the sketches for the opera. An early draft by Arnold Schoenberg shows that the question of materiality and the concretization of thought was a central aspect of his work on the opera. For him legal relationships and legalism presuppose the perception and acknowledgement of their media basis:

> TD63 (13r)
> The unconceivability of God | gives the result: | that belief in him | can provide | no foundation | of legal relationships.[184]

While Schoenberg writes, in a letter from 1933, that he has put the "the idea of the inconceivable God, of the Chosen People, and of the leader of the people"[185] in the foreground, Straub and Huillet seek the political aspect of this work in a precise debate with the materiality of perception and depiction, also as the concretization of a rebellion. The concept of tearing away, *s'arracher*, is understood in this material sense: "What I was interested in," says Straub in the interview, "is how a people succeeds in tearing away and liberating itself out of a con-

182 Translated from Paolo Virno, "Die Logik der Tumulte," in Isabell Lorey and others (eds.), *Inventionen 2*, Zurich 2012, pp. 17–26.

183 See somewhat differently in Walzer, *Exodus and Revolution*, which sees in the Exodus the model of twentieth-century protests against corrupt rule and the hope of land appropriation.

184 Translated from Schönberg, *Moses und Aron, Entstehungsgeschichte*, p. 166.

185 Schoenberg on March 15, 1933 to Walter Eidlitz, in *Letters*, p. 172.

crete situation, a 'situation' in the strict sense, in order to throw itself into a movement."[186]

The film of the opera therefore begins with the people's exit from the servitude of a seamlessly naive imaginary. Using the example of Straub and Huillet's cinematic reflection of the unconceivable—that fundamental disturbance of a synthesizing capacity of perception—it can be shown how the directors solve this problem by returning to the appearance of the material itself in the white- and black-screen sequences, through which they expose the historical production conditions of seeing itself before every conception, and consider the cinema in its pure, imageless effect.

Another level of materiality in the film is the linguistic, which regulates the opera as an act of speech as distinct from the singing voice. When Straub tells the journalists at the *Cahiers du Cinéma* that although the liberation of the people is theologically coded in the film it is in no way staged abstractly but is concretized through the insistently enunciated location in a specific historical genealogy, it's therefore a decisive argument that "Moses insists in saying, 'God of Abraham, Isaac, and Jacob.' It's a specific god, not some kind of idealistic one."[187] Historical specification realized through an act of speech that calls God and things by name, rhythmically. Not the rebellious act one might have expected in 1974, but resistance to the conventionalizing and conventionalized speech act is the politics that Straub and Huillet follow here. They examine language as a cultural code, which penetrates bodies as meter and rhythm to generate relationships. As a symptom, Moses's sentence "Thought is easy || speech is laborious," interrupted by a break, not only embodies powerlessness but also the impossibility of conceiving political truth without including the physical, the residual, the others.

As a staging of the imposition of every act of speech, the Schoenberg film is allied to earlier works by Straub and Huillet, which knock out the gesture of speaking from texts by Brecht, Kafka, and Corneille. Later they would examine the work of Friedrich Hölderlin in relation to language and speaking. Hölderlin's theory of tragedy and his linguistic-theoretical deliberations have clearly influenced Straub/Huillet, particularly in their work with actors—even though

186 Translated from Straub/Huillet, "Conversation," 1975, p. 18.

187 Ibid., pp. 18–19.

their great Hölderlin films were made after MOSES UND ARON. The two filmmakers rediscovered the theme of the political in a world beyond the scope of all comprehensive faculties and concepts in Hölderlin, again as a question of an unconceivable divinity. In the notes Hölderlin developed in 1803, having translated the tragedies of Sophocles, the relationship between the human being and God is associated with the relationship between language and speaking. All speech calls attention to the fact that there is an other, outer, alien, guiding principle at work at the core of the self, as Schiller knew before him.[188] Hölderlin shifts the approach, making out of it a call from the other, a provocation: every concrete act of speech challenges the law inherent in language, while at the same time objecting to this challenge.

The double structure can also be found in the musical form of the opera, in which its audible sounds expose the law of the twelve tones, but only implicitly, while every row is an objection and counter-movement to the equal distribution of the tones. The film version correspondingly brings in the symptomatically individual against the laws of media, when shot after shot refers to the rules of the game of spatial distribution, without revealing a playing space as a whole.

Hölderlin ascribes the two competing spaces he identifies to the spheres of the available and unavailable, the human and the divine. Tragedy then begins as a distinction between the realm of the gods and that of people, which turns out to be finite in this initial division: "The orbit of man's life" is doomed to violence, death, and forgetting. This confronts humans with a power beyond the human, which—for instance in the figure of Teiresias—"removes man from his orbit of life, the very mid-point of his inner life, to another world, and tears him off into the eccentric orbit of the dead."[189] But human organization requires from tragedy a whole series of further separations from the overall inhuman: "The representation of the tragic depends primarily on this: that the fearful enormity of God and man uniting and the power of nature becoming boundlessly one with man's innermost being in rage, thereby comprehends itself, that the infinite unification purifies itself through infinite separation."[190] The tragic shock that adjusts the relationship between gods and men, mortals and immortals, life and death

188 See the famous couplet "Why can the living spirit to the spirit no longer appear? // Soon as the soul begins to speak, alas, she speaks no more." Translated from Friedrich Schiller, *Schillers Werke in 2 Bänden*, vol. 1, Munich 1959, p. 200.

189 Hölderlin, "Notes on the Oedipus," p. 318.

190 Ibid., p. 323.

through the differentiation of a space without solid ground, core, or center, which Hölderlin also understands as purification, is translated by Schoenberg into a non-directional space of the twentieth century. Straub and Huillet reconstruct this space without direction as one of rifts, seams, and proximities. In speaking, people commit themselves to the possibility of what a word, a sound, an intervention can be in a godforsaken world that has to be constrained into reversal. Straub and Huillet also argue with tragic theory when they point out that justice isn't simply there but has to be continually realized. They argue Greek tragically in their stubborn clinging to the film's dedication, which endangered its broadcast: "It is regrettable to have to remind people that Holger Meins, whatever he was accused of, juristically died an innocent man. Apparently the cultural circumstances in the Federal Republic are worse than in the time of Creon—in antiquity—who forbade Antigone to bury a body, while in the Federal Republic it is not even permitted to mention the name of a dead man in public."[191] Such naming isn't credo, but it shows up the gap between law and justice.

Friedrich Hölderlin detects the endeavor of Greek tragedy to maintain the unbroken course of the world, a steady historical progress, in the "calculable law"[192] of its poetics. But he requires "content"[193] to be distinguished from such "calculation." Content resists the general law, extent, and principle of language, sets speaking against the performance of language and concreteness against generality. This becomes all the more urgent when poetry objects to crises and catastrophes, or wishes to become the court of history, the "trial for heresy."[194] The antagonisms between the law of language and the content of poetry become sharper the more distinctly poetry is applied "[It is a language for a world where, in a leisurely age, and amid plague, confusion of the mind and a universally awakened spirit of prophecy, God and man *communicate in the all-forgetting form of unfaithfulness.* This happens so that no gap occurs in the course of the world, and so that *the memory of the heavenly ones does not die out.* Divine unfaithfulness is retained best of all."[195] In crisis language turns against its law as speaking, but cuts itself short. The absence of the gods inscribes itself

191 Translated from Straub und Huillet in an interview with Gerd Conradt, in Conradt, "Eine Widmung," p. 183.

192 Hölderlin, "Notes on the Oedipus," p. 317.

193 Ibid.

194 Ibid., p. 324.

195 Ibid.

into human tragedy through such symptomatic faltering of language. Schoenberg proceeds analogously to this model when in the caesuras of speaking and the music he opens up the connection between Moses and people—which now replaces the connection between Moses and God—as absence or disloyalty in the exact sense. The people have left him. God is missing. Straub and Huillet amplify this with all media means.

A third thing links tragedy, as Hölderlin evacuates it from Ancient Greece, with the Moses opera and the forms of its film version: when the marking of language through speaking firstly shows the non-perceptible dynamic of language itself and secondly the idea itself appears out of this unconceivability, tragedy thirdly requires the embodiment of language in speech:

> For the tragic transport is essentially empty, and the most unbound of all. Hence the rhythmic succession of ideas wherein the transport manifests itself demands a counter-rhythmic interruption, a pure word, *that which in metrics is called a caesura*, in order to confront the speeding alternation of ideas at its climax, so that not the alternation of the idea, but the idea itself appears.[196]

For Hölderlin this political aspect of speaking, "reversal,"[197] permits two possible transformations: either towards openness *or* into a new structure; either into the smooth *or* the striated space; either into the desert *or* the apparatus of state, as he warns, "into wilderness or into new form."[198] The progress of history is thus led into a catastrophe at a boundary from which a reversal must be decided. Caesuras against the grain of unbroken history refer to the possibilities of intervention. A pan over the karstified Nile landscape is a call to intervention.

196 Ibid. p. 318.

197 Friedrich Hölderlin, "Notes on the Antigone," in *Essays and Letters*, pp. 325–332: 331.

198 Ibid., p. 331. At this point Hölderlin writes one of his most breathless, vocally barely realizable sentences on turmoil and the "national reversal" that this turmoil means: "And in a national reversal, where the whole shape of things changes, and nature and necessity, which always remain, tend to a new shape, whether going over into wilderness or into a new form, in a change like this, all mere necessities are biased in favour of the change; whence, in the eventuality of such change, even a neutral man (and not only one who is moved *against* the national form), can, by a spiritual violence of the time, be forced to be patriotic and present in an infinite form, in the religious, political and moral form of his fatherland."

In 2014 the film from 1974 shows that the reversal didn't happen. But it shows the possibility of caesura.

In Schoenberg's libretto there are many examples of such micro-caesuras. They include Moses' spoken sentence "Thought is easy || speech is laborious," with which the "inflexible tongue," the *kvad-peh* of the Bible, which is to a certain extent an "undirected" tongue, is supposed to bring out the pure word, of all things. They include the symmetrical sentence towards the end, "Thus, all was but madness that I believed before || and can || and must not be given voice," and the final sentence of or against the composition: "O word || thou word || that I lack!"[199]

Actors are resistances through which texts become spoken language. Harun Farocki reports that on asking Jean-Marie Straub, during the making of Class Relations, after Franz Kafka's unfinished novel *Amerika*, how an actor should articulate the pause in a Kafka text, Straub replied "[...] these pauses also have to do with the breathing of the individual performer. There are people who have more breath, through practice or physical reasons [...], but it isn't only to do with this; it also has to do with the texts themselves."[200] The resistance that actors in Straub/Huillet's productions bring to the process of language, and which they have to continue to attempt against their own resistance, makes relationships visible and audible that aren't conspicuous and certainly aren't perceived as power relationships in the conventional flow of speech and ideas. In speech and in sung articulation the film of *Moses und Aron* shows the interface of language and body: "There are no texts one can just recite, with one's spirit; that doesn't exist. Everything has to go through the body."[201] Speaking in the films of Straub and Huillet is conceived as the outcome of a self-inflicted verbal inability. When the relationship between signs, bodies, and law is addressed in the Mosaic story as a theological problem parallel with the identification of scripturality and legalism, then in Hölderlin's sense as political argumentation. Straub emphasizes this as the beginning of his interest in the opera:

199 See this broken transcription in Huillet, "Moses und Aron. Das Drehbuch," p. 248.

200 Translated from Harun Farocki, "Guten Tag, Herr Roßmann. Langsame Annäherung an Haltungen und Sprache," in *Die Zeit*, 1983, no. 27, p. 39.

201 Quoted in ibid.

> What first moved me was the theological side [*le côté théologique*]. When you want to make a film, it always proceeds from a core, and in this case the core was the final musical scene between Moses and Aron, after the Golden Calf has disappeared. The confrontation between Moses and Aron, with which the score ends, with both of them standing in front of the altar.[202]

In this key scene the dispute about the pure idea and its necessary articulation culminates, Aron's observation that ideas can only be conveyed as concrete and materialized drives Moses to a despair that, differently from how Freud reconstructs the Moses of Michelangelo, he can't control.[203] The shots in the film seem to remain in solidarity with Aron and his "practical rationality."[204] A film can also only convey ideas in their materiality, in images, sounds, light. Caesura and resistance to easy thinking in images, however, is provided by fade-ins and sequences of black or white screen, which can simply cause a shot of the Golden Calf to "be gone."[205] For the position of Aron such withdrawal is nothing other than the strategic operation with images. Aron calculates that the people, oriented to images and prohibitions, don't need to know about the law itself: "Unbewußt wird getan, wie du willst [Unbeknown, what you want will be done]."[206] Here Aron's artistic position becomes that of the Reich film minister, whose politics replaced laws with images.

Moses had previously insisted on the omnipotence of the idea, which enables legalism and thus radical resistance in the first place—against a world power, that of the Pharaoh, after all. Aron makes the case for accommodating the

202 Translated from Straub/Huillet, "Conversation," p. 6.

203 See Sigmund Freud, "The Moses of Michelangelo," in *The Standard Edition of the Complete Psychological Works of Sigmund Freud*, trans. James Strachey, Anna Freud, Alix Strachey, Alan Tyson. Volume XIII (1913–1914), *Totem and Taboo and other Works*, London. 1955.

204 Translated from Schönberg, *Moses und Aron, Entstehungsgeschichte*, p. 166.

205 See Moses' text, when he causes the Golden Calf to disappear in a fade-in:
Moses *off*:
Vergeh,
Du Abbild des Unvermögens, das Grenzenlose in ein Bild zu fassen!
[Be gone,
You image of pow'rlessness to enclose the boundless in an image!]
Schönberg, *Moses und Aron*, score II, act II, bar 980, and Huillet, "Moses und Aron. Das Drehbuch," p. 242.

206 Schönberg, *Moses und Aron*, score II, act II, bar 1048.

people on the path of the senses and comprehensibility. Yet both justify their positions as acting for the people, "serving the people."[207] Either—as Aron sings—to retain the people, or, as Moses warns, to conceive of uncorrupted freedom, so that they can emerge as a people at all:

> Aron *on*:
> Kein Volk erfasst mehr als einen Teil des Bildes,
> das den faßbaren Teil des Gedankens ausdrückt.
> So mache dich dem Volk verständlich auf ihm angemeß'ne Art.
>
> [No folk can grasp more than just a partial image,
> the perceivable part of the whole idea.
> Be understood by all the people in their own accustomed way.]
>
> Moses *off*:
> Ich soll den Gedanken verfälschen?
>
> [Am I to debase the idea?]

Upon which Aron replies with that analytical "Laß mich ihn auflösen"[208] [that "Let me dissolve it" not in the English libretto, *trans.*]. Life and thought are once again counterposed. The showdown, if you like, of this scene, the aporia acted out, lies in Aron's charge that Moses, as long as he lives, is tied to the idea, and as long as he thinks to life, to the materiality of things. These include the tablets bearing the law from Sinai No law without medium. Aron pronounces the words that annihilate Moses from above, in a medium shot to the right of the frame, while looking into the right *hors-champ*, into the open, as far as we know: "Du bist an deinen Gedanken gebunden! [You're bounden to your idea so closely!]." Then he turns to the left, acknowledging a field of Moses, while at the same time pinning him down to it. The space is redistributed. Everything has to go through the body and concrete matter. Aron's gesture follows the rhythm of

207 This is the formulation in the famous letter from Holger Meins to Manfred Grashof on October 31, 1974.

208 Schönberg, *Moses und Aron*, score II, act II, bars 1037–1042 and Huillet, "Moses und Aron. Das Drehbuch," p. 246.

language; language follows the rhythm of his argumentation, whose completeness drives Moses into a corner:

> Aron *on*:
> Du mußt leben!
> Du kannst nicht anders!
> Du bist an Deinen Gedanken gebunden!
>
> [Go on living!
> Aught else is futile.
> You're bounden to your idea so closely!]
>
> Moses *off*:
> Ja, an meinen Gedanken,
> wie ihn diese Tafeln ausdrücken...
>
> [Bounden to my idea
> as e'en do these tables set it forth.]
>
> Aron *on*:
> ... die auch nur ein Bild, ein Teil des Gedankens sind.
>
> [They're images also, just part of the whole idea.][209]

Now Moses flings the tablets out of the frame, but in such a way as to be missed by the camera. Another absence, a caesura. No catharsis in the shambles.

In the earliest drafts of *Moses und Aron* Arnold Schoenberg had literally made the relationship between idea, language, and speaking the subject of his deliberations. In a form of writing full of caesuras, which thus anticipates on paper the opera's staging and fields of conflict, he constructs the last debate between Moses and Aron about the relationship between ideas, words, images, and tones in regard to the law. Schoenberg notes his conceptual thought in a continually rhythmized text, so that one could assume it was produced while speaking. Sentences are split up, assumed relationships placed side by side unconnected,

209 Ibid., bars 1053–1057, and ibid., p. 246f.

gaps are noted as such through graphic markings and line breaks, which are given in the transcription, and here in the translation, of his manuscript along with the signs for the caesuras:

> TD84 (18r)
> Erection of the golden calf: victory of images over the word (Aron = the word) | collapse of the calf: | victory of the idea over images
> TD86 (20r)
> Stone tablets: a depiction | symbol of the | eternal existence of the chosen people | for the preservation of the idea | of the unconceivable God
> TD87 (20r)
> The Commandments: the word ... as paraphrase as resolution | as practical realization
> TD88 (20r)
> Breaking the tablets: an image!
> TD89 (20r)
> [...]
> Moses' faintheartedness: | doubt in the word | doubt in the possibility of the idea | to generalize.
> TD90 (20r)
> Moses' collapse victory of the word over the idea | victory of images over the word | Aron's victory, | as victory of practical reason.
> TI556 (18v)
> Moses victorious (victory of the idea over the word | the law: |this people should | see themselves as the idea | Aron: say it (?) | (5) with or without word (?) "the | 10 Commandments."
> Etc.[210]

In the caesuras Schoenberg distinguishes between idea, writing, and speaking, and relates them to one another at the same time. In the later written form of the libretto, as in the performance, in enunciation, the "victory of the word over the idea" is reversed into the verbal caesura, which generates a thought, and thus becomes the "victory of the idea over the word." This relationship precedes the formation of a people. The libretto is written in lines or verses, which

210 Translated from Schönberg, *Entstehungsgeschichte*, p. 166f.

appear in the score as an ongoing text. Schoenberg entered his sketchy text into the order of the score by distributing it among the actants on the one hand and the stage directions on the other; and by confronting the text with the movement of the music, bold tonal relationships, accelerating and syncopating rhythms, percussion on stage. The transformation of the text from Schoenberg's initial verse-like sketch to the score, then to the musical realization of the opera, and finally to the screenplay by Danièle Huillet and its cinematic realization can best be shown in "Moses' collapse."

As a running text transferred from the libretto to the score, the text of the Moses performer reads:

> Inconceivable God! Inexpressible, many sided idea, will you let it be so explained? Shall Aaron, my mouth, fashion this image?
> Then I have fashioned an image too, false, as an image must be. Thus I am defeated!
> Thus, all was but madness that I believed before, and can and must not be given voice. O word, thou word, that I lack![211]

The score contains a stage direction that for its part seems to come from the burning bush of the conductor's desk. At this point it orders freedom under the basic law: the call of "Inconceivable God!" should be intoned "with the Sprechstimme, which has complete freedom within the parts of the measure assigned to it from the strict march tempo,"[212] which comes as an off-beat. Here Schoenberg grants himself the complete freedom of dissolving the printed image from the line of the score. It becomes a veritable picture or rebus or notion that produces new relationships, in as much as it appears in nervous typography. In various scripts "Gongs, bells, bass drum a 3," are called for, and in between the repeated instruction "still in march tempo." The strings play intervals of more than three octaves at "Inconceivable God!" This is particularly noticeable in the study score, in which text and notation interweave.

Just as Schoenberg, in order to realize his idea, takes a path via the materiality of the signs in the score, and with his instructions for realizing the opera cuts through the order of the score itself, the cinematic staging by Straub and

211 Schoenberg, *Moses und Aron*, vocal score, act II, bars 1112–1136.
212 See Schönberg, *Moses und Aron*, score II, act II, bar 1112.

TD84 [18r]
1: *Aufrichtung des goldenen Kalbes* ist KE für *Das goldene Kalb.*

Aufrichtung des goldenen Kalbes: Sieg der Bilder über das Wort (Aron = Das Wort) | Zusammenbruch des Kalbes: | Sieg des Gedankens über die Bilder

TD86 [20r]
2–3: *Symbol des | Ewigen* ist KE für *Symbol des Gedankens: | des ewigen.*

Steinerne Tafeln: ein Abbild | Symbol des | Ewigen Bestehens des auserwählten Volkes | zur Bewahrung des Gedankens | des unvorstellbaren Gottes

TD87 [20r]

Die Gebote: Das Wort … als Umschreibung als Auflösung | als praktische Verwirklichung

TD88 [20r]

Zertrümmerung der Tafeln: ein Bild!

TD89 [20r]
1: Nach *Kleinmütigkeit:* ist *Verzweiflung* gestrichen.

Moses Kleinmütigkeit: | Zweifel am Wort | Zweifel an der Möglichkeit den Gedanken | zu verallgemeinern.

TD90 [20r]

Moses Zusammenbruch Sieg des Wortes über den Gedanken | Sieg der Bilder über das Wort | Arons Sieg, | als Sieg der praktischen Vernunft.

TI556 [18v]
4–5: Kaum mit Sicherheit lesbar.

Moses siegt (Sieg des Gedankens über das Wort | Das Gesetz: | Dieses Volk soll sich für | den Gedanken erhalten | Aron: Sag es [?] | [5] *mit oder ohne Wort*[?] *„die | 10 Gebote"*

"Erection of the golden calf."

Huillet takes its path via the transfer of the opera into a materiality of images, tones, and noises. Following the pauses in the score, Straub and Huillet put the text into a verse form that at the same time realizes the embodiment of all language in speaking—"with one's spirit; but that doesn't exist. Everything has to go through the body":[213]

> Moses:
> Inconceivable God!
> Inexpressible, many sided idea,
> will you let it be so explained?
> Shall Aaron, my mouth, fashion this image?
> Then I have fashioned an image too,

213 Quote translated from Farocki, "Guten Tag, Herr Roßmann," p. 39.

"Still in march tempo," Arnold Schönberg, *Moses und Aron, Oper in drei Akten*, study score.

false,
as an image must be.
Thus I am defeated!
Thus, all was but madness that I believed before,
and can
and must not be given voice.
O word,
thou word,
that I lack![214]

But before these linguistic caesuras, exactly in Hölderlin's sense, cause mutually interfering resistances between language, text, voice, body, music, and image, in order to "confront the speeding alternation of ideas at its climax so that not the alternation of the idea, but the idea itself appears,"[215] before the pauses structure the music or the act of speech interrupts language in the caesura or the breath, Straub and Huillet contrive an additional filmic caesura: before Moses' final exclamation, while the chorus are still singing of the way to the Promised Land, a long pan crosses the landscape from left to right, a reversal of the first long pan during the call from the burning bush. This one interrupts the brothers' argument about the way the people should be established, and in this respect it is once again linked to the missing figure or figure of thought of the people. Cut into the end of this pan is a frontal shot of Moses, which, if Straub and Huillet wouldn't categorically exclude this practice from their work, could very well be considered a countershot to the very first scene: Günter Reich, the Moses performer, his hands raised, embodies the text with his *Sprechstimme*, articulating the caesuras in such a way that the collapse doesn't only involve him but also the music, the sounds, the light. The call is issued with his back to the now conspicuously empty altar, so that the outside of this shot could be both the *hors-champ* of the landscape and an *off*; from out of the image, Moses cries "Inconceivable God ..."

Yosef Hayim Yerushalmi has described this with Foucault's term for the epistemological tear as a "cri déchirant,"[216] as a heart-rending, deafening cry that

214 Translated from Huillet, "Moses und Aron. Das Drehbuch," p. 248.
215 Hölderlin, "Notes on the Oedipus," p. 318.
216 Yerushalmi, "Le Moïse de Freud et le Moïse de Schönberg," p. 44.

at the same time tears the texture of the visible and audible world to pieces. He avoids taking the problem of the transfer into materiality that it raises seriously, however. It's the function of the words as words that is tragic for him: "When Moses breaks the tablets, he doesn't do so, as one might believe, because they are material objects. In a much more profound and endlessly tragic way he suddenly understands that words themselves are ultimately only images, icons, idols, not because they are engraved in stone but because they are words."[217]

There are probably reasons to comply with the idea that words are just images, but they dismiss the call to caesura, intervention, and reversal from the text and the opera. The film version raises an objection to such melancholy. Words aren't simply images or idols but aspirated weapons against the dull march of history. Straub and Huillet renew the tension between writing, speaking, and language with every shot.

In reference to Straub and Huillet's underlying texts Gilles Deleuze calls such procedures "s'arracher," using the exact same term that Straub applies to the initiative of the liberation of a people. For Deleuze this is also the abrupt transformation of texts into the materiality and mediality of thought processes. "The isolating of the pure speech-act, the properly cinematographic utterance or the sound image" must occur against the resistance of a text; "this act must be torn from its written support, text, book, letters, or documents."[218] In this respect the caesura doesn't simply stand in the tradition of epic theater, in which amateurs are supposed to quote their texts from figures in order to prevent "empathy with the screen characters";[219] on the contrary, Straub and Huillet, along with Hölderlin and Brecht, assume that the caesura must interrupt an ahistorical performance of language. Speaking, whether by amateur or professional actors, must take place as the dissection and tearing apart of the text, which reveals its texture in this way. Media-theoretical considerations that take the apparatuses of the archive contributing to our thinking into account would also incorporate images, icons, and idols, and all the more words, into a concretion of material as resistance to the law. In the context of tragedy the transition of words into their physical delivery is "infinitivement plus tragique," as Yerushalmi

217 Translated from ibid., p. 44.

218 Deleuze, *Cinema 2. The Time-Image*, p. 253.

219 As Anton Kaes understands it. Translated from *Deutschlandbilder. Die Wiederkehr der Geschichte als Film*, Munich 1987, p. 27.

emphasizes.[220] The tragic comes into play once more as a genealogy of the opera between Hellenism and Judaism.

In *Moses und Aron* the composition of the Exodus breaks off: the music ends with act II, but the text continues; the work culminates in words, and in a speaking no longer borne by music. The reason for the discontinuation has been the occasion for biographical, political, and artistic speculation, and Gertrud Schoenberg, in her short postscript to the score, closes with the fine testamentary words: "As it was, so it was to be."[221] From her selection of passages from letters before the text of act III it can be seen that until 1950 Schoenberg writes about the difficulty, but not of the impossibility, of composing the opera to its end, but that shortly before his death in 1951 he declared his agreement "that it is possible for the third act simply to be spoken, in case I cannot complete the composition."[222]

In the composition's discontinuation Philippe Lacoue-Labarthe discovers Schoenberg's coup of not understanding art as an end and not as a universalizing surrogate for religion, but as its caesura:

> But now Moses, although against his will—and one should certainly imagine Schönberg compelled and coerced, ultimately the fate of every modern artist—says that art is religion within the boundaries of a non-existing accord. Probably the end of religion. In every respect. Or to be more exact: the caesura of religion."[223]

The concept of the caesura, as Lacoue-Labarthe presents it here, marks the suspension of an agreement. In the discontinuation of the music he sees a halt in the work of art that reveals its aesthetic. Because the figure of Moses always speaks, the fault line of this caesura at the end of the work is present from the very beginning. Lacoue-Labarthe also sees the intervention into the immediacy and unity of the work as the suspension of any immediacy in the relationship to the law or a lawgiving deity.

220 Yerushalmi, "Le Moïse de Freud et le Moïse de Schönberg," p. 44.

221 Gertrud Schoenberg, "Remarks following the Score," in Arnold Schoenberg: *Moses und Aron*, vocal score, unpaginated.

222 Ibid., quoting from Arnold Schoenberg's letters.

223 Translated from Lacoue-Labarthe, "Zäsur der Religion," p. 476.

Proceeding from the function of this caesura, which silences the music and displaces the action into speaking, Lacoue-Labarthe's text follows the genealogy of the opera in the tradition of tragedy. He owes this trail to the film version: "This is why, if I admit to being guided by the very fine film version of *Moses* by Jean-Marie Straub and Danièle Huillet, I must also admit that their dramaturgical intuition in this case is decisive: to stage the first two acts, but not the remaining third, in a Greek arena, even though there was perhaps no other possibility given the position of the Roman theater of Alba Fucense, in Abruzzo. In its basic intention *Moses* is indeed a tragedy."[224]

Yet Straub and Huillet emphatically resist this concise term. In the first place, as already mentioned, after their extensive research trips they didn't in fact choose a Greek theater, and not the Hellenistic theater in Alba Fucense, for their location, but rather the syncretistic—both architecturally and dramaturgically—amphitheater. In it an architecture of hidden cellars, directed lines of sight, and the exhibited violence of Roman spectacle, in which the laws of an empire were stamped into bodies with punishing ruthlessness, encounters a space of the Greek tragedies—dramas of the word—open to the entire polis and opening outward.

Both forms of space, out of which a people may be constituted, are further modulated by Straub and Huillet in cinematic spaces, as transformations of the architectural. The idea that architecture and people are mutually dependent also stands in the tradition of the theory of tragedy and its concept of the chorus. Hegel, differently from his friend Hölderlin, sees a stable relationship in this: in his lectures on aesthetics he actually describes the chorus as part of a space in which architecture, physique, and sensibility combine into a coherent ensemble: "Just as the Greek theatre itself has its external terrain, its scene, and its surroundings, so the chorus, the people, is as it were the scene of the spirit; it may be compared, in architecture, with a temple surrounding the image of the gods, for here it is an environment for the heroes in the action.[225] Friedrich Nietzsche, studying the Greeks against their own heroics, and, here near to Hölderlin, seeing the beginning of all culture in a sense of the "terrors and horrors of existence,"[226] removes the chorus from the temple complex in

224 Ibid., p. 467.

225 Hegel, *Aesthetics*, vol. 2., p. 1211.

226 Nietzsche, "The Birth of Tragedy," pp. 22–25: 23.

Infringing the law, breaking the tablets, discontinuing the music.

a rereading of Schiller, and discovers in this a challenge to naturalism: “In his famous preface to the *Bride of Messina* Schiller betrayed an infinitely more valuable insight into the significance of the chorus when he considered it to be a living wall which tragedy draws about itself in order to shut itself off in purity from the real world and to preserve its ideal ground and its poetic freedom.”[227] Nietzsche instead interprets the Greek chorus in the cult of Dionysus as “the ‘ideal spectator’ inasmuch as it is the only *seer* (*Schauer*), the seer of the visionary world on the stage.”[228]

However, only the caesura into the Hellenistic permits the correspondence between the chorus and a liberated people, who are no longer located in the visionary or imaginary of the scene but break down the wall to reality. Straub and Huillet establish this caesura, against the fluid interpretation of Lacoue-Labarthe, through cinematic means. The dramaturgy of the focal lengths first, in particular, visualizes the physicality of speaking, or withdraws it in the relation of *off* and *on*. This becomes additionally clear from the perspective of the conflict between the spectacular and the tragic. Paradigmatic here is the staging of the chorus as a block, which sometimes breathes and articulates as a collective, and is sometimes dissolved into a plurality—gone with the wind of cinema—as the volatile agitation of a crowd. Sometimes the chorus is highlighted, sometimes it blocks the way and view out of the amphitheater, whose architecture it causes

227 Ibid., p. 38.
228 Ibid., p. 42.

to appear as a regulation of gazes and movements.[229] Second, the principle of the close-up organizes this syncretistic space. Third, especially the pans set up relationships between the spaces of historical performance practices and the space of material reality in which cinema exists. The images of the sky—which in Straub/Huillet's cinema, as otherwise only with Heine and Pasolini, is left to the sparrows, not the clerics—also have the function of creating a relationship between different historical spaces of seeing and visibility. In this way the stratified spaces of Alba Fucense are cinematically amplified in order to call to mind the history of media spaces as political.

The brothers' final discussion in act III is no longer staged in the arena but by a wide lake, Lago Matese, a glacial lake between high barren mountains, in the quite different light of a cold September sun, across which clouds pass, causing the faces and their expressions to change in the unstable illumination. The impression arises of the camp, the animals, and the people having been swept away by an apocalyptic flood, while the conflict between the godforsaken brothers about the salvation and liberation of the people continues unperturbed. Only now it has also left the musical space. The single scene of act III begins with an image of the muddy bank upon which Aron lies in chains, and ends with a pan in a long shot in which the surface of the lake horizontally divides the image into two, just as at the beginning of the film the first pan ends with a vertical doubling of the two mountains, a long pan that is repeated in the reverse direction shortly before the end of the second act, at the moment of Moses' defeat. Such

229 See Byg, *Landscapes of Resistance*, p. 147.

calculated shots and camera movements vary the compositional techniques of retrograde and inversion, even though images, differently from tones, don't form discrete series of elements. It's the movement, the "transport" of perception, and the caesura of the pan that makes both procedures comparable.

Straub sees the reason for Schoenberg's discontinuation of the project in the fact that a free people of the desert, who can look as closely and wherever they like had become unimaginable during the 1950s, and that Schoenberg had only been concerned with such a people, not with a state:

> Until 1949 or 1950 there are letters in which he writes: I will compose the music for the third act. In fact, I believe that given the content of this third act he got into, let's say, "ideological" difficulties. In my opinion it was the unleashing of fascism, the concentration camps, the annihilation of the Jews, and the founding of the state of Israel that prevented him from concluding the work. *Moses und Aron* is an anti-Zionist work. It's clear to me that Schoenberg never played with the idea of a state in Palestine.[230]

In the final scene by the lake Aron can be seen in chains with the lower bodies of two archaic-looking warriors to his right. The camera moves very irregularly towards him where he lies heavily in the mud of the flooded bank, while the absolute silence of this footage is an oppressive contrast to the diverse tone qualities of the now banished space of the opera-film music. Into this emptiness

230 Translated from Straub/Huillet, "Conversation," p. 7.

the voice of Moses intones, from the *off* and with surprisingly more reverberation than previously in the sandy arena: "Aron, nun ist es genug! [Aaron, now this must cease!]" Into the same stillness Aron replies, also surprising in his unknown speaking voice: "Willst du mich morden? [Will you then kill me?]"[231] In their film Straub and Huillet leave open whether Aron dies in the end. He is left in the *hors-champ* chained to his speech, from which "both word and image flee."[232] The camera pans from Aron on the ground to Moses standing alone before the ice-cold lake and the barren mountains, abandoned and lonely with a law that isn't human—and marks the condition of the human being for this very reason. We aren't in control of what determines existence and knowledge; we are subject to linguistic and technical orderings in their historicity. Once again, as in the first long pan of the burning bush, Straub and Huillet deploy camera movement as resistance to simple depiction. The brothers are linked by a camera movement for the first time in the film: "[T]here is never a pan linking Moses with Aron, or Aron with Moses, until the one in the final shot, where we leave Aron after his last sentence ('Für seine Freiheit, daß es ein Volk werde! [For their freedom – so that they would become a nation!]'). We leave him in a pan and see Moses as he will be seen until the end of the film. It's a glaring exception."[233] Once again the pan marks a historical rift. The people, which followed Aron and his politics of illustration, was a false people. And no one wants to follow the idea of God that Moses demands.

> And when Moses says "Set him free," you don't see Aron any more (he is *hors-champ*). We banished him from the field of vision with his last sentence ("For their freedom – so that they would become a nation!") [...] so as to put Moses there. Moses destroys Aron, but in doing this—it seemed evident to me, at least I hope so—he destroys himself. And is proved right when he sends the people back into the desert adding "in the wasteland you shall be victorious and achieve the goal."[234]

231 Schoenberg, *Moses und Aron*, vocal score, act III, unpaginated.

232 Ibid.

233 Translated from Straub/Huillet, "Conversation," p. 12.

234 Translated from Straub/Huillet, "Conversation," p. 8.

Jean-Marie Straub, apparently surprised by his own *mise en scène*, links the image beneath the grey sky of Lago Matese, over and above all national-theater debates and people's movements, to historical events when he associates the Aron of this scene with a revolutionary leader whose *nom de guerre* means "insurgent masses": "When we chained Aron in the film, I thought of Lumumba."[235] Patrice E. Lumumba, at the end of the film, would not least be an inversion of the figure standing at its beginning: Holger Meins, the man who certainly had no insurgent masses behind his rebellion—as his only film leads one to suppose—and didn't want any either. A renewed inversion, which clearly shows that the composition of the film doesn't pursue a political localization but a topology of politically motivated relationships. For Straub, as for the existentialists of the early 1960s, the murdered prime minister of the Congo stood for the vision of a future decolonized Africa, a Promised Land. The strength of this early liberation movement lay in its radical criticism of the legalism of old power and its willingness to chance the foundation of a new law, not in the success of its still pending realization. Today the Democratic Republic of Congo is still seen as an exploitable store of coltan, which is essential to the appliances that form and process our virtual worlds.

Through this last scene of the movie the film image is confronted with the prohibition of images once again. Moses' position is that the Promised Land is an image and thus comes under the prohibition, which Aron has disregarded:

> Moses, *off*:
> Da begehrtest du leiblich, wirklich, mit Füßen zu betreten
> ein unwirkliches Land, wo Milch und Honig fließt.
> [...]
> Du sagst es schlechter, als du es verstehst, denn du weißt,
> daß der Felsen ein Bild, wie die Wüste und der Dornbusch:
> drei, die dem Leib nicht geben, was er braucht, gegen den Geist,
> der Seele, was deren Wunschlosigkeit zu ewigem Leben genug ist.
> Auch der Felsen, wie alle Bilder,

235 Ibid., p. 8. Unexpectedly a further connection to the operatic fraternal conflict emerges: Patrice Lumumba's opponent, who led a secessionist movement in the southern province of Katanga, was in fact called Moïse Tshombé. Lumumba was later tortured and killed in Katanga. Joseph Mobutu was also supposed to have been involved in this murder along with Moïse Tshombé.

"In the wasteland you shall be victorious."

> gehorcht dem Wort, daraufhin er Erscheinung geworden war.
> So gewannst du das Volk nicht für den Ewigen, sondern für dich.
>
> [Moses, *off*:
> You desired, actually, physically, to tread with your feet
> upon an unreal land where milk and honey flowed.
> [...]
> You speak more simply than you understand, for you know
> that the rock is, like the wasteland and the burning bush –
> three that give not to the body what it needs with regard
> to spirit – is, I say, an image of the soul, whose very
> renunciation is sufficient for eternal life. And the rock,
> even as all images, obeys the word, from whence it came to
> be manifested. Thus, you won the people not for the eternal
> one but for yourself ...][236]

Physical space is interwoven with linguistic and political space in the film. Speaking itself raises an objection to any idea of a simple revolt against injustice. Speaking resists the equation of writing and legalism, but also the simple opposition of real and unreal. Straub establishes this first: "[Moses] says that the Promised Land is an image. He accuses Aron of always having been obsessed with setting his foot on real soil where milk and honey flows. For Moses it's

236 Schoenberg, *Moses und Aron*, vocal score, act III, unpaginated.

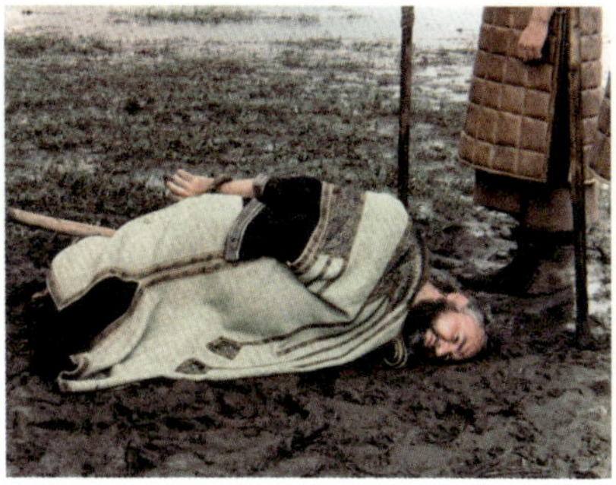

clear that this could only be an unreal land."[237] The relationship between reality and ideality, again with Hölderlin, should be turned around in speaking: "In the state between being and non-being, however, the possible everywhere becomes real and the real becomes ideal, and in the free imitation of art this is a terrible but divine dream."[238] What Lacoue-Labarthe sees as the caesura of religion is for Straub and Huillet a phsyical blueprint, in which, as Farocki recalls, the caesura regulates the breath and the breath the caesura. The alternative of Moses/Aron or real/unreal, or thought/image is politically irrelevant to the cinema of Straub and Huillet. Straub answers the question of the *Cahiers* journalists, "*Une terre irréelle contre des terres réelles?*" by referring to the fact that it isn't territorialization, real or unreal, but rather the kind of existence and movement in space that is subject to discussion: "No. Because people don't settle in the desert. The idea of Moses is the traversal of the desert without a goal. It's quite simply the nomadic idea."[239] The topology of the nomadic radicalizes the cinematic space precisely where the music is abandoned.

With an allusion to the halting in panoramic seeing, with the conjunctive "qu'est-ce qui se passerait si le pano s'ARRETAIT?"[240] Straub lets us know that the film of the opera, as in the Exodus itself, is concerned with the visualization and even the embodiment of caesuras and turning points, with thinking in

237 Translated from Straub/Huillet, "Conversation," p. 8.
238 Hölderlin, "'The declining fatherland ...'" in *Letters and Essays*, pp. 271–276.
239 Translated from Straub/Huillet, "Conversation," p. 8.
240 Ibid., p. 16.

topologies. For Straub and Huillet the people isn't something that forms itself as a mass or mob, no murmuring entourage, no Greek polis, nothing heroic, and no revolutionary *peuple* but an attitude of perception that explores new differences and thus creates new resistance. Liberation is only conceivable out of the recognition of one's own media-organized condition of hearing and seeing. The people isn't calculated according to class situation or historical crisis; it isn't a diverse association or multitude but a stance that differentiates autonomously and assumes that spaces have no above, below, right, or left before the directions are aligned. The film distills this from the opera of the old "royalist"[241] Schoenberg. This is why Straub can say, in view of the empty landscape and mountain lake, "... in the film only the people remains."[242]

241 See ibid., p. 10.

242 Translated from Straub/Huillet, "Conversation," p. 10.

5. CLOUDS, DESERTS

At the hour in which Moses ascended, a cloud settled before him. He did not know whether to sit upon it or embrace it. Then the cloud gaped open and he entered it, as is told: "And Moses went into the midst of the cloud" (Ex. 24:18) and "a cloud covered the mount" (see verse 15). Thereupon the cloud raised him up and he went into the citadel. There he encountered the archangel Chamuel, who was seated above twelve thousand angels of death at the entrance to the citadel. He shouted at Moses, saying What do you want among the high holy ones? You are from an impure place and come to a pure place? A man born of woman comes to a place of fire? I am, answered Moses, Amram's son. I am come to receive the law for Israel. When they did not let him alone he struck at them and put an end to them.

Pesikta Rabbati no. 20[1]

Before the law stands a doorkeeper. To this doorkeeper there comes a man from the country and prays for admittance to the Law. But the doorkeeper says that he cannot grant admittance at the moment. The man thinks it over and then asks if he will be allowed in later. "It is possible," says the doorkeeper, "but not at the moment."

Franz Kafka[2]

1 Translated from *Pesiqta Rabbati, Midrasch für den Festzyklus und die ausgezeichneten Sabbathe. Kritisch bearbeitet, commentiert durch neue handschriftliche Haggadas vermehrt, mit Bibel- und Personenindices versehen von Meir Friedmann,* Wien 1880, Tel Aviv 1963, p. 140.

2 Franz Kafka, "Before the Law," in Kafka, *The Complete Stories*, New York 1983, pp. 22–23: 22.

5.1. EXILE

On September 24, 1914 Arnold Schoenberg began a "War-Clouds Diary." With differently colored crayons he sketched and noted the signs and symptoms of the sky above Berlin and of his own perception. Cloud formations, cloud images might allow conclusions to be drawn about military operations and positions of the front. Observations of meteorological "tensions" are matched with tensions on the ground. The diary is interested in correspondences whose qualities remain speculative. It is recorded in the style of a semi-scientific, semi-artistic journal. The world is the laboratory, and Schoenberg's senses the gauge of the powers at work within it. Schoenberg opens the account with a short foreword. He hopes that others will participate in the research in order "once more accurate reports are available, since so far a number of war events could be premonitioned by the 'mood' of the sky."[3]

On this the diary's first day Schoenberg notes: "about 10:45 a.m.: icy cold mood, like in the circus before a very daring stunt: silence, tension, no wind; impression of the sky is at first predominantly clear, pure; only later I observe a slowly expanding cloud streak. Total impression: a daring operation which began under auspicious circumstances."[4] In 1914 Arnold Schoenberg was still hoping for a swift victory of the Central Powers, but the journal metaphorically discloses the shaky ground on which he was standing. Not only he. The metaphor of the circus artiste, in the dome, about to jump, expresses the constellation. At the moment of an imperceptible danger, of an irritation that suspends all known parameters of knowledge and being able to know, Schoenberg begins to observe, to draw, and write down anything he can decipher in order to give the unfathomable events a basis, framework, and context. In the "War-Clouds Diary" he seeks words, images, metaphors, purchase for the looming catastrophe that will later be named and numbered as the First World War. "Many people, like myself today, will have tried to interpret the events of war by the sky, since finally the belief in higher powers and also in God has returned."[5]

3 Arnold Schoenberg, "War-Clouds Diary," trans. Paul A Pisk, in *Journal of the Schoenberg Institute*, vol. XIV, no. 1, June 1986, pp. 53–77: 61.

4 Ibid.

5 Ibid.

In attempting to systematically apprehend the missing system of knowledge through cloud formations, Schoenberg follows a tradition of journal writers who also sought to determine the precarious relationship between signs and things, world and environment, atmospheric tensions, and social conditions through the vague object of the cloud: Albrecht Dürer, who struggled with the depiction of clouds, which have no place in the perspective world of *costruzione legittima,* in his woodcuts *The Apocalypse of Saint John* (1498), reconstructing the trance-like states of the apostle;[6] Galileo Galilei, who involuntarily became a cloud diarist in the *Sidereus Nuncius,* because clouds obscured his view of the object of his investigations, stars, in whose mechanical movements lay a new cosmic logic;[7] Goethe, who kept cloud journals in the terminology of Luke Howard's classifications in the preparation of his meteorological writings, transitions to the nineteenth-century science of distribution and thermodynamics, and links them to aesthetic and poetological questions, metamorphosis, and morphology. According to Joseph Vogl, who conceives the cloud in the register of becoming, interest in clouds as a nebulous third between sign and thing doesn't only relates to questions of semiotics; rather, "the thing about clouds—with Goethe and beyond—[shows] a new constellation between perception, aesthetics, and knowledge."[8] In the early 1940s Maurice Merleau-Ponty described forms of phenomenological perception in terms of cloud movements: "Sometimes I see the steeple motionless against the sky with clouds floating above it, and sometimes the clouds appear still and the steeple falls through space."[9] Only for phenomenologists is the cloud as stable and durable as any other object: "The looked-at object in which I anchor myself will always seem fixed, and I cannot take this meaning away from it except by looking elsewhere."[10] Around the same time Heidegger spoke in Freiburg of the typewriter as a "signless cloud" that

6 See Erwin Panofsky, *The Life and Art of Albrecht Dürer,* Princeton 1955, p. 39.

7 Galileo Galilei, *Sidereus Nuncius,* ed. Peter Barker, Oklahoma 2004; in general Joseph Vogl, "Wolkenbotschaft," in *Archiv für Mediengeschichte,* vol. 5, Weimar 2005, pp. 69–79. For cinema, in particular Friedrich Wilhelm Murnau, see Ute Holl, "Strahlen und Überstrahlen – Risse ins Bild der Geschichte. Zur filmischen Historiographie von F.W. Murnaus FAUST," in Daniel Tyradellis, Burkhardt Wolf (eds.), *Die Szene der Gewalt. Bilder, Codes und Materialitäten,* Frankfurt/Main 2007, pp. 157–174.

8 Translated from Vogl, "Wolkenbotschaft," p. 77.

9 Maurice Merleau-Ponty, "The Film and the New Psychology," in *Sense and Non-Sense,* trans. Hubert L. Dreyfus and Patricia Allen Dreyfus, Evanston 1964, pp. 48–59: 52.

10 Ibid.

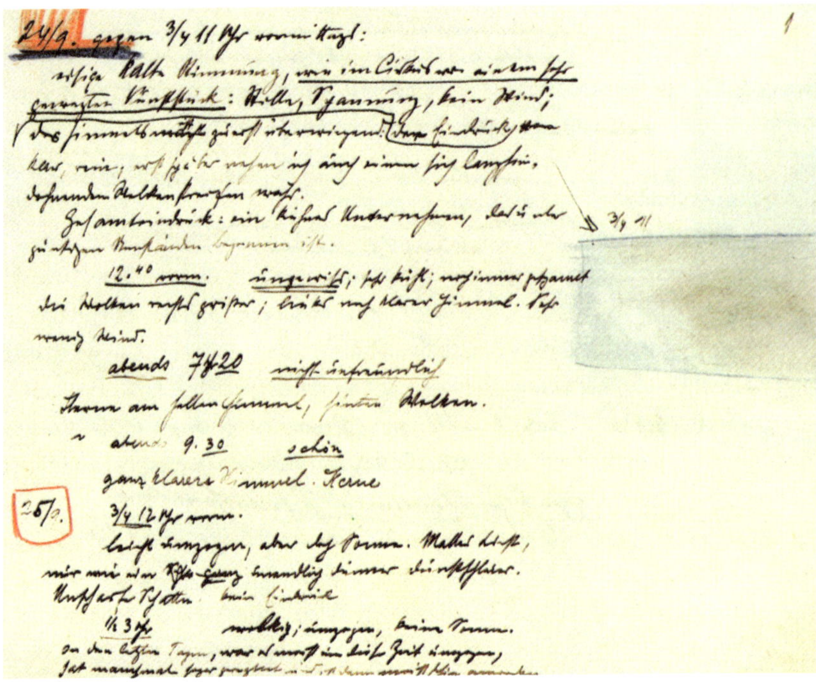

Arnold Schoenberg, "War-Clouds Diary."

unnoticeably veiled the basis of knowledge and brings about "a transformation in the relation of Being to man."[11] But in each case there is epistemological upheaval. Visions reveal themselves in cloud formations as projected knowledge.

Cinema is also involved in the reorganization of perception, aesthetics, and knowledge in the sense of the cloud. In 1926, his film of Goethe's *Faust*, Friedrich Wilhelm Murnau, who named himself after the small town in which a group of artists around Wassily Kandinsky experimented with invisible forces before the war, had the light refract and diffuse in the studio mists between enlightenment and bedazzlement. In this he repeated his experience as a pilot in the clouds of the First World War, which Schoenberg was drawing and describing in September 1914. Schoenberg's diary, experimenting between esoterics and

11 Heidegger, *Parmenides*, p. 86.

Arnold Schoenberg, "War-Clouds Diary."

science, thus captures the exceptional state of knowledge and sign regimes that could be written as a history of the cloud.[12] Clouds are epistemological in the sense suggested by Jörg Rheinberger: blurred, not even objects, of an "irreducible vagueness," which direct our exploration and questions into new fields.[13] They primarily come into view when the parameters of knowledge become precarious. Vogl applies this media-theoretically to a third thing: "Seeing clouds also means seeing, at the same time and decidedly, something invisible and impalpable."[14] Clouds are symptomatic, referring to forces for which there is neither concept nor model, and the experience of them can only be unclear.

12 See Hubert Damisch, *Theory of /Cloud/. Toward a History of Painting*, trans. Janet Lloyd, Stanford 2002.

13 Hans Jörg Rheinberger, *Toward A History of Epistemic Things. Synthesizing Proteins in the Test Tube*, Stanford 1997, p. 28.

14 Translated from Vogl, "Wolkenbotschaft," p. 72.

This certainly applies to Schoenberg's journal, which examines the conditions of being able to know. Above all the ability to know about war and violence.

In their film of the opera *Moses und Aron*, Jean-Marie Straub and Danièle Huillet characteristically transfer the motif of not knowing in the many shots of clouds and skies into the concrete, particular, and specific. Everything transcendent, everything adhering to the theological topos, is turned back to the earth, landscapes, light, and movement, to bodies and people, and their visibility or invisibility in the light of the world. Here cinema provides a new form of insight that has yet to establish itself as knowledge. The images of MOSES UND ARON aren't concerned with nature or natural beauty, but rather with the interconnection of diverse forces we know about and rely on: natural, cultural, artistic, linguistic, technical, and by all means historical. In the film's clouds and landscapes knowledge is subject to examination as seeing and wanting to know. This also applies to other unfathomable events dealt with in the Moses story. "Du hast die Greuel gesehen, die Wahrheit erkannt ... [You've seen your kindred enslaved, the truth you have known ...]."[15] The unfathomable has to be captured in such a way that it lends itself to political intervention. Hence the affinity to the sublime in this film. "... so kannst du nicht anders mehr: du musst dein Volk daraus befrein! [... so you can do nothing else, therefore you must set your folk fee!]."[16] The enlightened figure of a cooperation of sensuality and reason is thus strengthened as a form of research. And as the film's form of thought.

On the invitation of Wassily Kandinsky, Arnold Schoenberg had spent the summer of 1914 in Murnau, where he devoted himself with the other artists to the effects of forces and fields that operate invisibly but palpably in the world and the "experience of the emotions."[17] These effects are in turn inherent. In 1911/12, parallel to Schoenberg's *Theory of Harmony*, Kandinsky devoted his essay *Concerning the Spiritual in Art* to the effects of forms and colors. He explains the developing forces on the basis of electromagnetism, nuclear physics, and relativity theory. Invisible, unconceivable, and yet precisely calculable, these forces allow all natural movements to be translated into vibration ratios,

15 Schönberg, *Moses und Aron*, score I, act I, bars 23–25.

16 Ibid., bars 25–27.

17 Translated from Wassily Kandinsky, *Über das Geistige in der Kunst, insbesondere in der Malerei*, revised edition, Bern 2006, foreword to the first edition, January 1912, p. 21. This foreword was not included in the English translation.

which Kandinsky understands as values of "inner need"[18] and records in synaesthetically conceived taxonomic overviews (tableaus). He describes the struggle to capture the effect of non-material forces in the world as a struggle for knowledge: "Every day scientific theory finds bold discoverers who overstep the boundaries of prophecy and, forgetful of themselves, join the other soldiers in the conquest of some new summit and in the hopeless attack on some stubborn fortress."[19] Kandinsky's book documents that these experiments between art and military metaphors are conceived in proximity to the occult, to spiritism, theosophy, and anthroposophy.[20] The Murnau artists, the Blauer Reiter, and their circle dealt with invisible forces in visual and music as a disengagement from the model of a visible and imperturbable natural world. Like Kandinsky, Schoenberg had examined the logic of forces in his *Theory of Harmony*, and was beginning to explore their effects in the composition of a new kind of music: "Laws apparently prevail here. What they are, I do not know. Perhaps I shall know in a few years. Perhaps someone after me will find them. For the present the most we can do is describe."[21]

Schoenberg's and Kandinsky's texts are paradigmatic of a reevaluation of aesthetic fields, in which laws and systems of unknown effect can be found and invented. Causalities and genealogies that may have appeared reliable to the arts of the nineteenth century lose validity under the conditions of new fields of knowledge and new models of perception. Artistic research is carried on in parallel with science, or as science fiction: "Schönberg is endeavouring to make complete use of his freedom and has already discovered gold mines of new beauty in his search for spiritual harmony. His music leads us into a realm where musical experience is a matter not of the ear but of the soul alone – and from this point begins the music of the future."[22] Regarding this historical form of artistic research, Max Bill noted in his foreword to the new German edition

18 Kandinsky, *Concerning the Spiritual in Art*, trans. M.T.H. Sadler, New York 1977, p. 26.

19 Ibid., p. 12.

20 Ibid., p. 13. Wolfgang Hagen has examined the work and experiments of the extended Murnau circle in the context of a history of occult knowledge, within which he uncovers a genealogy of media science, particularly radio science: See Wolfgang Hagen, "Walter Ruttmanns Grosstadt-Weekend. Zur Herkunft der Hörcollage aus der ungegenständlichen Malerei," in Nicola Gess and others (eds.), *Hörstürze: Akustik und Gewalt im 20. Jahrhundert*, Würzburg 2005, pp. 183–200.

21 Schoenberg, *Theory of Harmony*, p. 421.

22 Kandinsky, *Concerning the Spiritual in Art*, p. 17.

of Kandinsky's book in 1965 that "artistic results ran ahead of physical ones."[23] The proximity of scientific, physical models and occult spiritism to no longer distinct boundaries between material and immaterial spheres requires aesthetic and epistemological freedom, which Kandinsky and Schoenberg take. The cloud diary belongs in this field.

It makes sense to put the observation and description of new phenomena and fields of knowledge in the context of the spread of technical media, which had long formed the experience of modernity by 1900. Photography and film, gramophone and records, the telephone and above all the radio, in its aesthetic modulations on unconceivable electromagnetic waves, suspended the older laws and offered new models of perception. But a current concept of media, developed much later, in the 1980s, recalling precisely the epistemological constellation around 1880, offers no conclusive means of ascribing the emerging ways of thinking to a basis or source. Media thinking instead draws circular-causal conclusions between established fields with the aid of epistemic indistinction. The concept of media initially only sharpens a field of questions discovered then and still relevant today.[24] The visible technical arrangements aren't decisive for the examination of unconscious, implicit, or media effects. The decisive thing is that physical and physiological functions become effective—beyond the threshold of human perception—and enable new differences and thus other caesuras and interventions. The functional points and empty spaces, as circuits, relays, interferences, that apparently regulate knowledge in the technical era, "silence, tension, no wind," only reveal themselves symptomatically. Kandinsky uses the image of Mount Sinai to describe this state of irritation under the new effects of invisible forces not yet called media: "The invisible Moses descends from the mountain and sees the dance round the golden calf. But he brings with him fresh stores of wisdom to man."[25]

Because Schoenberg returned to a "belief in higher powers and also in God,"[26] during the war in 1914, his involvement with the Moses complex, his musical staging of a camp before the law at the foot of Mount Sinai, can be dated to

23 Translated from Max Bill, "Vorwort zu Kandinsky," *Über das Geistige in der Kunst, insbesondere in der Malerei*, revised edition, Bern 2006, pp. 9–20: 16.

24 Erhard Schüttpelz, "Frage nach der Frage, auf die das Medium eine Antwort ist," in Albert Kümmel und ders. (eds.), *Signale der Störung*, Munich 2003, pp. 15–29.

25 Kandinsky, *Concerning the Spiritual in Art*, p. 8.

26 Schoenberg, "War-Clouds-Diary," p. 61.

this time. Even in the early months of the war his interest is not only religious but equally epistemological and media scientific *ante litteram*, and it raises the political question of behavior and action under a radical withdrawal of every epistemic matrix and an unclarity about social forms and the boundaries of knowledge. Schoenberg's composition handles the empty, unstable, and frightening space in which he found himself as a place of exile in which all the matrices of perception are in doubt.

Straub and Huillet film this exile as an unknown, unpredictable, unreliable space. They develop it from familiar cinematic and electro-acoustic forms, which they use contrary to all convention. From shots, camera movements, montage, from buildings, optics, and light they construct an unexpected space, conceive possibilities, invent forms of cinematic perception in an awareness of the tradition but against cinematic conventions: "I hate everything epigonic."[27] Straub/Huillet's spaces are neither transcendent nor esoteric. They invite the exploration of visuals and acoustics. They sound out, like Schoenberg, the boundaries of the audible and visible. Structure, laws, and aesthetic procedure can only be experienced recursively, much as in Schoenberg's music the law of composition and the rule of the tone row can only be reconstructed after the singular experience of their aural perception. Historicity under media conditions requires research as an exploration of feelings and affects.

Schoenberg, as his cloud diaries show, already felt himself to be in exile in 1914, before the passing of any laws to exclude people. After the First World War he spoke clearly of his experiences of racism. In a letter to Kandinsky on April 20, 1923 explaining his refusal to come to the Bauhaus in Weimar, although his "taste for teaching" was great, Schoenberg writes: "For I have at last learnt the lesson that has been forced upon me during this year, and I shall not ever forget it. It is that I am not a German, not a European, indeed perhaps scarcely even a human being (at least, the Europeans prefer the worst of their race to me), but I am a Jew."[28] Jean-Marie Straub and Danièle Huillet reconstructed this letter

27 Translated from Artem Demenok/Robert Bramkamp, "'Eine Hexe, die eine Menge Energie verbraucht …' Danièle Huillet & Jean-Marie Straub im Gespräch" in Klaus Volkmer et al. (eds), *Schönberg/Blonda/Huillet/Straub. Von Heute auf Morgen. Oper/Musik/Film*, Berlin 1997, pp. 87–99: 93.

28 Arnold Schoenberg, letter to Wassily Kandinsky, Mödling April 20, 1923, in Schoenberg, *Letters*, p. 88.

from the archive for their film INTRODUCTION TO ARNOLD SCHOENBERG'S ACCOMPANIMENT TO A CINEMATIC SCENE.

Schoenberg formulates it aggressively: "but I am a Jew." It is the others who prevent him from being German, Austrian, and European, forces that Kandinsky must know, as he warns in the letter. Exile is a network of relationships. Schoenberg writes: "Have you also forgotten how much disaster can be evoked by a particular mode of feeling?"[29] He is making the link between aesthetics, affects, and politics. Opera and film seek and establish further connections: between epistemological insecurity and racism, between the restructuring of all relationships and paranoid distinctions of friendship and enmity, between the reformation of all knowledge and hypertrophic nationalism, between the withdrawal of knowledge and violence, between new media and war. The opera *Moses und Aron* operates in these interstices, at the boundary between music and noises, speech and voice, function and identity, sign and disturbance. It explores thought in exile at the boundary to a perception deprived of any stable matrix. The position of Moses is in the open; Aron, however, decodes the sensory as a signal:

> *Aron off: [...]* Der Allmächtige gibt durch mich dem Volk ein Zeichen. *Moses:* Die Wolkensäule! *Aron off:* Sie führt uns bei Tag. *Moses:* Götzenbilder! *Aron off:* Gotteszeichen, wie der glühende Dornbusch. [...] *Moses:* [...] Darf Aron, mein Mund, dieses Bild machen? So habe ich mir ein Bild gemacht, falsch, wie ein Bild nur sein kann. So bin ich geschlagen!
>
> *Aaron off*: Thus through me has God giv'n a signal to the people. *Moses*: The cloudlike pillar! *Aaron off*: It leads us by day. *Moses*: Godless image! *Aaron off*: Godsent signal, burning bush again glowing [...] *Moses*: Shall Aaron, my mouth, fashion this image? Then I have fashioned an image too, false, as an image must be. Thus am I defeated!
> (act II, bars 1087–1124).

The film propels the opera further into the Moses position. Signs, images, and wonders don't stand for something else here. They don't refer, but are themselves circumstances and procedures in which a decision has to be made.

29 Arnold Schoenberg, letter Wassily Kandinsky, May 4, 1923 in Schoenberg, *Letters*, p. 91.

The film doesn't only eliminate semiotic structures but also the familiar order of cinematic spaces, in which a logic of *on* and *off*, shot and countershot, *champ* and *contre-champ* is ensured or in which a pan would be traced to human movement or the conventional stage view. Straub and Huillet set heightened concretion, exact shots, precise sound, and palpable relationships between elements against speculations about sense, being, and meaning. They direct their attention to what they frankly call beauty: the freedom to look at things in the entirety of their relationships and without pre-forming laws. They cause this beauty to emerge at the caesuras, which rupture familiar circumstances. Such caesuras can be edits, but also other cuts into the material of film, into language, breath, images, sounds. They expose a texture in which the opera- and moviegoers can and must decide for themselves how they form the visible and audible world, and how they see the others, the aliens, the strangers. On their own responsibility. Cloud images not only replace a Pythagorean and Newtonian world view with Bergsonian and ultimately cybernetic temporality; they also organize a communist time of decision, which arises from equal probability and equal status.[30]

5.2. NUMBERS

Arnold Schoenberg, as he explained in a jovial lecture at the University of Southern California in the summer of 1935, had been working since the 1920s on the technique of organizing musical material without a center and outside of predefined scales, on composing in the "constant and exclusive use of a set of twelve different tones,"[31] that is, of all twelve chromatic tones. Although not, as a concept of creation requires, "at once and in its ultimate perfection,"[32] but as the recursive development of musical thinking in relations, without a basic

30 See Norbert Wiener, *Cybernetics Or Control and Communication in the Animal and the Machine*, Cambridge MA 1965, p. 30. Wiener quotes the German lullaby: "Weißt du, wieviel Sternlein stehen, an dem blauen Himmelszelt? Weißt du, wieviel Wolken gehen, weithin über alle Welt" [Do you know how many little stars there are in the blue tent of the sky? Do you know how many clouds float all over the world?]. Wiener and all tired children know that no one can know such a thing, and only a computer could work it out approximately.

31 Schoenberg, "Composition with Twelve Tones," p. 218.

32 Ibid., p. 215.

tone: "[T]hese musical ideas must correspond to the laws of human logic; they are a part of what man can apperceive, reason and express."[33] With this concept Schoenberg's method becomes the model of structural thinking. In the overture to *Mythologica* Claude Lévi-Strauss juxtaposes the natural musical structures with those relationships that "according to Schönberg's significant formula, [...] are to be defined solely by 'the total system of relations of the sounds with one another'."[34] For Lévi-Strauss, cultural and physiological templates interlock in the experience of hearing, and provoke artistic operations of "a code independent of sense experience, as is the case in music with its sounds and rhythms"[35] and otherwise only mathematics.

But what has been mathematically equally divided doesn't simply generate equal distributions. Counting means exploring transition probabilities, organizing transitions. Organized in time and recursion, new and valuable structures reveal themselves in such procedures as the generation of inherent behavior, as Heinz von Foerster has system-theoretically described, taking into account the observer or listener in the process;[36] or in the sense of the inherent laws that, following stochastic models, can even be applied to the dynamics of human desire, as structural psychoanalysis calculates with Markov chains.[37] In these processes elements don't simply mount up but, arranged in groups and iterated, form new structures. Scansion and permutation, caesura and recursion, differentiation and repetition also generate distinctive effects, idiosyncratic structures, unexpected figures in sound and spaces in twelve-tone composition and the montage of independent visual elements. In contrast to the chance composition of his student John Cage, Schoenberg's row is already a particular organization of transitions, which show up and change in their musical implementation. Only in the sensitive disturbance of conventional ideas of hearing do hidden rules suddenly emerge that generate all relationships and transitions: in Schoenberg's serial music the row, in Straub/Huillet's film the rules of the game, which organize the spaces of acts I and II differently. When

33 Ibid., p. 220.

34 Claude Lévi-Strauss, *Mythologiques*, vol. I, *The Raw and the Cooked*, Chicago 1969, p. 21.

35 Ibid., p. 19.

36 Heinz von Foerster, "Gegenstände: Greifbare Symbole für (Eigen-)Verhalten," in Heinz von Foerster, *Wissen und Gewissen. Versuch einer Brücke*, Frankfurt/Main 1993, pp. 103–115.

37 Jacques Lacan, "Seminar on the 'The Purloined Letter'," trans. Jeffrey Mehlman, *Yale French Studies*, vol. 0, no. 48, *French Freud: Structural Studies in Psychoanalysis* (1972), pp. 39–72.

the familiar no longer holds or holds its tongue, implicit media orderings that precondition all hearing and seeing are revealed. Lévi-Strauss refers to the caesura, which organizes music, as it does language and mythology, "as a result of the selection made in the sound continuum by each type of scale, hierarchical relations are established among the notes."[38] Media differ in the forms with which they regulate relationships, particular transitions, differences, and difference phenomena as hierarchical or not. They also operate here on technical, physiological, and cultural levels. The hierarchical relationships resulting from the code of iteration, which Lévi-Strauss examines, produce tension between all three fields.

Thirty years after Schoenberg, and also in the United States, Jacques Derrida required post-structuralist thought to disband the center, against all totality. "By orienting and organizing the coherence of the system, the center of a structure permits the play of its elements inside the total form. And even today the notion of a structure lacking any center represents the unthinkable itself."[39] In Schoenberg's opera the unthinkable becomes the unconceivable invocation of God, in the double and recursive genitive. But the work also teaches the retrieval of the unconceivable into human and media effects, and the hearing of sound formations without a center.

The space that arises out of nothing—and this is also the risk of the Moses production—provides as little orientation as the smooth space of the desert: "Every musical configuration, every movement of tones has to be comprehended primarily as a mutual relation of sounds, of oscillatory vibrations, appearing at different places and times."[40] In an interview Jean-Marie Straub gives a different answer, which also refers to the risky form of aesthetic production: "I hate everything epigonic. When you film you really have to create emptiness, complete emptiness within you. EMPTINESS. If you don't create it, what you then make is probably not worth much."[41]

The film by Straub/Huillet develops the *coté théologique,* an imperceptible matrix of thinking and perception, as a historical side and as a media-aesthetic coté médiologique. The unthinkable is systematically returned to the

38 Lévi-Strauss, *The Raw and the Cooked*, p. 21.

39 Jacques Derrida, "Structure, Sign and Play in the Discourse of the Human Sciences," in Jacques Derrida, *Writing and Difference*, trans. Alan Bass, New York 1978, pp. 351–371: 352.

40 Schoenberg, "Composition with Twelve Tones," p. 223.

41 Demenok/Bramkamp, "Eine Hexe, die eine Menge Energie verbraucht ...," p. 93.

superimposition of very concrete arrangements to which it owes its existence: to echo and magnitude, the accessibilities and light effects of historical architecture, the conditions and mix of different recording situations, the concrete bodies of soloists and chorus. The film realizes a sound that is entirely of this world but assembled from complex vibrations and reverberations. And so it refers at the same time to a unity of sonic relationships under no one's command. A historicity is at work in this, also only mediated, as a *coté historique*.

It is at work on various levels. When human voices and instruments are closely apposed at the start of the opera, so that their sounds overlay into a third, alien other, historical cultural techniques are implicitly involved. For Europe new sounds and new music have their roots in the experimental cultures of the nineteenth century and the discovery of a logic of vibration in all things. Frequency structures became a shared quality that could bring the world's things and spaces down to a common denominator, which is general but not abstract, as Nietzsche remarked: "Accordingly, music, if regarded as an expression of the world, is in the highest degree a universal language that is related to the universality of concepts much as these are related to the particular things. Yet its universality is by no means that empty universality of abstraction, but is of quite a different kind; it is united with thorough and unmistakable distinctness. In this respect it is like geometrical figures and numbers, which are the universal forms of all possible objects of experience and are apriori applicable to them all, and yet are not abstract, but perceptible and thoroughly definite."[42]

Long before Schoenberg, melodies and sounds were no longer being arranged and blended only in harmonies but also from tone colors, superimpositions, and sound effects, and artistic, physical, and technical research was carried out in parallel in nineteenth-century music too. The voice from the burning bush, as simply *concertante* as it sounds, is the result of a genealogy of experiments, such as those from which Hermann von Helmholtz distilled music theory. The tone-color composition outlined by Schoenberg in his *Theory of Harmony*, along with serial composition, presupposes a history of technical media in the counting, combination, and arrangement of vibrations, realized by keys and electric cables. The voice from the burning bush that enters the stage at the beginning of *Moses und Aron* is a synthesized media voice. It can therefore be called and sound inhuman, but can nonetheless be analyzed historically. Schoenberg thus

42 Nietzsche, "The Birth of Tragedy," p. 77f.

musically combines the aesthetic and the political. The call of God in the opera contains a *coté théologique*, a *coté médiologique*, and a *coté historique*. Hearing correctly means being able to intervene.

In concerts the history of sounds and their cultural-technical preconditions usually remain implicit. Schoenberg, however, brings them back into perception in the opera house through the use of technical media such as telephone, radio, or electric cable. Straub and Huillet proceed analogously in their film when they juxtapose conventional and technically hybrid forms to bring the media aspect itself into play. But they actually don't show the apparatus as camera or projection, as in the enlightening gesture of cinema aesthetics from Vertov to Godard. Rather, they let us know what cinema can do, through montage, stratification, and displacement in the acoustic space and the visual one of buildings, landscapes, images of light and clouds. It isn't ahistorical nature or naturalness that appears in the footage of Abruzzo but images and sounds in a cultural-technical context linked to cinematic shots and montages. So it can be seen in the film and opera that mathematical composition, writing, or filming doesn't operate outside of the cultural. At least in the case of Schoenberg and Straub/Huillet it explores the basis of their own aesthetic procedures in vibrations and optics, in the electro-acoustic, and in forms of audiovisual transmission. Vowels, looks, dances show how historical knowledge is connected to bodies. What was once called transcendence then turns out to be the negotiation of relationships between code and body, economy, and aesthetics.

The perception of something other or strange as theological, mediological, and historical doesn't occur outside of the sensory, even if the enumerating code, as Lévi-Straus emphasizes, is "independent of sense experience."[43] The works of Schoenberg and Straub/Huillet systematically reconnect media aesthetics to their ordering by the senses, even if, in the technical media, this undercuts their perception or exceeds their framework. Symptoms of disturbance, such as interruption, rift, combination, or repetition point to this.

Political forms come into play with the media-aesthetic forms of counting. If democracy, as Jacques Rancière advises, should first be related back to the police practice of counting subjects, as the simulation of collectives on the basis of large numbers, statistics, data collections,[44] then new forms of counting and

43 Lévi-Strauss, *The Raw and the Cooked*, p. 19.

44 See Rancière, *Dis-agreement*, p. 83f.

enumeration, of placing people in space, should be developed. In their aesthetic procedures the works of Schoenberg and Straub/Huillet prove to be political concepts in this sense. New forms of counting construct new topologies, new places in which people can appear. The serial composition of sounds, the montage of images are in this sense techniques of relationship. Schoenberg's opening shows that everyone must and can decide, without having been assigned to a center or direction, without the police keeping count.

The film MOSES UND ARON doesn't simply make counting and topology available, however; rather, the figures are unthinkable outside this logic of force fields. They only come about from the entirety of relationships of words, song, instruments, and apparatuses, of landscapes, animals, movements, buildings. There is no psychology beyond it. Straub/Huillet develop this in the pan, which stands for the people: as a form of cinematic condensation, the pan produces unexpected relationships in which the people can get caught up and constitute themselves as a collective, even in the movie theater. This is the opposite of identification and immersion, and it makes the film recalcitrant. In the opera Schoenberg composed the figures as forces within the sound space. With the first sung O ______, as a vocalise or inhuman sound, a network of *dispositifs* and sciences is called up: alphabetization, phonetics, the history of technology as subjectivization processes in the sound space. We are entangled in this network manifested in sounds and images, even if we don't always know what it is we are hearing. Conversely, the protagonists of the film are constituted solely from aesthetic functions, rather than theological, historical, or political ones. Leader or rebel, people or God denote particular constellations of relationships rather than anything ontological; alterable constellations—like musical sound, like a camera movement. And new relationships are also produced in the abandonment or arrest of these constellations, *si le pano s'arretait.* If such knots of relationship are fixed culturally and in circular causality, they present themselves, according to Gregory Bateson, as gods. Monotheistic or not, they correct the "short-sighted purposiveness" of the individual. If only folk networked circularly. This we'd call the people.

5.3. THE PEOPLE

The people is a complex form of connectivity. It needs to be autonomous, and then constituted, subject to a law. The constitution, on the other hand, is a risk to autonomy. It should serve the idea, the Moses figure demands, rigorous against any form of impartition, incorruptible because without desire, because it lacks nothing. Distinction must be made in one's own judgment. The works dealing with Moses as opera, film, cultural history pursue this impossible position. Giorgio Agamben refers to a double meaning of the word "people," which "in modern European languages [...] also always indicates the poor, the disinherited, and the excluded,"[45] when he traces the absent people to a fundamental schism in the history of European states and law, to a split in the body politic. Because it is a "polar concept that indicates a double movement and a complex relation between two extremes,"[46] Agamben counts "people" among the "ur-words" in Freud's symptomatic analysis, those ambivalent terms that recall contrary processes: people "names both the constitutive political subject and the class that is, de facto if not de jure, excluded from politics."[47] The people, however, as represented in the polyphonic constellation of the double chorus in Schoenberg's opera, or the people that corresponds in Straub/Huillet's film to the equably floating observation of the pan, points to the necessity of a new form of differentiation. The people appears here as a symptom of what is lacking.

Looking at repetitions in history in his book *Moses and Monotheism*, Sigmund Freud developed an archaeological method that can be a model for all media historiography. Freud discovers gaps, rifts, and caesuras on the surface of landscapes or texts, of buildings, images, or names as traces that reveal the distortions, repetitions, and restorations of a hidden layer of historical dynamics. The dynamic that Freud attempts to clarify is that of the masses, the collective, the religions; the dynamic of a people and its conception of a "God suddenly 'choosing' a people"—a disconcerting idea, says Freud.[48] The dynamic of the masses

45 Giorgio Agamben, *Homo Sacer. Sovereign Power and Bare Life*, trans. Daniel Heller-Roazen, Stanford 1998, p. 176.

46 Ibid., p. 177.

47 Ibid., p. 176.

48 Freud, "Moses and Monotheism," p. 73.

also includes the temporary "people's falling away from the new religion,"[49] if only temporarily, the breaking of the law by the people, and, literally, in breaking the tablets, by the lawgiver himself.

Freud was already living in exile in London when he completed his Moses book, but in its rifts and caesuras the text refers to Vienna and Berlin in 1938, to the first post-war years, the European 1920s, and to the future, now. This can be read, differently in each case, from the 1940s, the German 1970s, or 2014 in the light of mass movements and their media, of caesuras left by wars, of wars that repeat and open up old fronts, of the violence that recurrently marks history, of the films that prefigured this as science fiction, precisely documenting historical dynamics.

In a first draft from 1934 Sigmund Freud described his book about Moses the man as a "historical novel."[50] More accurate would be "historiographical novel." Where in his research into a historical Moses he comes across names, figures, and events, these prove to be double and doubled:

> To the well-known *duality* of that history – *two peoples* who fuse together to form one nation, *two kingdoms* into which this nation divides, *two names* for the Deity in the source of the Bible – we add two new ones: the founding of *two* new religions, the first one ousted by the second and yet reappearing victorious, *two* founders of religions, who are both called by the same name Moses and whose personalities we have to separate from each other. And all these dualities are necessary consequences of the first: one section of the people passed through what may properly be termed a traumatic experience which the other was spared.[51]

Moses' message itself a repeated one: "When Moses gave to his people the conception of an Only God it was not an altogether new idea, for it meant the reanimation of primeval experience in the human family that had long ago faded

49 Ibid., p. 77.

50 See Grubrich-Simitis, *Freuds Moses-Studie*, p. 82ff. Yosef Hayim Yerushalmi, *Freud's Moses: Judaism Terminable and Interminable*, New Haven 1991, p. 17. For a different view see Peter Gay, *Freud:A Life for Our Time*, New York/London 2005. Gay calls the book "something of an oddity" (p. 648) in Freud's work.

51 Freud, *Moses and Monotheism*, p. 84.

from the conscious memory of mankind."[52] History is portrayed by families and fathers, family stories, and philosophy; history repeats family novels: Freud, father, son, child, man, Moses. Patrilineally, in monotheism.

In his 1938 work on Moses, his second after the one on Michelangelo's sculpture,[53] Freud shows that not only individuals, individual subjects, but also historical collectives and even territories can develop symptoms. These indicate a delayed and deferred return of the suppressed, the return of something whose first impression or impact overpowered, wounded, traumatized, or destroyed the consciousness and so couldn't be processed. Wherever or whatever a consciousness is unable to represent, the attention circles around an empty space and forms a center at the very point where there is none, where nothing is shown, where something is missing. Caesura and recursion, scansion and permutation, distinction, and repetition. In this dynamic, history generates new structures from the entirety of possible relationships. New correspondences are obscured or opened up. In everyday life, works of art, bodies, landscapes, and buildings, in images, films, and sounds, Freud's symptomatic model of recollection allows a sedimentary history and self-perpetuating power relationships to be found as traces of something not articulated. For suppression always forms a crypt, a storeroom, an archive in bodies, just as in landscapes or buildings.[54]

Repetitions point to futile repairs, bad restorations; traces of disturbance point to earlier soldering[55] of still active lines of struggle, to badly sewn tears, papered-over surfaces, and encrusted visions that had once formed as reactions to traumatic events. On the imperial stage, as Freud indicates, history performs its own march as a return, as a theater of regression and recursion: "History loves such restorations, in which later fusions are redissolved and former separations become once more apparent."[56] The example in Freud's text, written, altered, and rewritten between 1937 and 1938, when he was being persecuted because of his "race,"[57] isn't Palestine but the Reformation, which, "after an interval of more than a thousand years, [...] brought to light again the frontier

52 Ibid., p. 204.

53 Sigmund Freud, "The Moses of Michelangelo." For the text's history see Gay, *Freud: A Life for Our Time*, p. 604ff and Grubrich-Simitis, *Freuds Moses-Studie*, particularly p. 52ff.

54 For the concept of the crypt see Nicolas Abraham, Maria Torok, *The Wolf Man's Magic Word*, Minneapolis 1986.

55 See Freud, *Moses and Monotheism*, pp. 66, 67.

56 Ibid., p. 61.

57 Ibid., p. 61f.

between the Germania that had been Roman and the part that had always remained independent."[58] The Moses text seeks for the basis of the historical scar or darkness that tore or fell when Freud himself was driven from his home of Vienna at the age of seventy-eight, when he had to flee, to become a refugee, with many others. He traces this back and forward, handling history as wound and vision.

From the coded message of history, crypt, or soldering Freud develops an eye for a topology of the visible that reveals itself, under the pressure of historical antagonisms and power relationships, as spatialized history. The traces of the cryptic need to be deciphered. This determines both theory and practice. At the end of his text Freud begins to rewrite it, reading it again, from the beginning, in iterations, and recursively applying his method to his own writing and thought in "the scarcely altered repetition of what I said in the first section."[59] His repetitions are at the same time a re-establishment of what is missing. They are also deletions, suppressions, carried out under the pressure and impression of exile.

Layer by layer, like an archaeologist, like a dermatologist, Freud clears away historical truth in order to be able to read the psychology of the masses in the visible world. They don't behave irrationally but in the sense of the unconscious, whose content, as Freud again emphasizes, "is collective anyhow, a general possession of mankind."[60] Masses are all differently moved by the overcoming of an imagined act of violence at the beginning of history whose potential re-announces itself after very long periods of time. The monotheistic religions deal with this differently. Judaism, according to Freud, maintained a sense of guilt, which secured a feeling of ethical superiority and the good fortune of having been chosen. The "triumph of Christianity"[61] is based on "a Jew, Saul of Tarsus, who as a Roman citizen was called Paul"[62] having replaced the suppression of what Freud consistently holds to be a patricide with the consciousness of a general original sin. And this triumph also points to its link in the chain of violence: it is the delayed appearance of the "victory of the Amon priests over the god of

58 Ibid., p. 61.
59 Ibid., p. 205.
60 Ibid., p. 208.
61 Ibid., p. 142.
62 Ibid., p. 213.

Ikhnaton after an interval of a millennium and a half and over a larger region."[63] Latency and retrospective readability structure history, its writing, and writers. History visibly and audibly quotes itself in every event, entering in the iteration of its own memory.

In enumerating all doublings Freud repeats that his study "has been written twice over,"[64] once in Vienna, then rewritten and completed in London exile. In a surprising parallel with Schoenberg's repeated approaches to the composition of the Moses opera, Freud also broke off his Moses novel after the first two chapters, which he published successively in the journal *Imago*, just as Schoenberg interrupted work on the opera after the second act, only to take it up later in exile, without finishing the composition of the third act, however. In Freud's case the postponement wasn't indefinite, but one that, like all mental processes, accumulated affects and established force fields. In London exile, where he no longer felt obliged to spare either the Psychoanalytical Association or his health, he published the famous third part of the work, in whose fragmentary nature and overwriting, as Grubrich-Simitis notes, "the depth of the disturbance into which the Nazi terror had plunged Freud"[65] can be felt. But as in Schoenberg's case the interruption of Freud's writing should also be understood as a caesura that initiated an abrupt change in the medium of referentiality. In Schoenberg's opera, as Lacoue-Labarthe observes, the word, with the caesura of the third act, breaks into the unbroken collectivizing space of music and religion, and marks the suspension of all agreement. In the third part of his Moses study Freud repeats the logic of doubling, as developed in the first two parts, but he no longer emphasizes historical layers, referring instead to the disruptions that on the one hand can question an archive, on the other constitute it.

When at the end of his text Freud distinguishes between a material truth that indicates progress and a historical truth that recognizes the layers of threat, violence, and fear as historical factors, and even that "delusions contain a piece of forgotten truth,"[66] this perception introduces the method and problem of all historiography. It applies equally to the reconstruction of the history of the Moses figure as to the history of Freud's present and our own. Understanding

63 Ibid., p 142f.
64 Ibid., p. 164.
65 Translated from Grubrich-Simitis, *Freuds Moses-Studie als Tagtraum*, p. 77.
66 Freud, *Moses and Monotheism*, p. 137.

history means discovering latencies and distillations from which events, wars, and oppression draw their energy. And discovering violence as something that stabilizes rather than dissolves power relationships. The dynamic of history is determined by recursion, not causality. And thus what is called memory, recollection, archive, or media-theoretically storage also changes. Technology is no bulwark against the history of latency. On the contrary, it is probably its tool.

Freud's thesis challenges scientific nature and a subject of knowledge in general, remarks Jacques Derrida in reference to the Moses book: "this *project* for a science at least, which is called psychoanalysis, claims to transform the very status of the historian's object, the structure of the archive, the concept of 'historical truth', indeed a science in general, the methods of deciphering the archive, the implication of the subject in the space he claims to objectize, and notably the topology of all the internal/external partitions that structure this subject and make of him a place for archives in relation to which no objectivization is pure, nor in truth rigorously possible, which is to say, complete and terminable."[67]

The archive itself should be thought of historically, as an unstable store in which old orderings organize knowledge but overwrite it through new storage and readdressing, and their consignations, as Derrida puts it, are rewritten. In this lies the risk and responsibility of those who make a distinction, divide and separate a space, at once reconstruct and constitute the archive through the placement of new relationships after the parameters of new media: Freud, Schoenberg, Straub/Huillet. Reorganizing the order of the archive with violence, without experience of reliable media traditions, without knowing where decisions will carry, is Moses' risky mission before the law—and also the risky mission of the project of psychoanalysis. For this reason Derrida severely takes Yosef Hayim Yerushalmi to task for reading Freud's Moses book as an example of the "deferred obedience" with which Freud simply follows an old instruction from his father.[68] For Derrida the politically bold construction of the foundation of the law and history, along with the risk of thinking without a center, of writing in an empty space, of an unsecured historiography between family novel and historical catastrophe in which delusion also contains traces of truth, disappears in such a reading. The missing center, deleted in Freud's text along

67 Derrida, *Archive Fever*, p. 37.

68 Ibid., p. 40.

with the father principle, returns only as symptom and specter, as voice without body, neither outside nor inside, neither knowledge nor consciousness, a third thing, returning in the burning bush, in Hamlet's father or Schreber's God, in media whose message switches over the store called psyche. According to Freud the only stability is in the endless, unconscious, reckless return to the moment of buried historical violence, which controls what he called the death wish.

Freud's analytical historiography does away with the idea of a primeval image. There is no home for the alien, no original to the reproducible, only sinister, violence-laden history, which demands repetition. In every archive, Derrida concludes, the destruction of the old consignations is at work, a devastation that belongs to the new archive but isn't ordered within it. It rumbles anarchivally in the order of memory, thus producing the future. Derrida sees a heart here, but it's the heart of a function, as his feverish book shows, a table, a stylus, a relay, or an algorithm.[69] Moses is a media complex.

What can be remembered only comes to consciousness through the order of memory, through its organization and inherencies. There is no other access to what has been except the archive and its architecture. But no entrance is granted in the here and now. The archive is also a future one because it organizes the future. Cinema functions in exactly the same way. The past always comes to us from the future there, soon, on a site that has to remain white in the meantime, very nearby. As a view of the media realm, the empty site of everything to come, as waiting in front of the empty screen, the "Freudian deletion" of the father function is complementary to the "*Freudian signature*,"[70] from which Derrida proceeds in his study of the "mal d'archive" as both rereading and subversion of the prohibition of images, which now means not dealing with figures but exploring their basis and relationships in movements headed for a blank.

The opera and film proceed in the same way. Schoenberg doesn't avoid the prohibition of images by devoting himself to music, as Adorno supposed; rather, he addresses it in the negative, as an absent center. Schoenberg deletes

69 Ibid., p. 51: "If repetition is thus inscribed at the heart of the future to come, one must also import there, *in the same stroke*, the death drive, the violence of forgetting, *superrepression* (suppression and repression), the anarchive, in short, the possibility of putting to death the very thing, whatever its name, which *carries the law in its tradition*: the archon of the archive, the table, *what* carries and *who* carries the table, the subjectile, the substrate, and the subject of the law." Italics in the original.

70 Ibid., p. 11.

familiar relationships and figurations of sounds in favor of an equal distribution of tones from which new forms and figures arise through caesura and permutation. The rules of these formations, the law of the tone row, can only be discerned recursively, in the imagination of the listeners once they have relied on their senses. Only when the whole row has sounded and been heard can conclusions be drawn about its order, and not because of a basic tone, as in traditional harmony. There is no ur-image, as a scale or cosmos, in serial music.

For Schoenberg a musical space isn't an existing one in which music can be made to sound but one that only emerges with the vibrations of the music, one that results, in the middle of emptiness, from the individual tones and their common oscillation. For this reason he erases the prefigured logic of harmonic vibration, and makes each individual and independent tone the starting point of the sounds. Schoenberg's music doesn't return to a cosmic, harmonic, or otherwise ontological order, but creates a new access. Schoenberg generates an extensive coming-into-being from nothing but foreignness: "Though the elements of these ideas appear separate and independent to the eye and the ear, they reveal their true meaning only through their co-operation, even as no single word alone can express a thought without relation to other words. All that happens at any point of this musical space has more than a local effect. It functions not only in its own plane, but also in all other directions and planes, and is not without influence even at remote points."[71]

So too do Straub and Huillet erase an existing cinematic law of space or time that could determine the logic of the camera movement or the montage. Cinema also has no ur-image; at most it has recurring topoi, from which its cultural and social history insistently announces itself as difference and repetition.[72] Cinematic images don't follow preformed spaces that should be reproduced as accurately as possible; neither do they depict things as they are. The camera eye sees how it wants to. It assembles unknown forms, and distorts what it records with every shot. Hence the films of Straub/Huillet, and Moses und Aron in particular, fix the recording rules. They follow them in the time the music, cinema, and life need for sounds and texts to connect with bodies and landscapes. Then they interrupt the connections with breath, edits, white screen, and black leader so

71 Schoenberg, "Composition with Twelve Tones," p. 220.

72 See Wolfgang Ernst, Harun Farocki, "Towards an Archive for Visual Concepts," in Thomas Elsaesser (ed.), *Working on the Sight-Lines*, Amsterdam 2006, pp. 261–286.

that resistance forms and seeing becomes visible and hearing audible, and what is missing manifest. They rely on the effects of an undefined *off* or a singular *hors-champ* that aren't complementary to the visible shot but form an obstinate, unconnected other. Only in retrospect is the topology of these films noticeable.

In 1937 and still in Vienna, Sigmund Freud, in his Moses book, returned to the art of distortion its double meaning, which opera and film also expound: "One could wish to give the word 'distortion' the double meaning to which it has a right, although it is no longer used in this sense. It should mean not only 'to change the appearance of,' but also 'to wrench apart,' 'to put in another place.' That is why in so many textual distortions we may count on finding the suppressed and abnegated material hidden away somewhere, though in an altered shape and torn out of its original connection. Only – it is not always easy to recognize it."[73] Where there used to be law there is now distortion, and the distortion points to the broken law. Jacob Taubes also read Freud's Moses book as a double change in the law: "This is a subversive program. How is it possible to suspend the law? For the law is now not only Mosaic law – though it means that too – but it means civil law, bourgeois custom, which gives human beings all these neuroses."[74] Freud, like Schoenberg and Straub/Huillet, envisages a new law of uniform structures requiring an equable, receptive attention, a law of the desert, the nomads, the migrants.

Jan Assmann's study on Moses remains closer to media-historical considerations in deciphering Moses principally as a figure of memory, while Freud had presented him as something that "oscillates strangely between being a figure of memory and being a figure of history."[75] The Egyptologist Assmann is initially interested in a distinction between cultures that manifested in disassociation from Egyptian religious practices, primarily the cult of the image: "The Mosaic distinction was therefore a radically new distinction which considerably changed the world in which it was drawn. The space which was 'severed or cloven' by this distinction was not simply the space of religion in general, but that of a very specific kind of religion. We may call this new type of religion 'counter-religion' because it rejects and repudiates everything that went before and what

73 Freud, *Moses and Monotheism*, p. 70.
74 Taubes, *Paulus*, p. 90.
75 Assmann, *Moses the Egyptian*, p. 148.

is outside itself as 'paganism'."[76] The distinction establishes a new space of perception that also excludes according to the biblical text with which Straub and Huillet head their film: "her zu myr wer den HERRN angehört"[77] [Who is on the LORD's side? *let him come* unto me]. The children of Levi gather around Moses, and he orders them to kill. Friend and foe, the distinction of the camp.

Freud's symptomatic procedure, the opera, and the film, however, permit the understanding of the Mosaic distinction as a method of discovering new cultural techniques of communication. The distinction results from the experience of a failure of communication, of a noisy channel, of an incomprehensibly other language and culture, of an unconceivable law. Assmann develops this in the light of the cultural technique of translation: "Counter-religion," he writes, "no longer functioned as a means of intercultural translation; on the contrary, it functioned as a means of intercultural estrangement."[78] Only in an involvement with strangers and the alien can translation be thought of in terms of caesura and difference, and thus opens up a mnemohistorical exploration of the present as psychohistory.[79] Here the symptomatic, which for both Freud and Assmann manifests as the rise of violence in the context of monotheism, has to be deciphered in both directions: not only does the return of the suppressed point to violence at the beginning and in the dynamic of a progression to sensibility; conversely, it can be argued media-archaeologically and exactly in the tradition of the Canadian school of media studies that with the rise of new technical media— today still electronic according to McLuhan—an uneasiness in culture and memory is actualized and acts on the subject as unreliable and palpably foreign forces, as violent powers that also descend on collectives. The media caesura appears as a caesura of the evil alien, as the bearded Tartar before the gates of the archive. Analytical distinction means seeing the effect of media at work instead of a god. The media caesura provides the key to the doors of the archive, doors of perception, which not only open but are even unguarded. Freud considered both possibilities in 1937 for psychoanalysis under the conditions of the occupation: to close its archive so that it would survive undamaged as a crypt of knowledge, or to make public the theory of mass movements as the superior

76 Ibid., p. 3.

77 Quoted from the shot of the Luther Bible at the beginning of the film.

78 Assmann, *Moses the Egyptian*, p. 3.

79 See ibid., p. 160f.

knowledge of an alien and an alienation, and so put himself and psychoanalysis in danger. In 1994 Derrida reads this as a call to further distort and scatter the archive, precisely so that someone will remember psychoanalysis and its symptomatic thinking, its founder and alienation as the only equality among people: "Because if it is just to remember the future and the injunction to remember, namely the archontic injunction to guard and to gather the archive, it is no less just to remember the others, the other others and the others in oneself, and that the other peoples could say the same thing – in another way. And that tout autre est tout autre, as we can say in French: every other is every other, is altogether other."[80] How must a text, an opera, a film be ordered? What must be ordered in order to remember the strangers? With the order of an archive that changes in the practice of memory, the Moses project returns to the people, which is missing in the very place one had expected it.

5.4. MEDIUM, CAMP

As a place without law, under emergency rule or the conventions of war, the camp is a heterotopia that stands in the twentieth century for internment and murder by the National Socialists, and at the same time, as a form of political negotiation outside the law, as a peace or protest camp, for utopias of immediate communication. And through this term runs the ambivalent rift of Freudian ur-words. One meaning wants to seal itself off from the others, in vain Giorgio Agamben has described the camp as paradigm of modernity. In the excluded people Agamben recognizes the "bare" life, the Greek *bios*, which in contrast to *zoe* can't be represented. He returns to Walter Benjamin's critique of a law-giving and boundary-drawing, bloody, mythic "violence over life and death."[81] Agamben puts this in the context of modern biopolitics. The bare life is that of the *homo sacer*, "the life of the exile [...], who may be killed but not sacrificed,"[82] and Agamben contrasts it with sovereignty. Freud also discusses

80 Derrida, *Archive Fever*, p. 50.

81 See Benjamin, "Critique of Violence," p. 286. The original German term is "bloßes Leben," which Agamben's translator renders as "bare life" (*trans.*).

82 Agamben, *Homo Sacer*, p. 110.

the status of *sacer* in his Moses book in the ambivalence of holy and heinous, a paradoxical figure of thought whose history Agamben rediscovers in anthropology and sociology as that of the taboo, ruling and inviolable.[83] Agamben does in fact write this genealogy of the bare life in a form of "deferred obedience" and complementary to Carl Schmitt's concept of the exception. According to the famous first sentence of *Political Theology*, from 1922, "Sovereign is he who decides on the exception," the decision itself is declared to be the founding act of sovereignty for the entire history of the West.[84] This paradoxical figure of a sovereignty that stands both within and without the law, radicalizes the topos "before the law." While a sovereignty, according to Franz Kafka, would at least be confronted with its coming judgment as a lawgiver or law taker, Schmitt's sovereignty spares itself this calamity. So with Agamben, who is obedient to Schmitt, the life of *homo sacer* can't be one that offers resistance.

Agamben's attempt to project Michel Foucault's concept of biopolitics, as the disposition of a people that is no longer ruled as a polis but on the basis of the exploitability of its inherent biological qualities, onto the twentieth century and the concentration camps leads to a surprising universalization of both the "*sacratio*"[85] and of the camp. It isn't only refugees, who, as Hannah Arendt never tired of warning, have no legal status, are outlawed[86] and threatened by the exception; "we" all are, the philosophy professor claims, "because we are all virtually *homines sacri*."[87] The situation of "indistinction of fact and law, of life and juridical rule"[88] corresponds to a political omnipresence of the concept

83 Freud, *Moses and Monotheism* p. 230. Agamben pursues the fate of this ambivalent term from its late-Victorian genealogy via Wilhelm Wundt to French sociology, Mauss, Durkheim, Callois, Bataille, and notes that Freud takes this ambivalence into account in *Totem and Taboo* after reading William Robertson's *Lectures on the Religion of Semites*. See Agamben, *Homo Sacer*, p. 75ff.

84 Carl Schmitt, *Political Theology. Four Chapters on the Concept of Sovereignty*, trans. Georg Schwab, Chicago/London 2005, p. 5. Georg Schwab adds a footnote here: "In the context of Schmitt's work, a state of exception includes any kind of severe economic or political disturbance that requires the application of extraordinary measures. Whereas an exception presupposes a constitutional order that provides guidelines on how to confront crises in order to reestablish order and stability, a state of emergency need not have an existing order as a reference point because *necessitas non habet legem*."

85 Here Agamben quotes the jurist Rodolphe Jhering, *Homo Sacer*, p. 104.

86 Hannah Arendt, "We Refugees," in Marc Robinson (ed.), *Altogether Elsewhere. Writers on Exile*, ed. Marc Robinson, Boston 1994, pp. 110–119: 119.

87 Agamben, *Homo sacer*, p. 115.

88 Ibid., p. 185.

of the camp, which Agamben calls the "absolute political space."[89] The camp became the "biopolitical paradigm of the modern,"[90] the exception commonplace.[91]

The situation or the camp before the law is also the site of the Moses complex. Friedrich Engels, in a military-historical article for the *New American Cyclopædia*, remarked in 1858, when siege discourses were in mode: "One of the most ancient camps mentioned in history is that of the Israelites at their exodus from Egypt," adding honestly, "but the form, the dimensions, and the intrenchments of the regular military camps of the Hebrews, or their enemies, can scarcely be traced."[92]

When Schoenberg makes this camp, as an unconstituted space, lacking and in expectation of the law, the setting for his opera, he not only poses the question of the law but also of legalism; he examines the suspension of the law, and puts sovereignty forward for discussion. He deals with despotism, violence, and the necessity of a foundation from the nothingness of the desert as a problem of knowledge and a correspondingly justified rebellion, of a necessary liberation of a people from oppression. In this he handles both the historical situation and his own. He also approaches the topos self-reflectively, aesthetically, in regard to his own constitution of a new archive of new tonal sequences, sound forms, sonic spaces. With the caesuras of the composition, after a term of Walter Benjamin's, he has something other, alien interrupt, or more exactly: he has the lacking word interrupt the music.[93] Marking the lacking word, the missing voice, multiplies the perspectives on legalism, the prohibition of images, and the formation of a people. Violence isn't celebrated as decisiveness in the

89 Ibid., 153.

90 Ibid., p. 117.

91 This argument, not least since the turn of the millennium and unexpected, unconceivable attacks on the pacified West, has woken the interest of further academics who worried about the determination of the political after Carl Schmitt and its distinction between friend and foe. See, for example, Joseph Vogl (ed.), *Gesetz und Urteil. Beiträge zu einer Theorie des Politischen*, Weimar 2003.

92 Friedrich Engels, "Camp" (1858), in *The New American Cyclopædia. A popular Dictionary of General Knowledge*, ed. George Ripley and Charles A.. Dana, vol. IV, New York, London 1869. pp. 312–313: 312.

93 See Walter Benjamin, "Goethe's Elective Affinitites," in *Selected Writings, Volume 1 1913-1926*, ed. Marcus Bullock, and Michael W. Jennings, Cambridge 2002, pp. 297–359: 341: "Indeed, one could not characterize this rhythm any more aptly than by asserting that something beyond the poet interrupts the language of the poetry."

conflict between Moses and Aron but as a dreadful moment of decision, when the word is lacking and deeds are inappropriate. We may speculate that Schoenberg was uneasy about this unavoidable violence, which begins when there is no constituted legal basis and law is asserted, or when in the floating space of the twelve tones a clear hierarchy, an above and below, are fixed. Schoenberg's unease is more aesthetically than politically founded. In the libretto he at least ascribes a speech act of judgment to the Moses figure in act III, that Aron should not be murdered for the sake of the living—"Es geht nicht um *Dein* Leben [It is not a matter of *your* life]," says Moses to Aron at the beginning of act III (emphasis added)—but be allowed to die in God's name. It isn't clear what musical structure could carry this. Nor the extent to which a musical solution for concrete violence, which Schoenberg himself experienced, as described in letters and diaries, was excluded. Nor whether ambivalence, the position between two attracting forces, could be realized in a floating musical space. Straub believes, plausibly, in "ideological difficulties," which at the end of the opera make the radical aesthetic and political decision that at the beginning of the work requires the autocratic setting of a structure as the distinction between burning bush and voice, noise and message, no longer possible.[94] For the political side Straub frankly chooses the term that analyzed the opera in the time of its composition: "Between the two [Moses and Aron] there is a kind of political seizure of power, which doesn't happen with Schoenberg. Or let's say, there is a seizure of power by Moses, which we have put back in."[95]

Straub and Huillet abruptly put the rise of violence, which is also emphasized in the Old Testament text, at the beginning of their film, where even before the titles they show a page from the Luther Bible in which verses 25–28 from Exodus 32 are underlined in red pen. Danièle Huillet reads this passage aloud, in which Moses, returning from the mountain calls those of the people on the side of the Lord to him: a distinction that requires a decision on the part of the people. Moses gives the gathered Levites the instruction to kill: "bynde ein iglicher seyn schwerd auff seyne lenden und durch geht hyn und wider von eynem thor zum andern ym lager, und erwurge eyn iglicher seynen bruder, freund, und nehisten" [Put every man his sword by his side, *and* go in and out from gate to gate throughout the camp, and slay every man his brother, and every man his

94 See Straub/Huillet, "Conversation," p. 7.

95 Translated from ibid., p. 8.

companion, and every man his neighbour].[96] So in the film the murder hangs over the scene for three acts. Neither in the context of Near Eastern nomadic movements nor in the Peasant Wars and church schism—which Freud names as examples of returning rifts in the topography of the German memory—does the Moses complex manage without violence.

Straub and Huillet then put the scene of violence into the *off*, leaving decision and judgment in the matter of the prohibition of images to cinematic thought. While Schoenberg ends his opera with the death of Aron, in order, with Moses' final words, to dismiss the people into the freedom and contentment of the desert,[97] Straub and Huillet avoid the discourse of transcendence and eschatology. Instead they expect the viewers to keep in mind the missing *off* themselves and think independently, in order to notice that the respectively introduced *off* or *hors-champ* completely changes the visible scenery. They can leave the shots so open because they rely on their exact setting of the historicity, concretion, power and—for the present of the shoot—class relationships that become visible. The images work conversely on the ideas of the viewers. Violence doesn't come from somewhere up above, remarks Straub against Schoenberg, but is the result of power relationships, which the film shows in detail. But above all the decision to take part in violence or not is one that must be taken. There is no "we" that would permit automatism or determinism in this situation. Nor are there media to determine it: Straub and Huillet deploy them not as a simple order but as arrangements of options. Straub once again remembers the letters to Kandinsky censored in the edition of Schoenberg's letters when he makes the point that Schoenberg appeared in America as a conservative, and, in Straub's words, had exactly the political idea that he aesthetically excluded from the opera as aniconism: "Schoenberg's idea is that of a power from above, even if he says that Moses is inhuman, even if he says (these are the sentences that were cut out of the letters to Kandinsky), that all idealists have blood on their hands. And he doesn't deny that Moses has blood on his hands. At this point he openly names Lenin, Stalin, and I don't know who else. Schoenberg provocatively portrayed himself as a royalist, even at the last meeting with Brecht

96 Quoted from Huillet, "Moses und Aron. Das Drehbuch," p. 203. It is the translation of Exodus 32:27. English from the King James Bible.

97 "*Moses*: 'Gebt ihn frei, und wenn er es vermag, so lebe er!' *Aron, frei, steht auf und fällt tot um [Moses: Set him free, and if he desires, he may live].*" Schoenberg, *Moses und Aron*, vocal score, act III, unpaginated.

in front of some drugstore somewhere in California."[98] In their film Straub and Huillet set aesthetic communism against Schoenberg's conservatism without further ado. In the musical work Schoenberg proves that nowhere is he interested in the nature of sovereignty, rather in the differentiation of the entirety of possible relationships. The limited and not very complex binary distinctions like we or they, friend or foe, Jew or not are neither politically nor aesthetically useful. No one is bare life.

5.5. LAWLESS: CLOUDS REPRISE

Jean-Marie Straub declared the Moses complex to be nomadic, a concept that was doing the rounds in 1974, shortly after the publication of *Anti-Oedipus*, by Gilles Deleuze and Félix Guattari.[99] But in their film and writings on it Straub and Huillet transfer the nomadic to both concrete aesthetic procedures and concrete historical and political constellations. This is documented to start with in the "Small Historical Digression"[100] that Danièle Huillet wrote during her studies and researches. In it she critically reconstructs the cultural techniques and economies of nomads at the time of the Exodus, compares biblical stories with other historical sources, taking a look along the way at the question of the postcolonial, the nation states, and their strategies of settlement in the Middle East at the time of working on the film. The preparations for filming connect historical and contemporary views of things and events, of landscapes, buildings, and cultural techniques. Straub and Huillet crisscross—literally and in a borrowed Citroën—Italy and the Middle East, traveling as far as Egypt in order to discover the layers, rifts, soldering, and scars of historically antagonistic cultures. So in 1974 the film MOSES UND ARON keeps in sight the visible and audible history of colonialism and fascism, while opening up a perspective on the time in

98 Translated from Straub/Huillet, "Conversation," p. 10.

99 See Gilles Deleuze and Félix Guattari, *Anti-Oedipus. Capitalism and Schizophrenia*, trans. Robert Hurley, Mark Seem, and Helen R. Lane, Minneapolis 1983, p. 110: "[A] nomadic and polyvocal use of the conjunctive syntheses is opposed to the segregative and biunivocal use made of them." The concept of nomadism is only fully elaborated in 1980 in Deleuze/Guattari, *A Thousand Plateaus. Capitalism and Schizophrenia*, ed. Brian Massumi, Minneapolis 1987, p. 351–424.

100 Huillet, "Kleiner Historischer Exkurs."

which Arnold Schoenberg wrote the opera, and on our present. In this way the migrant trail runs through the Moses complex. The decisive thing is that Straub and Huillet understand the historical procedure as a media one, as the exposition of productive differences. The difficulty isn't in filming class situations but class relationships—as the work of Straub and Huillet could be summarized in general. Their solution is insistent: they coin ideas from extreme concretion. In the process of working on Schoenberg's opera they develop from this material a form of media historiography, which has to prove itself in the individual shots, the décor, the sound, and the montage.

It's primarily a particular concept of historicity in the visible and audible that comes to fruition in the film Moses und Aron and shows surprising correspondences to one developed by Sigmund Freud in his treatment of the Moses complex. It's based on the distinction between "material" and "historical" truth, which turns out to be a media differentiation. Historical truth is subject to a "certain distortion,"[101] as Freud says. A "written [...] report"[102] is challenged and transformed by oral communications, but through this is fixed anew in a "permanent trace"[103] that is symptomatically passed on from generation to generation. What's missing gives form to process and readability. From the symptoms of its return the trace can be analyzed as withdrawal and deciphered in regard to historical processes.

This symptomatic procedure has characterized the theory and practice of such cinematic forms between fictionalization and documentary that for want of a better word can be called essay films. Chris Marker has formulated it as the fundamental principle of cinematic memory: "We do not remember, we rewrite memory."[104] For mnemohistory Jan Assmann considers it in connection with his Moses book, which he describes in its subtitle as "Seen as an individual and as a social capacity, memory is not simply the storage of the past 'facts' but the ongoing work of reconstructive imagination."[105] The work of cinema consists in the development and reflection of such reconstructive strategies. Cinematic

101 Freud, *Moses and Monotheism* p. 204.

102 Ibid., p. 111.

103 Ibid., p. 129.

104 Chris Marker, voiceover in the film Sans Soleil (F 1982). See Ute Holl, "'Man erinnert sich nicht, man schreibt das Gedächtnis um.' Modelle und Montagen filmischer Bildatlanten," in Sabine Flach, Inge Muenz-Koenen, Marianne Streisand (eds.), *Der Bildatlas im Wandel der Künste und Medien*, Munich 2005, pp. 251–270.

105 Assmann, *Moses the Egyptian*, p.. 14.

forms and formulations of rift and lack, the revelation of materialities in their formats and fragmentariness, the showing of false colors, surface effects, overexposures, and blurs, or the insistent use of black and white screen and complex *off* and *hors-champ* structures through camera movements and sound mixing confront what the image is with its withdrawal. They connect experiences and visions in circularly organized perception. Calculated relationships between knowing and not knowing, consciousness and unconsciousness, organize the imagination, which continually reconstructs what the image is.

The concept of history that Freud develops from the Moses figure as a model of "progress in spirituality" (*Geistigkeit*)[106] seems barely compatible with film aesthetics, as cinema develops its thought from sensory, physical perception, from images and sounds, and precisely not from abstraction and conception. On the other hand a progress in spirituality, which Freud maps as the way from aniconism to the asceticism of the renounced urge, would mean "deciding against the direct sense perception in favour of the so-called higher intellectual processes, that is to say, in favour of memories, reflection and deduction."[107] But it is these very processes–cinematic memories, reflection, and deduction–with which both avant-garde film forms and mainstream cinema experiment. Cinema performs and presents perception. The caesuras and differences of the images are constitutive of its specific techniques and made up of both material and conceptual procedures. Thinking isn't detained in the realm of spirituality but insists, in contact with the physical, as difference, symptom, and montage from shot to shot. Differently than the concept of projection suggests, the cinematic image should be understood as an interjection between apparatus, screen, and individual perception.

The aesthetic procedures of necessary distortion, in which opera, cultural theory, and cinema treat the Moses complex, are the basis of a perception of historicity as a recursive process that only shows itself in retrospect. "The irreducibility of the "effect of deferment," such is no doubt Freud's discovery. [...] In *Moses and Monotheism* (1937), the efficacy of deferment is at work over large historical intervals."[108] The space of historical truth knows no linear depiction,

106 Freud, *Moses and Monotheism* p. 176.

107 Ibid., p. 186.

108 Jacques Derrida, "Freud and the Scene of Writing," trans. Jeffrey Mehlman, *Yale French Studies*, no. 48, *French Freud: Structural Studies in Psychoanalysis* (1972), pp. 74–117: 81f.

The cloud, not a sign, not an image.

no above and below, no earlier or later, but only relations: distortions, displacements, and shifts, as well as delays, additions, anticipations; in short, a circular suspension of time. Retrospect constitutes what was previously neither visible nor audible. The space of Moses is both founded and opened through the recursive decision to hear a voice in the noise from the burning bush.

The cloud proves to be a reciprocal structure to the burning bush. In no way should it become a sign, like Aron wished for, "a signal to the people" (act II, bar 1089); it must, as Moses demands, remain in the recursive openness of the meteorological, thermodynamic temporality of becoming, beyond the image, as in the desert. Then comes the double traverse: cut and distortion. "L'idée de Moïse, c'est que la traversée du désert est sans fin. C'est l'idée du nomadisme, tout simplement."[109]

109 Straub/Huillet, "Conversation," p. 8.

4/11 1915 about 6:30 [...] Today I make notes because the day is as beautiful as those of last autumn which I especially noticed. And because yesterday the sky was especially peculiar. Half an hour later it is raining! But very strangely; in the background it's still bright and in the foreground [are] very black rainclouds.[110]

110 Schoenberg, "War-Clouds Diary," p. 75.

5.6. IN RETROSPECT, TOO LATE

> Art saves him, and through art life saves him—for itself
> *Friedrich Nietzsche* [111]

> Sauve qui peut (la vie)
> *Jean-Luc Godard* [112]

In 1974, the hundredth anniversary of the birth of Arnold Schoenberg, Jean-Marie Straub and Danièle Huillet filmed MOSES UND ARON, which was scheduled to be broadcast on German television for the Christian festival of Easter, but was banned because of its dedication to Holger Meins and ultimately broadcast on March 29, 1975 without it. In 1914 Schoenberg wrote his cloud diary. In 2014 the Europeans sent a camera seven million miles into space to a stinking small comet supposed to contain news about the formation of the world. In 1943 Hannah Arendt wrote about the life of Jewish immigrants in the United States: "In order to forget more efficiently we rather avoid any allusion to concentration or internment camps we experienced in nearly all European countries – it might be interpreted as pessimism or lack of confidence in the new homeland. [...] After so much bad luck we want a course as sure as a gun. Therefore, we leave the earth with all its uncertainties behind and we cast our eyes up the sky." Ahrend means it cynically: "The stars will tell us – rather than the newspapers – when Hitler will be defeated and when we shall become American citizens."[113] Schoenberg, however, sees in the sky the inexact, risky, dangerous aspect of transition, impersonated by Aron in his libretto is:

> Bei meinem Haus, wie eine leuchtende Wolke, kam er eben vorbei. Er schwebte mehr, als er ging, kaum berührt' sein Fuß den Weg und rasch schwand er aus dem Auge.

111 Nietzsche, "The Birth of Tragedy," p. 40. Nietzsche is referring to the Hellene.

112 SAUVE QUI PEUT (LA VIE). (CH, A, F, FRG 1986), dir.: Jean-Luc Godard.

113 Arendt, "We Refugees," p. 111.

> [He passed by my house, as would a luminous cloud pass, even so came he by. He floated rather than walked. Hardly indeed did he touch the ground. He quickly passed from my vision.][114]

In 2014 wars spread in the Near and Middle East, in the name of monotheistic religions. The distribution of the last remaining resources is currently being forced. At the same time boundaries are coming back or cracking open. After a latency of almost a hundred years, borders set down in the Sykes-Picot Agreement between England and France in 1916 insist on the violence with which they were once asserted and recurrently transgressed. "History loves such restorations, in which later fusions are reversed and earlier divisions reappear."[115] Alliances change fast. Religions differentiate themselves. War recalls violence that couldn't be remembered, and spreads exponentially. As an archive of human history religions become the possible conditions of a future archive. On January 6, 1935 Sigmund Freud wrote to Lou Andreas-Salomé: "Religions owe their compulsive power to the *return of the repressed*; they are awakened memories of very ancient, forgotten, highly emotional episodes of human history. I have already said this in *Totem and Taboo*; I express it now in the formula: the strength of religion lies not in its *material*, but in its *historical* truth."[116] Freud codified the suppressed act of violence at the source of history, which breaks through cyclically as repetition and death wish in wars and less official murders among peoples and individuals, as patricide. Deleuze and Guattari and, at the same time, Straub and Huillet replaced this family codification with a political one. Whether proceeding from affect economies or media organizations of power, in this context they meet the challenge, thrown up by Immanuel Kant with the sublime, of a threefold threat to the political by the indeterminate: the affect or horror of fear, the unconstituted people, and the devastation of the planet. Currently, when people talk of the monotheistic religions as a transition from slavery in the desert and from the desert into the camp of the sedentary, ecological aspects are also crucial. Historical truth should be sought in the interlocking of visible and audible events and the technical, cultural, and

114 Schönberg, *Moses und Aron*, score I, act I, bars 267–276.

115 Freud, *Moses and Monotheism*, p. 61.

116 Sigmund Freud an Lou Andreas-Salomé, *Letters*. Edited by Ernst Pfeiffer. Translated by William and Elaine Robson-Scott. New York London 1985, S. 205.

political constellations in which they were possible. In meteorology there are no constellations, only states in transition. In music it's called suspension. Meteorology is the science of things in the balance. They require decisions, distinctions. As far as politics is concerned, it can't be separated from artistic practices that change, distort and displace cultural dividing, cutting, decision, and combination. "It must appear cynical after what has happened in Europe, and what continues to threaten, to lavish time and mental energy on the deciphering of esoteric questions on the technique of modern composition. Moreover, the obstinate artistic disputes of the text often enough appear as if they directly address a reality that is uninterested in them"[117] wrote Adorno in 1948 in the foreword to the *Philosophy of New Music*, which so annoyed Schoenberg in California. Violence isn't mystified, has no basis in myth. Violence springs from the empty space within class relationships and race relationships that anyone can discover and decide upon. Visual and sound relationships perform and present this. In 2014, while touring their new album *Who's Bad*, the Goldene Zitronen projected the film MOSES UND ARON during their concerts, having the audience dance around a Golden Calf. Around a really false image.

The film MOSES UND ARON, as realized by Straub and Huillet, doesn't exist. The 35 mm copy in the Berlin archive of the Freunde der Deutschen Kinemathek has become quite discolored in the time that life takes. The archive hasn't rewritten but recolored. The ascetic film has become a psychedelic experience. The sand of the arena at Alba Fucense runs into Bordeaux, the Nile shines violet against a pink sky, the black leader is aubergine red and the white screen pink. What I wanted to write about no longer exists. Only the acoustic level has been preserved very well in optical sound; the audible experience of this opera recording is extraordinary.

But there is an excellent DVD from the *Editions Montparnasse*, scanned and color corrected from the copy in the archive in Bois d'Arcy in Paris. This version is very fine, but it doesn't convey the same images as the original film. Depending on the digital projection the skies are more monochrome or show more artifacts; the apparently white images take on different shadings. The digital logic works on the images, just as Schoenberg assumed for the entirety of the elements in the space of serial music. The greatest difference is musical. The optical sound of the 35 mm copy unfolds a field of tone colors and musical

117 Adorno, *Philosophy of New Music*, p. 4.

What I wanted to write about no longer exists.

layers of suspensions, superimpositions, and interferences that can't be heard in the digital compression. In 2014, only forty years after the film's premiere, its effects are more difficult to reconstruct than archaeological finds in the desert around Gizeh. On the other hand, more people than ever before are seeing this film in its digital circulation. The archive reconstitutes itself. As a form of knowing, cinema has barely touched the path and disappears again.

At 10:06 on October 31, 2012 Harun Farocki <harun.farocki@farocki-film.de> wrote:

[...]

I was recently in the Regenbogenkino to "introduce" 2 films by the Straubs (can't understand them otherwise). No one there under 55, unfortunately!

I complained about this, but pointed out that at least your book was coming out soon.

In Kassel about 100 people sat in the theater and watched Straub from 9 in the morning till 3 at night. The copy of Moses und Aron was almost entirely red.

For some the dedication to Holger Meins was more important than anything else.

[...]

Yours, Harun

Digital procedures to generate knowledge and resistance from the cloud and identify historical dynamics in their historical appearances once again require a distinction between figure and topology. And artistic strategies for producing music and images that make the historicity in the material audible and visible outside of hierarchical orders. Schoenberg enables us to hear that differentiation in an undirected space is the construction of a new sound space purified of old power relationships. In their film Straub and Huillet bring out the violence of differentiation, seeing in Moses' path-breaking into the desert a self-destructive process that also puts Aron's images, signs, and wonders on trial. But the figures are functions of the images and sounds, borne by the constellations in which they appear. The art of describing circumstances in such a way that new decisions can be imagined comes about in the Moses complex. The idea of the devastation of the planet making strangers of everyone, the idea of nomadism, was a utopia for Straub: "Seen historically it's clearly a utopia. At least until we reach the point when capitalism ruins the planet." It was a utopia for as long as capitalism hadn't ruined the planet. Now we're seeing the horrors. What art will help to differentiate? Noise, O ______.

LITERATURE

Abraham, Nicolas and Maria Torok, *The Wolf Man's Magic Word*, Minneapolis 1986.

Adachi-Rabe, Kayo, *Abwesenheit im Film. Zur Theorie und Geschichte des hors-champ*, Münster 2005.

Adorno, Theodor W., "Sacred Fragment. Schoenberg's Moses and Aron," in Theodor W. Adorno, *Quasi una Fantasia. Essays on Modern Music*, trans. Rodney Livingstone, London 1998, pp. 225–249.

Adorno, Theodor W., *Prisms*, trans. Samuel and Shierry Weber, Cambridge 1983.

Adorno, Theodor W., *Negative Dialectics*, trans. E.B. Ashton, London 1973

Adorno, Theodor W., "Filmtransparente," in Theodor W. Adorno, *Ohne Leitbild. Parva Aesthetica*, Frankfurt/Main 1967, pp. 79–88.

Adorno, Theodor W., *Aesthetic Theory*, trans. Robert Hullot-Kentor, London 2002.

Adorno, Theodor W., *Philosophy of New Music*, trans., ed. Robert Hullot-Kentor, Minneapolis 2006.

Adorno, Theodor W., "Is Art Lighthearted?" in Theodor W. Adorno, *Notes to Literature*, vol. 2, ed. Rolf Tiedemann, New York 1992, pp. 247–253.

Adorno, Theodor W., "Music, Language and Composition," in *The Musical Quarterly*, vol. 77, no. 3, 1993, pp 401–414.

Adorno, Theodor W., "Über die musikalische Verwendung des Radios," in Theodor W. Adorno, *Gesammelte Schriften*, Bd. 15: *Kompositionen für den Film. Der getreue Korrepetitor*, hg. v. Rolf Tiedemann u.a., Frankfurt/Main 2003, pp. 369–401.

Adorno, Theodor W., *Prismen. Kulturkritik und Gesellschaft I*, Bd. 10.1: *Prismen. Ohne Leitbild*, München 2003.

Adorno, Theodor W. and Pierre Boulez, "Gespräche über den Pierrot lunaire," in Heinz-Klaus Metzger, Rainer Riehn (ed.), *Schoenberg und der Sprechgesang. Musik-Konzepte 112/113*, VII, 2001, pp. 82–96.

Adorno, Theodor W. and Hanns Eisler, *Composing for the Films*, London 2007.

Adorno, Theodor W. and Siegfried Kracauer, *Briefwechsel 1923–1966. 'Der Riss der Welt geht auch durch mich,'* ed. Wolfgang Schopf, Frankfurt/Main 2008.

Agamben, Giorgio, *Homo Sacer. Sovereign Power and Bare Life*, trans. Daniel Heller-Boazen, Stanford 1998.

Akerman, Chantal, in Nicole Brenez, *Chantal Akerman, The Pajama Interviews*, Vienna 2011.

Albright, Daniel, "Series Editor's Forword," in Charlotte M. Cross, Russell A. Berman, *Political and Religious Ideas in the Works of Arnold Schoenberg*, New York 2000.

Allende-Blin, Juan, "Über Sprechgesang. Auf Spurensuche," in Metzger, Heinz-Klaus and Rainer Riehn (ed.), *Schoenberg und der Sprechgesang. Musik-Konzepte* 112/113, 2001, VII.

Arendt, Hannah, "We Refugees," in Marc Robinson (ed.), *Altogether Elsewhere. Writers on Exile*, ed. Marc Robinson, Boston 1994, pp. 110–119

Arnheim, Rudolf, *Film as Art*, Berkeley 1957.

Assmann, Jan, *Moses the Egyptian. The Memory of Egypt in Western Monotheism*, Cambridge 1997,

Auerbach, Erich, *Mimesis. The Representation f Reality in Western Literature*, trans. Willard Trask, Princeton 2003.

Auerbach, Erich, *Mimesis. Dargestellte Wirklichkeit in der abendländischen Kultur*, Bern 1942, 8th edition 1988

Balázs, Béla, *Early Film Theory: Visible Man and The Spirit of Film*, trans. Rodney Livingstone, ed. Erica Carter, New York/Oxford 2010.

Bateson, Gregory, "Letter to Warren McCulloch," December 20, 1967, in Gregory Bateson., "'*They threw God out of the garden': letters from Gregory Bateson to Philip Wylie and Warren McCulloch*," ed. Rodney E. Donaldson, *CoEvolution Quarterly*, 32 (winter), 1982, pp. 62–67.

Baudry, Jean-Louis, "The Apparatus: Metapsychological Approaches to the Impression of Reality in Cinema," in Leo Braudy and Marshall Cohen (eds.), *Film Theory and Criticism: Introductory Readings*, New York 1999, pp. 690—707.

Baur, Detlev, *Der Chor im Theater des 20. Jahrhunderts. Typologie des theatralen Mittels Chor*, Tübingen 1999.

Bazin, André, "The Evolution of the Language of Cinema," in André Bazin, *What is Cinema?* trans. Hugh Gray, Berkeley 2005, pp. 23–41.

Bazin, André, "Painting and Cinema.", in André Bazin, *What is Cinema?* trans. Hugh Gray, Berkeley 2005, pp. 164–173

Bazin, André, "Theater and Cinema, I and II," in André Bazin, *What is Cinema?* vol. I, trans. Hugh Gray, Berkeley 1967, pp. 76–95.

Benjamin, Walter, "Goethes Wahlverwandtschaften," in *Gesammelte Schriften*, ed. Rolf Tiedemann and Hermann Schweppenhäuser, vol. I. 1, *Abhandlungen*, Frankfurt/Main 1980, pp. 123–201.

Benjamin, Walter, *The Work of Art in the Age of Mechanical Reproduction*, second version, ed. Michael W. Jennings, Brigid Doherty, and Thomas Y. Levin, trans. Edmund Jephcott, Rodney Livingstone, Howard Eiland, et al., Cambridge 2008

Benjamin, Walter, "Über den Begriff der Geschichte, Anmerkungen," in *Gesammelte Schriften*, ed. Rolf Tiedemann and Hermann Schweppenhäuser, vol. I. 3, *Abhandlungen*, Frankfurt/Main 1980, pp. 1223–1266.

Benjamin, Walter, *On the Concept of History*, trans. Dennis Redmond, New York 2009.

Benjamin, Walter, "Critique of Violence", in Walter Benjamin, *Reflections. Essays. Aphorisms. Autobiographical Writings*, ed. and intro. Peter Demetz, New York, 1986, pp. 277–300.

Benjamin, Walter, *The Arcades Project*, trans. Howard Eiland and Kevin McLaughlin, Cambridge 2002.

The Bible. Authorized King James Version, ed. intro. and notes by Robert Carroll and Stephen Prickett, Oxford, New York 1997.

Bitsch, Annette, *"Always Crashing in the Same Car." Jacques Lacans Mathematik des Unbewußten*, Weimar 2001.

Bill, Max, "Vorwort zu Kandinsky," *Über das Geistige in der Kunst, insbesondere in der Malerei*, revised edition, Bern 2006, pp. 9–20.

Bodenheimer, Alfred, "Biblische Wege. Jüdisches Wandern in Werken Arnold Schönbergs und Franz Werfels," in Ekkehard John, Heidy Zimmermann (ed.), *Jüdische Musik? Fremdbilder, Eigenbilder*, Cologne 2004, pp. 149–156.

Bodenheimer, Alfred, *Haut Ab!*, Göttingen 2012.

Böhme, Hartmut, "Das Steinerne. Anmerkung zur Theorie des Erhabenen aus dem Blick des 'Menschenfremdesten'," in Christine Pries (ed.), *Das Erhabene*, Weinheim 1989, pp. 119–141.

Bonitzer, Pascal, *Peinture et cinéma. Décadrages*, Paris 1985.

Bordwell, David and Kristin Thompson, *Film Art. An Introduction*, New York 2008.

Brecht, Bertolt, "A Short Organum for the Theatre" (1948), in Bertolt Brecht, *The Development of an Aesthetic*, trans. John Willet, New York 1977, pp. 179–205.

Brecht, Bertolt, *Arbeitsjournal, Erster Band, 1938–1942*, ed. Werner Hecht, Frankfurt/Main 1973.

Brecht, Bertolt, *Journals* 1934–1955. New York, 1995 Bertolt Brecht.

Bresson, Robert, *Notes On Cinematography*, trans. Jonathan Griffin, New York 1977.

Buber, Martin, *Moses*, Zurich 1994.

Bucerius, Gerd, "Zensur! Zensur?" in *Die ZEIT*, 16/1975, April 11, 1975, p. 20.

Burch, Noel, *Theory of Film Practice*, Princeton 1981.

Burch, Noel, "Building a Haptic Space," in Noel Burch, *Life to Those Shadows*, Berkeley 1990, pp. 162–185.

Byg, Barton, *Landscapes of Resistance. The German Films of Danièle Huillet and Jean-Marie Straub*, Berkeley 1995.

Cage, John, *A Year from Monday, New Lectures and Writings*, Middletown 1970.

Cage, John, "Experimental Music," in John Cage, *Silence*, Cambridge 1971, pp. 7–13.

Cage, John "The Future of Music I", in John Cage, *Silence*, Cambridge 1971, pp. 2–7.

Cherlin, Michael, "Schoenberg's Representation of the Divine in Moses und Aron," in *Journal of the Arnold Schoenberg Institute*, vol. IX, 1986, no. 2.

Chion, Michel, *Sound. An Acoulogical Treatise.* Edited and introduced by James A. Steintrager, Durham/London 2016.

Conrad, Tony, *Slapping Pythagoras,* Table of Elements 1995 (audio CD).

Conradt, Gerd, "Eine Widmung. Begegnung mit Jean-Marie Straub und Danièle Huillet, Rom, August 1999," in Gerd Conradt (ed.), *Starbuck Holger Meins. Ein Porträt als Zeitbild,* Berlin 2001, pp. 182–185.

Damisch, Hubert, *The Origin of Perspective,* trans. John Goodman, Cambridge 1995.

Damisch, Hubert, *Theory of /Cloud/. Toward a History of Painting,* trans. Janet Lloyd, Stanford 2002.

de Brigard, Emilie, "The History of Ethnographic Film," in Paul Hockings (ed.), *Principles of Anthropology,* Berlin 1995, pp. 13–43.

De Koven Ezrahi, Sidra, "Our Homeland, The Text ... Our Text, The Homeland ... Exile and Homecoming in the Modern Jewish Imagination," in *Michigan Quarterly Review* 31, no. 4, 1992, pp. 463–497.

de la Motte-Haber, Helga, "Aufbruch in das Klanguniversum," in:Helga de la Motte-Haber (ed.), *Edgar Varèse: die Befreiung des Klangs,* Hofheim 1992, pp. 41–55.

de Lauretis, Teresa and Stephen Heath (eds.), *The Cinematic Apparatus,* New York 1980.

Deleuze, Gilles, *Negotiations,* New York 1995.

Deleuze, Gilles, *Cinema 1. The Movement-Image,* trans. Hugh Tomlinson and Barbara Habberjam, Minneapolis 1986.

Deleuze, Gilles, *Cinema 2. The Time-Image,* trans. Hugh Tomlinson and Robert Galeta, Minneapolis 1989.

Deleuze, Gilles and Félix Guattari, *Anti-Oedipus. Capitalism and Schizophrenia,* trans. Robert Hurley, Mark Seem, and Helen R. Lane, Minneapolis 1983.

Deleuze, Gilles and Félix Guattari, *A Thousand Plateaus. Capitalism and Schizophrenia,* ed. Brian Massumi, Minneapolis 1987.

Deleuze, Gilles, "What Is the Creative Act?" in Gilles Deleuze, *Two Regimes of Madness, Texts and Interviews 1975-1995. Semiotext(e),* New York 2007, pp. 317–329.

Demenok, Artem and Robert Bramkamp, "'Eine Hexe, die eine Menge Energie verbraucht ...' Danièle Huillet & Jean-Marie Straub im Gespräch," in Klaus Volkmer et al. (eds), *Schönberg/Blonda/Huillet/Straub. Von Heute auf Morgen. Oper/Musik/Film,* Berlin 1997, pp. 87–99.

Derrida, Jacques, "Freud and the Scene of Writing," trans. Jeffrey Mehlman, *Yale French Studies,* no. 48, *French Freud: Structural Studies in Psychoanalysis* (1972), pp. 74–117.

Derrida, Jacques, "Structure, Sign and Play in the Discourse of the Human Sciences," in Jacques Derrida, *Writing and Difference,* trans. Alan Bass, New York 1978, pp. 351–371.

Derrida, Jacques, "Force of Law: the 'Mystical Foundation of Authority'," in Jacques Derrida, *Acts of Religion,* ed. Gil Anidjar, New York 2002.

Derrida, Jacques, *Of Grammatology,* trans. Gayatri Chakarvorty Spivak, Baltimore 1976.

Derrida, Jacques, “Archive Fever. A Freudian Impression,” trans. Eric Prenowitz, *Diacritics*, vol. 25, no. 2 (summer 1995).

Dolar, Mladen, *His Master’s Voice. Eine Theorie der Stimme*, Frankfurt/Main 2007.

Douglas, Mary, *In the Wilderness. The Doctrine of Defilement in the Book of Numbers* (Sheffield 1993), paperback reprint 2004.

Eco, Umberto, “Articulations of the Cinematic Code,” in Bill Nichols (ed.), *Movies and Methods*, Berkeley 1976, pp. 590–607.

Edgerton, Samuel Y., *The Renaissance Rediscovery of Linear Perspective*, New York 1975.

Eisler, Hanns, *Gespräche mit Hans Bunge. Fragen Sie mehr über Brecht*, Leipzig 1975.

Elsaesser, Thomas, “Early Film Form: Articulations of Space and Time. Introduction,” in Thomas Elsaesser (ed.), *Early cinema: Space – Frame – Narrative*, London 1990, pp. 11–31.

Engell, Lorenz, “Erzählung. Historiographische Technik und kinematographischer Geist,” in Eva Hohenberger et al. (eds.), *Die Gegenwart der Vergangenheit. Dokumentarfilm, Fernsehen und Geschichte*, Berlin 2003, pp. 247–275.

Engels, Friedrich, “Camp” (1858), in *The New American Cyclopædia. A popular Dictionary of General Knowledge*, ed. George Ripley and Charles A. Dana, vol. IV, New York, London 1869. pp. 312–313.

Ernst, Wolfgang and Harun Farocki, “Towards an Archive for Visual Concepts,” in Thomas Elsaesser (ed.), *Working on the Sight-Lines*, Amsterdam 2006, pp. 261–286.

Farocki, Harun, “Guten Tag, Herr Roßmann. Langsame Annäherung an Haltungen und Sprache,” in *DIE ZEIT*, 1983, no. 27.

Farocki, Harun, “Shot/Countershot: the Most Important Expression in Filmic Law of Value” in Susanne Gaensheimer, Nikolaus Schaffhausen (eds.), *Nachdruck/Imprint. Texte/Writings*, Berlin 2001, pp. 86–111.

Farocki, Harun, »Das Vorbild jeder stilisierten Jugendunsicherheit muss James Dean sein«, in: Gerd Conradt (Hg.), *Starbuck Holger Meins. Ein Porträt als Zeitbild*, Berlin 2001, S. 178–182.

Felderer, Brigitte, “Stimm-Maschinen. Zur Konstruktion und Sichtbarmachung menschlicher Sprache im 18. Jahrhundert,” in: Friedrich Kittler u.a. (ed.), *Zwischen Rauschen und Offenbarung. Zur Kultur- und Mediengeschichte der Stimme*, Berlin 2002, S. 257–278.

Fichte, Hubert, *Eine glückliche Liebe. Die Geschichte der Empfindlichkeit*. Band 4, Frankfurt/Main 1988.

Fischer, Alexander Achilles, *Der Text des Alten Testaments. Neubearbeitung der Einführung in die Biblia Hebraica von Ernst Würthwein*, Stuttgart 2009.

Fischer-Appelt, Peter, “Die ‘göttlichen Stimmen’ in Schönbergs Oper ‘Moses und Aron’”, in: Christian Meyer (Hg.), *Arnold Schönberg und sein Gott: Bericht zum Symposium Juni 26.–29. Juni 2002*, Vienna 2003, S. 373–383.

Foucault, Michel, *The Order of Things*, London 1989.

Foucault, Michel, "Un 'fantastique' de bibliothèque", in Foucault, *Schriften zur Literatur*, Frankfurt/Main 1979, pp. 157–177.

Foucault, Michel, *"Society Must Be Defended." Lectures at the Collège de France*, 1975–76, ed. Mauro Bertani and Alessandro Fontana, trans. David Macey, New York 1997.

Foucault, Michel, *Security, Territory, Population. Lectures at the Collège de France 1977–1978*, London 2004.

Foucault, Michel, "My Body, This Paper, This Fire," in ibid. *Aesthetics, Method, and Epistemology*, ed. James D. Faubion, New York 1998, pp. 393–417.

Freud, Sigmund, "The Moses of Michelangelo," in *The Standard Edition of the Complete Psychological Works of Sigmund Freud*, trans. James Strachey, Anna Freud, Alix Strachey, Alan Tyson. Volume XIII (1913–1914), *Totem and Taboo and other Works*, London. 1955.

Freud, Sigmund, *Moses and Monotheism*, ed Katherine Jones, London 1939.

Friedmann, Meir, *Pesiqta Rabbati, Midrasch für den Festzyklus und die ausgezeichneten Sabbathe. Kritisch bearbeitet, commentiert durch neue handschriftliche Haggadas vermehrt, mit Bibel- und Personenindices versehen von Meir Friedmann, Wien 1880*, Tel Aviv 1963.

Galilei, Galileo, *Sidereus Nuncius*, ed. Peter Barker, Oklahoma 2004.

Gasché, Rodolphe, "Über Kritik, Hyperkritik und Dekonstruktion: der Fall Benjamin," in Anselm Haverkamp (ed.), *Gewalt und Gerechtigkeit, Derrida-Benjamin*. Frankfurt/Main 1994, pp. 196–216.

Gay, Peter, *Freud: A Life for Our Time*, London/New York 1988.

Gehler, Fred and Ulrich Kasten, *Friedrich Wilhelm Murnau*, Berlin 1990.

Gelb, Ignace Jay, *A Study of Writing: the Foundation of Grammatology*, Chicago 1974.

Gielen, Michael, "Bericht über die Wiener Tonaufnahmen im April/Mai 1974. Schönbergs 'Moses und Aron'," in *Filmkritik 221/222*, 1876, pp. 276–278.

Gielen, Michael, "'Aus einem Gespräch mit Michael Gielen.' Wolfram Schütte spricht mit Michael Gielen," in *Filmkritik* 221/222, 1975, pp. 280–283.

Gielen, Michael, *Unbedingt Musik. Erinnerungen*, Leipzig 2005.

Goehr, Alexander, "Schoenberg's 'Gedanke' Manuscript," in *Journal of the Arnold Schoenberg Institute* II, 1977, no. 1, pp. 4–25.

Göttert, Karl-Heinz, *Geschichte der Stimme*, Munich 1998.

Goldstein, Bluma, "Schoenberg's *Moses und Aron*. A Vanishing Biblical Nation," in Charlotte M. Cross, Russell A. Berman (eds.), *Political and Religious Ideas in the Works of Arnold Schoenberg*, New York 2000, pp. 159–192.

Goldstein, Bluma, *Reinscribing Moses: Heine, Kafka, Freud, and Schoenberg in a European Wilderness*, Cambridge 1992.

Goodman, Steve, *Sonic Warfare. Sound, Affect, and the Ecology of Fear*, Cambridge 2010.

Gould, Glenn, "Arnold Schönberg – A Perspective," in *The Glenn Gould Reader*, edited and with an introduction by Tim Page, New York, 1984, pp. 107–122.

Gould, Glenn, "Music and Technology," in *The Glenn Gould Reader*, pp. 353–357.

Gould, Glenn, "The Grass is Always Greener in the Outtakes: An Experiment in Listening," in *The Glenn Gould Reader*, pp. 357–368.

Grafe, Frieda, "Übersetzung und Rezeption von Maurice Merleau-Pontys 'Das Kino und die Neue Psychologie'," in *Filmkritik* 11, 1969, pp. 695–702.

Grubrich-Simitis, Ilse, *Freuds Moses-Studie als Tagtraum. Ein biographischer Essay*, revised new edition, Frankfurt/Main 1994.

Grun, Constantin, *Arnold Schönberg und Richard Wagner: Spuren einer außergewöhnlichen Beziehung*, vol. 1: *Werke*, Göttingen 2006.

Gugerli, David, "Die Suche nach dem Muster: Horst Herold", in David Georgi, *Suchmaschinen. Die Welt als Datenbank*, Frankfurt/Main 2009, S. 52–69.

Gunning, Tom, "An Unseen Energy Swallows Space. The Space in Early Film and Its Relation to American Avant-Garde Film," in John L. Fell (ed.), *Film Before Griffith*, Berkeley 1983, pp. 355–366.

Gunning, Tom, "The Cinema of Attractions: Early Film, Its Spectator and the Avantgarde," in *Wide Angle* 8, 3–4, 1986, pp. 63–70.

Guthrie, Sylvan, *The Life of Pythagoras by Iamblichus of Syrian Chacis*, New York, 1919.

Haftmann, Werner, "Über die Funktion des Musikalischen in der Malerei des 20. Jahrhunderts," in Lucius Grisebach et al. (eds.), *Hommage à Schönberg. Der Blaue Reiter und das Musikalische in der Malerei der Zeit*, Berlin 1974, üü. 8–41 (exhib. cat.),

Hagen, Wolfgang, "Silencetechno: Cage und das Radio," in Rösing, Helmut (ed.): *Step across the Border. Neue musikalische Trends – neue massenmediale Kontexte: musikalische Aufbrüche und die Medien*, Karben 1997, pp. 73–91.

Hagen, Wolfgang, *Gegenwartsvergessenheit. Studien zu Lazarsfeld, Adorno, Innis und Luhmann*, Berlin 2003.

Hagen, Wolfgang, "Walter Ruttmanns Grosstadt-Weekend. Zur Herkunft der Hörcollage aus der ungegenständlichen Malerei," in Gess, Nicola et al. (eds), *Hörstürze: Akustik und Gewalt im 20. Jahrhundert*, Würzburg 2005, pp. 183–200.

Haselstein, Ulla, *Entziffernde Hermeneutik: Zum Begriff der Lektüre in der psychoanalytischen Theorie des Unbewußten*, Munich 1991.

Haverkamp, Anselm, "Kritik der Gewalt und die Möglichkeit von Gerechtigkeit: Benjamin in Deconstruction," in Anselm Haverkamp (ed.), *Gewalt und Gerechtigkeit. Derrida – Benjamin*, Frankfurt/Main 1994, pp. 7–50.

Heath, Stephen, *Questions of Cinema*, Bloomington 1981.

Hegel, Georg Wilhelm Friedrich, *Aesthetics. Lectures on Fine Art*, vol. 1 and 2, trans. Tim M. Knox, Oxford, New York 1975.

Heidegger, Martin, *Parmenides*, trans. André Schuwer and Richard Rojcewicz, Bloomington 1992.

Herder, Johann Gottfried, *Abhandlung über den Ursprung der Sprache*, Stuttgart 1966.

Herold, Horst, *Kriminalität und Gesellschaft. Rationalisierung und Automation in der Verbrechensbekämpfung*. RIAS Funkuniversität, 1975 (79th lecture, broadcast Monday July 7, 1975), typewritten manuscript of RIAS, Berlin 1975.

Heuner, Ulf, *Tragisches Handeln in Raum und Zeit. Raum-zeitliche Tragik und Ästhetik in der sophokleischen Tragödie und im griechischen Theater*, Stuttgart 2001.

Hickethier, Knut, *Film- und Fernsehanalyse*, 3rd revised edition, Stuttgart, Weimar 2001.

Hockings, Paul (ed.), *Principles of Anthropology*, Berlin 1995.

Hölderlin, Friedrich, "'The declining fatherland ...'" in Friedrich Hölderlin, *Essays and Letters*, ed. trans. Jeremy Adler and Charles Louth, London, 2009, pp. 271–276.

Hölderlin, Friedrich "Notes on the *Oedipus*" in F. Hölderlin, *Essays and Letters*, ed. trans. Jeremy Adler and Charles Louth,London 2009, pp. 317–324.

Hölderlin, Friedrich, "Notes on the Antigone," in F. Hölderlin, *Essays and Letters*, ed. trans. Jeremy Adler and Charles Louth,London 2009, pp. 325–332.

Hofmann, Beate, "Zur Bedeutung der Wüste im pharaonischen Ägypten," in Uwe Lindemann und Monika Schmitz-Emans (ed.), *Was ist eine Wüste? Interdisziplinäre Annäherungen an einen interkulturellen Topos*, Würzburg 2000.

Hohmann, Katharina and Fritz von Klinggräff, "Die guten Götter Hölderlins. Ein Gespräch mit Danielle [sic.] Huillet und Jean-Marie Straub über ihren neusten Streifen 'Cézanne' und die Zernichtung ihres Sujets," in *tageszeitung*, May 5, 1990, pp. 34–36.

Holert, Tom, "Strudel und Wüsten des Politischen. Michelangelo Antonioni, Robert Smithson und Michael Snow," in *MedienKunstNetz*, http://www.medienkunstnetz.de/themen/kunst_und_kinematographie/wuesten_des_politischen/ (accessed April 16 2014).

Holl, Ute, *Kino, Trance und Kybernetik*, Berlin 2002.

Holl, Ute, "'Man erinnert sich nicht, man schreibt das Gedächtnis um.' Modelle und Montagen filmischer Bildatlanten," in Sabine Flach, Inge Muenz-Koenen, Marianne Streisand (eds.), *Der Bildatlas im Wandel der Künste und Medien*, Munich 2005, pp. 251–270.

Holl, Ute, "'Ich kann beim besten Willen kein Blut sehen.' Gesellschaftsvertrag und rote Farbe in Godards WEEK-END," in Anja Lauper (ed.), *Transfusionen. Blutbilder und Biopolitik in der Neuzeit*, Zürich 2005, pp. 243–266.

Holl, Ute, "Strahlen und Überstrahlen – Risse ins Bild der Geschichte. Zur filmischen Historiographie von F.W. Murnaus FAUST," in Tyradellis, Daniel and Burkhardt Wolf (eds.), *Die Szene der Gewalt. Bilder, Codes und Materialitäten*, Frankfurt/Main 2007.

Holl, Ute, "Vierzehn Versuche, eine Oberfläche zu beschreiben," in Doris Kern and Sabine Nessel (eds.), *Unerhörte Erfahrungen. Texte zum Kino. Festschrift für Heide Schlüpmann zum Geburtstag*, Frankfurt/Main 2008, pp. 341–366.

Holl, Ute, "Vom Teuflischen, der Kybernetik und der Ethik des Kinos in Robert Bressons Le diable probablement (1977)," in *RISS, Zeitschrift für Psychoanalyse*, special edition on cinema, ed. Andreas Cremonini, Zurich 2009, pp. 53–76.

Huillet, Danièle, "Moses und Aron. Das Drehbuch. Beschreibungen – Texte – Photogramme," in *Filmkritik* 221/222, 1975, pp. 203–252.

Huillet, Danièle, "Kleiner historischer Exkurs," in *Filmkritik* 221/222, 5/6/1975, pp. 194–202.

Huillet, Danièle, "Appunti sul giornale di lavorazione di Gregory," in *Filmkritik* 225, 9/1975, pp. 398–419.

Iamblichos Chelcidensis, *Pythagoras. Legende, Lehre, Lebensgestaltung*, hg. v. Michael von Albrecht, Zurich 1963.

Idel, Moshe, *Hasidism. Between Ecstasy and Magic*, Albany 1995.

Jakobson, Roman, *Six leçons sur le son et le sens* (1942/43), Paris 1976.

Jeremias, Brigitte, "Ein sakraler Monolith, mitten in die Landschaft gestellt. Jean-Marie Straubs Moses und Aron-Verfilmung," in *Frankfurter Allgemeine Zeitung*, no. 49, February 27, 1975, p. 21.

Journal of the Arnold Schoenberg Institute, vol. X, no. 2, November 1987.

Kaes, Anton, *Deutschlandbilder. Die Wiederkehr der Geschichte als Film*, Munich 1987.

Kafka, Franz, "Before the Law," in Kafka, *The Complete Stories*, New York 1983, pp. 22–23:22.

Kandinsky, Wassily, *Concerning the Spiritual in Art*, trans. M.T.H. Sadler, New York 1977.

Kandinsky, Wassily, *Über das Geistige in der Kunst, insbesondere in der Malerei*, revised edition, Bern 2006.

Kant, Immanuel, *Critique of Judgement*, trans. James Creed Meredith, ed. Nicholas Walker, Oxford, New York 2007.

Kerling, Marc M., *"O Wort, du Wort, das mir fehlt": Die Gottesfrage in Arnold Schönbergs Oper "Moses und Aron." Zur Theologie eines musikalischen Kunst-Werkes des 20. Jahrhunderts*, Mainz 2004.

Kittler, Friedrich (ed.), *Austreibung des Geistes aus den Geisteswissenschaften: Programme des Poststrukturalismus*, Paderborn 1980.

Kittler, Friedrich, *Aufschreibesysteme 1800/1900*, Munich 1985.

Kittler, Friedrich, *Grammophon, Film, Typewriter*, Berlin 1986.

Kittler, Friedrich, "Weltatem," in Friedrich Kittler et al. (eds.), *Diskursanalysen*, vol. 1: *Medien*, Opladen 1987, pp. 94–107.

Kittler, Friedrich, "Signal-Rausch-Abstand," in Friedrich Kittler, *Draculas Vermächtnis, Technische Schriften*, Leipzig 1993, pp. 161–181.

Kittler, Friedrich et al. (eds.), *Zwischen Rauschen und Offenbarung. Zur Kultur- und Mediengeschichte der Stimme*, Berlin 2002.

Kittler, Friedrich, "Das Werk der Drei. Vom Stummfilm zum Tonfilm," in Kittler et al. (eds.), *Zwischen Rauschen und Offenbarung*, pp. 357–370.

Kittler, Friedrich, *Musik und Mathematik I*, vol. 1. *Hellas 1: Aphrodite*, Munich 2006.

Kleinspehn, Thomas, *Der flüchtige Blick. Sehen und Identität in der Kultur der Neuzeit*, Hamburg 1989.

Koch, Gertrud, "*Moses und Aron*, Musik, Text, Film und andere Fallen der Rezeption," in Gertrud Koch, *Die Einstellung ist die Einstellung. Visuelle Konstruktionen des Judentums*, Frankfurt/Main 1992, pp. 30–52.

Koch, Gertrud, "In Sachen Moses gegen Aron. Die Kritische Theorie und das Kino," in Gertrud Koch, *Die Einstellung ist die Einstellung. Visuelle Konstruktionen des Judentums*, Frankfurt/Main 1992, pp. 12–114.

Köckert, Matthias, "Wie kam das Gesetz an den Sinai?" in *Vergegenwärtigung des Alten Testaments. Beiträge zur biblischen Hermeneutik. Festschrift für Rudolf Smend zum 70. Geburtstag*, ed. Christoph Bultmann et al., Göttingen 2002, pp. 13–27.

Koschorke, Albrecht, *Die Geschichte des Horizonts. Grenze und Grenzüberschreitung in literarischen Landschaftsbildern*, Frankfurt/Main 1990.

Kracauer, Siegfried "The Task of the Film Critic," in Martin Jay, Anton Kaes (eds.) *The Weimar Republic Source Book*, Berkeley 1995.

Kracauer, Siegfried, *Theory of Film. The Redemption of Physical Reality*, Princeton 1997.

Kracauer, Siegfried, *Jacques Offenbach und das Paris seiner Zeit*, in Siegfried Kracauer, *Werke*, ed. Inka Mülder-Bach and Ingrid Belke, vol. 8, Frankfurt/Main 2005.

Krämer, Ulrich, "Zur Notation der Sprechstimme bei Schönberg," in Heinz-Klaus Metzger and Rainer Riehn (eds.), *Schoenberg und der Sprechgesang. Musik-Konzepte* 112/113, 2001, VII.

Kraus, Karl, *The Last Days of Mankind*, trans. Alexander Gode and Sue E. Wright, New York 2000.

Kursell, Julia und Armin Schäfer, "Das Band, das die Zeit macht," in Lorenz Engell et al. (ed.), *Archiv für Mediengeschichte – 1950*, Weimar 2004, pp. 45–57.

Lacan, Jacques, "Seminar on the 'The Purloined Letter'," trans. Jeffrey Mehlman, *Yale French Studies*, vol. 0, no. 48, *French Freud: Structural Studies in Psychoanalysis* (1972), pp. 39–72.

Lacan, Jacques, *Das Seminar VII, Die Ethik der Psychoanalyse (1959–1960)*, Berlin 1996.

Laclau, Ernesto, *On Populist Reason*, London 2005.

Laclau, Ernesto, "Why do Empty Signifiers Matter to Politics?" in Ernesto Laclau, *Emancipation(s)*, London, New York 1996, pp. 36–45.

Lacoue-Labarthe, Philippe, "Die Zäsur der Religion. Zu Schönbergs Moses und Aron," in Christiaan L. Hart Nibbrig (ed.) *Was heißt Darstellen?*, Frankfurt/Main 1974, pp. 451–479.

Lange, Britta, "Ein Archiv von Stimmen. Kriegsgefangene unter ethnographischer Beobachtung," in Wegmann, Nikolaus, Harun Maye and Cornelius Reiber (eds.), *Original/Ton. Zur Mediengeschichte des O-Tons*, Konstanz 2007, pp. 317–341.

Lenzen, Verena, "Vom Bilderverbot zum jüdischen Gebet bei Arnold Schönberg," in Michael J. Rainer and Hans-Gerd Janßen (eds.), *Bilderverbot. Jahrbuch politische Theologie 2*, Münster 1997, pp. 239–251.

Lévi-Strauss, Claude, *Mythologiques*, vol. I, *The Raw and the Cooked*, Chicago 1969.

Lewin, David, "Moses und Aron: Some General Remarks and Analytic Notes for Act 1 Scene 1," in *Perspectives of New Music*, vol. 6, no. 1, 1967, pp. 1–17.

Lindenberger, Herbert, *Opera in History. From Monteverdi to Cage*, Stanford 1998.

Lipowatz, Thanos, *Der "Fortschritt in der Geistigkeit" und der "Tod Gottes,"* Würzburg 2005.

Lohmann, Johannes, "Die Geburt der Tragödie aus dem Geiste der Musik," in *Archiv für Musikwissenschaft* 37, ed. H 3, 1980, pp. 167–186.

Lyotard, Jean-François, *The Inhuman. Reflections on Time*, trans. Geoffrey Bennington and Rachel Bowlby, Cambridge 1991.

Macho, Thomas, "Glossolalie in der Theologie," in Friedrich Kittler et al. (eds.), *Zwischen Rauschen und Offenbarung. Zur Kultur- und Mediengeschichte der Stimme*, Berlin 2002, pp. 3–17.

Macho, Thomas, "Zeit und Zahl. Kalender und Zeitrechnung als Kulturtechnik," in Sybille Krämer, Horst Bredekamp (eds.) *Bild – Schrift – Zahl*, Munich 2003, pp. 179–192.

Melchinger, Siegfried, *Das Theater der Tragödie, Aischylos, Sophokles, Euripides auf der Bühne ihrer Zeit*, Munich 1974.

Menke, Bettine, "Benjamin vor dem Gesetz: Die Kritik der Gewalt in der Lektüre Derridas," in Anselm Haverkamp (ed.), *Gewalt und Gerechtigkeit, Derrida–Benjamin*, Frankfurt/Main 1994, pp. 217–275.

Menke, Bettine, "Die Stimme der Rhetorik – die Rhetorik der Stimme," in Friedrich Kittler et al (eds.), *Zwischen Rauschen und Offenbarung. Zur Kultur- und Mediengeschichte der Stimme*, Berlin 2002, pp. 115–132.

Menke, Christoph, *Die Gegenwart der Tragödie. Versuch über Urteil und Spiel*, Frankfurt/Main 2005.

Merleau-Ponty, Maurice, "The Film and the New Psychology," in Maurice Merleau-Ponty, *Sense and Non-Sense*, trans. H. Dreyfus and P. Dreyfus, Evanston 1964, pp. 48–59.

Mertens, Joseph, *Alba Fucens*, Bruxelles 1981.

Metzger, Heinz-Klaus and Rainer Riehn (eds.), *Schoenberg und der Sprechgesang. Musik-Konzepte 112/113*, VII, 2001.

Meyer, Christian (ed.), *Arnold Schönberg und sein Gott: Bericht zum Symposium Juni 26.–29. Juni 2002*, Vienna 2003.

Meyer, Christian and Therese Muxeneder (eds.), *Arnold Schönberg. Catalogue raisonné*, 2 vols., Vienna 2005.

Meyer-Kalkus, Reinhart, *Stimme und Sprechkünste im 20. Jahrhundert*, Berlin 2001.

Michelson, Annette, "'The Man with a Movie Camera': From Magician to Epistemologist," in *Artforum* X, 1972, no. 7, pp. 60–72.

Mitry, Jean, *The Aesthetics and Psychology of the Cinema*, Indiana 2000.

Mowitt, John, *Radio: Essays in Bad Reception*, Berkeley 2011.

Münsterberg, Hugo, *The Photoplay; A Psychological Study. The Silent Photoplay in 1916*, New York 1916/1970.

Nattiez, Jean-Jacques and Robert Samuels (eds.), *The Boulez-Cage Correspondence*, Cambridge 1993.

Nau, Peter, *Zur Kritik des politischen Films. 6 analysierende Beschreibungen und ein Vorwort »Über Filmkritik«*, Cologne 1978.

Nietzsche, Friedrich, "The Birth of Tragedy" in Nietzsche *The Birth of Tragedy and Other Writings* (1999), ed. Raymond Geuss, Ronald Spiers (trans.), Cambridge 2007, pp. 1–116.

Olender, Maurice, *The Languages of Paradise, Race, Religion, and Philology in the Nineteenth Century*, trans. Arthur Goldhammer, Cambridge 1992.

Panofsky, Erwin, *The Life and Art of Albrecht Dürer*, Princeton 1955.

Pasolini, Pier Paolo, *Empirismo eretico*, Milan, 1972.

Powell, Barry B., *Homer and the Origin of the Greek Alphabet*, Cambridge 1991.

Rancière, Jacques, *Dis-agreement. Politics and Philosophy*, trans. Julie Rose, Minneapolis 1999.

Rancière, Jacques, "Arithmetics of the People," http://www.diagonalthoughts.com/?p=1605.

Reisz, Karel and Gavin Millar, *The Technique of Film Editing*, London 1953.

Revill, David, *Roaring Silence. John Cage: A Life*, New York 1992.

Rheinberger, Hans Jörg, *Toward A History of Epistemic Things. Synthesizing Proteins in the Test Tube*, Stanford 1997.

Rheinberger, Hans Jörg, *Experimentalsysteme und epistemische Dinge. Eine Geschichte der Proteinsynthese im Reagenzglas*, Göttingen 2001.

Ringer, Alexander L., "Schoenberg and the Politics of Jewish Survival," in *Journal of the Arnold Schoenberg Institute*, vol. III, no. 1, March 1979, pp. 11–48.

Roccati, Alessandro, "La Conception Rituelle du Désert chez les Anciens Égyptiens," in Christe Yves (ed.), *Le Désert, Image et Réalité. Actes du Colloque de Cartigny 1983*, Leuven 1989.

Ruschkowski, André, *Elektronische Klänge und musikalische Entdeckungen*, Stuttgart 1998.

Salt, Barry, "The Early Development of Film Form," in *Film Form*, 1976, no. 1, pp. 91–106.

Sarasin, Philipp, *Michel Foucault zur Einführung*, Hamburg 2005.

Schaeffer, Pierre, *Traité des objets musicaux. Essai interdisciplines*, Paris 2002.

Schafer, Murray R., *Soundscape. Our Sonic Environment and the Tuning of the World*, Rochester 1993.

Scherer, Wolfgang, *Hildegard von Bingen: Musik und Minnemystik*, Freiburg 1987.

Scherer, Wolfgang, *Klavier-Spiele: die Psychotechnik der Klaviere im 18. und 19. Jahrhundert*, München 1989.

Schiller, Friedrich, "On the Employment of the Chorus in Tragedy," trans. George Gregory, in *Fidelio*. vol. 2, no. 1, 1993, pp. 60–64.

Schivelbusch, Wolfgang, *Geschichte der Eisenbahnreise. Zur Industrialisierung von Raum und Zeit im 19. Jahrhundert*, Munich 1977.

Schlüpmann, Heide, *Abendröthe der Subjektphilosophie. Eine Ästhetik des Kinos*, Frankfurt/Main 1998.

Schlüpmann, Heide, "Das Aufklärungsversprechen des Kinos oder: die Ablösung der Metaphysik durch die Medien," in *montage AV* "Erfahrung," 19/1 2010, p. 161–174.

Schmidt, Matthias, "Musik ohne Noten. Arnold Schönbergs 'Pierrot lunaire' und Karl Kraus," in *Studien zur Musikwissenschaft*, 47, 1999, pp. 365–393.

Schmidt, Matthias, "Vor dem Gesetz. Zur religiösen Dimension eines musikalischen Begriffs bei Schönberg," in Christian Meyer (ed.), *Arnold Schönberg und sein Gott. Bericht zum Symposium 26.–29. Juni 2002*, Vienna 2003, pp. 299–310.

Schmitt, Carl, *Constitutional Theory*, Durham, London 2008.

Carl Schmitt, *The Nomos of the Earth in the International Law of the Jus Publicum Europaeum*, trans. G.L. Ulmen, New York 2006.

Schmitt, Carl, *Political Theology. Four Chapters on the Concept of Sovereignty*, trans. Georg Schwab, Chicago/London 2005.

Schöll, Salome, "'Der biblische Weg' und der Zionismus in den 1920er Jahren," in Christian Meyer (ed.): *Arnold Schönberg und sein Gott*, pp. 239–246.

Schoenberg, Arnold, "A Four-Point Program for Jewry," in *Journal of the Arnold Schoenberg Institute*, vol. III, no. 1, March 1979, pp. 48–67.

Schoenberg, Arnold, *Begleitmusik zu einer Lichtspielszene (drohende Gefahr, Angst, Katastrophe)*, Wilhelmshaven 1930.

Schoenberg, Arnold, "Composition with Twelve Tones," in *Arnold Schoenberg: Style and Idea*, ed., Leonard Stein, London 1975, pp. 214–245.

Schoenberg, Arnold ""Eartraining through Composing," in *Arnold Schoenberg: Style and Idea*, ed., Leonard Stein, London 1975, pp. 377–382.

Schoenberg, Arnold, *Letters*, ed. Erwin Stein, trans. Eithne Wilkins and Ernst Kaiser, London/Boston 1964.

Schoenberg, Arnold, *Moses und Aron. Oper in drei Akten, miniature score*, Mainz 1958.

Schoenberg, Arnold, *Moses und Aron. Oper in drei Akten, vocal score*, Mainz 1957.

Schoenberg, Arnold, "New Music: My Music," in *Arnold Schoenberg: Style and Idea*, ed., Leonard Stein, London 1975, pp. 99–104.

Schoenberg, Arnold, "New Music, Outmoded Music, Style and Idea," in Arnold Schoenberg, *Style and Idea*, ed. Leonard Stein, London 1975, pp. 113–124.

Schoenberg, Arnold, *Theory of Harmony* (1911), trans. Roy. E Carter, Berkeley, 1987.

Schoenberg, Arnold, "War-Clouds Diary," trans. Paul A Pisk, in *Journal of the Schoenberg Institute*, vol. XIV, no. 1 June 1986, pp. 53–77.

Schönberg, Arnold, *Sämtliche Werke*, section III, stage works, series A, vol. 8, parts 1 and 2, *Moses und Aron. Oper in drei Akten*, ed. Christian Martin Schmidt, Mainz 1977.

Schönberg, Arnold, *Sämtliche Werke*, section III, stage works, series A, vol. 8, parts 1 and 2, *Moses und Aron. Oper in drei Akten, Entstehungsgeschichte. Texte und Textentwürfe zum Oratorium und zur Oper*, ed. Christian Martin Schmidt, Mainz, Vienna 1998.

Schoenberg, Gertrud, "Remarks following the Score," in Arnold Schoenberg: *Moses und Aron, study score, unpaginated*, Mainz 1958.

Schüttpelz, Erhard, "Frage nach der Frage, auf die das Medium eine Antwort ist," in Albert Kümmel and Erhard Schüttpelz (eds.), *Signale der Störung*, Munich 2003, pp. 15–29.

Seeber, Guido, *Der Trickfilm. Der Praktische Kameramann Band II. Schriftenreihe des deutschen Filmmuseums*, Frankfurt/Main 1979.

Seidensticker, Bernd, *Das Antike Theater*, Munich 2010.

Sekula, Allan, *Fish Story*, Rotterdam 2005.

Shannon, Claude E., "Eine mathematische Theorie der Kommunikation (1948)," in Claude E. Shannon, *Ein/Aus. Ausgewählte Schriften zur Kommunikations- und Nachrichtentheorie*, ed. Friedrich Kittler et al., Berlin 2000, pp. 7–100.

Siegert, Bernhard, *Passage des Digitalen. Zeichenpraktiken der neuzeitlichen Wissenschaften 1500–1900*, Berlin 2003.

Sievers, Eduard, "Über Sprachmelodisches in der deutschen Dichtung," in Eduard Sievers, *Rhythmisch-melodische Studien: Vorträge und Aufsätze*, Heidelberg 1912.

Sievers, Eduard, *Ziele und Wege der Schallanalyse. Zwei Vorträge*, Heidelberg 1924.

Silverman, Kaja, *The Acoustic Mirror. The Female Voice in Psychoanalysis*, Bloomington-Indianapolis 1988.

Simondon, Gilbert, *Du mode d'existence des objets techniques*, Paris 1958.

Souriau, Etienne, "La structure de l'univers filmique et le vocabulaire de la filmologie," in *Revue International de Filmologie*, no. 7–8, Paris 1951, pp. 231–241.

Steiner, George, "Schoenberg's *Moses und Aron*," in George Steiner, *A Reader*, London 1984, pp. 234–245.

Steiner, George, "Pessimisten sind lächerlich," in *Die Zeit*, no. 17, April 16, 2014, p. 45.

Stephan, Rudolf, "Wege zur neuen Musik," in Helga de la Motte-Haber (ed.), *Edgard Varèse: Die Befreiung des Klangs. Symposium Edgard Varèse Hamburg 1991*, Hofheim 1992, pp. 11–16.

Sternberger, Dolf and Joachim Neugroschel, "Panorama of the 19th Century," in *October*, vol. 4 (fall 1977), pp. 3–20.

Straub, Jean-Marie and Danièle Huillet "Conversation avec Jean-Marie Straub et Danièle Huillet (Moïse et Aaron). Par Jacques Bontemps, Pascal Bonitzer et Serge Daney," in *Cahiers du Cinéma* 258/259, 1975, pp. 5–24.

Straub, Jean-Marie and Danièle Huillet, "Direct Sound: An Interview with Jean-Marie Straub and Danièle Huillet," in Elisabeth Weis and John Belton (eds.), *Theory and Practice of Film Sound*, New York 1985, pp. 150–153.

Stuckenschmidt, Hans Heinz, *Schoenberg – His Life, World and Works*, Richmond 1977.

Taubes, Jacob, *The Political Theology of Paul*, Stanford, 2004.

Theuring, Gerhard, "Tagebucheintragungen," in *Filmkritik* 9, 1975, pp. 394–397.

Theweleit, Klaus, *Buch der Könige*, vol. 2y: *Recording angels' mysteries*, Frankfurt/Main 1994.

Tholen, Georg Christoph, *Die Zäsur der Medien. Kulturphilosophische Konturen*, Frankfurt/Main 2002.

Tompkins, Dave, *How to Wreck a Nice Beach. The Vocoder from World War II to Hip Hop. The Machine Speaks*, New York 2010.

Ullmann, Jakob, "zwei sprachen," in Heinz-Klaus Metzger and Rainer Riehn (eds.), *Schönberg und der Sprechgesang, Musik-Konzepte* 112/113, 2001.

Vertov, Dziga, *Kino-Eye. The Writings of Dziga Vertov*, ed. Annette Michelson, trans. Kevin O'Brien, Berkeley 1984.

Virilio, Paul, *The Paul Virilio Reader*, trans. Michael Degener, London 2002.

Virno, Paolo, "Die Logik der Tumulte," in Isabell Lorey et al. (eds.), *Inventionen 2*, Zurich 2012, pp. 17–26.

Vismann, Cornelia, *Medien der Rechtsprechung*, Frankfurt/Main 2011.

Vogl, Joseph, "Medien-Werden. Galileis Fernrohr," in Engell, Lorenz and Joseph Vogl (eds.), *Mediale Historiographien. Archiv für Mediengeschichte*, Weimar 2001, pp. 115–123.

Vogl, Joseph (ed.), *Gesetz und Urteil. Beiträge zu einer Theorie des Politischen*, Weimar 2003.

von Clausewitz, Carl, *Vom Kriege*, Schleswig 1963.

von Dewitz, Bodo and Werner Nekes (eds.), *›Ich sehe was, was Du nicht siehst‹. Sehmaschinen und Bilderwelten. Die Sammlung Werner Nekes*, Göttingen 2002.

von Foerster, Heinz, "Gegenstände: greifbare Symbole für (Eigen-) Verhalten," in Heinz von Foerster, *Wissen und Gewissen. Versuch einer Brücke*, Frankfurt/Main 1993, pp. 103–115.

von Foerster, Heinz, "Perception of the Future and the Future of Perception," in Heinz von Foerster, *Understanding Understanding: Essays in Cybernetics and Cognition*, New York 2003, pp. 199–210.

von Helmholtz, Hermann, *On the Sensation of Tone as a Physiological Basis for the Theory of Music*, trans. Alexander J. Ellis, London 1895.

Walzer, Michael, *Exodus and Revolution*, New York 1985.

Warnke, Martin u.a., *EbsKart – Die Ebstorfer Weltkarte in hypermedialer Aufbereitung*, http://weblab.uni-lueneburg.de/kulturinformatik/projekte/ebskart/content/start.html (accessed March 13, 2008).

Weber, Samuel "In the Name of the Law," in *Deconstruction and the Possibility of Justice*, ed. Drucilla Cornell, Michel Rosenfeld and David Gray Carlson, New York 1992, pp. 232–258.

Weber, Samuel, "Deconstruction before the Name: Some Preliminary Remarks on Deconstruction and Violence," in *Cardozo Law Review*, vol. 13 / 1991–1992, pp. 1188–1191.

Welsch, Wolfgang, "Adornos Ästhetik: eine implizite Ästhetik des Erhabenen," in Christine Pries (ed.), *Das Erhabene: zwischen Grenzerfahrung und Größenwahn*, Weinheim 1989, pp. 185–213.

Wiener, Norbert, *Cybernetics Or Control and Communication in the Animal and the Machine*, Cambridge MA 1965.

Wittmann, Matthias, "Am Anfang war das Blackout. Zur Konstruktion des Gedächtnisses in der Erfahrung des Films," in *Zeitschrift für Medienwissenschaft*, no. 2, April 2010, pp. 41–52.

Woods, Gregory, "Ein Arbeitsjournal," in *Filmkritik* 221/222, 1974, pp. 254–273.

Wundt, Wilhelm, *Völkerpsychologie. Eine Untersuchung der Entwicklungsgesetze von Sprache, Mythus und Sitte*, vol. 1, *Die Sprache*, Leipzig 1900.

Yerushalmi, Yosef Hayim, "Le Moïse de Freud et le Moïse de Schönberg," in Pierre Nora (ed.), *Le Débat* (1993), no. 73, January/February 1993, pp. 39–55.

Yerushalmi, Yosef Hayim, *Freud's Moses: Judaism Terminable and Interminable*, New Haven 1991.

Zelinsky, Hartmut, "Arnold Schönberg – der Wagner Gottes. Anmerkungen zum Lebensweg eines deutschen Juden aus Wien," in *Neue Zeitschrift für Musik* 04/1986, pp. 7–19.

ILLUSTRATIONS

p. 101: "Far in the distance Moses and Aaron suddenly appear. They approach in the manner described by the choruses," Schönberg, *Moses und Aron*, score I, act I, bars 419–420.

p. 116: The rules of the game of the visible, Gregory Woods, "Ein Arbeitsjournal," in *Filmkritik* 221/222, 1974, pp. 254–273: 256.

p. 117: The rules of the game of the composition. Basic row and retrograde forms, Arnold Schoenberg, "Composition with Twelve Tones," in *Arnold Schoenberg: Style and Idea*, ed, Leonard Stein, London 1975, pp. 214–245: 224.

p. 124: Singers, singly in the wind and at the same time a desert-colored ensemble, Moses und Aron, BRD 1974, shots no. 19, 21, 23, 48, 49 according to Huillet, "Moses und Aron. Das Drehbuch."

p. 130: Michael Gielen: sketch of the line-up of the chorus in the ORF sound studio, from Gielen, "Bericht über die Wiener Tonaufnahmen im April/Mai 1974. Schönbergs *Moses und Aron*," in *Filmkritik* 221/222, 1975, pp. 276–278: 277.

p. 144: Reconstruction of the development of the text "Aron explains and hands over the gold calf," Schönberg, *Entstehungsgeschichte*, p. 143.

p. 145: Reconstruction of the development of the text "Slaughter, preparations, livestock is dragged in," Schönberg, *Entstehungsgeschichte*, p. 144.

p. 148–150: Letting environmental sounds into the music, Moses und Aron, BRD 1974, shot no. 53 according to Huillet, "Moses und Aron. Das Drehbuch."

p. 159: The Dance of the Butchers, at once archaic and modern, Moses und Aron, BRD 1974, shots no. 54, 56 according to Huillet, "Moses und Aron. Das Drehbuch."

p. 161: Tableaus staged in very fine lighting, Moses und Aron, BRD 1974, shots no. 61, 62, 70 according to Huillet, "Moses und Aron. Das Drehbuch."

p. 163: Symmetrical arrangement, ascetic ritual, Moses und Aron, BRD 1974, shot no. 63 according to Huillet, "Moses und Aron. Das Drehbuch."

p. 174: "Rain" in the tone colors of *Pierrot lunaire*, Hanns Eisler, "Fourteen Ways to Describe Rain," in Theodor W. Adorno and Hanns Eisler, *Composing for the Films*, London 2005, p. 108.

p. 195–198: Pan across the Nile, scanning the face of the earth, Moses und Aron, BRD 1974, shots no. 42, 43 according to Huillet, "Moses und Aron. Das Drehbuch."

p. 216–218: The idea of the people, cinematically bound to the pan, represented by the chorus, Moses und Aron, BRD 1974, shot no. 37 according to Huillet, "Moses und Aron. Das Drehbuch" (excerpts from the pan).

p. 237: "Auflösen" [dissolve], Schönberg, *Moses und Aron*, score II, act II, bars 1041–1042.

p. 246–247: "An image of light, this side of transcendence, Moses und Aron, BRD 1974, shot no. 73 according to Huillet, "Moses und Aron. Das Drehbuch."

p. 248–249: Giving life its time; life takes its time, Moses und Aron, FRG 1974, shots no. 52, 73, 51, 55 according to Huillet, "Moses und Aron. Das Drehbuch."

p.252–253: Unprotected: rural population, extras, people, Moses und Aron, FRG 1974, shot no. 58 according to Huillet, "Moses und Aron. Das Drehbuch."

p. 265: "Erection of the golden calf," in Schönberg, *Moses und Aron, Entstehungsgeschichte*, p. 142.

p. 266: "Still in march tempo," Arnold Schönberg, *Moses und Aron, Oper in drei Akten, study score*, Mainz 1958, act II, bar 1116.

p. 271–273: Infringing the law, breaking the tablets, discontinuing the music, Moses und Aron, FRG 1974, shots no. 76, 78 according to Huillet, "Moses und Aron. Das Drehbuch."

p. 276–277: "In the wasteland you shall be victorious," Moses und Aron, FRG 1974, shot no. 82 according to Huillet, "Moses und Aron. Das Drehbuch."

p. 282–283: Arnold Schoenberg, "War-Clouds Diary," trans. Paul A Pisk, in *Journal of the Schoenberg Institute*, vol. XIV, Nr. 1 June 1986, pp. 53–77.

p. 313: The cloud, not a sign, not an image, Moses und Aron, FRG 1974, shot no. 10 according to Huillet, "Moses und Aron. Das Drehbuch."

p. 318: What I wanted to write about no longer exists, shot no. 49 according to Huillet, "Moses und Aron. Das Drehbuch" (frame with optical sound).

MOSES UND ARON, FRG 1974

Directors: Jean-Marie Straub, Danièle Huillet

Screenplay: Jean-Marie Straub, Danièle Huillet

Camera: Ugo Piccone

Camera assistants: Saverio Diamanti, Giovanni Canfarelli, Renato Berta

Lighting: Francesco Ragusa, Alvaro Nannicini, Gianfranco Baldacci

Set: Francesco Ragusa, Alvaro Nannicini, Gianfranco Baldacci

Costumes: Cantini, Renata Morroni, Augusta Morelli, Mariateresia Stefanelli

Hairdresser: Guerrino Todero

Editing: Danièle Huillet, Jean-Marie Straub

Sound: Louis Hochet, Ernst Neuspiel, Georges Vaglio, Jeti Grigioni

Mix: Louis Hochet

Music: Arnold Schoenberg

Conductor: Michael Gielen, Bernard Rubenstein (assistant)

Chorus master: Gottfried Preinfalk

Performers:

Günther Reich: Moses

Louis Devos: Aron

Eva Csapò: Young Girl

Roger Lucas: Young Man

Richard Salter: Another Man

Werner Mann: Priest

Ladislav Illavsky: Ephraimite

Friedl Obrowsky: Invalid Woman

Helmut Baumann: dancer

Jürg Burth: dancer

Nick Farrant: dancer

Wolfgang Kegler: dancer

Michael Molnar: dancer

Procuktion company: Straub-Huillet (Rome), NEF-Diffusion (Paris), Taurus Film (Munich), Janus Film und Fernseh-Produktion GmbH (Frankfurt am Main), Radiotelevisione Italiana (RAI) (Rome), commissioned by Österreichischer Rundfunk (ORF) (Vienna), Hessischer Rundfunk (HR) (Frankfurt am Main)

Producer: Klaus Hellwig

Produktion management: Danièle Huillet

Length: 3010 m; duration: 110 mins.

Format: 35 mm, 1:1.37

Image/sound: Eastmancolor, mono

Censor: FSK-Prüfung (FRG): March 5, 1975, 47216, from the age of 12 / not on religious public holidays

Screening: premiere (NL): February 1975, Rotterdam, IFF

1ST EDITION
ISBN 978-3-03734-623-5

WWW.DIAPHANES.NET

LAYOUT AND PRINTING PREPARATION: 2EDIT, ZURICH
PRINTING: STEINMEIER, DEININGEN